Peterson's

# MASTER AP

# ENGLISH LITERATURE

# & COMPOSITION

Margaret C. Moran
W. Frances Holder

2nd Edition

# PETERSON'S

A **nelnet** COMPANY

# PETERSON'S

A **nelnet** COMPANY

## OTHER RECOMMENDED TITLES

*Peterson's AP European History*

*Peterson's AP World History*

*Peterson's Master AP Calculus AB & BC*

*Peterson's Master AP Chemistry*

*Peterson's Master AP English Language & Composition*

*Peterson's Master AP U.S. Government & Politics*

*Peterson's Master AP U.S. History*

# Contents

# Acknowledgments

Peterson's gratefully acknowledges the following publishers:

Poem 621, "The Wind—tapped like a tired Man . . ." reprinted by permission of the publishers and the Trustees of Amherst College from *The Poems of Emily Dickinson,* ed. by Ralph W. Franklin, Cambridge, Mass.: The Belknap Press of Harvard University Press, Copyright 1998 by the President and Fellows of Harvard College. Copyright 1951, 1955, 1979 by the President and Fellows of Harvard College.

Text from the Preface of *Modern American Poetry,* 5th Revised Edition, ed. by Louis Untermeyer. Copyright 1919, 1921, 1925, 1930, 1936 by Harcourt, Brace & Company, Inc. Reprinted by permission of Professional Publishing Service.

Text excerpt from "Politics and the English Language" from *Shooting an Elephant and Other Essays* by George Orwell. Copyright 1946 by Sonia Brownell Orwell and renewed 1974 by Sonia Orwell. Reprinted by permission of Harcourt, Inc., and A. M. Heath & Company, Ltd.

"Fueled" from *Serve Me a Slice of Moon* by Marcie Hans. Copyright 1965 by Marcie Hans and renewed 1993 by Ernestine Hans. Reprinted by permission of Harcourt, Inc.

"Address to the Graduating Class" from *Essays, Speeches & Public Letters by William Faulkner,* ed. by James B. Meriweather. Copyright 1951 by William Faulkner. Reprinted by permission of Random House, Inc., and Chatto & Windus, Ltd.

"Night Clouds" from *The Complete Poetical Works of Amy Lowell.* Copyright 1955 by Houghton Mifflin Company. Copyright renewed 1983 by Houghton Mifflin Company, Brinton P. Roberts, and G. D'Andelot Belin, Esq. Reprinted by permission of Houghton Mifflin Company. All rights reserved.

"Douglass" from *The Complete Poems of Paul Laurence Dunbar.* Originally published by Dodd, Mead & Company.

# Acknowledgments

Abridged excerpt from *The House of the Dead* by Fyodor Dostoyevsky, trans. by Constance Garnett. Translation copyright 1923 by Macmillan Publishing Company. Reprinted by permission of Simon & Schuster and Random House UK Ltd.

"July Storm" from *Down Half the World* by Elizabeth Coatsworth. Copyright 1924, 1926, 1946, 1949, 1950, 1952, 1953, 1954, 1955, 1956, 1957, 1958, 1959, 1963, 1964, 1968 by Elizabeth Coatsworth Beton. Reprinted by permission of Macmillan Publishing Company.

# Before You Begin

## HOW THIS BOOK IS ORGANIZED

Whether you have five months, nine weeks, or just two short weeks to prepare for the exam, *Peterson's Master AP English Literature & Composition* will help you develop a study plan that caters to your individual needs and timetable. These step-by-step plans are easy to follow and remarkably effective.

- **Top 10 Strategies to Raise Your Score** gives you tried and true test-taking strategies

- **Part I** includes the basic information about the AP English Literature & Composition test that you need to know.

- **Part II** provides a diagnostic test to determine your strengths and weaknesses. Use the diagnostic test as a tool to improve your objective test-taking skills.

- **Part III** provides the review and strategies for answering the different kinds of multiple-choice questions on prose and on poetry and numerous opportunities to practice what you are learning. It is a good idea to read the answer explanations to all of the questions because you may find ideas or tips that will help you better analyze the answers to questions in the next Practice Test you take. You will also find "quick" reviews of grammar and literary terms.

- **Part IV** includes three additional practice tests. Remember to apply the test-taking system carefully, work the system to get more correct responses, and be careful of your time in order to answer more questions in the time period.

- The **Appendix,** College-by-College Guide to AP Credit and Placement, provides an easy reference to the AP credit guidelines at more than 400 selective colleges and universities.

## SPECIAL STUDY FEATURES

*Peterson's Master AP English Literature & Composition* was designed to be as user-friendly as it is complete. It includes several features to make your preparation easier.

### Overview

Each chapter begins with a bulleted overview listing the topics that will be covered in the chapter. You know immediately where to look for a topic that you need to work on.

### Summing It Up

Each strategy chapter ends with a point-by-point summary that captures the most important points. The summaries are a convenient way to review the content of these strategy chapters. In addition, be sure to look in the page margins for the following test-prep tools:

### Bonus Information

#### NOTE

*Notes* highlight critical information about the test.

#### TIP

*Tips* draw your attention to valuable concepts, advice, and shortcuts for tackling the exam. By reading the tips, you will learn how to approach different question types, pace yourself, and remember what was discussed previously in the book.

#### ALERT!

Whenever you need to be careful of a common pitfall, you'll find an *Alert!* This information reveals and eliminates the misperceptions and wrong turns many people take on the exam. By taking full advantage of all features presented in *Peterson's Master AP English Literature & Composition,* you will become much more comfortable with the exam and considerably more confident about getting a high score.

## APPENDIX

Peterson's College-by-College Guide to AP Credit and Placement gives you the equivalent classes, scores, and credit awarded at more than 400 colleges and universities. Use this guide to find your possible placement status, credit, and/or exemption based on your AP English Literature & Composition score.

## YOU'RE WELL ON YOUR WAY TO SUCCESS

Remember that knowledge is power. You will be studying the most comprehensive guide available and you will become extremely knowledgeable about the exam. We look forward to helping you raise your score.

## GIVE US YOUR FEEDBACK

Peterson's, a Nelnet company, publishes a full line of resources to help guide you through the college admission process. Peterson's publications can be found at your local bookstore, library, and high school guidance office, and you can access us online at www.petersons.com.

We welcome any comments or suggestions you may have about this publication and invite you to complete our online survey at www.petersons.com/booksurvey.

Your feedback will help us to provide personalized solutions for your educational advancement.

## TABLE OF LITERARY WORKS

The following list represents all the works of literature discussed in this book, broken out by chapter.

## TOP 10 STRATEGIES TO RAISE YOUR SCORE

When it comes to taking an AP, some test-taking skills will do you more good than others. There are concepts you can learn and techniques you can follow that will help you do your best. Here are our picks for the top 10 strategies to raise your score:

1. **Create a study plan and follow it.** The right study plan will help you get the most out of this book in whatever time you have.

2. **Choose a place and time to study every day,** and stick to your routine and your plan.

3. **Complete the diagnostic and practice tests in this book.** They will give you just what they promise: practice—practice in reading and following the directions, practice in pacing yourself, practice in understanding and answering multiple-choice questions, and practice in writing timed essays.

4. **Complete all of your assignments for your regular AP English class.** Ask questions in class, talk about what you read and write, and enjoy what you are doing. The test is supposed to measure your development as an educated and thinking reader.

5. **If the question is a *main idea* or *theme* question,** look for the answer that is the most general and can be supported by evidence in the selection.

6. **All elements in an answer must be correct for the answer to be correct.**

7. **Don't rely on your memory; refer to the passage.** For poetry, read a line or two above and a line or two below the reference.

8. **With *not/except* questions, ask yourself if an answer choice is true about the selection.** If it is, cross it out, and keep checking answers.

9. **If you aren't sure about an answer but know something about the question, eliminate what you know is wrong and make an educated guess.**

10. **Finally, don't cram.** Relax. Go to a movie, visit a friend—but not one who is taking the test with you. Get a good night's sleep.

# PART I

## AP ENGLISH LITERATURE & COMPOSITION BASICS

CHAPTER 1    All About the AP English
            Literature & Composition Test

# All About the AP English Literature & Composition Test

## OVERVIEW

- 10 facts about the AP English Literature & Composition Test
- Basic information about the multiple-choice section
- Scoring the AP English Literature & Composition Test
- Suggested reading
- Creating a plan of attack
- Summing it up

This chapter provides basic information about the AP English Literature & Composition Test as well as suggestions for developing a strategy for attacking the multiple-choice portion of the test. Chapters 3 and 4 will help you master effective techniques for answering the specific types of multiple-choice questions that you will find on the test.

You have answered hundreds, probably thousands, of multiple-choice questions during your school life. The multiple choice questions on the AP English Literature & Composition Test are not that different. Of course, there is a lot riding on the AP test, but, just like other tests, if you have studied and know some test-taking techniques, you can do well.

## 10 FACTS ABOUT THE AP ENGLISH LITERATURE & COMPOSITION TEST

**① The Advanced Placement Program Offers Students an Opportunity to Receive College Credit for Courses They Take in High School.**

The AP program is a collaborative effort of secondary schools, colleges and universities, and the College Board through which students who are enrolled in AP or honors courses in any one or more of thirty-eight subject areas may receive credit or advanced placement for college-level work completed in high school. While the College Board makes recommendations about course content, it does not prescribe content. As a result, the annual testing program ensures a degree of comparability among courses in the same subject.

**② Thousands of Colleges and Universities in the United States and 30 Other Countries Participate in the AP Program.**

Neither the College Board nor your high school awards AP credit. You need to find out from the colleges to which you are planning to apply whether they grant credit and/or use AP scores for placement. It is IMPORTANT that you obtain each school's policy IN WRITING so that when you actually choose one college and register, you will have proof of what you were told.

**③ The AP English Literature & Composition Test Measures Your Ability to Read and Write Analytically.**

According to the College Board's course description, an AP English Literature & Composition course should prepare students to read literature in order to experience, interpret, and evaluate it, and to write about literature to understand, explain, and evaluate it. The test will ask you to use the skills you have developed in close reading and analytical writing to examine, answer questions about, and discuss pieces of literature that most likely are unfamiliar to you.

**④ The AP English Literature Test Has Two Parts: Multiple Choice and Essays.**

**TIP**

See Chapters 3–4 for multiple-choice strategies.

See Chapters 5–10 for strategies for writing essays.

Typically, Section I: Multiple Choice has about 50 questions divided among two poems and two prose passages (about 10 to 15 questions for each passage). This section counts for 45 percent of your total score, and you have 60 minutes to complete it.

In Section II, you have three essays to write: a free response essay analyzing a poem, a free response essay analyzing a prose passage, and an open essay on a topic that you are given. The essays count for 55 percent of your total score, approximately 18 percentage points for each essay. You have 40 minutes to write each essay (120 minutes total).

**⑤ The Poetry and Prose Passages Cover English and American Literature from the English Renaissance to the 21st Century.**

**TIP**

See "Suggested Reading," p. 9.

On occasion, translations of European literature appear on the test, but for the most part, you will find poetry and prose passages (fiction, nonfiction, and drama) that were originally written in English. That means the authorship could also be African, Australian, Canadian, Indian, or West Indian. There is no way you can read every possible piece of literature that might appear, but you can hone your skills and work up example pieces.

**6** **There Is No Required Length for Your Essays.**

It is the quality, not the quantity, that counts. Realistically, a one-paragraph essay is not going to garner you a high mark because you cannot develop a well-reasoned analysis and present it effectively in a single paragraph. An essay of five paragraphs is a good goal. By following this model, you can set out your ideas with an interesting introduction, develop a reasoned body, and provide a solid ending.

**7** **You Will Get a Composite Score for Your Test.**

The College Board reports a single score from 1 to 5 for the two-part test, with 5 being the highest. By understanding how you can balance the number of questions you need to answer correctly against the essay score you need to receive in order to get at least a "3," you can relieve some of your anxiety about passing the test.

**8** **Educated Guessing Can Help.**

No points are deducted for questions that go unanswered on the multiple-choice section, and don't expect to have time to answer them all. A quarter of a point is deducted for each wrong answer. The College Board suggests guessing IF you know something about a question and can eliminate a couple of the answer choices. Call it "educated guessing."

**TIP**

See "Scoring the AP English Literature & Composition Test," p. 6.

**9** **The Test Is Given in Mid-May.**

Most likely, the test will be given at your school, so you do not have to worry about finding a strange school building in a strange city. You will be in familiar surroundings—that should reduce your anxiety a bit. If the test is given in another school, be sure to take identification with you.

**10** **Studying for the Test Can Make a Difference.**

The first step is to familiarize yourself with the format and directions for each part of the test. Then, you will not waste time on the day of the test trying to understand what you are supposed to do. The second step is to put those analytical skills you have been learning to work, dissecting and understanding the kinds of questions you will be asked. The third step is to practice "writing-on-demand" for the essays. So let's get started.

**TIP**

Stop first at p. 17 and read "Nine-Week Practice Plan for Studying for the AP English Literature & Composition Test."

## BASIC INFORMATION ABOUT THE MULTIPLE-CHOICE SECTION

**1** Section I generally consists of about 50 multiple-choice questions. You are given five possible answers for each question.

**2** Section I typically has two prose passages and two poetry passages. Each selection has 10 to 15 questions.

③ You will have 60 minutes to answer all of the questions.

④ The multiple-choice questions fall into two categories: six types of comprehension questions and two kinds of factual knowledge questions.

⑤ You receive one point for each correct answer you give. You receive no points for each question you leave blank. If you answer incorrectly, a quarter of a point is subtracted. This is the guessing penalty.

⑥ Section I accounts for 45 percent of your final composite score.

Besides the obvious importance of understanding the material, you have probably discovered during your educational career that there are three significant considerations when taking multiple-choice tests:

❶ Accurate reading and analysis of test material

❷ Time management

❸ Educated guesses

The consequences of failing to do any of the above can be disastrous to your score:

- If you fail to read the selections or the questions carefully, you may make errors that are unnecessary.

- If you neglect time, you may miss opportunities for showing what you know.

- If you do not make educated guesses to answer questions you are not sure of, then you are missing out on a higher score.

How do you prevent these things from happening and ensure your highest score? You need to develop a plan to read effectively, to manage your time well, and to use all of your knowledge to the best possible effect.

## SCORING THE AP ENGLISH LITERATURE & COMPOSITION TEST

Around early July, you and the colleges you designate will receive a score from 1 to 5, with 5 being the highest, for your AP English Literature & Composition Test. Your high school will receive its report a little later. The multiple-choice section is graded by machine, and your essays are graded during a marathon reading session by high school and college teachers.

A different reader grades each of your essays. None of the readers knows who you are (that's why you fill in identification information on your Section II booklet and then seal it) or how the others scored your other essays. Each reader is familiar with the work discussed in the essay question she or he is reading. Even your open essay choice is read by someone familiar with the work. The grading is done on a holistic system; that is, the overall essay is scored, not just the development of your ideas, your spelling, or your punctuation. For each essay, the

College Board works out grading criteria for the readers to use, much as your teacher uses a rubric to evaluate your writing.

## What the Composite Score Means

The College Board refers to the composite score as weighted because a factor of about 1.3 (the exact number varies from year to year) for the multiple-choice questions and a factor of 3.0556 for the essay questions are used to determine a raw score for each section. That is, the actual score you get on the multiple-choice questions—say 35—is multiplied by about 1.3 (1.2273 for 55 questions in a recent year). The actual score that you get on the essay test—say 21—is multiplied by 3.0556. Those two numbers, your raw scores, are then added, and the resulting score—somewhere between 0 and 150 (107, based on the above example)—is then equated to a number from 5 to 1. A score of 107 is good enough to get you a "5" for the test.

## What Does All of This Mean To You?

You can leave blank or answer incorrectly some combination of 20 questions on a 55-question multiple-choice section, get a 7 for each of your three essays, and still earn a score of 5. It is not as easy as it may seem, or the majority of students would not fall into the "3" range, although a 3 may be good enough to get you college credit or advanced placement. A score of 4 certainly will.

Take a look at the charts below. It takes work, but raising your score may not be impossible. Sometimes the difference between a 3 and a 4 or a 4 and a 5 is only a couple of points.

| POSSIBLE SCORE DISTRIBUTION FOR A 55-QUESTION MULTIPLE-CHOICE SECTION | | | | | |
|---|---|---|---|---|---|
| SCORE = 5 | | SCORE = 4 | | SCORE = 3 | |
| MC | Essays (3) | MC | Essays (3) | MC | Essays (3) |
| 25 | 25 (8.33 ) | 25 | 21 (7) | 25 | 14 (4.66) |
| 30 | 23 (7.66) | 30 | 19 (6.33) | 30 | 12 (4) |
| 35 | 21 (7) | 35 | 17 (5.66) | 35 | 10 (3.33) |
| 40 | 19 (6.33) | 40 | 15 (5) | 40 | 8 (2.66) |
| 45 | 17 (5.66) | 45 | 13 (4.33) | 45 | 6 (2) |

The highest score you can receive on an essay is a 9, so the highest total essay score is 27. It is possible to get a variety of scores on your essays—7, 5, 5, for example. The chances are that you will not get a wide range of individual essay scores like 6, 2, 5. Even if you did, you could still get at least a 3 and possibly a 4, depending on how many correct answers you have in the multiple-choice section weighed against how many wrong answers you have.

| AP Grade | AP Qualifier | Composite Scores | Probability of Receiving Credit |
|---|---|---|---|
| 5 | Extremely Well Qualified | 107–150 | Yes |
| 4 | Well Qualified | 93–106 | Yes |
| 3 | Qualified | 73–92 | Probably |
| 2 | Possibly Qualified | 43–72 | Rarely |
| 1 | No Recommendation | 0–42 | No |

According to the College Board, about three quarters of the students who took the test in a recent year received a 3 or better. The cut-off point for passing grades may change from year to year, but it remains in this range. This chart shows the actual conversion scale in a recent year. What it means is that you do not have to answer all the questions, nor do you have to answer them all correctly, nor write three "9" essays to receive your AP credit.

## Some Things to Remember

NOTE

These are important facts straight from the College Board.

❶ The multiple-choice section is worth 45 percent of your total score.

❷ The College Board says that "students who perform acceptably on the free-response section" can receive a 3 if they answer correctly 50 to 60 percent of the multiple-choice questions.

❸ There is no deduction for unanswered questions.

❹ There is a quarter-point deduction for wrong answers.

❺ The three essays together account for 55 percent of your total score, with each essay being counted equally; that is, the open essay counts for the same number of percentage points as the other two essays.

## Why Are We Telling You These Facts?

Because you can use them to your advantage.

❶ It is important to spend time practicing the kinds of questions that you will find in the multiple-choice section because 45 percent of your score comes from that section. You do not have to put all your emphasis on the essay questions.

**②–③** You can leave some questions unanswered and still do well. Even though you will be practicing how to pace yourself as you use this book, you may not be able to complete all 50 or so questions the day of the test. If you come across a really incomprehensible passage, you can skip it and come back to it later and still feel that you are not doomed to a low score.

**④** There is a guessing penalty. If you do not know anything about the question or the choices, do not take a chance. However, if you know something about the question and can eliminate one or more of the answer choices, then it is probably worth your while to choose one of the other answers. Rather than calling it guessing, call it EDUCATED GUESSING. Even the College Board suggests this strategy.

**⑤** Because all three essays count for the same number of points, the open essay is no more important than the other two. It may seem more important because it provides you with so many choices, but you can make it manageable, as you will see in Chapter 9.

**TIP**

The diagnostic and practice tests will help you pace yourself on the exam.

**TIP**

See Chapters 3 and 4 for strategies for educated guessing.

**TIP**

Chapter 9 offers strategies for being prepared for the open essay.

## SUGGESTED READING

The following list of novelists, short story writers, dramatists, poets, essayists, and diarists draws heavily from the selection of writers that the College Board suggests students read during an AP English literature course. The works have been chosen from a variety of sources to provide representative examples of literary types and periods. In studying for the test, use this list to practice developing essay responses.

### Poetry

Auden, W. H., "The Unknown Citizen," "Lay Your Sleeping Head, My Love"

Bishop, Elizabeth, *North & South—A Cold Spring*

Blake, William, "London," "The Tyger," "The Marriage of Heaven and Hell"

Bradstreet, Anne, *Contemplations,* "To My Dear and Loving Husband"

Braithwaite, Edward Kamau, *Third World Poems*

Brooks, Gwendolyn, *Annie Allen, Riot*

Browning, Robert, "My Last Duchess," "The Bishop Orders His Tomb"

Byron, George Gordon, Lord, "Childe Harold's Pilgrimage: Canto III," "When we two parted," "So we'll go no more a-roving"

Chaucer, Geoffrey, *Canterbury Tales*

Cervantes, Lorna Dee, *Emplumada*

Coleridge, Samuel Taylor, "The Rime of the Ancient Mariner"

cummings, e.e., "anyone lived in a pretty how town," "buffalo bill's defunct"

Dickinson, Emily, "Success is counted sweetest," "I cannot live with you," "There came a day at Summer's full," "There's a certain slant of light"

Donne, John, "A Valediction Forbidding Mourning," "The Flea"

Dove, Rita, *The Yellow House on the Corner, Thomas and Beulah*

Eliot, T. S., "The Hollow Men," "The Love Song of J. Alfred Prufrock," "The Waste Land"

Frost, Robert, "The Road Not Taken," "The Wood-Pile," "Birches"

H. D. (Hilda Doolittle), *Sea Garden, The Walls Do Not Fall*

Heaney, Seamus, *Station Island, North*

Herbert, George, "The Pulley," "Easter Wings"

Hongo, Garrett, *Yellow Light, The River of Heaven*

Hopkins, Gerard Manley, "The Windhover," "The Caged Skylark," "Spring and Fall," "The Wreck of the Deutschland"

Hughes, Langston, "Dreams," "My People," "The Negro Speaks of Rivers"

Jarrell, Randall, *The Woman at the Washington Zoo*

Keats, John, "To Autumn," "The Eve of St. Agnes," "Ode on a Grecian Urn," "La Belle Dame sans Merci"

Lowell, Robert, *Lord Weary's Castle, The Dolphin*

Marvell, Andrew, "To His Coy Mistress," "The Garden"

Milton, John, *Paradise Lost,* "On His Blindness," "Lycidas"

Moore, Marianne, *Collected Poems*

Plath, Sylvia, *Collected Poems*

Poe, Edgar Allan, "The Raven," "The Bells"

Pope, Alexander, "The Rape of the Lock"

Rich, Adrienne, *Diving into the Wreck*

Sexton, Anne, *Live or Die, Transformation*

Shakespeare, William, *Sonnets*

Shelley, Percy Bysshe, "Ozymandias," "Ode to the West Wind," "Mutability"

Silko, Leslie Marmon, *Laguna Women: Poems*

Song, Cathy, *Picture Bride*

Tennyson, Alfred Lord, "Morte d'Arthur," "The Lotus-Eaters," "Ulysses"

Walcott, Derek, *Collected Poems, 1948–1984*

Whitman, Walt, "Song of Myself," "Crossing Brooklyn Ferry," "Beat! Beat! Drums"

Wilbur, Richard, *Things of This World*

Williams, William Carlos, *Pictures from Brueghel, Paterson*

Wordsworth, William, "Lucy Gray," "Daffodils," "Ode: Intimations of Immortality"

Yeats, William Butler, "The Lake Isle of Innisfree," "When You Are Old"

## Drama

Aeschylus, *Orestes Trilogy*

Albee, Edward, *Who's Afraid of Virginia Woolf?*

Baraka, Amiri, *The Dutchman*

Beckett, Samuel, *Waiting for Godot, Endgame*

Chekhov, Anton, *The Cherry Orchard, The Sea Gull*

Congreve, William, *The Way of the World*

Eliot, T. S., *Murder in the Cathedral, The Cocktail Party*

Goldsmith, Oliver, *She Stoops to Conquer*

Hansberry, Lorraine, *Raisin in the Sun*

Hellman, Lillian, *The Little Foxes*

Hwang, David Henry, *M. Butterfly*

Ibsen, Henrik, *A Doll's House, Hedda Gabler, Enemy of the People*

Ionesco, Eugene, *Rhinoceros, The Bald Soprano*

Jonson, Ben, *Volpone*

Mamet, David, *Glengarry Glen Ross, American Buffalo*

Miller, Arthur, *Death of a Salesman, The Crucible, All My Sons*

Moliere, *Tartuffe, The Physician in Spite of Himself*

O'Casey, Sean, *Juno and the Paycock, The Plough and the Stars*

O'Neill, Eugene, *Long Day's Journey Into Night, Mourning Becomes Electra*

Pinter, Harold, *The Birthday Party, Master Harold and the Boys*

Pirandello, Luigi, *Six Characters in Search of an Author*

Shakespeare, William, *Hamlet, Macbeth, Richard III, Othello, King Lear, Twelfth Night, Antony and Cleopatra*

Shaw, George Bernard, *Major Barbara, Arms and the Man, Pygmalion*

Shepard, Sam, *Buried Child*

Sheridan, Richard Brinsley, *The Rivals, The School for Scandal*

Sophocles, *Antigone, Electra, Oedipus Rex*

Stoppard, Tom, *Rosencrantz and Guildenstern Are Dead*

Valdez, Luis, *Zoot Suit*

Wilde, Oscar, *The Importance of Being Earnest*

Williams, Tennessee, *The Glass Menagerie, A Streetcar Named Desire*

Wilson, August, *The Piano Player, Joe Turner's Come and Gone, Fences*

## Fiction

Achebe, Chinua, *Things Fall Apart*

Amis, Kingsley, *Lucky Jim*

Atwood, Margaret, *The Handmaid's Tale*

Austen, Jane, *Northanger Abbey, Pride and Prejudice*

Baldwin, James, *Go Tell It on the Mountain*

Bellow, Saul, *Herzog, Humboldt's Gift*

Brontë, Charlotte, *Jane Eyre*

Brontë, Emily, *Wuthering Heights*

Carver, Raymond, *Will You Please Be Quiet, Please?*

Cather, Willa, "Paul's Case"

Cheever, John, *The Wapshot Scandal, The Wapshot Chronicle, The Stories of John Cheever*

Chopin, Kate, *The Awakening*

Cisneros, Sandra, *The House on Mango Street, Woman Hollering Creek*

Colette, *Gigi, The Cat, Cheri*

Conrad, Joseph, *Heart of Darkness, Lord Jim*

Crane, Stephen, "The Open Boat"

Desai, Anita, *Clear Light of Day*

Dickens, Charles, *Tale of Two Cities, David Copperfield, Nicholas Nickleby*

Eliot, George, *Middlemarch*

Ellison, Ralph, *Invisible Man*

Erdrich, Louise, *Love Medicine, The Beet Queen*

Faulkner, William, *As I Lay Dying, The Sound and the Fury, Light in August*

Fielding, Henry, *Tom Jones*

Fitzgerald, F. Scott, *The Great Gatsby*

Ford, Ford Maddox, *The Good Soldier*

Forster, E. M., *Passage to India*

Hardy, Thomas, *Return of the Native, Tess of the D'Urbervilles, Jude the Obscure*

Hawthorne, Nathaniel, *The Scarlet Letter*

Hemingway, Ernest, *The Sun Also Rises, A Farewell to Arms, The Old Man and the Sea*

Hijuelos, Oscar, *The Mambo Kings Play Songs of Love*

Hurston, Zora Neale, *Their Eyes Were Watching God*

Ishiguro, Kazuo, *Remains of the Day*

James, Henry, *Daisy Miller, The Americans, Portrait of a Lady*

Joyce, James, *The Dubliners* (collection), *Portrait of the Artist as a Young Man*

Kogawa, Joy, *Obasan*

Kingston, Maxine Hong, *The Woman Warrior*

Laurence, Margaret, *This Side Jordan, A Jest of God*

Lawrence, D. H., *Sons and Lovers, Women in Love*

Malamud, Bernard, *The Assistant*

Mansfield, Katherine, *Bliss, The Garden Party* (both collections)

Márquez, Gabríel Garcia, *Chronicle of a Death Foretold*

Mason, Bobbie Ann, *Shiloh and Other Stories*

McCullers, Carson, *The Heart Is a Lonely Hunter, Member of the Wedding, The Balled of the Sad Café* (collection)

Melville, Herman, *Moby Dick,* "Benito Cereno"

Morrison, Toni, *The Bluest Eye, Beloved*

Mukherjee, Bharati, *Jasmine*

Naipaul, V. S., *A Bend in the River*

O'Connor, Flannery, *A Good Man Is Hard to Find, Everything That Rises Must Converge* (both collections)

Ozick, Cynthia, *Heir to the Glittering World*

Paton, Alan, *Too Late the Phalarope; Cry, the Beloved Country*

Porter, Katherine Anne, *Flowering Judas; Pale Horse, Pale Rider* (both collections)

Rhys, Jean, *Wide Sargasso Sea*

Swift, Jonathan, *Gulliver's Travels,* "A Modest Proposal"

Tan, Amy, *The Kitchen God's Wife*

Tolstoy, Leo, *Anna Karenina, War and Peace*

Twain, Mark, *Pudd'nhead Wilson*

Tyler, Anne, *Dinner at the Homesick Restaurant*

Updike, John, *Rabbit Is Rich*

Valenzuela, Luisa, *Clara*

Walker, Alice, *The Color Purple*

Waugh, Evelyn, *Brideshead Revisited*

Welty, Eudora, *The Optimist's Daughter*

Wharton, Edith, *Ethan Frome, The House of Mirth, The Age of Innocence*

Wideman, John Edgar, *Brothers and Keepers*

Woolf, Virginia, *To the Lighthouse, Mrs. Dalloway*

Wright, Richard, *Native Son*

## Nonfiction

Angelou, Maya, *I Know Why the Caged Bird Sings*

Addison, Joseph, *The Tatler, The Spectator*

Arnold, Matthew, *Culture and Anarchy*

Baldwin, James, *Notes of a Native Son*

Boswell, James, *Life of Samuel Johnson*

Carlyle, Thomas, *On Heroes, Hero-Worship, and the Heroic in History*

Colón, Jesús, *Puerto Ricans in New York*

Emerson, Ralph Waldo, "Self-Reliance," "Nature"

Hazlitt, William, *Sketches and Essays*

Johnson, Samuel, *The Rambler, The Idler*

Lamb, Charles, *Essays of Elia*

Mailer, Norman, *The Armies of the Night, A Fire on the Moon*

Mencken, H. L., *Prejudices*

Mill, John Stuart, *On Liberty*

Orwell, George, "Shooting an Elephant"

Steele, Richard, *The Tatler, The Spectator*

Thomas, Lewis, *Et Cetera, Et Cetera: Notes of a Word Watcher*

Thoreau, Henry David, *Walden*

Tuchman, Barbara, *The Guns of August, Practising History* (collection)

Woolf, Virginia, *A Room of One's Own*

## CREATING A PLAN OF ATTACK

Consider the following four steps to help you create an effective plan of attack for Section I:

**1** Pace yourself.

**2** Review the selections to decide which passage and set of questions to do first and which to do last.

**3** Read the selections, using different strategies for poetry and for prose.

**4** Answer the questions.

### Pacing Yourself

**NOTE**

Be sure to take a watch with you so you can pace yourself. Be courteous—don't use the alarm.

The first part of the strategy for acing the multiple-choice section is time awareness. Since you have 60 minutes for Section I, give yourself approximately 14 minutes for each of the four passages. (You will see under *Setting Priorities* why it's not 15 minutes.) Use that 14 minutes per selection as a guideline. If you find you are spending significantly more time per selection, speed up. In the unlikely event that you finish with time to spare, revisit any problem passages to see if you can answer any of the questions you left blank.

If, as the hour comes to an end, you find that you have only five or so minutes and another passage to complete, try this technique. Do not read the passage; read the questions instead. Some questions, such as those asking about vocabulary, can be answered just by reading the lines that are identified. Others ask specific questions about specific portions of the selection. Answer these sorts of questions when time is short. And remember, you only need to answer 50 to 60 percent of the questions correctly to set the groundwork for a score of "5."

### Setting Priorities

The first active step to take is prioritizing the passages. Quickly scan the four passages (this is where the extra 4 minutes come in) to find which ones seem difficult to you and which seem easier. You do not have to complete questions or passages in the order they appear on the test. Do the most difficult one last and the easiest one first. Since many students only finish three passages, you will score more points by working on the passages you are most comfortable with and leaving the most difficult for last.

### Reading Passages: Effective Strategies for Prose and Poetry

This step is obvious—read the selections. Do not forget that you are reading in a test situation. You must answer questions on the material. However, you do not need to memorize the passage or retain the content for long. For all passages, whether they are poetry or prose, first skim the passage to get a general sense of the major ideas and the writer's purpose. How you will proceed from this point depends on the type of literature you must read.

## READING PROSE PASSAGES

Begin by scanning the selection. When you scan a prose selection, take only 30 or so seconds to do so. You want an overview here; don't worry about details. Then concentrate and read the selection carefully. Read for a clear, specific understanding of the writer's main idea. The main idea is the underlying communication that the writer is trying to make. It is not details, but the fundamental message you, the reader, are to receive. Ask yourself what the author's purpose is in writing and what is revealed about the subject. Be aware of your reactions to the piece. Make predictions about conclusions. Mentally summarize important points and supporting details.

CAUTION: Rarely will you find a topic sentence or a literal thesis statement in AP selections. You will need to interpret the literature to find the key concept of the passage.

## READING POETRY PASSAGES

Poetry's special requirements call for some techniques different from those for reading other types of literature. First, skim the poem for the general sense. Then read it carefully and slowly, but do not read the poem line by line. Read it sentence by sentence, and then phrase by phrase, paying attention to the punctuation. Ask yourself what the poet seems to be saying to you and question the meaning of the language and the impact of the images. Then read the poem again more quickly to gauge the effect the poem has on you. Listen to the musical qualities, the rhythm, and the rhyme. Pause to summarize where appropriate, even paraphrase mentally. Pull the details together to understand the meaning.

If you still do not understand the whole poem, do not spend any more time on it. Some unintelligible phrases (or a line or two) will not make that much difference to your total score.

## Attacking the Questions: Practical Advice

When you take the AP examination, you will want to have every advantage possible. Of course, the ideal is to know the correct answer as soon as you read the question, but that does not always happen. Here are some methods to help you score well.

As we said above, you do not have to do anything on the exam in the order presented. You can and should answer the questions in the order that works for you. By showing yourself that you know answers, you build self-confidence. Remember that as you work through the questions, you can return to the passage to find answers you do not immediately recall. Often the question will have the line numbers identified for reference.

One technique that is especially helpful for achieving your best score is educated guessing. Use this technique when you do not know the correct answer immediately.

- First, ignore answers that are obviously wrong.

- Discard choices in which part of the response is incorrect.

**TIP**

Check the "Nine-Week Practice Plan for Studying for the AP English Literature & Composition Test," p. 17.

- Revisit remaining answers to decide which seems more correct. Remember to eliminate any response that has anything wrong about it.

- Choose the answer that you feel is right. Trust yourself. Your subconscious will usually guide you to the correct choice. Do not argue with yourself.

You are probably thinking about the quarter-point penalty for an incorrect answer, and you are wondering if taking a chance is worth the possible point loss. Recognize that if you use this technique, your chances are excellent of scoring higher. You are not guessing, but making an educated guess. You will have to answer four questions incorrectly to lose a single point. If you have an idea about which choice is correct, act on it. Even the College Board suggests that you guess as long as you can eliminate some answer choices.

## Analyzing the Types of Questions

Most multiple-choice questions test how carefully you read and how well you interpret what you read. Comprehension questions fall into six categories: main idea, detail, inference, definition, tone and purpose, and questions about form. There are also two types of factual knowledge questions that may appear. If you can identify the type of question you are facing, you can employ the best strategies to answer it correctly.

### COMPREHENSION QUESTIONS

- **Main Idea Questions.** This type of question asks you to determine the subject of an entire passage. A main idea question may require you to identify the subject or to select the choice that best describes what the passage is about. Skimming the first and last paragraphs of a passage is a helpful technique for answering these questions because writers often state their topic in the beginning or end of a selection—although not in a single neat sentence in the selections that the College Board chooses.

- **Detail Questions.** Detail questions are ones that you can usually get right because they almost always tell you where to look in the passage to interpret an aspect of the passage.

- **Inference Questions.** These are probably the most difficult to answer because the answers are not stated directly in the selection. You must piece together facts and make a generalization based on those facts. Most inference questions include key words such as *think, predict, indicate, feel, probably, seem, imply, suggest, assume, infer,* and *most likely.* When you come upon a question that contains one of these terms, return to the selection to find the specific sentences that the question refers to and make a generalization based on the clues. Remember, in answering an inference question you are making a guess, but the best guess is based upon facts from the selection.

- **Definition Questions.** These are basically vocabulary questions about difficult words in a passage or about ordinary words that are used with a special meaning. Go to the selection and read the sentence in which the word appears, and then substitute each of the possible choices to see which is closest in meaning. You may need to read the sentences that surround the one containing the word or phrase in question to get the full sense of the idea. Avoid choosing a word or phrase just because it looks or sounds like the word or phrase to be defined, unless you have checked it in context.

- **Tone and Purpose Questions.** These questions ask you to determine how or why the author wrote the material. The tone reflects the writer's attitude toward the subject and the audience. The purpose defines the effect the author wants to have on the audience. Understanding the tone helps you understand the purpose. Writers convey the purpose through their choice of words and the impression those words create. Some possible tones are *admiration, adoration, optimism, contempt, pride, objectivity, disappointment, respect, surprise, anger, regret, irony, indignation, suspicion, pessimism,* and *amusement.*

- **Form Questions.** Form is the method of organization that a writer uses. As you read, observe the patterns of organization used. While some authors will use only one form, others may use a combination. When analyzing poetry, be sensitive to rhythm and rhyme schemes, numbers of lines, and stanzas. With prose, look for comparison and contrast, cause and effect, order or importance, logical sequence of events, and spatial order.

## FACTUAL KNOWLEDGE QUESTIONS

- **English Language Questions.** These questions may test your knowledge of English grammar, punctuation, or mechanics. Remember that often these are comprehension questions. Other questions test your understanding of literary terminology.

- **Cultural Questions.** This question type tests your knowledge of facts that are a part of our civilization. Well-educated people should know this type of information. There are very few of these questions on the AP test.

## Nine-Week Practice Plan for Studying for the AP English Literature & Composition Test

The following plan should be followed for nine weeks. The best study plan is one that continues through a full semester. Then you have time to think about ideas and to talk with your teacher and other students about what you are learning, and you will not feel rushed. Staying relaxed about the test is important. A full-semester study plan also means that you can apply what you are learning here to classwork—your essay writing—and apply your classwork—everything that you are reading—to test preparation. The plan is worked out so that you should spend about 3 hours on each lesson.

## WEEK 1

**First:** Take the *Practice Test 1: Diagnostic,* pp. 27–60, and complete the self-scoring process. List the areas that you had difficulty with, such as timing, question types, and writing on demand.

**Then:** Reread the basic information and facts about the test and its scoring, pp. 3–9.

## WEEK 2

### Lesson 1

- Read *Top 10 Strategies to Raise Your Score.*

- Reread pp. 6–9 to remind yourself that a score of at least "3" is achievable.

- Review the list you made after the *Practice Test 1: Diagnostic* to see what you need to learn about the multiple-choice section.

- Read Chapter 1, *All About the AP English Literature & Composition Test,* p. 3.

- Read Chapter 3, *About the Multiple-Choice Questions Related to Prose,* p. 63.

- Do two sets of Exercises at the end of the chapter and review the answers.

### Lesson 2

- Review Chapter 3, *About the Multiple-Choice Questions Related to Prose,* and do another two sets of Exercises at the end of the chapter.

- Review the answers for these Exercises.

## WEEK 3

### Lesson 1

- Reread *Top 10 Strategies to Raise Your Score.*

- Reread *Scoring the AP English Literature & Composition Test,* pp. 6–9, to remind yourself that a score of at least "3" is achievable. It may seem boring by now, but it is important to remember that the test score does not ride on the essays.

- Review Chapter 1, *All About the AP English Literature & Composition Test.*

- Review the list you made after the *Practice Test 1: Diagnostic* to see what you need to learn about the multiple-choice section.

- Read Chapter 4, *About the Multiple-Choice Questions Related to Poetry.*

- Do two sets of Exercises at the end of the chapter and review the answers.

### Lesson 2

- Review Chapter 4, *About the Multiple-Choice Questions Related to Poetry,* and do another two sets of Exercises at the end of the chapter.

- Review the answers for these Exercises.

**WEEK 4**

*Lesson 1*

- Answer the multiple-choice section of *Practice Test 2* and complete the self-scoring process.
- Compare the score to the score on the *Practice Test 1: Diagnostic*. Which question types continue to be a concern?
- Reread Chapters 1, 3, and 4 as needed.

*Lesson 2*

- Read Chapter 5, *About the "9" Essay,* p. 121, and practice the activities.
- Read Chapter 11, *A Quick Review of Grammar* et al.

**WEEK 5**

*Lesson 1*

- Read Chapter 6, *About the Free Response Essay on Prose* and write one of the *Practice Essays* at the end of the chapter. Use the 10-step process on the *Free Response Guides,* pages 182–185, as a guide.
- Complete the self-scoring process and compare your score to the score on the *Practice Test 1: Diagnostic* prose essay.
- Ask a responsible friend, an AP classmate, or a teacher to evaluate your essay using the scoring guide.

*Lesson 2*

- Read Chapter 7, *About the Free Response Essay on Poetry* and write one of the *Practice Essays* at the end of the chapter. Use the 10-step process on the *Free Response Guides,* pages 182–185, as a guide.
- Complete the self-scoring process, and compare your score to the score on the *Practice Test 1: Diagnostic* poetry essay.
- Again, ask a responsible friend, an AP classmate, or a teacher to evaluate your essay using the scoring guide.

**WEEK 6**

*Lesson 1*

- Complete the free response essays (not the open essay question) on *Practice Test 2,* and score your essays against the rubrics.
- Again, ask a responsible friend, an AP classmate, or a teacher to evaluate your essay using the scoring guide.
- Compare your scores to the scores on the *Practice Test 1: Diagnostic.* Where did you improve? Where does your writing still need work?
- Reread Chapters 6 and 7 as needed.

### Lesson 2

- Read Chapter 9, *About the Open Essay* and write one of the *Practice Essays*. Use the 10-step process on the *Open Response Guides*, pages 232–235, as a guide.

- Complete the self-scoring process and compare your score against the score on the *Practice Test 1: Diagnostic*.

- Again, ask a responsible friend, an AP classmate, or a teacher to evaluate your essay using the scoring guide. Where did you improve? Where does your writing still need work?

- Reread Chapter 9 as needed.

### WEEK 7

### Lesson 1

- Answer the open essay question on *Practice Test 2* and score your essay against the rubric.

- Ask a responsible friend, an AP classmate, or a teacher to evaluate your essay using the scoring guide as well. Compare it to the score on the *Practice Test 1: Diagnostic*.

- Choose a book or play that you have studied and work it up using the suggestions in Chapter 9 as a guide.

### Lesson 2

- Choose another book or play that you have studied and work it up using the chapter suggestions as a guide.

### WEEK 8

### Lesson 1

- Take *Practice Test 3* and complete the self-scoring process. Compare it to your scores for the other two tests. Work on your weaknesses for the next two weeks.

### Lesson 2

- Just to prove that you know more than you may think about literary analysis, choose a book that you have read but not studied in class and work it up for the test. Look at the list of writers in *Suggested Reading* and see if there is an author whose work you have read that you could use for practice.

### WEEK 9

### Lesson 1

- Take *Practice Test 4* and complete the self-scoring process. Check your results against the other three tests.

### Lesson 2

- If you are still unsure about some areas, review those chapters, including the answers to the practice activities.

- Review the suggestions in Chapter 9 and the examples you have worked up for the test.

- Reread *Scoring the AP English Literature & Composition Test* and *Top 10 Strategies to Raise Your Score.*

## The Panic Plan

Eighteen weeks, nine weeks—how about two weeks? If you are the kind of person who puts everything off until the last possible minute, here is a two-week Panic Plan. Its objectives are to make you familiar with the test format and directions, to help you get as many right answers as possible, and to write the best open essay you can.

### WEEK 1

- Read *Top 10 Strategies to Raise Your Score* and *Scoring the AP English Literature & Composition Test.*

- Take the *Practice Test 1: Diagnostic.* Read the directions carefully and use a timer for each section.

- Complete the self-scoring process. You can learn a lot about the types of questions in the multiple-choice section by working through the answers.

### Multiple Choice

- Answer the multiple-choice section on *Practice Test 2.*

- Complete the self-scoring process and see where you may still have problems with question types.

- Read all the answer explanations, including those you identified correctly.

- Answer the multiple-choice section on *Practice Test 3,* concentrating on the question types that are still tricky.

- Complete the self-scoring process.

- Read all the answer explanations, including those you identified correctly.

### Essays

- Complete the essay section on *Practice Test 2.*

- Score your essays using the rubrics. List your weaknesses.

- Write one practice essay on poetry and one on prose using practice questions in Chapters 6 and 7, *About the Free Response Essay on Prose* and *About the Free Response Essay on Poetry.*

- Score your essays against the rubrics, noting areas that need improvement.

- Ask a responsible friend, an AP classmate, or a teacher to evaluate your essays using the scoring guide as well. Compare to the score on the *Practice Test 1: Diagnostic.*

- Complete the essay section on *Practice Test 3,* concentrating on the areas of weakness.

- Score your essays against the rubrics, noting areas for improvement.

- Again, ask a responsible friend, an AP classmate, or a teacher to evaluate your essays using the scoring guide. Compare to the score on the *Practice Test 1: Diagnostic.*

## WEEK 2

- Reread *Top 10 Strategies to Raise Your Score* and *Scoring the AP English Literature & Composition Test.*

- Complete *Practice Test 4* and score the multiple-choice and essay sections.

### Multiple Choice

- Work on at least two practice sets of multiple-choice questions in Chapters 3 and 4, *About the Multiple-Choice Questions Related to Prose* and *About the Multiple-Choice Questions Related to Poetry.*

### Essays

- Read Chapter 9, *About the Open Essay.*

- Choose two books you have studied in class and prepare them using the suggestions in the chapter.

- Choose one book that you have read from the list of authors in *Suggested Reading* but have not studied in class, and work it up using the suggestions in Chapter 11.

- Write another set of essays—free response and open—from practice questions in Chapters 6, 7, and 9, working on strengthening your weaknesses. Score your practice essays against their rubrics.

- Ask a responsible friend, an AP classmate, or a teacher to evaluate your essays using the scoring guide.

**TIP**

The 10-step process in the *Free Response* and *Open Response Essay Guides* can help you with planning, pacing, and organizing your essays.

## SUMMING IT UP

- The AP Program offers an opportunity to receive college credit for courses taken in high school.

- The AP English Literature & Composition course prepares students to read literature and to experience, interpret, and evaluate it.

- Section I: Multiple Choice contains about 50 questions testing poetry and prose passages; Section II requires writing 3 essays.

- The multiple-choice questions include the following types:

    - Main Idea

    - Detail

    - Inference

    - Definition

    - Tone and Purpose

    - Form

    - Factual Knowledge

- The multiple-choice section is graded by machine and the essays are graded during a reading session by high school and college teachers.

- The highest score you can receive on an essay is a 9, so the highest total essay score is 27.

- The three essays together account for 55 percent of the total score.

- The suggested reading list draws heavily from the selection of writers that the College Board suggests students read during their AP literature course.

# PART II
## DIAGNOSING STRENGTHS AND WEAKNESSES

CHAPTER 2    Practice Test 1: Diagnostic

# ANSWER SHEET PRACTICE TEST 1: DIAGNOSTIC

## SECTION I

1. Ⓐ Ⓑ Ⓒ Ⓓ Ⓔ
2. Ⓐ Ⓑ Ⓒ Ⓓ Ⓔ
3. Ⓐ Ⓑ Ⓒ Ⓓ Ⓔ
4. Ⓐ Ⓑ Ⓒ Ⓓ Ⓔ
5. Ⓐ Ⓑ Ⓒ Ⓓ Ⓔ
6. Ⓐ Ⓑ Ⓒ Ⓓ Ⓔ
7. Ⓐ Ⓑ Ⓒ Ⓓ Ⓔ
8. Ⓐ Ⓑ Ⓒ Ⓓ Ⓔ
9. Ⓐ Ⓑ Ⓒ Ⓓ Ⓔ
10. Ⓐ Ⓑ Ⓒ Ⓓ Ⓔ
11. Ⓐ Ⓑ Ⓒ Ⓓ Ⓔ
12. Ⓐ Ⓑ Ⓒ Ⓓ Ⓔ
13. Ⓐ Ⓑ Ⓒ Ⓓ Ⓔ
14. Ⓐ Ⓑ Ⓒ Ⓓ Ⓔ
15. Ⓐ Ⓑ Ⓒ Ⓓ Ⓔ
16. Ⓐ Ⓑ Ⓒ Ⓓ Ⓔ
17. Ⓐ Ⓑ Ⓒ Ⓓ Ⓔ

18. Ⓐ Ⓑ Ⓒ Ⓓ Ⓔ
19. Ⓐ Ⓑ Ⓒ Ⓓ Ⓔ
20. Ⓐ Ⓑ Ⓒ Ⓓ Ⓔ
21. Ⓐ Ⓑ Ⓒ Ⓓ Ⓔ
22. Ⓐ Ⓑ Ⓒ Ⓓ Ⓔ
23. Ⓐ Ⓑ Ⓒ Ⓓ Ⓔ
24. Ⓐ Ⓑ Ⓒ Ⓓ Ⓔ
25. Ⓐ Ⓑ Ⓒ Ⓓ Ⓔ
26. Ⓐ Ⓑ Ⓒ Ⓓ Ⓔ
27. Ⓐ Ⓑ Ⓒ Ⓓ Ⓔ
28. Ⓐ Ⓑ Ⓒ Ⓓ Ⓔ
29. Ⓐ Ⓑ Ⓒ Ⓓ Ⓔ
30. Ⓐ Ⓑ Ⓒ Ⓓ Ⓔ
31. Ⓐ Ⓑ Ⓒ Ⓓ Ⓔ
32. Ⓐ Ⓑ Ⓒ Ⓓ Ⓔ
33. Ⓐ Ⓑ Ⓒ Ⓓ Ⓔ
34. Ⓐ Ⓑ Ⓒ Ⓓ Ⓔ

35. Ⓐ Ⓑ Ⓒ Ⓓ Ⓔ
36. Ⓐ Ⓑ Ⓒ Ⓓ Ⓔ
37. Ⓐ Ⓑ Ⓒ Ⓓ Ⓔ
38. Ⓐ Ⓑ Ⓒ Ⓓ Ⓔ
39. Ⓐ Ⓑ Ⓒ Ⓓ Ⓔ
40. Ⓐ Ⓑ Ⓒ Ⓓ Ⓔ
41. Ⓐ Ⓑ Ⓒ Ⓓ Ⓔ
42. Ⓐ Ⓑ Ⓒ Ⓓ Ⓔ
43. Ⓐ Ⓑ Ⓒ Ⓓ Ⓔ
44. Ⓐ Ⓑ Ⓒ Ⓓ Ⓔ
45. Ⓐ Ⓑ Ⓒ Ⓓ Ⓔ
46. Ⓐ Ⓑ Ⓒ Ⓓ Ⓔ
47. Ⓐ Ⓑ Ⓒ Ⓓ Ⓔ
48. Ⓐ Ⓑ Ⓒ Ⓓ Ⓔ
49. Ⓐ Ⓑ Ⓒ Ⓓ Ⓔ
50. Ⓐ Ⓑ Ⓒ Ⓓ Ⓔ

answer sheet

## SECTION II

**Essay Question 1**

_____

_____

_____

_____

_____

_____

_____

_____

_____

_____

_____

_____

_____

_____

_____

_____

_____

_____

_____

_____

_____

_____

**answer sheet**

**Essay Question 2**

_____

_____

_____

_____

_____

_____

_____

_____

_____

_____

_____

_____

_____

_____

_____

_____

_____

_____

_____

_____

_____

_____

_____

_____

answer sheet

**Essay Question 3**

_____

_____

_____

_____

_____

_____

_____

_____

_____

_____

_____

_____

_____

_____

_____

_____

_____

_____

_____

_____

_____

_____

_____

_____

answer sheet

# Practice Test 1: Diagnostic

## SECTION I

*50 QUESTIONS • 60 MINUTES*

**Directions:** This section consists of selections of literature and questions on their content, style, and form. After you have read each passage, choose the answer that best answers the question and mark the space on the answer sheet.

**QUESTIONS 1 THROUGH 10 REFER TO THE FOLLOWING POEM. READ THE PASSAGE CAREFULLY AND THEN CHOOSE THE ANSWERS TO THE QUESTIONS.**

### A Valediction: Forbidding Mourning

Line As virtuous men pass mildly away,
    And whisper to their souls to go,
Whilst some of their sad friends do say
    The breath goes now, and so say, No;

5 So let us melt, and make no noise,
    No tear-floods, nor sigh-tempests move,
'Twere profanation of our joys
    To tell the laity of love.

Moving of th' earth brings harms and fears,
10     Men reckon what it did and meant;
But trepidation of the spheres,
    Though greater far, is innocent.

Dull sublunary lovers' love
    (Whose soul is sense) cannot admit
15 Absence, because it doth remove
    Those things which elemented it.

But we by a love, so much refined
    That our selves know not what it is,
Inter-assured of the mind,
20     Care less, eyes, lips, and hands to miss.

35

Our two souls therefore, which are one,
　　Though I must go, endure not yet
A breach, but an expansion,
　　Like gold to airy thinness beat.

25　If they be two, they are two so
　　As stiff twin compasses are two;
Thy soul, the fixt foot, makes no show
　　To move, but doth, if th' other do.

And though it in the center sit,
30　　Yet when the other far doth roam,
It leans and hearkens after it,
　　And grows erect, as that comes home.

Such wilt thou be to me, who must
　　Like th' other foot, obliquely run;
35　Thy firmness makes my circle just,
　　And makes me end where I begun.

　　　　　—John Donne (1572–1631)

**1.** The speaker in this poem is a

  **(A)** man who wants to get away
from his lover
  **(B)** friend of a dying man
  **(C)** churchman
  **(D)** man who wants to travel
  **(E)** lover who must leave on a
journey

**2.** Which of the following best describes
the speaker's point of view in stanzas
3, 4, and 5?

  **(A)** True lovers can separate without
causing major disturbances.
  **(B)** Earthquakes cause more
problems than the movement of
heavenly bodies.
  **(C)** People who depend on physical
love are similar to the stars and
planets.
  **(D)** A person should not miss his
lover's lips and eyes.
  **(E)** Lovers have better minds and
senses than other people.

**3.** All of the following are figurative
images in the poem EXCEPT

  **(A)** virtuous men
  **(B)** trepidation of the spheres
  **(C)** eyes, lips, and hands
  **(D)** gold to airy thinness beat
  **(E)** the fixt foot (of a compass)

**4.** The subject of the poem is

  **(A)** death
  **(B)** true lovers parting
  **(C)** a compass
  **(D)** the nature of the earth
  **(E)** a journey

**5.** The tone of the poem is

  **(A)** sanguine
  **(B)** paradoxical
  **(C)** humorous
  **(D)** melancholy
  **(E)** sardonic

**6.** The poem's major conceit is

  **(A)** lovers as a compass
  **(B)** earthquakes and celestial
movement
  **(C)** virtuous men and death
  **(D)** love as thin gold
  **(E)** virtuous men and love

7. The phrase "laity of love" in line 8 refers to

(A) clergymen in love
(B) lovers who need physical sensation for their love
(C) lovers who can abide absences
(D) love remaining after death
(E) nonreligious people who worship love

8. According to Donne, true love

(A) can tolerate separation
(B) belongs to the "laity of love"
(C) dies like virtuous men
(D) is the "trepidation of the spheres"
(E) is "sublunary lovers' love"

9. "A Valediction: Forbidding Mourning" is what kind of a poem?

(A) Ode
(B) Sonnet
(C) Narrative
(D) Elegy
(E) Lyric

10. In the last stanza, the speaker talks of

(A) dying
(B) leaving his lover
(C) returning to his lover
(D) making a trip similar in route to a circle
(E) missing his lover

**QUESTIONS 11 THROUGH 25 REFER TO THE FOLLOWING SELECTION. READ THE PASSAGE CAREFULLY AND THEN CHOOSE THE ANSWERS TO THE QUESTIONS.**

## From *Pride and Prejudice*

Line It is a truth universally acknowledged that a single man in possession of a good fortune must be in want of a wife.

However little known the feelings or views of such a man may be on his first entering a neighborhood, this truth is so well fixed in the minds of the surrounding
5 families, that he is considered as the rightful property of some one or other of their daughters.

"My dear Mr. Bennet," said his lady to him one day, "have you heard that Netherfield Park is let at last?"

Mr. Bennet replied that he had not.
10 "But it is," returned she; "for Mrs. Long has just been here, and she told me all about it."

Mr. Bennet made no answer.

"Do you not want to know who has taken it?" cried his wife impatiently.

"*You* want to tell me, and I have no objection to hearing it."
15 This was invitation enough.

"Why, my dear, you must know, Mrs. Long says that Netherfield is taken by a young man of large fortune from the north of England; that he came down on Monday in a chaise and four to see the place, and was so much delighted with it, that he agreed with Mr. Morris immediately; that he is to take possession before Michaelmas,
20 and some of his servants are to be in the house by the end of next week."

"What is his name?"

"Bingley."

"Is he married or single?"

"Oh! Single, my dear, to be sure! A single man of large fortune; four or five thou-
25 sand a year. What a fine thing for our girls!"

"How so? How can it affect them?"

"My dear Mr. Bennet," replied his wife, "how can you be so tiresome! You must know that I am thinking of his marrying one of them."

"Is that his design in settling here?"

**GO ON TO THE NEXT PAGE** ➡

30    "Design! Nonsense, how can you talk so! But it is very likely that he *may* fall in love with one of them, and therefore you must visit him as soon as he comes."

"I see no occasion for that. You and the girls may go, or you may send them by themselves, which perhaps will be still better, for as you are as handsome as any of them, Mr. Bingley might like you the best of the party."

35    "My dear, you flatter me. I certainly *have* had my share of beauty, but I do not pretend to be anything extraordinary now. When a woman has five grown-up daughters, she ought to give over thinking of her own beauty."

"In such cases, a woman has not often much beauty to think of."

"But, my dear, you must indeed go and see Mr. Bingley when he comes into the
40    neighborhood."

"It is more than I engage for, I assure you."

"But consider your daughters. Only think what an establishment it would be for one of them. Sir William and Lady Lucas are determined to go, merely on that account, for in general, you know, they visit no newcomers. Indeed you must go, for it will be
45    impossible for *us* to visit him if you do not."

"You are overscrupulous, surely. I dare say Mr. Bingley will be very glad to see you; and I will send a few lines by you to assure him of my hearty consent to his marrying whichever he chooses of the girls: though I must throw in a good word for my little Lizzy."

50    "I desire you will do no such thing. Lizzy is not a bit better than the others; and I am sure she is not half so handsome as Jane, nor half so good-humored as Lydia. But you are always giving *her* the preference."

"They have none of them much to recommend them," replied he; "they are all silly and ignorant, like other girls: but Lizzy has something more of quickness than her
55    sisters."

"Mr. Bennet, how can you abuse your own children in such a way. You take delight in vexing me. You have no compassion on my poor nerves."

"You mistake me, my dear. I have a high respect for your nerves. They are my old friends. I have heard you mention them with consideration these twenty years at
60    least."

"Ah! You do not know what I suffer."

"But I hope you will get over it, and live to see many young men of four thousand a year come into the neighborhood."

"It will be no use to us, if twenty such should come, since you will not visit them."

65    "Depend on it, my dear, that when there are twenty, I will visit them all."

Mr. Bennet was so odd a mixture of quick parts, sarcastic humor, reserve, and caprice, that the experience of three-and-twenty years had been insufficient to make his wife understand his character. *Her* mind was less difficult to develop. She was a woman of mean understanding, little information, and uncertain temper. When she was discontented,
70    she fancied herself nervous. The business of her life was to get her daughters married; its solace was visiting and news.

—Jane Austen

11. Which of the following best characterizes the conversation between Mr. and Mrs. Bennet?

(A) Mr. Bennet is understanding, and Mrs. Bennet is realistic.
(B) Mr. Bennet is sarcastic, and Mrs. Bennet is pensive.
(C) Mr. Bennet is questioning, and Mrs. Bennet is fantasizing.
(D) Mr. Bennet is realistic, and Mrs. Bennet is pessimistic.
(E) Mr. Bennet is facetious, and Mrs. Bennet is negative.

12. What does this passage reveal about the author's feelings toward her characters and their values?

(A) Austen feels that their preoccupation with the proper forms for behavior is overstressed.
(B) Middle-class women are humorless.
(C) After having five children, most women are not so beautiful as they were in their youth.
(D) The author finds the Bennets ridiculous.
(E) The British middle class has standards of behavior that all people should emulate.

13. What conflict is clear from this excerpt?

(A) The Bennet daughters are in conflict with their parents.
(B) Mrs. Bennet has a conflict with Lizzy.
(C) Mr. Bingley is in conflict with Mrs. Bennet.
(D) Mrs. Bennet has a conflict with her husband.
(E) Lizzy is in conflict with her sisters.

14. What best characterizes the way Mr. Bennet expresses himself when he says, "Is that his design in settling here?" (line 29)

(A) Sarcasm
(B) Astonishment
(C) Disgust
(D) Anger
(E) Delight

15. From this excerpt, it is possible to predict that Austen will continue to develop the story as a

(A) romance
(B) criticism of the middle class
(C) tragic comment on the condition of women in the late eighteenth and early nineteenth centuries
(D) genial satire
(E) subtle cautionary tale

16. Which of the following best explains how Mr. and Mrs. Bennet view their daughters?

(A) While both parents love their daughters, Mrs. Bennet loves the girls more than Mr. Bennet.
(B) Mrs. Bennet sees them idealistically; Mr. Bennet sees them as imperfect.
(C) Mr. Bennet believes they are loving; Mrs. Bennet believes they are sophisticated.
(D) Mrs. Bennet thinks them witty; Mr. Bennet views them as dull.
(E) Mr. Bennet enjoys their company; Mrs. Bennet thinks they are lazy.

17. Which of the following best summarizes the meaning of the first paragraph?

(A) Single men look for their fortune with wealthy women.
(B) Wealthy single men are looking for someone to marry.
(C) Wealthy single men like to move to new neighborhoods.
(D) People welcome wealthy single men to their neighborhoods.
(E) Families with unmarried daughters search for neighborhoods with wealthy single men.

**GO ON TO THE NEXT PAGE**

18. What is the meaning of the sentence "It is more than I engage for, I assure you," spoken by Mr. Bennet?

    (A) I understand what you are saying.
    (B) It is more than I intend to do.
    (C) I will do as you ask.
    (D) We are in agreement.
    (E) I will be involved.

19. Which of the following is an example of irony?

    (A) Mr. Bennet's discussion of Lizzy's qualities
    (B) Mrs. Bennet's desire to call on Mr. Bingley
    (C) Mr. Bennet's description of his wife's nerves
    (D) The fast-moving pace of the conversation
    (E) The emphasis on proper behavior

20. In the last paragraph, Jane Austen sums up the character of Mr. Bennet. Which of the following qualities does she not attribute to him?

    (A) Lively intelligence
    (B) Whimsical
    (C) Ironic
    (D) Aloof, self-restrained
    (E) Irritable

21. Which statement best characterizes this excerpt?

    (A) It is a discussion about the impact of a new neighbor on the lives of a family.
    (B) It is a discussion about getting the Bennets' daughter, Lizzy, married.
    (C) It is a satire of the relationship between Mr. and Mrs. Bennet.
    (D) It is a parody of the upper classes.
    (E) It is a portrait of the Bennets through their daughters' eyes.

22. What does the word "establishment" mean in the sentence spoken by Mrs. Bennet: "Only think what an establishment it would be for one of them" (lines 42–43)?

    (A) Engagement
    (B) Accomplishment
    (C) Attachment
    (D) Celebration
    (E) Sacrifice

23. What is Mr. Bennet saying in line 65: "Depend on it, my dear, that when there are twenty, I will visit them all"?

    (A) Mr. Bennet has agreed to go see Mr. Bingley.
    (B) Mr. Bennet is going to see twenty people.
    (C) Mr. Bennet is sending his wife and daughters to see Mr. Bingley.
    (D) Mr. Bennet is looking for wealthier neighbors for his daughters.
    (E) Mr. Bennet is saying he does not intend to see Mr. Bingley.

24. What is Mr. Bennet doing when he says "Lizzy has something more of quickness than her sisters" (lines 54–55)?

    (A) He is agreeing with Mrs. Bennet.
    (B) He is praising his daughter because he wants her to marry first.
    (C) He is defending his position.
    (D) He admires his daughter's intelligence.
    (E) He wants Lizzy to stay at home.

25. In the last paragraph, Jane Austin sums up the character of Mrs. Bennet. What qualities does she attribute to her?

    (A) Cleverness, above average intelligence
    (B) Modesty, timidity
    (C) Great beauty, elegance
    (D) Narrowness, an inferior mind
    (E) Impatience, irritability

QUESTIONS 26 THROUGH 35 REFER TO THE
FOLLOWING POEM. READ THE PASSAGE
CAREFULLY AND THEN CHOOSE THE
ANSWERS TO THE QUESTIONS.

**Night Clouds**

Line    The white mares of the moon rush
            along the sky
        Beating their golden hoofs upon the
            glass Heavens;
5       The white mares of the moon are all
            standing on their hind legs
        Pawing at the green porcelain doors of
            the remote Heavens.
        Fly, Mares!
10      Strain you utmost.
        Scatter the milky dust of stars,
        Or the tiger sun will leap upon you
            and destroy you
        With one lick of his vermilion tongue.
                                    —Amy Lowell

26. What is the writer describing in this
    poem?
    (A) A rainy night
    (B) A morning in the jungle
    (C) A partly cloudy dawn
    (D) A moonlit night
    (E) Midday on the ocean

27. What are the white mares?
    (A) Stars
    (B) Clouds
    (C) Statues
    (D) Ghosts
    (E) Waving trees

28. What is the poet describing in the
    last two lines?
    (A) A tiger attacking an animal
    (B) Moonrise
    (C) The sun burning off clouds
    (D) Sunrise in the jungle
    (E) An argument

29. The expression "tiger sun" is an
    example of:
    (A) A simile
    (B) A metaphor
    (C) Figurative language
    (D) Personification
    (E) Alliteration

30. This poem is an example of what
    type of poetry?
    (A) Sonnet
    (B) Lyric
    (C) Elegy
    (D) Ode
    (E) Narrative

31. Which of the following best describes
    the writer's tone in this poem?
    (A) Solemn
    (B) Introspective
    (C) Playful
    (D) Serious
    (E) Insightful

32. Why is the poet urging the mares
    to fly?
    (A) To avoid being eaten
    (B) To get home
    (C) To win the race
    (D) To keep from disappearing with
        the sunrise
    (E) To go higher in the sky

33. What is the best interpretation of the
    expression "glass Heavens"?
    (A) A clear but restricted ceiling
    (B) A high point in the skies
    (C) The road the mares are on
    (D) A reflection of life
    (E) An opening to the other side of
        the world

34. What does the word "vermilion"
    mean in the last line?
    (A) Sticky
    (B) Catlike
    (C) Wet
    (D) Red
    (E) Hard

35. Which of the following senses is the
    poet appealing to the most?
    (A) Taste: flavor
    (B) Sound: volume
    (C) Sight: color
    (D) Sound: hearing
    (E) Touch: feeling

**GO ON TO THE NEXT PAGE** ➤

**QUESTIONS 36 THROUGH 50 REFER TO THE FOLLOWING SECTION. READ THE PASSAGE CAREFULLY AND THEN CHOOSE THE ANSWERS TO THE QUESTIONS.**

### From the Preface of *Modern American Poetry, A Critical Anthology*

Line    It may be difficult, if not impossible, to determine the boundaries as well as the beginnings of "modernism," but only a few appraisers will deny that American litera-ture became modern as well as American with the advent of Mark Twain, Herman Melville, and Walt Whitman. In the history of poetry the line may be drawn with a
5    measure of certainty, and it is with the Civil War and the publication of the third edition of *Leaves of Grass* that modern American poetry is defined.

**Aftermath of the Civil War**

The Civil War inspired volumes of indignant, military, religious, and patriotic verse without adding more than four or five memorable pieces to the anthologies; the
10    conflict produced a vast quantity of poems but practically no important poetry. Its end marked the end of an epoch—political, social, and literary. The arts declined; the New England group began to disintegrate. The poets had overstrained and outsung them-selves; it was a time of surrender and swan-songs. Unable to respond to the new forces of political nationalism and industrial reconstruction, the Brahmins (that
15    famous group of intellectuals who had dominated literary America) withdrew into their libraries. Such poets as Longfellow, Bryant, Taylor, turned their eyes away from the native scene, [. . .] or left creative writing altogether and occupied themselves with translations. "They had been borne into an era in which they had no part," writes Fred Lewis Pattee (*A History of American Literature Since 1870*), "and they contented
20    themselves with reëchoings of the old music." For them poetry ceased to be a reflection of actuality, "an extension of experience." Within a period of six years, from 1867 to 1872, there appeared Longfellow's *Divina Commedia,* C. E. Norton's *Vita Nuova,* T. W. Parson's *Inferno,* William Cullen Bryant's *Iliad* and *Odyssey,* and Bayard Taylor's *Faust.*
25    Suddenly the break came. America developed a national consciousness; the West discovered itself, and the East discovered the West. Grudgingly at first, the aristo-cratic leaders made way for a new expression; crude, jangling, vigorously democratic. The old order was changing with a vengeance. All the preceding writers—poets like Emerson, Lowell, Longfellow, Holmes—were not only products of the New England
30    colleges, but typically "Boston gentlemen of the early Renaissance." To them, the new men must have seemed like a regiment recruited from the ranks of vulgarity. Walt Whitman, Mark Twain, Bret Harte, John Hay, Joaquin Miller, Joel Chandler Harris, James Whitcomb Riley—these were men who had graduated from the farm, the frontier, the mine, the pilothouse, the printer's shop! For a while, the movement
35    seemed of little consequence; the impact of Whitman and the Westerners was averted. The poets of the transition, with a deliberate art, ignored the surge of a spontaneous national expression; they were even successful in holding it back. But it was gathering force.

—Louis Untermeyer

36. What is the meaning of the expression "overstrained and outsung themselves" (lines 12–13)?

    (A) Tired out
    (B) Lost creativity
    (C) Worked too hard
    (D) Went beyond their knowledge
    (E) Sought new insights

37. This selection is an example of which mode of writing?

    (A) Description
    (B) Narration
    (C) Persuasion
    (D) Exposition
    (E) Argument

38. What is the best explanation of the expression "an extension of experience" (line 21)?

    (A) A reference to existentialism in poetry
    (B) Poetry is a reflection of the real world
    (C) A definition of modern poetry
    (D) A reflection of the universal nature of poetry
    (E) Poetry as an art form

39. Which of the following is the thesis that the author explores?

    (A) The Civil War inspired volumes of indignant, military, religious, and patriotic verse without adding more than four or five memorable pieces to the anthologies.
    (B) It may be difficult, if not impossible, to determine the boundaries as well as the beginnings of "modernism."
    (C) Only a few appraisers will deny that American literature became modern as well as American with the advent of Mark Twain, Herman Melville, and Walt Whitman.
    (D) The conclusion of the Civil War marked the end of an epoch—political, social, and literary.
    (E) The Brahmins withdrew from the literary scene because they could not respond to the changes made by the Civil War.

40. Which of the following changed the role of the Brahmins?

    (A) The Civil War and Reconstruction
    (B) Religious freedom and politics
    (C) Political nationalism and industrial reconstruction
    (D) Industrial growth and the westward movement
    (E) Philosophical creativity and the scientific revolution

41. Longfellow's *Divina Commedia* is an example of the author's contention that

    (A) modernism began with the end of the Civil War
    (B) the New England poets no longer created vibrant, original verse, but turned to translations
    (C) modernism developed along political lines
    (D) modern literature grew slowly in most areas
    (E) the New England writers provided a more studied view of life

42. What is meant by the expression "reëchoings of the old music" (line 20)?

    (A) Tired old songs
    (B) Rewriting old material
    (C) Hearing influences from the past
    (D) Metaphorical sounds of the past
    (E) Redone philosophical treatises

43. The author contends that the Brahmins viewed the new poets as

    (A) vulgar
    (B) intellectual
    (C) uneducated
    (D) simple
    (E) insightful

44. What does the author mean in the first lines of the final paragraph: "Suddenly the break came. America developed a national consciousness; the West discovered itself, and the East discovered the West"?

    (A) People in the East were moving west.
    (B) There was a break in thought between the East and West.
    (C) American modern poetry found itself.
    (D) The Brahmins and modern poets were in conflict.
    (E) Poetry from the West became the dominant verse.

45. Which of the following is the best characterization of the tone of this passage?

    (A) Harsh and scathing
    (B) Scholarly and informative
    (C) Condescending and irritating
    (D) Humorous and witty
    (E) Dry and pretentious

46. Which of the following best summarizes the thoughts of the author in this piece?

    (A) The Brahmins' poetry, although superior to modern poetry, was lost after the Civil War.
    (B) The more liberated modern American poetry outshone the older styles.
    (C) The Brahmins were essentially the fathers of modern American poetry.
    (D) The Civil War marked the beginning of modern American poetry.
    (E) The experiences of the Civil War formed the basis of some of the Brahmins' work.

47. The author would agree with which of the following statements about the Civil War?

    (A) It produced a quantity of poems, but little poetry.
    (B) It produced many poets.
    (C) It developed the skills of the Brahmins.
    (D) It created new advocates for poetry.
    (E) It produced a number of forums for poets.

48. What is the meaning of the sentence beginning on line 36: "The poets of the transition, with a deliberate art, ignored the surge of a spontaneous national expression"?

    (A) The transitional poets were deliberate in their poetry.
    (B) The Brahmins worked to prevent changes in American poetry.
    (C) The Brahmins paid little attention to the changes in poetry.
    (D) The spontaneous growth of modern American poetry overwhelmed the Brahmins.
    (E) There was little support for the Brahmins' poetry.

49. The author characterizes the new poets as

    (A) brash and arrogant
    (B) spiritual and philosophical
    (C) malleable and whimsical
    (D) forceful and inventive
    (E) crude and cutting edge

50. The author characterizes the Brahmins as

    (A) educated and mercurial
    (B) stuffy and intransigent
    (C) lighthearted and introspective
    (D) serious but easygoing
    (E) brilliant and forgiving

**STOP** If you finish before time is called, you may check your work on this section only. Do not turn to any other section in the test.

# SECTION II

*3 QUESTIONS • 2 HOURS*

> **Directions:** The passage that follows is from *The House of the Dead*. In the book, author Fyodor Dostoyevsky, a political prisoner, writes about his experiences in a Siberian prison camp. Read the passage carefully. Then write a well-organized essay concerning the methods by which the author portrays the subject and the substance of the portrait itself. Be sure to consider such literary elements as diction, imagery, mood, and point of view.

## Essay Question 1

*SUGGESTED TIME—40 MINUTES*

**From *The House of the Dead***

Line He was a little grey-headed man of sixty. He made a vivid impression on me from the first minute. He was so unlike the other convicts, there was something so calm and gentle in his expression that I remember I looked with a peculiar pleasure at his serene, candid eyes, which were surrounded with tiny wrinkles like rays. I often
5 talked to him and I have rarely met a more kindly, warm-hearted creature in my life. He had been sent there for a very serious offense. Among the Starodubovsky Old Believers, some converts to the Orthodox Church were made. The government gave them great encouragement and began to make great efforts for the conversion of the others. The old man resolved with other fanatics to stand up for the faith, as he
10 expressed it. An orthodox church was being built and they burnt it down. As one of the instigators, the old man was sent to penal servitude. He had been a well-to-do trades-man and left a wife and children behind him, but he went with a brave heart into exile, for in his blindness he considered it "martyrdom for the faith." After spending some time with him, one could not help asking oneself how this meek old man, as
15 gentle as a child, could have been a rebel. Several times I talked to him of "the faith"; he would never yield an inch in his convictions, but there was no trace of anger or of hatred in his replies. And yet he had destroyed a church and did not deny doing it. It seemed that from his convictions he must have considered his action and his suffering for it a glorious achievement. But, however closely I watched him and studied him, I
20 never detected the faintest sign of pride or vanity in him. . . . He was of a very communicative disposition. He was merry, often laughing, not with the coarse cynical laugh of the other convicts, but with a gentle candid laugh, in which there was a great deal of childlike simplicity that seemed peculiarly in keeping with his grey hair. I may be mistaken, but I fancy that one can know a man from his laugh, and if you like a
25 man's laugh before you know anything of him, you may confidently say that he is a good man. Though the old man had gained the respect of all throughout the prison, he was not the least conceited about it. The convicts used to call him grandfather, and they never insulted him. I could partially imagine the sort of influence he must have had on his fellow believers. But in spite of the unmistakable courage with which he

30 endured his punishment, there was also a deep inconsolable melancholy in his heart, which he tried to conceal from all. I lived in the same room with him. One night, I woke at three o'clock and heard the sound of quiet, restrained weeping. The old man was sitting on the stove (the same stove on which the Bible reader who threw the brick at the major used to pray at night). He was saying his prayers over his manu-

35 script book. He was weeping and I could hear him saying from time to time, "Lord, do not forsake me! Lord, give me strength! My little ones, my darling little ones, I shall never see you again!" I can't describe how sad it made me.

—Fyodor Dostoyevsky

**Directions:** William Cullen Bryant stated that the main strength of "To a Waterfowl" was its "completeness," and the poem's "rounded and didactic termination has done wonders." Read the poem carefully. Then write a well-organized essay in which you discuss the ways by which the author created such a complete work. Be sure to consider such literary elements as diction, imagery, rhyme, rhythm, and structure.

## Essay Question 2

*SUGGESTED TIME—40 MINUTES*

### To a Waterfowl

Line      Whither, midst falling dew,
While glow the heavens with the last steps of day,
Far, through their rosy depths, dost thou pursue
    Thy solitary way?

5      Vainly the fowler's eye
Might mark thy distant flight to do thee wrong,
As, darkly seen against the crimson sky,
    Thy figure floats along.

     Seek'st thou the plashy brink
10  O weedy lake, or marge of river wide,
Or where the rocking billows rise and sink
    On the chafed ocean-side?

     There is a Power whose care
Teaches thy way along that pathless coast—
15 The desert and illimitable air—
    Lone wandering, but not lost.

     All day thy wings have fanned,
At that far height, the cold, thin atmosphere,
Yet stoop not, weary, to the welcome land,
20    Though the dark night is near.

     And soon that toil shall end;
Soon shalt thou find a summer home, and rest,
And scream among thy fellows; reeds shall bend
    Soon, o'er thy sheltered nest.

25    Thou'rt gone, the abyss of heaven
Hath swallowed up thy form; yet, on my heart
Deeply has sunk the lesson thou hast given,
    And shall not soon depart.

     He who, from zone to zone,
30 Guides through the boundless sky thy certain flight,
In the long way that I must tread alone,
    Will lead my steps aright.

           —William Cullen Bryant

**Directions:** In some works of literature, the passage from one state to another—in growth, in belief, in understanding, in knowledge—is a terrifying process.

Choose a novel or play of literary merit and write an essay in which you show how such a change in a character was a frightening process and led to destruction or violent cleansing. You may wish to discuss how the author develops this change of state through the action, theme, or character development. Avoid plot summary.

You may select a work from the list below, or you may choose another work of comparable literary merit suitable to the topic.

## Essay Question 3

*SUGGESTED TIME—40 MINUTES*

Orwell, *1984*

Sophocles, *Antigone*

Morrison, *Beloved*

Dostoyevsky, *Crime and Punishment*

Marlowe, *Doctor Faustus*

Shakespeare, *Hamlet*

Conrad, *Heart of Darkness*

Brontë, *Jane Eyre*

Shakespeare, *Macbeth*

Flaubert, *Madame Bovary*

Euripedes, *Medea*

Melville, *Moby Dick*

Sophocles, *Oedipus Rex*

Euripedes, *Orestes*

Shakespeare, *Othello*

Conrad, *Lord Jim*

Hemingway, *The Old Man and the Sea*

Crane, *The Red Badge of Courage*

Hawthorne, *The Scarlet Letter*

Lee, *To Kill a Mockingbird*

**S T O P** If you finish before time is called, you may check your work on this section only. Do not turn to any other section in the test.

*diagnostic test*

# ANSWER KEY AND EXPLANATIONS

## Section I

| | | | | |
|---|---|---|---|---|
| 1. E | 11. C | 21. A | 31. C | 41. B |
| 2. A | 12. A | 22. B | 32. D | 42. B |
| 3. C | 13. D | 23. E | 33. C | 43. A |
| 4. B | 14. A | 24. C | 34. D | 44. C |
| 5. A | 15. D | 25. D | 35. C | 45. B |
| 6. A | 16. B | 26. C | 36. B | 46. D |
| 7. B | 17. B | 27. B | 37. D | 47. A |
| 8. A | 18. B | 28. C | 38. B | 48. B |
| 9. E | 19. C | 29. C | 39. C | 49. E |
| 10. C | 20. E | 30. B | 40. A | 50. B |

1. **The correct answer is (E).** Line 21, which refers to two souls that are one, is a clear reference to lovers. That eliminates choices (B), (C), and (D). Choice (A) cites a lover, but the poet makes no reference to a desire to leave the lover. In fact, the poem is about a departure that is necessary but perhaps not welcome.

2. **The correct answer is (A).** The last two lines of the fifth stanza indicate that the lovers are assured of each other's love, and absence can be tolerated because they are true lovers, not just physical lovers. Choice (D) is incomplete because it does not address the reason the physical separation can be tolerated. Choices (B) and (C) are distractors because they mention images from the poem but do not relate to the overall sense of the poem. The same is true of choice (E), although on a quick reading you might think it is a restatement of the theme.

3. **The correct answer is (C).** The "eyes, lips, and hands" are tangible objects with no alternative meaning in this poem. Choices (A), (B), (D), and (E) create comparisons or associations that the reader can interpret imaginatively.

4. **The correct answer is (B).** Lovers are identified in line 21. Parting is suggested in the first stanza and reinforced in later stanzas. Choice (B) is the only one containing both these elements. Choices (A), (C), (D), and (E) are only partially correct.

5. **The correct answer is (A).** The word *sanguine* means cheerful or optimistic. The lovers' positive viewpoint that their love can survive and even be strengthened by separation is optimistic. Choices (B) and (E) are negative in tone, choice (C) is humorous, and choice (D) is sad.

6. **The correct answer is (A).** A conceit is an unusual or startling extended metaphor and/or an extended metaphor comparing two dissimilar objects. In this case, the two lovers are compared to a compass, the lover staying home being the "fixt foot." A conceit has a powerful effect, and the only answer contained in the poem that fits the definition of a conceit is choice (A). Choices (B), (C), (D), and (E) do not meet the criteria.

7. **The correct answer is (B).** *Laity* means people who are not clergy, so choice (A) can be eliminated. While death and absence are mentioned, the contexts do not coincide with choices (C) and (D), so those two choices are incorrect. Although choice (E) may be a literal reading of the phrase, it does not relate to the phrase in the context of the poem.

8. **The correct answer is (A).** The concluding stanza makes reference to leaving and returning by a lover who would go away and come back. The lovers view such a situation as tolerable. Choices (B) and (C) do not represent the important ideas in the poem, and choices (D) and (E) are distortions of those ideas.

9. **The correct answer is (E).** A lyric poem is subjective and reflective, with a regular rhyme scheme. Lyric poetry reveals the poet's inner thoughts, just as Donne has written in this poem. To be a sonnet, choice (B), the poem has too many lines and the wrong rhyme scheme. It does not tell a story, so it is not a narrative, choice (C). Since an ode is a type of lyric poem, choice (A) is a possibility, but odes are written to praise someone or something, which is not the case with this poem. An elegy, choice (D), is a lament, mourning someone's death. While the first few lines might seem to be about death, the poem is really about love.

10. **The correct answer is (C).** The stanza says "th'other foot, obliquely run . . . and makes me end where I begun." Leaving and coming back is implied in "returning," choice (C). Choices (B) and (E) discuss portions, but not all, of this idea. *Dying*, in choice (A), is a part of a simile, not to be taken literally. Choice (D) is a literal interpretation.

11. **The correct answer is (C).** Mr. Bennet may be considered understanding, choice (A); sarcastic, choice (B); questioning, choice (C); realistic, choice (D); or facetious, choice (E). However, Mrs. Bennet is not realistic, choice (A); pensive, choice (B); pessimistic, choice (D); or negative, choice (E). Mrs. Bennet is fantasizing, choice (C), so only choice (C) is correct in both conditions.

12. **The correct answer is (A).** In choice (B), Austen makes Mrs. Bennet humorless, but that cannot be expanded to be a comment on all middle-class women from this excerpt. In choice (C), Mrs. Bennet's beauty is mentioned, but not as an expression of the author. In choice (D), the Bennets are not portrayed as ridiculous as much as having differing opinions. Choice (E) can be eliminated because Austen does not cast these standards in a broader context.

13. **The correct answer is (D).** Choices (A) and (E) are incorrect because there is no mention of either in the excerpt. Mrs. Bennet sticks up for her other daughters, but there is no mention of conflict with Lizzy, choice (B). Choice (C) is not correct because the Bennets have not yet met Mr. Bingley, so a conflict cannot have developed.

14. **The correct answer is (A).** Mr. Bennet is responding to a statement made by his wife that she wants Mr. Bingley to marry one of their daughters. Mr. Bennet's question is presented as a humorously sarcastic comment on his wife's aspirations. His question is not presented with astonishment, choice (B); in disgust, choice (C); in anger, choice (D); or with delight, choice (E).

15. **The correct answer is (D).** Austen is using satire to comment on marriage. The first sentence sets the tone of playful irony and gentle criticism. Austen is making fun of the staid conventions of her era. Choice (B) is a broader response than could be determined by the passage. Choices (A), (C), and (E) are not relevant or addressed.

16. **The correct answer is (B).** Choice (A) is not discussed in the passage. The characteristics of loving and sophisticated, choice (C); witty and dull, choice (D); and lazy, choice (E), as well as whether Mr. Bennet enjoys his daughters' company, are not discussed. Mrs. Bennet argues in her daughters' favor despite the imperfections pointed out by Mr. Bennet. This is consistent with choice (B).

17. **The correct answer is (B).** Choice (B) forms the basis for all of Mrs. Bennet's subsequent comments to her husband. While they might be true, all the other answers are not relevant to the passage. There is no mention of wealthy women, choice (A), or neighborhoods, choices (C), (D), and (E).

18. **The correct answer is (B).** Mr. Bennet has been reluctant to agree to go see Mr. Bingley. Choice (B) is the only answer to express Mr. Bennet's feelings. The sentence does not convey that he understands his wife's comments, choice (A); gives in to her wishes, choice (C); agrees with her, choice (D); or wishes to be involved, choice (E).

19. **The correct answer is (C).** Irony has a hint of mockery, as when Mr. Bennet refers to his wife's nerves in the following manner: "They are my friends. I have heard you mention them with consideration these twenty years at least." Choices (A), (B), (D), and (E) do not fit the definition of irony.

20. **The correct answer is (E).** Austen describes Mr. Bennet as "a mixture of quick parts, sarcastic humor, reserve, and caprice." Even if you did not know the meaning of the words in Austen's characterization, you should know that Mr. Bennet is ironic from question 19. His lack of irritation at his wife shows that he is not irritable, choice (E). Therefore, the other answers must be incorrect.

21. **The correct answer is (A).** Choice (B) is restricted to Lizzy, but all of the daughters are considered eligible for marriage. Austen is not satirizing the relationship between the Bennets, nor is she creating a parody of the upper classes, choices (C) and (D). The daughters are not commenting in this passage; therefore, choice (E) is incorrect.

22. **The correct answer is (B).** To settle or achieve is an obsolete use of the word *establishment*. Mrs. Bennet's comment is made about her daughters successfully meeting and marrying Mr. Bingley, thus an accomplishment. From context, you should be able to eliminate choice (E) since Mrs. Bennet views marriage as a happy prospect. Neither choice (A) nor choice (C) necessarily will end in marriage, and choice (D) does not make sense.

23. **The correct answer is (E).** Mr. Bennet is being ironic again. His real intent is to say that he has no plans to go see Mr. Bingley. Choices (A), (B), (C), and (D) do not reflect or convey his sense of irony.

24. **The correct answer is (C).** The question is not asking for what Mr. Bennet's opinion may be but for what his response represents in this situation. He is defending his position, choice (C), by saying that Lizzy is a little quicker or smarter than her sisters. Mr. Bennet has said that he will "throw in a good word for his little Lizzy." Mrs. Bennet argues that no daughter should be singled out for special consideration. Mr. Bennet does not agree with his wife, choice (A). Whether he admires his daughter's intelligence, choice (D); wants her to stay at home, choice (E); or wants her married, choice (B), is irrelevant to the question.

25. **The correct answer is (D).** In the last paragraph, Austen says that Mrs. Bennet is "of mean understanding, little information, and uncertain temper." These characteristics are best described by choice (D), with "mean" meaning narrow or small. Choice (A) is the direct opposite of Austen's view of Mrs. Bennet. Mrs. Bennet shows neither modesty nor timidity in her desire to go after Mr. Bingley for her daughters, choice (B). The conversation about beauty is a form of flattery between the Bennets, but it is not part of Austen's comments on Mrs. Bennet, choice (C). Mrs. Bennet does not display impatience or irritability with her husband, but assumes she will have her way, choice (E). Most importantly, only choice (D) relates to Austen's description.

26. **The correct answer is (C).** There is no reference to rain, a jungle, or the ocean, thereby eliminating choices (A), (B), and (E). Although it may be moonlit, choice (D), the "tiger sun" is coming up, making it an early dawn setting.

27. **The correct answer is (B).** Lowell has the "white mares" moving across the sky. This eliminates the stars, statues, and waving trees in choices (A), (C), and (E). The ghosts, choice (D), do not relate to other elements in the poem, such as the "tiger sun," but clouds do. In addition, the poem's title provides another clue to the correct answer. (Did you even notice the title? This is a reminder to read everything about a selection, including its title.)

28. **The correct answer is (C).** The reference to the "tiger sun" destroying the mares with its reddish orange tongue creates the image of the sun burning off the clouds. There is no additional animal image or reference to a jungle—choices (A), (D), and (E). The moon, but not moonlight, is mentioned in this stanza; therefore, choice (B) is incorrect.

29. **The correct answer is (C).** The expression does not have "like" or "as," so choice (A) is incorrect. No comparison is made, so it is not a metaphor—choice (B). Human qualities are not given to the sun, choice (D), and continuous sounds, choice (E) are not used.

30. **The correct answer is (B).** A lyric poem expresses subjective ideas or feelings. Lowell is giving the reader a feeling for the sunrise she observed. A sonnet, choice (A), is a fourteen-line poem. An elegy, choice (C), is a lament for a person. An ode, choice (D), is a lengthy poem that normally has a serious theme. A narrative, choice (E), tells a story. None of these apply to "Night Clouds."

31. **The correct answer is (C).** The use of the references to the horses and the tiger gives the poem an almost childlike quality. This is most closely associated with choice (C), playful. The poem does not have the heavier mood of solemnity, choice (A); introspection, choice (B); seriousness, choice (D); or insightfulness, choice (E), thereby eliminating those answers.

32. **The correct answer is (D).** The mares are fleeing the "tiger sun" to avoid being burned off by the heat of the sun and disappearing. The sun will destroy them, not eat them, choice (A). The poem mentions "remote Heavens" but does not indicate that this is home, choice (B), or someplace higher in the sky, choice (E). Choice (C) may seem correct if you think of sunrise as a race, but it is not so complete an answer as choice (D). Choice (E) could confuse you on a quick reading because stars are mentioned in the poem.

33. **The correct answer is (C).** The vision that Lowell creates is that the mares are running across the sky, but they are seen from below, hence the "glass heavens." Choice (A) is merely a definition with no literary basis in the poem. While choice (B) might seem logical, the mares are stepping on the ceiling, so it must be a road or trail. There is no reference in the poem to life, choice (D), or a place on the other side of the world, choice (E).

34. **The correct answer is (D).** The definition of the word *vermilion* is a vivid red to reddish orange color. This is similar to the color that can be seen in the rays from the sun at sunrise and sunset. Guessing this one would be hard because choices (A), (B), (C), and (E) might seem correct if you did not know what vermilion means, but a careful reading of the imagery could lead you to choose the color, especially after answering question 35.

35. **The correct answer is (C).** The poet appeals to the reader's sense of sight with references such as "white mares," "golden hoofs," "green porcelain doors," and "vermilion tongue." There are no other outstanding sensory images referring to taste, choice (A); sound, choices (B) and (D); or touch, choice (E).

36. **The correct answer is (B).** The context is that the New England group of poets was beginning to fall apart. As poets, this means that they were beginning to lose their creativity. Although choices (A), (C), (D), and (E) may express some of the feelings and experiences of the New England group, none addresses the core problem of these poets in the manner that choice (B) does.

37. **The correct answer is (D).** This selection is not descriptive, so the mode cannot be description, choice (A). It does not attempt to argue or persuade, so it cannot be persuasive, choice (C), or argumentative, choice (E), writing. Nor does it tell a story; therefore, it is not a narrative, choice (B). It simply presents the facts—exposition, choice (D).

38. **The correct answer is (B).** The sentence cited contains the statement "a reflection of actuality, 'an extension of experience.'" Choice (B) closely matches that thought. There is no discussion of an existential subject, choice (A). Modern poetry is not defined, choice (C). Choices (D) and (E) are similarly not discussed in the excerpt.

39. **The correct answer is (C).** All of these statements are true. The trick here is to figure out which gives the author's main idea. The writer is discussing the beginning of modern American writing. That is what choice (C) states. The other choices, (A), (B), (D), and (E), are facts that support and illuminate the writer's thesis.

40. **The correct answer is (A).** The correct answer is developed in the first paragraph by benchmarking the start of modern poetry with the Civil War. In the second paragraph, a link is shown between the close of the Civil War and the decline of the New England group, also known as the Brahmins. Religious freedom and politics, choice (B), were never shown to be an issue. Political nationalism, industrial growth, and philosophical creativity were also never developed as an influence on the Brahmins, choices (C), (D), and (E).

41. **The correct answer is (B).** In the second paragraph, Louis Untermeyer states that some of the Brahmins "occupied themselves with translations." *Divina Commedia* is such a translation. This makes choice (B) the correct answer. Choice (A) is true, but it is incorrect because it is not relevant to the question. Choices (C), (D), and (E) are not related to the question, and the author does not explore them.

42. **The correct answer is (B).** The context of this expression is another way that Untermeyer shows that the creativity of the Brahmins had been lost. In this case, he is saying that the Brahmins were satisfied with the sounds of old music, an allusion to their focus on translations of old writings. The author is not speaking of sounds *per se*. That eliminates choices (A), (C), and (D). The author is not speaking of philosophical concepts, choice (E).

43. **The correct answer is (A).** This question is from the point of view of the Brahmins, not the author. It probably does not reflect the thoughts of the author. In the third paragraph, Untermeyer writes "To them [the Brahmins], the new men must have seemed like a regiment recruited from the ranks of vulgarity." This passage is a direct response to the question and is represented by choice (A). Choices (B), (C), (D), and (E) do not express the point of view of the New England poets.

44. **The correct answer is (C).** The passage from the third paragraph is the identification by the author of the change from the Brahmin-influenced era to modern American poetry. This can be most readily seen by Untermeyer's comment that "America developed a national conscience." Choices (A) and (D) are true, but do not reflect the writer's thoughts in this passage. Choices (B) and (E) are neither true nor relevant.

45. **The correct answer is (B).** Although the Brahmins might have been harsh and scathing in their commentary about modern American poets, the passage itself does not have that tone; therefore, choice (A) is incorrect. There is no wit or humor in the excerpt, making choice (D) incorrect. The remaining two answers have some elements that may be seen to be true. A reader may see the article as dry or even irritating, but not condescending, choice (C), or pretentious, choice (E). Only one of these three answer choices has both elements that are true. Choice (B), scholarly and informative, correctly answers the question.

46. **The correct answer is (D).** The author never made a judgment about which type of poetry was superior, so choice (A) is incorrect. The same can be said of choice (B). The Brahmins were not identified as the fathers of modern American poetry, choice (C). The author specifically said that the Civil War produced little quality poetry, eliminating choice (E). The author develops the Civil War as the starting point of modern American poetry in the first two paragraphs, choice (D).

47. **The correct answer is (A).** The author says in the first sentence of the second paragraph "the Civil War . . . produced a vast quantity of poems but practically no important poetry." Choice (A) mirrors Untermeyer's commentary. If Untermeyer says that no poetry was produced, that implies that no poets were produced, so that choice (B) cannot be correct. Choices (C), (D), and (E) do not accurately reflect this passage.

48. **The correct answer is (B).** The sentence taken from the end of the concluding paragraph is a reference to the Brahmins' attempt to keep their style of poetry the dominant form. Untermeyer does not suggest that the poets of transition were deliberate in the execution of their art as indicated in choice (A). The author proposes that the poets of transition resisted the change; therefore, they were aware of it, making choice (C) incorrect. The author states neither of the meanings described in choices (D) and (E).

49. **The correct answer is (E).** In the third sentence of the final paragraph, Untermeyer identifies the new poetic expression as "crude, jangling, and vigorously democratic." Choice (E) repeats the description as crude, and it relies on the reader to recognize that a democratic form of poetry was cutting edge. The descriptions of the poets in choices (A), (B), (C), or (D) are not consistent with this description or even mentioned by the author.

50. **The correct answer is (B).** Untermeyer describes the Brahmins as educated, but he does not contend that they are mercurial, choice (A). The author leaves the reader with the impression that the Brahmins are anything but lighthearted or easygoing, choices (C) and (D). They are portrayed as brilliant, but not forgiving; thus, choice (E) is incorrect. This leaves choice (B) as the correct answer. Untermeyer does give the impression that the Brahmins were stuffy and intransigent.

## Section II

### SUGGESTIONS FOR ESSAY QUESTION 1

The following are points that you might have chosen to include in your essay on *The House of the Dead* by Fyodor Dostoyevsky. Consider them as you do your self-evaluation. (Use the Self-Evaluation Rubic form on pp. 59–60.) Revise your essay using points from this list that will strengthen it.

### *Form or Mode*

- Nonfiction

### *Theme*

- Found toward the end of the passage
- Theme statement: People can be different than they appear.
- Theme statement: Courage manifests itself in different ways.
- Theme statement: The gentlest of people can become so ferocious in their dedication to a cause that they are willing to be cast out of society fighting for it.

### *Characters*

- The old man, an Old Believer
- The narrator, Dostoyevsky
- Prisoners in a Siberian camp

### *Dialogue*

- At the end of the passage
- "Lord, do not forsake me! Lord, give me strength! My little ones, my darling little ones, I shall never see you again!"
- A prayer
- Powerful impact since only dialogue in a long description

### *Conflict*

- A man against the establishment, the Orthodox Church
- A man against himself
- His principles and religious beliefs versus his love for his family

### *Plot*

- The old man burned an Orthodox church.
- Action in support of his faith
- Sent to prison for life

- Respected there
- Secretly misses his family

### Setting

- A prison camp in Siberia
- A room within the camp
- "The old man was sitting on the stove (the same stove on which the Bible reader who threw the brick at the major used to pray)."

### Point of View

- First-person observer

### Diction

- Simple and effective
- Excellent descriptions
- "He was a little grey-headed man of sixty. . . . he was so unlike the other convicts, there was something so calm and gentle in his expression that I remember I looked with a peculiar pleasure at his serene, candid eyes . . ."
- Peaceful, pleasant tone makes ending a powerful surprise

## SUGGESTIONS FOR ESSAY QUESTION 2

The following are points that you might have chosen to include in your essay on "To a Waterfowl" by William Cullen Bryant. Consider them as you do your self-evaluation. Revise your essay using points from this list that will strengthen it.

### Type

- A lyric poem from the Romantic period; written in quatrains with an *abab* rhyme
- The Romantic concern with individual, personal experience evident
- Emphasis on the heart rather than the mind

### Themes

- Romantic poetry often about nature
- Exploration of the relationship between humanity and nature
- Nature as a source of inspiration and understanding

### Speaker/Others

- Uses his imagination concerning the bird's destination
- Speaker interested in the bird for divine sustenance; fowler interested in bird for bodily sustenance
- Speaker's belief: trusts he will be guided on his way like the waterfowl was

### Tone

- Emotional
- Humble
- Contemplative

### Figurative Language

- Waterfowl as symbol of divine sustenance
- Power and mystery of nature

### Imagery

- Vivid images, or word pictures, that illustrate the beauty of nature
- For example, "While glow the heavens with the last steps of day,/ Far, through their rosy depths, dost thou pursue/ Thy solitary way"

## SUGGESTIONS FOR ESSAY QUESTION 3

The following are points about character development that you might have chosen to discuss in your essay on character change. Consider them as you do your self-evaluation. Revise your essay using points from this list that will strengthen it.

### Character

- What you know about a character is determined by what the author tells you.
- Information coming from other characters must be considered carefully. Define the relationship between the character and the informant to understand better.
- Words of a character are good indicators of who he or she truly is. However, proceed cautiously because characters, like people in real life, lie, pretend, or disguise themselves.
- Actions speak louder than words. Consider what characters do as well as what they say.
- Take into account who is telling the story. Narrators can influence your perception.
- Protagonists and antagonists deserve most of the attention.
- The protagonist often brings a message from the writer, and that message usually relates to the theme.
- Identifying the protagonist is sometimes difficult and not always necessary. Doing so makes you think about the elements of the literature.
- Characters can encounter forces that are other than human. How the characters react reveals a great deal about them.
- How people cope with economic, social, or political forces reveals character.
- The struggle between the protagonist and the antagonist is crucial to a literary work. How it is resolved gives you insight into the characters and the meaning of the piece.

## SELF-EVALUATION RUBRIC FOR THE ADVANCED PLACEMENT ESSAYS

| | 8–9 | 6–7 | 5 | 3–4 | 1–2 | 0 |
|---|---|---|---|---|---|---|
| **Overall Impression** | Demonstrates excellent control of the literature and outstanding writing competence; thorough and effective; incisive | Demonstrates good control of the literature and good writing competence; less thorough and incisive than the highest papers | Reveals simplistic thinking and/or immature writing; adequate skills | Incomplete thinking; fails to respond adequately to part or parts of the question; may paraphrase rather than analyze | Unacceptably brief; fails to respond to the question; little clarity | Lacking skill and competence |
| **Understanding of the Text** | Excellent understanding of the text; exhibits perception and clarity; original or unique approach; includes apt and specific references | Good understanding of the text; exhibits perception and clarity; includes specific references | Superficial understanding of the text; elements of literature vague, mechanical, overgeneralized | Misreadings and lack of persuasive evidence from the text; meager and unconvincing treatment of literary elements | Serious misreadings and little supporting evidence from the text; erroneous treatment of literary elements | A response with no more than a reference to the literature; blank response, or one completely off the topic |
| **Organization and Development** | Meticulously organized and thoroughly developed; coherent and unified | Well-organized and developed; coherent and unified | Reasonably organized and developed; mostly coherent and unified | Somewhat organized and developed; some incoherence and lack of unity | Little or no organization and development; incoherent and void of unity | No apparent organization or development; incoherent |
| **Use of Sentences** | Effectively varied and engaging; virtually error free | Varied and interesting; a few errors | Adequately varied; some errors | Somewhat varied and marginally interesting; one or more major errors | Little or no variation; dull and uninteresting; some major errors | Numerous major errors |
| **Word Choice** | Interesting and effective; virtually error free | Generally interesting and effective; a few errors | Occasionally interesting and effective; several errors | Somewhat dull and ordinary; some errors in diction | Mostly dull and conventional; numerous errors | Numerous major errors; extremely immature |
| **Grammar and Usage** | Virtually error free | Occasional minor errors | Several minor errors | Some major errors | Severely flawed; frequent major errors | Extremely flawed |

Rate yourself in each of the categories. Choose the description that most accurately reflects your performance, and enter the numbers on the lines below. Be as honest as possible so you will know what areas need work. Then calculate the average of the six numbers to determine your final score. It is difficult to score yourself objectively, so you may wish to ask a respected friend or teacher to assess your writing for a more accurate reflection of its strengths and weaknesses. On the AP test itself, a reader will rate your essay on a scale of 0 to 9, with 9 being the highest.

Rate each category from 9 (high) to 0 (low).

## Essay Question 1

**SELF-EVALUATION**

Overall Impression _____
Understanding of the Text _____
Organization and Development _____
Use of Sentences _____
Word Choice (Diction) _____
Grammar and Usage _____

TOTAL _____
    Divide by 6 for final score _____

**OBJECTIVE EVALUATION**

Overall Impression _____
Understanding of the Text _____
Organization and Development _____
Use of Sentences _____
Word Choice (Diction) _____
Grammar and Usage _____

TOTAL _____
    Divide by 6 for final score _____

## Essay Question 2

**SELF-EVALUATION**

Overall Impression _____
Understanding of the Text _____
Organization and Development _____
Use of Sentences _____
Word Choice (Diction) _____
Grammar and Usage _____

TOTAL _____
    Divide by 6 for final score _____

**OBJECTIVE EVALUATION**

Overall Impression _____
Understanding of the Text _____
Organization and Development _____
Use of Sentences _____
Word Choice (Diction) _____
Grammar and Usage _____

TOTAL _____
    Divide by 6 for final score _____

## Essay Question 3

**SELF-EVALUATION**

Overall Impression _____
Understanding of the Text _____
Organization and Development _____
Use of Sentences _____
Word Choice (Diction) _____
Grammar and Usage _____

TOTAL _____
    Divide by 6 for final score _____

**OBJECTIVE EVALUATION**

Overall Impression _____
Understanding of the Text _____
Organization and Development _____
Use of Sentences _____
Word Choice (Diction) _____
Grammar and Usage _____

TOTAL _____
    Divide by 6 for final score _____

# PART III

## AP ENGLISH LITERATURE & COMPOSITION REVIEW

# About the Multiple-Choice Questions Related to Prose

## OVERVIEW

- **Recommendations for acing prose questions**
- **Practicing**
- **Summing it up**

On the Advanced Placement test, you will discover that most of the multiple-choice questions test how carefully you read and how well you interpret what you read. Chapter 3 presents techniques that you can apply to the questions about prose selections. Remember, in order to earn an overall grade of at least 3, you will need to answer approximately 50 to 60 percent of the questions correctly and write reasonably good essays. The more questions you answer correctly, the less pressure you will have to do exceptionally well on the three essays.

The prose selections on the AP English Literature & Composition Test may vary from a few short paragraphs to lengthy sections. Some passages may be from plays, others may come from short stories, and still others may be taken from essays. By following the recommendations offered here, you may gain those extra points that will give you a great score going into Section II.

## RECOMMENDATIONS FOR ACING PROSE QUESTIONS

### Reading the Selections

- Most prose passages are not given titles. If a selection is titled, think about what it tells you about the work. You may get a sense of the subject and theme just from the title.

- If there is no title, look for the topic sentence or thesis statement. In most writing, you will find it near the beginning. However, because AP exams ask you about challenging literature, you may find the topic sentence at the end or in the middle of the selection, or the thesis will be implied rather than stated outright.

- As you read, observe patterns of organization that the writer employs. Patterns may follow a certain sequence or order, set up a compare and contrast situation, offer a problem and solution, show cause and effect, or offer a series of examples. Some authors may use more than one system of organization.

**NOTE**

See Chapter 1 for more on reading prose passages.

- As you read, highlight words and sentences that seem significant. However, do not spend a lot of time doing this. Make it part of your second reading.

- When you read a passage, keep in mind the 5 Ws and H: *who, what, where, when, why,* and *how.* Answers to these questions will help you to recall specific information about the selection.

**TIP**

If paraphrasing does not come easily to you, try writing paraphrases of the selections in this book for practice.

- Mentally paraphrase the passage that you have just read. Paraphrasing helps you discover the subject and the organization of the selection or the thesis and supporting arguments. The writer's style, transitions, sentence types, language, and literary devices become clear. You see the framework of the passage in a paraphrase.

## Identifying the Question Type

- Remember that there are six types of multiple-choice questions: main-idea, detail, inference, definition, tone or purpose, and form. You may also find a few factual knowledge questions dealing with language and with culture related to literature.

- Look for the main idea of the passage, its central point. If you paraphrased well, recognizing the main idea will come easily.

- When answering a main-idea question, the correct choice must be entirely true and include as much relevant information as possible. In many questions, two or three choices might seem to be correct. However, the answer that is most complete is the one to choose.

- When you are asked to make judgments about what is inferred or implied in a selection, you must put together clues from the passage. You must be able to support your answer with specific facts or examples from the selection.

- Questions that ask about the meaning of words or phrases are best answered by substituting your answer choice in the sentence or paragraph. If the answer makes sense, you have the correct choice.

- In answering a question about tone or purpose, pay attention to word choice. That type of question asks you to determine how or why the writer created the selection. Authors convey that information through diction.

## Answering the Questions

- Reread lines, sentences, or paragraphs that are identified in the questions. In fact, scan or reread any selection if you do not immediately know the answer for a question.

- Just as you choose the order to attack the passages, choose the order for how you wish to answer the multiple-choice questions. If you understand the passage, answer the questions in order.

- If you are not confident about a passage, skip difficult questions and answer the easy ones first. Be sure to mark in the test booklet the ones you have not answered. If you do skip a question, check to be sure you also skip that number on your answer sheet.

- Look for consistency in the answers to the questions about a passage. If a choice seems contradictory to other answers you have given, rethink that choice.

- Many times the key to finding the correct answer is to narrow down the choices and make an intelligent guess. Eliminate some answers by finding those that are obviously unrelated, illogical, or incorrect. Having reduced the number of choices, you can make an educated guess from among the remaining possibilities. Use the techniques presented in the chart below to reduce the number of choices.

**TIP**

The more questions you answer in order the less chance you have of filling in the wrong answer ovals on the answer sheet.

| STRATEGIES FOR ANSWERING OBJECTIVE QUESTIONS/ MAKING EDUCATED GUESSES | |
| --- | --- |
| **ANSWER CHOICE** | **REASON TO ELIMINATE** |
| 1. too narrow | too small a section of the selection covered, based on the question |
| 2. too broad | an area wider than the selection covered, based on the question |
| 3. irrelevant | • nothing to do with the passage<br>• relevant to the selection but not the question |
| 4. incorrect | • distortion of the facts in the selection<br>• contradiction of the facts in the selection |
| 5. illogical | • not supported by facts in the passage<br>• not supported by cited passage from the selection |
| 6. similar choices | GO BACK AND REVIEW 1–5 TO TEASE OUT THE DIFFERENCES. |
| 7. *not/except* | answers that correctly represent the selection |

The *not/except* questions are tricky. You can forget what it is you are looking for and choose a correct answer, which is really a wrong answer, because you are answering a *not/except* question. Convoluted? Yes; as you go through each answer, ask yourself, "Is this statement true about the selection?" If yes, cross it out and keep going until you find a choice that you can answer "no" to.

**NOTE**

Always read all the explanations given for correct answers in the "Answer Key and Explanations" sections in this book. You may learn something new about taking the test or about a piece of literature.

## PRACTICING

Read the short story "Hearts and Hands" by O. Henry that begins on the next page. After you have read the story, jot down your answers to the questions in the margin or on a separate piece of paper. Even though this is a fairly easy passage, you may not be able to answer every question correctly. This is practice.

If you do not understand the question, you may check the explanation immediately. You may refer to the answers question by question, or you may wish to score the entire section at one time. No matter which method you choose, read all the explanations. The reasoning involved may point out to you concepts or details that you missed. Once you have read the story, look at the questions.

# EXERCISE 1

**Directions:** This section consists of selections of literature and questions on their content, style, and form. After you have read each passage, choose the answer that best answers the question.

**QUESTIONS 1 THROUGH 14 REFER TO THE FOLLOWING SHORT STORY BY O. HENRY. READ THE PASSAGE CAREFULLY AND THEN CHOOSE THE ANSWERS TO THE QUESTIONS.**

### Hearts and Hands

Line At Denver there was an influx of passengers into the coaches on the eastbound B. & E. express. In one coach there sat a very pretty young woman dressed in elegant taste and surrounded by all the luxurious comforts of an experienced traveler. Among the newcomers were two young men, one of handsome presence with a bold, frank counte-
5 nance and manner; the other, a ruffled, glum-faced person, heavily built and roughly dressed. The two were handcuffed together.

As they passed down the aisle of the coach the only vacant seat offered was a reversed one facing the attractive young woman. Here the linked couple seated themselves. The young woman's glance fell upon them with a distant, swift disinter-
10 est; then with a lovely smile brightening her countance and a tender pink tingeing her rounded cheeks, she held out a little gray-gloved hand. When she spoke, her voice, full, sweet, and deliberate, proclaimed that its owner was accustomed to speak and be heard.

"Well, Mr. Easton, if you *will* make me speak first, I suppose I must. Don't you ever
15 recognize old friends when you meet them in the West?"

The younger man roused himself sharply at the sound of her voice, seemed to struggle with a slight embarrassment which he threw off instantly; and then clasped her fingers with his left hand.

"It's Miss Fairchild," he said, with a smile. "I'll ask you to excuse the other hand;
20 it's otherwise engaged just at the present."

He slightly raised his right hand, bound at the wrist by the shining "bracelet" to the left one of his companion. The glad look in the girl's eyes slowly changed to a bewildered horror. The glow faded from her cheeks. Her lips parted in a vague, relaxing distress. Easton, with a little laugh, as if amused, was about to speak again when the
25 other forestalled him. The glum-faced man had been watching the girl's countenance with veiled glances from his keen, shrewd eyes.

"You'll excuse me for speaking, miss, but I see you're acquainted with the marshal here. If you'll ask him to speak a word for me when we get to the pen he'll do it, and it'll make things easier for me there. He's taking me to Leavenworth prison. It's seven
30 years for counterfeiting."

"Oh!" said the girl, with a deep breath and returning color. "So that is what you are doing out here? A marshal!"

"My dear Miss Fairchild," said Easton, calmly. "I had to do something. Money has a way of taking wings unto itself, and you know it takes money to keep step with our
35 crowd in Washington. I saw this opening in the West, and—well, a marshalship isn't quite as high a position as that of ambassador, but—"

"The ambassador," said the girl, warmly, "doesn't call any more. He needn't ever have done so. You ought to know that. And so now you are one of these dashing Western heroes, and you ride and shoot and go into all kinds of dangers. That's
40 different from the Washington life. You have been missed from the old crowd."

The girl's eyes, fascinated, went back, widening a little, to rest upon the glittering handcuffs.

"Don't you worry about them, miss," said the other man. "All marshals handcuff themselves to their prisoners to keep them from getting away. Mr. Easton knows
45 his business."

"Will we see you again soon in Washington?" asked the girl.

"Not soon, I think," said Easton. "My butterfly days are over, I fear."

"I love the West," said the girl irrelevantly. Her eyes were shining softly. She looked away out the car window. She began to speak truly and simply, without the gloss of
50 style or manner: "Momma and I spent the summer in Denver. She went home a week ago because father was slightly ill. I could live and be happy in the West. I think the air here agrees with me. Money isn't everything. But people always misunderstand things and remain stupid—"

"Say, Mr. Marshal," growled the glum-faced man. "This isn't quite fair. Haven't had
55 a smoke all day. Haven't you talked long enough? Take me in the smoker now, won't you? I'm half dead for a pipe."

The bound travelers rose to their feet, Easton with the same slow smile on his face.

"I can't deny a petition for tobacco," he said lightly. "It's the one friend of the unfortunate. Goodbye, Miss Fairchild. Duty calls, you know." He held his hand for
60 a farewell.

"It's too bad you are not going East," she said, reclothing herself with manner and style. "But you must go on to Leavenworth, I suppose?"

"Yes," said Easton, "I must go on to Leavenworth."

The two men sidled down the aisle into the smoker.
65 The two passengers in a seat nearby had heard most of the conversation. Said one of them: "That marshal's a good sort of chap. Some of these Western fellows are all right."

"Pretty young to hold an office like that, isn't he?" asked the other.

"Young!" exclaimed the first speaker, "why—Oh! Didn't you catch on? Say—did you
70 ever know an officer to handcuff a prisoner to his right hand?"

—O. Henry

1. The primary purpose of this selection is to present

   **(A)** a social commentary on the criminal justice system in the United States in the late 1900s
   **(B)** ordinary people in a situation that surprises and entertains the audience
   **(C)** satires on the elegant manners of upper-class Americans
   **(D)** a regional tale of the Wild West
   **(E)** a dramatization of a true event in the history of Colorado

2. Which of the following best explains the main idea of the passage?

   **(A)** Crime does not pay.
   **(B)** Elegant manners and courtesy often make difficult situations easier to handle.
   **(C)** The law is sometimes forgiving.
   **(D)** A love of money may be hurtful in many ways.
   **(E)** Appearances can be deceiving.

3. This story is an excellent example of which of the following literary techniques?

   **(A)** A romance
   **(B)** A surprise ending
   **(C)** Regional style
   **(D)** A red herring
   **(E)** Development of suspense

4. Which one of the following choices best describes the past relationship between Miss Fairchild and Mr. Easton?

   (A) They know each other from Washington, D.C.
   (B) There was more than friendship between them.
   (C) Mr. Easton and Miss Fairchild moved in high social circles.
   (D) They had been engaged to be married.
   (E) Mr. Easton and the ambassador fought a duel over Miss Fairchild.

5. Which of the following best describes the glum-faced man?

   (A) The man was a criminal convicted of counterfeiting.
   (B) He was addicted to tobacco.
   (C) Although he appeared rough, he was sensitive and perceptive.
   (D) Many passengers knew him since he was a well-known figure in the West.
   (E) He did not like Miss Fairchild or Mr. Easton.

6. What impression does the author seek to create in this story?

   (A) Mr. Easton is the marshal and he is taking his prisoner to Leavenworth.
   (B) Mr. Easton and Miss Fairchild will resume their engagement.
   (C) Mr. Easton is actually the prisoner.
   (D) Miss Fairchild finds the marshal attractive.
   (E) The two passengers know the reputation of the marshal.

7. Which of the following sentences does not hint at the ending?

   (A) "He slightly raised his right hand, bound at the wrist by the shining 'bracelet' to the left one of his companion." (lines 21–22)
   (B) "'Not soon, I think,' said Easton. 'My butterfly days are over, I fear.'" (line 47)
   (C) "The girl's eyes, fascinated, went back, widening a little, to rest upon the glittering handcuffs." (lines 41–42)
   (D) "All marshals handcuff themselves to their prisoners to keep them from getting away. Mr. Easton knows his business." (lines 43–45)
   (E) "I must go on to Leavenworth." (line 63)

8. The statement "'Yes,' said Easton, 'I must go on to Leavenworth,'" (line 63) is an example of

   (A) a surprise ending
   (B) a complex sentence
   (C) sarcasm
   (D) irony
   (E) satire

9. What is the significance of the fact that the prisoner's crime is counterfeiting?

   (A) The crime of counterfeiting involves making and spending fake money. The prisoner is "counterfeit" since he passes himself off as a marshal.
   (B) A nonviolent crime such as counterfeiting makes Mr. Easton less threatening.
   (C) It establishes that money is important to Mr. Easton.
   (D) Counterfeiting is something that Miss Fairchild could understand.
   (E) People are not always what they appear to be.

exercises

10. What literary device is found in the sentence: "Money has a way of taking wings unto itself. . . ." (lines 33–34)?

    (A) Personification
    (B) Alliteration
    (C) Analogy
    (D) Metaphor
    (E) Figurative language

11. What is the inference that the author encourages readers to make from this description: "Among the newcomers were two young men, one of handsome presence with a bold, frank countenance and manner; the other, a ruffled, glum-faced person, heavily built and roughly dressed. The two were handcuffed together." (lines 3–6)?

    (A) The well-dressed man is the law-enforcement officer.
    (B) One man is more well-to-do than the other.
    (C) Miss Easton was interested in the better-dressed man.
    (D) The well-dressed man is a Washington, D.C., official.
    (E) The glum-faced man is a U.S. marshal.

12. Which of the following was probably not a reason that the marshal deceived Miss Fairchild?

    (A) He found her attractive.
    (B) He perceived her fondness for Mr. Easton.
    (C) The marshal noticed that Miss Fairchild was concerned when she saw the handcuffs.
    (D) The marshal wanted to protect her feelings.
    (E) The marshal wanted her to feel more comfortable.

13. Grammatically, the phrase "had been watching" in the sentence, "The glum-faced man had been watching the girl's countenance with veiled glances from his keen, shrewd eyes," (lines 25–26) indicates which of the following?

    (A) Past perfect
    (B) Past emphatic
    (C) Past progressive
    (D) Present perfect progressive
    (E) Past perfect progressive

14. Explain the use of the colon in the following quotation: "Said one of them: 'That marshal's a good sort of chap. Some of these Western fellows are all right.'" (lines 65–67)

    (A) The colon is incorrect. The writer should have used a semicolon.
    (B) The colon introduces a list, in this case, two sentences.
    (C) The colon punctuates an introductory statement.
    (D) A colon is used to separate explanatory words in a formal or lengthy quotation.
    (E) The colon joins two sentences of almost equal weight that say essentially the same thing.

This selection is longer than most of those you will encounter on the Advanced Placement examination. The longer passages allow for more variety in the practice questions. Some prose selections may have only ten questions. Longer passages may have up to fifteen.

Turn to the next page. There you will find the explanations clarifying the reasoning behind the correct answers and showing you why the other choices are incorrect. Notice the techniques used to answer each type of question.

## ANSWER KEY AND EXPLANATIONS

| | | | | |
|---|---|---|---|---|
| 1. B | 4. B | 7. C | 10. E | 13. E |
| 2. E | 5. C | 8. D | 11. A | 14. D |
| 3. B | 6. A | 9. A | 12. A | |

1. **The correct answer is (B).** Did you recognize this as a purpose question? You need to consider O. Henry's choice of words and the tone of the story. If you recognized that the tone is wryly humorous or amusing, you could immediately pick choice (B). Educated guessing would eliminate choice (A), because there is no criticism of the criminal justice system in the story. Although the author makes such slight references to manners, choice (C), it can hardly be his purpose. The setting is the West, choice (D), but that is not essential to the tale. What is important is that Miss Fairchild and Mr. Easton are no longer in Washington. Nowhere is there any indication that this actually happened, choice (E). In fact, it seems improbable that it could have happened.

2. **The correct answer is (E).** This question asks about your overall understanding of the passage. You must look for the answer that is entirely correct and general enough, without going beyond the limits of the story. Choices (A) and (D) are true but too general. Choice (B) may be true; however, there is no evidence supporting it in the story. Likewise, choice (C) is only partially complete and therefore partially wrong.

3. **The correct answer is (B).** This question tests your knowledge of the conventions of fiction. If you are familiar with O. Henry, this question is a snap. He was one of the first to perfect the surprise ending. If you did not recall this fact, then try eliminating answers. Choice (A) is incorrect because a romance is a story of love, adventure, and excitement. Although the story is set in the West, the setting is unimportant, thus eliminating choice (C). A red herring, choice (D), is used in this story, but to accomplish a surprise ending, making choice (B) a more accurate answer. Because this story has a surprise ending, there is no development of suspense, choice (E).

4. **The correct answer is (B).** This is an inference question. The correct answer is supported by the facts of the story. Miss Fairchild makes sure that Mr. Easton knows she was not interested in the ambassador, and she also makes it clear that she would love to live in the West. Choices (A) and (C), while true, are too broad; they are details that support choice (B). Choice (D) is illogical when you consider the characters' behavior. Choice (E) is irrelevant and not referenced in the story.

5. **The correct answer is (C).** This question tests your understanding of an important character, and in doing so tests your comprehension of the entire story. The plot rests on the true marshal's observant and considerate personality. Choice (A) contradicts the facts in the story. Choices (B) and (D) are irrelevant and not supported by facts. The marshal must have liked the two young people or he would not have behaved as he did, choice (E).

6. **The correct answer is (A).** This is one of those questions with an answer that you could figure out through other questions. Because you know that the purpose of the story (question 3) is to create a surprise for the reader, you can logically assume that somewhere something in the story must be misleading. Choice (B) is not supported by any statement in the story, so it is irrelevant. Choice (D) is vague—which marshal?—since Easton is not really a marshal. Choice (C) is the truth, and that makes it the wrong answer. Choice (E) is not supported by the facts. If it were correct, both passengers would have recognized the real marshal.

7. **The correct answer is (C).** Did you see the *not* in this question? Choices (A), (B), (D), and (E) all hint that Mr. Easton is not what he seems. While choice (C) does mention handcuffs, an important clue in the story, this choice does not indicate anything ironic about them or about the situation.

8. **The correct answer is (D).** Irony is the recognition of the difference between reality and appearance. Mr. Easton uses verbal irony, a contrast between what is said and what is actually meant. If you did not identify the irony, you could make some educated guesses that would eliminate other answers. While choice (A) is true of the story, Mr. Easton's speech is not relevant to the surprise ending. Choice (B) is both irrelevant and inaccurate. Choices (C) and (E) are inconsistent with the tone O. Henry creates in his story.

9. **The correct answer is (A).** Since there is truth in all of the choices, this question demands that you choose the best answer. Counterfeiting is a nonviolent crime and Mr. Easton is nonthreatening, choice (B), but those facts are not important to the development of the story. Choice (C) is too broad; obviously money was important to him or he would not have committed a crime. The point is so basic that it is a poor choice. We have no information that supports choice (D), so it is irrelevant. Choice (E) is an aphorism that is the main idea of the story, but it does not explain the significance of counterfeiting as Mr. Easton's crime.

10. **The correct answer is (E).** This question tests your knowledge of English literature. To answer this question easily, you must know the various literary devices used by writers. Mr. Easton is making an association that is to be interpreted imaginatively rather than literally. You might have thought choice (A) was correct, but a personification gives human, nonanimal characteristics to nonhuman things; wings belong to birds, not people. Alliteration, choice (B), is the repetition of consonant sounds at the beginning of words in a series. An analogy, choice (C), is a comparison of two similar but different things, whereas a metaphor, choice (D), states that one thing is another.

11. **The correct answer is (A).** If you understand O. Henry's purpose, to create a surprise ending, this question is easy. You can infer that the author wants readers to misjudge the roles of Mr. Easton and the actual marshal. Choice (E), of course, is the reverse of the correct answer. Choices (B) and (C) are irrelevant to the quotation, and choice (D) is an interpretation of the passage that is not supported by any facts.

12. **The correct answer is (A).** Did you see the word *not*? This question asks you to eliminate all answers that are correct and have a bearing on the story. There is evidence to support all answers except choice (A). The marshal may have found Miss Fairchild attractive, but there is no mention of that in the story.

13. **The correct answer is (E).** This is one type of grammar question that you might come across on the actual test. The *-ing* form of the verb makes the tense progressive. The past form of the auxiliary verbs *to have* and *to be* make the verb phrase past and perfect.

14. **The correct answer is (D).** Although you might consider that the colon is used improperly here, it cannot be corrected by replacing it with a semicolon, choice (A). Colons do introduce lists, but these sentences do not constitute a list, choice (B). Choices (C) and (E) correctly state uses of the colon, but neither applies to this question. If you did not answer this question correctly, remember that there are very few of these questions on the actual examination.

# EXERCISE 2

**Directions:** This section consists of selections of literature and questions on their content, style, and form. After you have read each passage, choose the answer that best answers the question.

**QUESTIONS 1 THROUGH 10 REFER TO THE FOLLOWING SELECTION. READ THE PASSAGE CAREFULLY AND THEN CHOOSE THE ANSWERS TO THE QUESTIONS.**

### From *Hard Times*

Line   "Now, what I want is, Facts. Teach these boys and girls nothing but Facts. Facts alone are wanted in life. Plant nothing else, and root out everything else. You can only form the minds of reasoning animals upon Facts; nothing else will ever be of any service to them. This is the principle on which I bring up my own children, and this is the
5      principle on which I bring up these children. Stick to Facts, sir!"

The scene was a plain, bare, monotonous vault of a schoolroom, and the speaker's square forefinger emphasized his observations by underscoring every sentence with a line on the schoolmaster's sleeve. The emphasis was helped by the speaker's square wall of a forehead, which had his eyebrows for its base, while his eyes found commodi-
10     ous cellarage in two dark caves, overshadowed by the wall. The emphasis was helped by the speaker's mouth, which was wide, thin, and hard set. The emphasis was helped by the speaker's voice, which was inflexible, dry, and dictatorial. The emphasis was helped by the speaker's hair, which bristled on the skirts of his bald head, a plantation of firs to keep the wind from its shining surface, all covered with knobs, like the crust
15     of a plum pie, as if the head had scarcely warehouse-room for the hard facts stored inside. The speaker's obstinate carriage, square coat, square legs, square shoulders— nay, his very neckcloth, trained to take him by the throat with an unaccommodating grasp, like a stubborn fact, as it was—all helped the emphasis.

"In this life, we want nothing but Facts, sir; nothing but Facts!"
20     The speaker, and the schoolmaster, and the third grown person present, all backed a little, and swept their eyes the inclined plane of little vessels and there arranged in order, ready to have imperial gallons of facts poured into them until they were full to the brim.

—Charles Dickens

1.  This selection could best be characterized as a(n)

    **(A)**  amusing but pointed satire
    **(B)**  invective against British education
    **(C)**  solemn view of the importance of the scientific method
    **(D)**  objective description of the nineteenth-century world
    **(E)**  laudatory view of teachers

2.  Which of the following literary techniques does Dickens effectively employ in this selection?

    **(A)**  Parallel structure
    **(B)**  Stream of consciousness
    **(C)**  Hyperbole
    **(D)**  Repetition
    **(E)**  Limited omniscient narrator

3. Which of the following best describes the character that Dickens portrays in the second paragraph?

   (A) Warm and understanding
   (B) Malleable and open-minded
   (C) Opinionated and intransigent
   (D) Educated and erudite
   (E) Scholarly and pedantic

4. What does the word "commodious" mean in the following sentence: "The emphasis was helped by the speaker's square wall of a forehead, which had his eyebrows for its base, while his eyes found commodious cellarage in two dark caves, overshadowed by the wall." (lines 8–10)?

   (A) Dark
   (B) Foreboding
   (C) Spacious
   (D) Friendly
   (E) Serious

5. What is Dickens referring to when he speaks of "little vessels" in the last paragraph, line 21?

   (A) Toy boats
   (B) Students
   (C) Containers
   (D) Travel
   (E) Assistants

6. The phrase "a plantation of firs to keep the wind from its shining surface" (lines 13–14) is an example of

   (A) metaphor
   (B) simile
   (C) synecdoche
   (D) repetition
   (E) allusion

7. What inference can be drawn about what Dickens wants the reader to think about his character, the speaker?

   (A) The speaker is to be admired.
   (B) The speaker is pompous.
   (C) The speaker is insightful.
   (D) The speaker is to be liked.
   (E) Dickens presents the speaker as an educated man.

8. The phrase "the inclined plane of little vessels" (line 21) functions as what sentence part?

   (A) Subject
   (B) Predicate
   (C) Direct object
   (D) Indirect object
   (E) Object of a preposition

9. In the second paragraph, what is the author suggesting in describing the knobs on the speaker's head?

   (A) He is old.
   (B) His head is filled with data.
   (C) He is soft in the head.
   (D) He bumped his head.
   (E) He is bald.

10. The setting of this excerpt is a(n)

   (A) auditorium
   (B) conference room
   (C) classroom
   (D) college
   (E) dormitory

## ANSWER KEY AND EXPLANATIONS

| | | | | |
|---|---|---|---|---|
| 1. A | 3. C | 5. B | 7. B | 9. B |
| 2. D | 4. C | 6. A | 8. D | 10. C |

1. **The correct answer is (A).** The use of educated guessing can be useful in determining the correct answer to this question. Look at the answers in this fashion:

   - Is it amusing, choice (A)? Yes, it is funny and satirical.

   - Is it an invective (abusive discourse), choice (B)? No, the speaker may be inveighing against education but Dickens's intent is satirical.

   - Does it discuss scientific method, choice (C)? No, just because it talks about facts does not mean it is about the scientific method.

   - Does it describe the nineteenth-century world, choice (D)? No, not at all.

   - Does it praise teachers, choice (E)? No, there is no mention of teachers, just what they should teach.

2. **The correct answer is (D).** Make sure that you understand all of the terms contained in this question. In this case, the two closest responses are parallel structure, choice (A), and repetition, choice (D). Repetition is used for emphasis (no pun intended!), which is the author's intention here, so choice (D) is the correct answer. In stream of consciousness, choice (B), the reader is privy to the continuous, chaotic flow of thoughts and impressions of the character. In this passage, the character is actually speaking, so choice (B) is incorrect. Hyperbole, choice (C), is deliberate exaggeration to create humor, and we already determined in question 1 that the passage is humorous. A limited omniscient narrator, choice (E), is a third person who narrates the thoughts of one character, and in this passage the character is speaking directly and the writer is an objective narrator.

3. **The correct answer is (C).** In each of these paired answers, try to eliminate one portion as being incorrect. If one part is wrong, the entire answer is wrong. The speaker was not warm, choice (A), or open-minded, choice (B). Whether he is educated, choice (D), or scholarly, choice (E), is unknown based on this passage. His words show that he is both opinionated and intransigent, choice (C). If you did not know what *intransigent* meant, eliminating the other pairs will bring you to this one by default.

4. **The correct answer is (C).** If you do not know the meaning of the word *commodious,* this can be a difficult question because several of the responses contain the feeling that the author wants you to have of the individual. Although the character is certainly not friendly, choice (D), he could be described as dark, choice (A); foreboding, choice (B); or serious, choice (E). These are subjective expressions, however, and the author is making a straightforward description of the character's eye sockets—they are spacious.

5. **The correct answer is (B).** If the answer is not immediately apparent, you can eliminate some of the responses. Two of these, travel, choice (D), and assistants, choice (E), have no relation to the passage. Vessels can be both containers, choice (C), and boats, choice (A). In the context of the referenced sentence, these containers are being filled with facts. The only answer that meets that criterion is choice (B), students.

6. **The correct answer is (A).** In this case, the speaker's head is compared with a "plantation of firs," but there is neither "like" nor "as," so it is a metaphor, not a simile, choice (B). A synecdoche, choice (C), is a figure of speech in which a part of something is used to represent a whole. There is no repetition, choice (D), involved in this phrase. An allusion, choice (E), is a reference to another work or famous figure.

7. **The correct answer is (B).** In questions that ask you to make an inference, it is useful to think of the overall tone or feeling of the excerpt. For example, is the feeling of the speaker that Dickens gives you a positive or negative one? In this case you would have to say negative; therefore, choices (A), (C), and (D) can be eliminated. Choice (E) is wrong not only because the image is positive but also because his education is not mentioned in the passage.

8. **The correct answer is (D).** When questions about sentence structure appear on the exam, do not expect them to be based on simple sentence structure. In this example, restate the clause so that it reads: "The speaker, and the schoolmaster, and the third grown person . . . swept their eyes (over) the inclined plane of little vessels." It then becomes clear that the phrase is the indirect object.

9. **The correct answer is (B).** This question tests your comprehension of the excerpt. It is, however, easily answered once you put the question into context. The problem is, where is it? When you read the passages, make sure that you have a feel for the author's overall points, but also try to keep in mind that the excerpt is like an encyclopedia, that is, you do not have to know everything, just where to find it. In this example, you know the question deals with the description of the speaker. You also know that the speaker is described in the second paragraph. Scan that paragraph looking for key words such as *knobs* and *head*. Once you have found the phrase, read the surrounding sentences to put the question into context. In this case, you will readily see that the reference is to the speaker's head being stuffed with data.

10. **The correct answer is (C).** The approach to answering this question is a combination of eliminating wrong answers and scanning. First, eliminate those answers that are most likely incorrect, based on the excerpt. This means choice (B), but the balance of choices can be associated with education, the subject matter of the passage. Second, try to find a reference in the passage to where the characters might be. Unlike question 9, there is no single paragraph devoted to the physical description of the location, but the answer is there in the author's wording in the first sentence of the second paragraph—schoolroom, choice (C).

## EXERCISE 3

**Directions:** This section consists of selections of literature and questions on their content, style, and form. After you have read each passage, choose the answer that best answers the question.

QUESTIONS 1 THROUGH 10 REFER TO THE FOLLOWING SELECTION. READ THE PASSAGE CAREFULLY AND THEN CHOOSE THE ANSWERS TO THE QUESTIONS.

**From the third essay of *Letters from an American Farmer***

Line  What attachment can a poor European emigrant have for a country where he had
nothing? The knowledge of the language, the love of a few kindred as poor as himself,
were the only cords that tied him: his country is now that which gives him land,
bread, protection, and consequence. *Ubi panis ibi patria** is the motto of all emigrants.
5     What then is the American, this new man? He is either an European, or the descen-
dant of an European, hence that strange mixture of blood, which you will find in no
other country. I could point out to you a family whose grandfather was an English-
man, whose wife was Dutch, whose son married a French woman, and whose present
four sons have now four wives of different nations. *He* is an American, who, leaving
10    behind him all his ancient prejudices and manners, receives new ones from the new
mode of life he has embraced, the government he obeys, and the new rank he holds.
He becomes an American by being received in the broad lap of our great *Alma
Mater*.** Here individuals of all nations are melted into a new race of men, whose
labors and posterity will one day cause great changes in the world. Americans are the
15    western pilgrims, who are carrying along with them that great mass of arts, sciences,
vigor, and industry which began long since in the east; they will finish the great circle.
The Americans were once scattered all over Europe; here they are incorporated into
one of the finest systems of population which has ever appeared, and which will
hereafter become distinct by the power of the different climates they inhabit. The
20    American ought therefore to love this country much better than that wherein either
he or his forefathers were born. Here the rewards of his industry follow with equal
steps the progress of his labor; his labor is founded on the basis of nature, *self-interest;*
can it want a stronger allurement? Wives and children, who before in vain demanded
of him a morsel of bread, now, fat and frolicsome, gladly help their father to clear
25    those fields whence exuberant crops are to arise to feed and to clothe them all;
without any part being claimed, either by a despotic prince, a rich abbot, or a mighty
lord. Here religion demands but little of him; a small voluntary salary to the minister,
and gratitude to God; can he refuse these? The American is a new man, who acts upon
principles; he must therefore entertain new ideas, and form new opinions. From
30    involuntary idleness, servile dependence, penury, and useless labor, he has passed to
toils of a very different nature, rewarded by ample subsistence.—This is an American.

—Hector St. John de Crèvecoeur

---

\* Where bread is, there is one's country.
\*\* beloved mother

1.  Which of the following best describes
    the author's view of America?

    **(A)**  A melting pot
    **(B)**  Lacking in prejudices
    **(C)**  Devoid of principles
    **(D)**  Class conscious
    **(E)**  Lawless

2.  How can this selection be best
    characterized?

    **(A)**  An eloquent expression of the
           American dream
    **(B)**  A charming narrative
    **(C)**  An ironic discourse
    **(D)**  A subtle criticism of the new
           American nation
    **(E)**  A commentary directed at
           reforming European countries

3.  Which of the following is not a
    reason for Americans to love this
    country more than that of their
    ancestors?

    **(A)**  Religion demands little of them.
    **(B)**  Rewards follow their labor.
    **(C)**  Abbots, princes, or lords do not
           confiscate crops.
    **(D)**  The labor of Americans is
           founded upon their own self-
           interest.
    **(E)**  Charity is freely given.

4.  In this sentence, "From involuntary
    idleness, servile dependence, penury,
    and useless labor, he has passed to
    toils of a very different nature,
    rewarded by ample subsistence."
    (lines 29–31), what is the meaning of
    the word "penury"?

    **(A)**  Largess
    **(B)**  Imprisonment
    **(C)**  Destitution
    **(D)**  Hard work
    **(E)**  Corporal punishment

5.  Why is there a semicolon after the
    word "Europe," in the following
    sentence: "The Americans were once
    scattered all over Europe; here they
    are incorporated into one of the
    finest systems of population which
    has ever appeared, and which will
    hereafter become distinct by the
    power of the different climates they
    inhabit"?

    **(A)**  To set off two or more indepen-
           dent clauses
    **(B)**  To separate items in a series
    **(C)**  To separate parenthetical
           elements
    **(D)**  To establish a new thought
    **(E)**  To set off an introductory
           phrase

6.  How does the author describe the
    "American"?

    **(A)**  A hard-working person
    **(B)**  A new principled person
    **(C)**  An indolent individual
    **(D)**  A class-conscious person
    **(E)**  An educated individual

7.  What does de Crèvecoeur say he had
    in common with Americans when he
    came to this country?

    **(A)**  Farming skills and some money
    **(B)**  Education and desire
    **(C)**  Language and poor relatives
    **(D)**  Religion and education
    **(E)**  Wife and children

8.  Which of the following is a source of
    a new prejudice that an American
    will embrace?

    **(A)**  Religion
    **(B)**  Race
    **(C)**  National origin
    **(D)**  American government
    **(E)**  Class structure

9. What is the best synonym for the word "exuberant" as it is used in this sentence: "Wives and children, who before in vain demanded of him a morsel of bread, now, fat and frolic-some, gladly help their father to clear those fields whence *exuberant* crops are to arise to feed and to clothe them all; without any part being claimed, either by a despotic prince, a rich abbot, or a mighty lord"?

   **(A)** Sparse
   **(B)** Abundant
   **(C)** Harvested
   **(D)** Withered
   **(E)** Enthusiastic

10. Which statement best presents the writer's theme?

    **(A)** Americans will be self-absorbed.
    **(B)** The new nation will become imperialistic.
    **(C)** America will cause worldwide changes.
    **(D)** American citizens will develop a rigid class structure.
    **(E)** The people will destroy their own country because of their excesses.

exercises

## ANSWER KEY AND EXPLANATIONS

| 1. A | 3. E | 5. A | 7. C | 9. B |
|------|------|------|------|------|
| 2. A | 4. C | 6. B | 8. D | 10. C |

1. **The correct answer is (A).** The challenge on this question is to sift through the responses to select the one that is the best. The information in the first four responses are all mentioned in the passage, so you might select one of these four because they sound familiar. Choice (E) is not mentioned and can be eliminated. A scanning of the passage shows that the only one that truly reflects the author's words is choice (A). Choice (B) is a detail that supports choice (A). Choices (C) and (D) actually contradict information in the passage.

2. **The correct answer is (A).** Sometimes the obvious is the answer. Choices (C), (D), and (E) do not reflect the tone or subject matter addressed by the author. Your choice should be between (A) and (B). Choice (B) is in the running only because of the word *charming*. The piece is arguably charming, but clearly it is not a narrative.

3. **The correct answer is (E).** The key to choosing the correct answer is to notice the word *not* in the question. You are looking for the one answer in the series that is either opposite to or not included in the writer's thesis. In this case, the subject of charity, choice (E), is never mentioned in the passage.

4. **The correct answer is (C).** This is a straightforward vocabulary question. That makes it easy if you happen to know the definition of the word. There are ways, however, to improve your chances even if you are uncertain of the meaning of the word. First, you must find the word in context and substitute the answers. In so doing, some may be eliminated and one may clearly become the correct answer. In this case, inserting the answer choices in context easily eliminates choices (A) and (D) because gifts and hard work would not logically appear in the same series as involuntary idleness and useless labor. That leaves imprisonment, choice (B); destitution, choice (C); and corporal punishment, choice (E). Involuntary idleness might mean imprisonment or unemployment, so in case it means imprisonment, choice (B) should be eliminated. Corporal punishment does not seem to fit in a series about work or not working, so that leaves choice (C).

5. **The correct answer is (A).** Choice (B) can be eliminated because there is no series, nor is there a parenthetical element, eliminating choice (C). Choice (D) is not a grammar rule, and there is no introductory phrase, choice (E), in the quotation. There are two independent clauses, choice (A).

6. **The correct answer is (B).** You may find this to be a difficult question because it is asking you to find a small, but important, element in the excerpt. It is helpful to start by eliminating responses that are inconsistent with the overall theme. Choices (C) and (D) can quickly be seen to vary from the author's arguments. Choice (A) misses the point that Americans are working for themselves; they are not necessarily hard working. Once again, in choice (E), the response suggests something that is not in the passage.

7.  **The correct answer is (C).** This question tests your ability to recall or find specific facts in the passage. Remember that the easiest way to approach the question is to look for one incorrect element in a set of paired answers. If you look at each of the four incorrect responses, you can see that one, if not both, are either not mentioned or are stated incorrectly in the answer.

8.  **The correct answer is (D).** The author touches on all these answers in this passage, but in only one case is it in the context of a new American prejudice. As you read the excerpt, it is important to keep in mind the location in the passage of points that the author is making. If you did so in this case, it would be possible to quickly review that section (lines 10–13) and arrive at the proper answer.

9.  **The correct answer is (B).** This is not so much a vocabulary drill as it is a test of your comprehension. None of the responses is an exact synonym for the word *exuberant* as we use the word today. You must determine the definition from the context of the sentence. Substitute each of the proposed responses and select the one that makes the most sense, keeping in mind the tone and theme of the author. Neither sparse, choice (A), nor withered, choice (D), would be likely choices given the rest of the sentence. Harvested, choice (C), does not make sense before the crops grow. Enthusiastic, choice (E), is a synonym for exuberant, but it does not make sense. Abundant, choice (B), makes the best fit.

10. **The correct answer is (C).** You can eliminate all but the correct answer in this question by keeping in mind the general tone and theme of the author. The writer is very positive about America and America's future. Four of the five possibilities, choices (A), (B), (D), and (E), are negative. Proof of the answer can be found in the sentence, "Here individuals of all nations are melted into a new race of men, whose labors and posterity will one day cause great changes in the world."

## EXERCISE 4

**Directions:** This section consists of selections of literature and questions on their content, style, and form. After you have read each passage, choose the answer that best answers the question.

QUESTIONS 1 THROUGH 10 REFER TO THE FOLLOWING SELECTION. READ THE PASSAGE CAREFULLY AND THEN CHOOSE THE ANSWERS TO THE QUESTIONS.

From *A Vindication of the Rights of Women*

Line    It is difficult for us purblind mortals to say to what height human discoveries and improvements may arrive when the gloom of despotism subsides, which makes us stumble at every step; but, when mortality shall be settled on a more solid basis, then, without being gifted with a prophetic spirit, I will venture to predict that woman will
5       be either the friend or slave of man. We shall not, as a present, doubt whether she is a moral agent, or the link which unites man with brutes. But, should it then appear, that like the brutes they were principally created for the use of man, he will let them patiently bite the bridle, and not mock them with empty praise; or, should their rationality be proved, he will not impede their improvement merely to gratify his
10      sensual appetites. He will not, with all the graces of rhetoric, advise them to submit implicitly their understanding to the guidance of man. He will not, when he treats of the education of women, assert that they ought never to have the free use of reason, nor would he recommend cunning and dissimulation to beings who are acquiring, in like manner as himself, the virtues of humanity.
15      Surely there can be but one rule of right, if morality has an eternal foundation, and whoever sacrifices virtue, strictly so called, to present convenience, or whose *duty* it is to act in such a manner, lives only for the passing day, and cannot be an accountable creature.
        The poet then should have dropped his sneer when he says
20      "If weak women go astray,
        The stars are more in fault than they."
        For that they are bound by the adamantine chain of destiny is most certain, if it be proved that they are never to exercise their own reason, never to be independent, never to rise above opinion, or to feel the dignity of a rational will that only bows to
25      God, and often forgets that the universe contains any being but itself and the model of perfection to which its ardent gaze is turned, to adore attributes that, softened into virtues, may be imitated in kind, though the degree overwhelms the enraptured mind.
        If, I say, for I would not impress by declamation when Reason offers her sober light, if they be really capable of acting like rational creatures, let them not be treated like
30      slaves; or, like brutes who are dependent on the reason of man, when they associate with him; but cultivate their minds, give them the salutary, sublime curb of principle, and let them attain conscious dignity by feeling themselves only dependent on God. Teach them, in common with man, to submit to necessity, instead of giving, to render them more pleasing, a sex to morals.
35      Further, should experience prove that they cannot attain the same degree of strength of mind, perseverance, and fortitude, let their virtues be the same in kind, though they may vainly struggle for the same degree; and the superiority of man will be equally clear, if not clearer; and truth, as it is a simple principle. Which admits of no modification, would be common to both. Nay. The order of society as it is at present
40      regulated would not be inverted, for woman would then only have the rank that

reason assigned her, and arts could not be practised to bring the balance even. Much
less to turn it.

These may be termed Utopian dreams. Thanks to that Being who impressed them
on my soul, and gave me sufficient strength of mind to dare to exert my own reason,
45   till, becoming dependent only on him for support of my virtue, I view, with indignation, the mistaken notions that enslave my sex.

I love man as my fellow; but his sceptre, real, or usurped, extends not to me, unless
the reason of an individual demands my homage; and even then the submission is to
reason, and not to man. In fact, the conduct of an accountable being must be regulated
50   by the operations of its own reason; or on what foundations rests the throne of God?

It appears to me necessary to dwell on these obvious truths, because females have
been insulated, as it were; and, while they have been stripped of the virtues that
should clothe humanity, they have been decked with artificial graces that enable them
to exercise a short-lived tyranny. Love, in their bosoms, taking place of every nobler
55   passion, their sole ambition is to be fair, to raise emotion instead of inspiring respect;
and this ignoble desire, like the servility in absolute monarchies, destroys all strength
of character. Liberty is the mother of virtue, and if women be, by their very constitution, slaves, and not allowed to breathe the sharp invigorating air of freedom, they
must ever languish like exotics, and be reckoned beautiful flaws in nature.

—Mary Wollstonecraft

1.  This selection conveys which of the
    following sentiments?

    **(A)**  God created women for men's
          pleasure.
    **(B)**  The future for women is bright.
    **(C)**  A fervent sense of the unjust
          status of women
    **(D)**  The helpful nature of women
    **(E)**  A plea for understanding
          between the sexes

2.  Wollstonecraft argues that

    **(A)**  men are inferior to women
          intellectually
    **(B)**  women are the stronger gender
          emotionally
    **(C)**  women are more independent
          than men
    **(D)**  women should have the same
          education as men
    **(E)**  women provide more stability to
          a society than men

3.  The writer would agree with which of
    the following?

    **(A)**  Women need to develop their
          intuitive powers.
    **(B)**  Women are obligated to develop
          their rational powers to the
          fullest extent.
    **(C)**  Women need to follow the lead
          of men and be more demonstra-
          tive.
    **(D)**  Women must break their chains
          and enter the business and
          political arenas.
    **(E)**  Women cannot change their
          status without the help of men.

4.  What is the meaning of "adamantine"
    (line 22)?

    **(A)**  Extensive
    **(B)**  Elastic
    **(C)**  Unyielding
    **(D)**  Self-imposed
    **(E)**  Fragile

5. Which of the following is true about the tone of this selection?

   (A) Argumentative and over-wrought
   (B) Appealing to reason and convincing
   (C) Subtly persuasive
   (D) Desultory and emotional
   (E) Optimistic and uplifting

6. According to Wollstonecraft, what qualities did the society of her time value in women?

   (A) To be attractive and cause men to admire them
   (B) To inspire respect and consideration
   (C) To love liberty and freedom
   (D) To be servile and deceitful
   (E) To fight for female suffrage

7. "Utopian dreams" is an example of a(an)

   (A) allegory
   (B) allusion
   (C) aphorism
   (D) conundrum
   (E) synecdoche

8. In the sentence "Liberty is the mother of virtue, and if women be, by their very constitution, slaves, and not allowed to breathe the sharp invigorating air of freedom, they must ever languish like exotics, and be reckoned beautiful flaws in nature," there are examples of which literary devices?

   (A) Personification and conundrum
   (B) Simile and allusion
   (C) Alliteration and onomatopoeia
   (D) Hyperbole and metaphor
   (E) Personification and simile

9. In the first sentence, what does the author mean by the word "purblind"?

   (A) A hiding place for hunters
   (B) Direction
   (C) Chauvinistic
   (D) Enlightened
   (E) Lacking in vision and understanding

10. With which of the following statements would Wollstonecraft agree?

    (A) The rationality of women need not be a concern to men as long as they pay compliments to women.
    (B) When women are deprived of opportunities, all of society is diminished.
    (C) Women are superior in intellect to men.
    (D) By their nature, women are more virtuous than men.
    (E) Women live in their imaginations where they create a perfect world for themselves.

## ANSWER KEY AND EXPLANATIONS

| | | | | |
|---|---|---|---|---|
| 1. C | 3. B | 5. B | 7. B | 9. E |
| 2. D | 4. C | 6. A | 8. E | 10. B |

1. **The correct answer is (C).** This is a main idea question. The word *fervent* should provide a clue. The tone of the selection is certainly passionate. Choice (A) is contrary to the theme of the selection. While the writer may hope that the future will be bright for women, choice (B), there is no evidence of this in the passage. Both choices (D) and (E) represent some truth, but both are too general to be the best answer, and choice (D) is not particularly supported by the passage.

2. **The correct answer is (D).** This is another type of main idea question in that you are asked the author's solution to the issue of inequality. Wollstonecraft argues that women may be the intellectual equal of men, choice (A), but does not say they are their superior. The emotional issue in choice (B) distorts the main point. Choices (C) and (E) are irrelevant to this question and illogical in relation to the selection.

3. **The correct answer is (B).** Being aware of consistency in answers (ideas) will help you with this question. If you answered questions 1 and 2 correctly, you recognized that developing rational powers is consistent with Wollstonecraft's theories about education and the unjust treatment of women by society. You might argue that choice (D) is also consistent, but the author does not mention business or politics. Choices (A) and (E) are inconsistent with Wollstonecraft's thesis, while choice (C) is not mentioned in the passage. Choice (E) is tricky, but Wollstonecraft is making the point that women should not depend on men; they need only depend on God and they will find themselves equal to men in reason.

4. **The correct answer is (C).** If you did not know the meaning of *adamantine,* you could substitute the answer choices in the sentence to see which made the most sense. Consider that a chain is made of something hard and difficult to break, like iron, so that choices (B) and (E) would be inaccurate. Extensive, choice (A), is a not a good fit then, nor is choice (D) consistent with the thesis. You probably also realized that the correct answer is very similar to *adamant,* a word that you most certainly know.

5. **The correct answer is (B).** Remember, a writer communicates the tone through diction. Tone reflects the writer's attitude toward the subject and the audience. You might think that choice (A) is a good possibility, especially if you do not agree with Wollstonecraft. However, her arguments are very logical and her development is sound. The word choice, which might seem overwrought to you, is typical of the Romantic period. Choice (C) is incorrect; this piece is frank and forthright. Choice (D) is only partially correct. Choice (E) is illogical.

6. **The correct answer is (A).** This question is tricky, not because of what it asks but how it asks it. Did you notice that the question asked what society valued, not what the author valued? If you chose choices (B) or (C), you probably misread the question because these are qualities Wollstonecraft judged important. Choice (D) is illogical, not only in terms of the selection, but also in terms of real life. Very few, if any, societies value deceit. While the writer would heartily agree with choice (E), it is irrelevant and not supported by facts.

7. **The correct answer is (B).** This question tests your knowledge of English literature. The reference, or allusion, is to Sir Thomas Moore's *Utopia*. If you did not know that, you could still eliminate answers and make an educated guess. An allegory, choice (A), is a story or tale with several levels of meaning, one literal and another symbolic. This is not a tale, and the meaning is plainly stated. An aphorism, choice (C), is a general truth or observation about life, usually stated concisely. While this selection qualifies by the first standard, it is hardly concise. A conundrum, choice (D), is a puzzling question or problem, most often in the form of a riddle. A synecdoche, choice (E), a figure of speech, occurs when a part is used for the whole. A hint here: If you are sure you have never seen a word before, eliminate the choice. It was probably included to confuse you.

8. **The correct answer is (E).** To answer this question correctly, you must first find the literary devices and identify them correctly. Then remember that both parts in an answer choice must be correct for the answer to be the right one. Choices (A) and (B) are partly correct (personification and simile), but not entirely (conundrum and allusion). Choices (C) and (D) are completely wrong.

9. **The correct answer is (E).** If you were unfamiliar with the word, you could determine the correct answer by substituting the answer choices in the sentence. Also, the root word *–blind* is a clue. Yes, a blind can be a hiding place for hunters, choice (A), but that makes no sense in the context of the sentence and the essay. Choice (B) is a noun, and, therefore, does not fit. Choice (C) is incorrect because it modifies "us mortals," which includes women. Choice (D) contradicts the selection.

10. **The correct answer is (B).** Often on the AP English Literature & Composition Test, you will find the same kinds of information tested in different ways. Remember that the test is really about comprehension, what you understand about what you read. Choice (B) is consistent with the correct answers to questions 1, 2, and 3. Choice (A) is illogical because no facts support it. Choice (C) is contradictory to the writer's argument. Choices (D) and (E) are incorrect because both are distortions of Wollstonecraft's points.

## EXERCISE 5

**Directions:** This section consists of selections of literature and questions on their content, style, and form. After you have read each passage, choose the answer that best answers the question.

QUESTIONS 1 THROUGH 10 REFER TO THE FOLLOWING SELECTION. READ THE PASSAGE CAREFULLY AND THEN CHOOSE THE ANSWERS TO THE QUESTIONS.

### From *The Time Machine*

Line "I looked about me to see if any traces of animal life remained. A certain indefinable apprehension still kept me in the saddle of the machine. But I saw nothing moving, in earth or sky or sea. The green slime on the rocks alone testified that life was not extinct. A shallow sandbank had appeared in the sea and the water had receded from
5 the beach. I fancied I saw some black object flopping about upon the bank, but it became motionless as I looked at it, and I judged that my eye had been deceived, and that the black object was merely a rock. The stars in the sky were intensely bright and seemed to me to twinkle very little.

"Suddenly I noticed that the circular westward outline of the sun had changed; that
10 a concavity, a bay, had appeared in the curve. I saw this grow larger. For a minute perhaps I stared aghast at this blackness that was creeping over the day, and then I realized that an eclipse was beginning. Either the moon or the planet Mercury was passing across the sun's disk. Naturally, at first there is much to incline me to believe that what I really saw was the transit of an inner planet passing very near the earth.
15 "The darkness grew apace; a cold wind began to blow in freshening gusts from the east. And the showering white flakes in the air increased in number. From the edge of the sea came a ripple and whisper. Beyond these lifeless sounds the world was silent. Silent? It would be hard to convey; the stillness of it. All the sounds of man, the bleating of sheep, the cries of birds, the hum of insects, the stir that makes the
20 background of our lives—all that was over. As the darkness thickened, the eddy flakes grew more abundant, dancing before my eyes; and the cold of the air more intense. At last, one by one, swiftly, one after the other, the white peaks of the distant hills vanished into blackness. The breeze rose to a moaning wind. I saw the black central shadow of the eclipse sweeping towards me. In another moment the pale stars alone
25 were visible. All else was rayless obscurity. The sky was absolutely black.

"A horror of this great darkness came on me. The cold, that smote to my marrow, and the pain I felt in breathing, overcame me. I shivered, and a deadly nausea seized me. Then like a red-hot bow in the sky appeared the edge of the sun. I got off the machine to recover myself. I felt giddy and incapable of facing the return journey. As I
30 stood sick and confused I saw again the moving thing upon the shoal—there was no mistake now that it was a moving thing—against the red water of the sea. It was a round thing, the size of a football perhaps, or, it may be, bigger, and tentacles trailed down from it; it seemed black against the weltering blood-red water, and it was hopping fitfully about. Then I felt I was fainting. But a terrible dread of lying helpless
35 in that remote and awful twilight sustained me while I clambered upon the saddle."

—H. G. Wells

1. Which of the following best describes the tone of the passage?

    (A) Cold but comforting
    (B) Suspenseful and frightening
    (C) Futuristic and spiritual
    (D) Depressing and realistic
    (E) Fanciful and complex

2. What is the point of view of the excerpt?

    (A) Objective
    (B) Omniscient
    (C) Limited omniscient
    (D) Stream of consciousness
    (E) First person

3. What inference can be drawn about the time setting from the title and the first and third paragraphs?

    (A) It is in the long-ago past.
    (B) It is in the future.
    (C) It is present day, but somewhere not on this earth.
    (D) It is not on an earthly time scale.
    (E) No inference can be drawn.

4. H. G. Wells creates an image of the sun in lines 9–10. Which of the following most closely resembles that image?

    (A) A biscuit with a bite taken out of it
    (B) An ocean estuary
    (C) A concave mirror
    (D) A deformed ball
    (E) An incomplete sphere

5. All of the following are true of Wells's diction EXCEPT

    (A) it creates a sense of menace
    (B) it uses a variety of sentence structures
    (C) Wells uses sensory words to great effect
    (D) Wells creates an effect by playing off a rational description of the character's surroundings against the irrationality of what the character is describing
    (E) it is precise

6. The narrator in this selection experienced which climatic conditions?

    (A) Cold and rain
    (B) Cold and dry
    (C) Warm and humid
    (D) Cold and snow
    (E) Warm and breezy

7. The use of the word "moaning" to describe the wind in line 23 is an example of both:

    (A) alliteration and metaphor
    (B) personification and allusion
    (C) onomatopoeia and personification
    (D) metaphor and onomatopoeia
    (E) simile and alliteration

8. This selection is an example of which form of discourse?

    (A) Description
    (B) Persuasion
    (C) Interrogation
    (D) Narration
    (E) Exposition

9. What does Wells mean by "rayless obscurity" in the third paragraph?

    (A) The speaker's eyes were blurry.
    (B) Time was at a standstill.
    (C) There was no sunlight.
    (D) The stars provided no light.
    (E) The black form was obscure.

10. In the last paragraph, the author uses the word "red" to describe several elements in the scene. How does that word affect the tone?

    (A) Conveys a feeling of warmth and hope
    (B) Presents a contrast to the black object
    (C) Expresses a feeling of anger
    (D) Creates a feeling of foreboding and dread
    (E) Demonstrates a change in tone

## ANSWER KEY AND EXPLANATIONS

| | | | | |
|---|---|---|---|---|
| 1. B | 3. B | 5. B | 7. C | 9. C |
| 2. E | 4. A | 6. D | 8. D | 10. D |

1.  **The correct answer is (B).** In paired answers, you can eliminate choices by looking for the wrong choice in each pair. In this case the scene may be cold, choice (A); futuristic, choice (C); depressing, choice (D); and complex, choice (E). But it is not comforting, choice (A); spiritual, choice (C); or realistic, choice (D). The scene may be imaginative but not fanciful, choice (E), which connotes playfulness or whimsy. That leaves choice (B) as having two correct parts.

2.  **The correct answer is (E).** The use of "I" indicates that the point of view is first person. Stream of consciousness, choice (D), is first person point of view but from inside the character's mind, making the reader privy to the continuous, disconnected flow of half-formed thoughts and impressions. Although the character describes the scene for the reader, there is nothing free-form about the passage, so choice (D) is incorrect. The other choices are all third person. Objective narrator, choice (A), reports only what would be visible to a camera; no thoughts or feelings are described. An omniscient narrator, choice (B), is able to see into each character's mind and understands all the action. Limited omniscient point of view, choice (C), tells the story from the point of view of only one character's thoughts.

3.  **The correct answer is (B).** The title frames the question as moving between points of time. The word *remained* in the first sentence of the first paragraph and the phrase "all that was over" in the third paragraph are indications that the setting is in the future. Choice (A) is, therefore, incorrect. Choice (C) is incorrect because all the indications—sounds of humans, birds, sheep, and insects and the clause "the stir that makes the background of our lives"—are that this is Earth. There is no evidence to support choice (D), and choice (E) is clearly incorrect and meant as a distractor. It seems as though it might be correct.

4.  **The correct answer is (A).** The author is describing an eclipse of the sun. Do not be fooled by words in the answer that are similar to words in the passage, such as estuary and bay. Create an image in your mind of a planet passing in front of the sun; it should be most closely associated with the bitten biscuit.

5.  **The correct answer is (B).** Did you keep the word *except* in mind as you read the answer choices? Choices (A), (C), (D), and (E) are true about the passage, so choice (B) is the correct answer. Wells does use a variety of sentence structures, but diction deals with word choice, not sentence structure.

6.  **The correct answer is (D).** Read the pairs in each answer, and look for one of the words in each pair to be incorrect so you can eliminate the entire answer. For example, there are three answers that correctly identify the setting as being cold. One of those says it is rainy, choice (A), and another says it is dry, choice (B). Neither of these is correct. The "snowy" answer, choice (D), is correct based on the author's reference to "white flakes" and "eddy flakes." Choices (C) and (E) are irrelevant to the passage and can be eliminated completely.

7. **The correct answer is (C).** Again, read each pair and look for one of the words in each pair to be incorrect. In this case, "moaning" is a human characteristic, so in literary terminology, it is personification. Also, "moaning wind" resembles the sound of someone moaning, so it is also onomatopoeia. Alliteration is the repetition of initial consonant sounds in a series, and metaphor states that something is something else, choice (A). In choice (B), personification is correct, but this is not a reference to a famous person or another literary work (allusion), so the whole answer is incorrect. Half of choice (D) (onomatopoeia) is correct, but metaphor is not. A simile compares something to another using *like* or *as* choice (E).

8. **The correct answer is (D).** In this question, choice (C) can be eliminated because it is not a form of discourse. The author is recounting a story, the classic form of narration. Choice (A) may seem to be correct, because the author is vividly describing the scene, but the purpose is to tell the reader what was happening. The tone is not persuasive, choice (B). The selection sets the scene, choice (E), but that is not the purpose of the author.

9. **The correct answer is (C).** In this question, you can eliminate three of the five answer choices merely by recognizing that the reference is to light in some form. Only choices (C) and (D) have this attribute. To eliminate choice (D), check the passage around the phrase and you will find the sentence "In another moment the pale stars alone were visible."

10. **The correct answer is (D).** There is a trap in this question. The color "red" is often used to convey heat, choice (A), or anger, choice (C). If you have not read the passage, you might be inclined to select one of these traditional references. In this case, you would be wrong, because the author is using the color to express foreboding and dread, choice (D). This would be analogous to the red of spilled blood. The color does contrast with the black object, choice (B), but it is not the most important reason why a writer would choose the word in this context. Choice (E) is inaccurate because the word does not change the tone but heightens it.

# SUMMING IT UP

- The prose selections vary from a few short paragraphs to lengthy selections. Some passages may be from plays, others may come from short stories and essays.

- As you read, observe patterns of organization that the writer employs.

- Highlight words and sentences that seem significant during your second reading.

- Keep in mind the 5 Ws and H: *who, what, where, when, why,* and *how.*

- Remember there are six types of multiple-choice questions: *main idea, detail, inference, definition, tone or purpose,* and *form.*

- If you are not confident about a passage, skip difficult questions and answer the easy ones first. Be sure to mark in the test booklet the ones you haven't answered.

- Many times, the key to finding the correct answer is tp narrow down the choices and make an intelligent guess.

# About the Multiple-Choice Questions Related to Poetry

## OVERVIEW

- **Recommendations for acing poetry questions**
- **Practicing**
- **Summing it up**

As you learned in Chapter 3, Section I of the Advanced Placement test asks about 50 multiple-choice questions about prose and poetry. Many people, not just students, shy away from poetry because they think it is too difficult, too obscure, too irrelevant, or too emotional. However, poetry shares many characteristics with prose. Both create an imaginative statement through language. Both have certain elements in common, such as speaker or narrator, point of view, tone, style, and theme.

However, there are important differences between the two forms of literature. Economy of words, imagery, rhythm, and sound define poetry. Because of these elements, you must read poetry differently. This chapter presents strategies for reading a poem so you can understand it and answer questions about it correctly. In addition, the chapter will remind you of the strategies for answering multiple-choice questions that you learned in Chapter 3, which you can also apply to the questions about poetry selections.

At least two selections in Section I will be poems. The poetry you will find on the examination will probably be more difficult than the prose selections. (For that reason alone, you may wish to answer the prose selections first, saving the poetry for later.) However, by using the suggestions offered here about reading poetry and answering questions about it, you may find the poetry questions easier than you anticipated.

## chapter 4

# RECOMMENDATIONS FOR ACING POETRY QUESTIONS

## Reading a Poem—Carefully

- Remember that the language of poems is compact and economical, with every word of a poem carrying part of the impact and meaning.

- You must bring your own experience to a poem as well as what you know about literature.

- If possible, read a poem four times.

- The first two times you read a poem, read it sentence by sentence, not line by line. If you focus your reading on line endings and ignore a poem's syntax (word arrangement), you may become confused.

- The first time, read it straight through. You might consider this your skimming stage. Do not worry about strange words or difficult passages. You are looking for the "layout" of the poem.

- When you read the poem the second time, take more time and care. Now deal with obscure language and confusing sentences. After you have finished this second reading, you should have a good understanding of what the poet is saying.

- As you read the poem a second time, highlight words, phrases, and sentences that seem significant. However, do not spend a lot of time at this.

- The third time, read the poem aloud, that is, aloud in your mind since you will be in a test situation. Hear the music of the poem and evaluate the contribution of the rhythm, rhyme, and sound to the meaning. This information will deepen your understanding of the poem.

- Finally, during your last read you should paraphrase the poem. Again, in a test situation you cannot take the time to write out your paraphrase, but you can "write" it in your mind. This will help you solidify your understanding of the poem.

## Understanding the Poem

**NOTE**

Most of the multiple-choice questions test how carefully you read and how well you interpret.

- If a poem has a title, consider it carefully. Some titles may tell you nothing, while others tell you exactly what the poem is about. A third type of title hints at the content or the setting. You may not be sure what the theme will be, but a title might suggest the subject the poet has chosen to write about. Think about what the title tells you about the selection.

- Use the footnotes. They may help you understand an archaic word or explain a difficult reference.

- Ask yourself what the individual words mean and what each word suggests. This is important for words that are unfamiliar or words used in unfamiliar ways. Consider the implications of familiar words used in unfamiliar ways. How do they contribute to the imagery and impact of the poem?

- Figure out *who* or *what* is speaking. Rarely are the speaker and the poet one and the same. Ask yourself who is inside and who is outside the poem. Notice how pronouns are used. Is the poem written in the first person, second person, or third person?

- Quickly establish the poem's setting and situation. Always figure out as much as you can about the *where* and the *when* of a poetry passage.
- Determine the subject of the poem. In other words, figure out the general or specific topic that the poem presents.
- Figure out the theme (main idea). Ask yourself what general or specific ideas the poem explores. Decide what the writer is trying to tell you.
- Identify the conventions of poetry used in the selection. Determine how the poet uses literary devices and figurative language. Understanding these will help clarify meaning for you.

Determining the information as suggested in these eight steps can prove difficult, and a great deal of thoughtful work can be involved. However, if you follow these steps as you read a poem, you will have an excellent understanding of that poem. Practicing the steps in this book will make unraveling the meaning of poems easier on the day of the test.

## Answering the Questions

The following two strategies are especially effective when working with a poem.

- When reading a poem to find an answer, read the phrases around the reference. A line or two before and a line or two after should be sufficient to understand the context.
- Do not be too concerned about scansion since there are only a few questions about it on the test. Check "meter" and "foot" in *A Quick Review of Literary Terms,* p. 253.

Virtually everything we said in Chapter 3 about multiple-choice questions for prose can be applied to poetry questions.

- Remember to scan the selections to prioritize the order in which you choose to tackle them.
- There are six types of multiple-choice questions: main-idea, detail, inference, definition, tone or purpose, and form. You may also find one or two questions about grammar and culture.
- When answering a main-idea question, the correct choice must be entirely true and include as much relevant information as possible. The answer that is most complete is the one to choose.
- You must be able to find evidence in the selection or cited portions to support your answer.
- When answering questions about the meaning of words or phrases, substitute your choice in the sentence or line.
- Answer questions in the order you wish. If you are not confident, skip difficult questions, and answer the easier ones first.
- Be sure to mark the questions you skip so you can find them later if you have time. Also, be sure to skip the answer oval for that number on the answer sheet.

**NOTE**

Read all the explanations in the "Answer Key and Explanations" sections in this book. You may learn something new about the test or about a piece of literature.

- Look for consistency in the answers to the questions about a passage. If a choice seems contradictory to other answers you have given, rethink that choice.

- Many times, the key to finding the correct answer is to narrow down the choices and make an educated guess. Eliminate some answers by finding those that are obviously unrelated, illogical, or incorrect. Having reduced the number of choices, you can make an educated guess from among the remaining possibilities. Use the techniques presented in the chart below to reduce the number of choices.

| STRATEGIES FOR ANSWERING OBJECTIVE QUESTIONS/ MAKING EDUCATED GUESSES | |
|---|---|
| **ANSWER CHOICE** | **REASON TO ELIMINATE** |
| 1. too narrow | too small a section of the selection covered, based on the question |
| 2. too broad | an area wider than the selection covered, based on the question |
| 3. irrelevant | • nothing to do with the passage<br>• relevant to the selection but not the question |
| 4. incorrect | • distortion of the facts in the selection<br>• contradiction of the facts in the selection |
| 5. illogical | • not supported by facts in the passage<br>• not supported by cited passage from the selection |
| 6. similar choices | GO BACK AND REVIEW 1–5 TO TEASE OUT THE DIFFERENCES. |
| 7. *not/except* | answers that correctly represent the selection |

The *not/except* questions are tricky. As you go through each answer, ask yourself, "Is this statement true about the selection?" If yes, cross it out, and keep going until you find a choice that you can answer "no" to.

## PRACTICING

Read the poem "La Belle Dame Sans Merci" by John Keats. Jot down your answers to the questions in the margin or on a separate piece of paper. In choosing answers, apply the recommendations and strategies you have just learned.

If you do not understand a question, check the explanation immediately. You may refer to the answers question by question, or you may wish to score the entire section at one time. No matter which method you choose, read all the explanations. The reasoning involved may point out concepts or details that you missed, and the explanations will show you how the strategies can work for you. This poem is not easy, so you may not be able to answer every question correctly. That is why it is good practice.

## EXERCISE 1

> **Directions:** This section consists of selections of literature and questions on their content, style, and form. After you have read each passage, choose the answer that best answers the question.

**QUESTIONS 1 THROUGH 12 REFER TO THE FOLLOWING POEM. READ THE POEM CAREFULLY AND THEN CHOOSE THE ANSWERS TO THE QUESTIONS.**

### La Belle Dame Sans Merci

Line   O what can ail thee, knight-at-arms,
       Alone and palely loitering?
   The sedge has withered from the lake,
       And no birds sing.

5   O what can ail thee, knight-at-arms,
       So haggard and so woe-begon?
   The squirrel's granary is full,
       And the harvest's done.

   I see a lily on thy brow,
10       With anguish moist and fever dew,
   And on thy cheeks a fading rose
       Fast withereth too.

   I met a lady in the meads,*
       Full beautiful—a faery's child,
15   Her hair was long, her foot was light,
       And her eyes were wild.

   I made a garland for her head,
       And bracelets too, and fragrant zone;**
   She looked at me as she did love,
20       And made sweet moan.

   I set her on my pacing steed,
       And nothing else saw all day long,
   For sidelong would she bend and sing
       A faery's song.

25   She found me roots of relish sweet,
       And honey wild, and manna dew,
   And sure in language strange she said—
       "I love thee true."

---

\* meadow
\*\* sweet-smelling plant

She took me to her elfin grot,
30     And there she wept, and sighed full sore,
And there I shut her wild wild eyes
     With kisses four.

And there she lullèd me asleep,
     And there I dreamed—Ah! Woe betide!
35   The latest dream I ever dreamed
     On the cold hill's side.

I saw pale kings and princes too,
     Pale warriors, death-pale were they all;
They cried–"La Belle Dame Sans Merci
40     Hath thee in thrall!"

I saw their starved lips in the gloam,
     With horrid warning gaped wide,
On the cold hill's side.

And this is why I sojourn here,
45     Alone and palely loitering
Though the sedge has withered from the lake,
     And no birds sing.

                             —John Keats

1. What is one of the themes of this poem?

   **(A)** Experience destroys innocence.
   **(B)** One should not trust magical beings.
   **(C)** Death is similar to a nightmare or unpleasant dream.
   **(D)** Medieval women had no pity.
   **(E)** Beauty enslaves men.

2. Which of the following does not characterize the lady?

   **(A)** She is extremely beautiful.
   **(B)** Her hair is very long.
   **(C)** She sings enchanting songs.
   **(D)** She is the daughter of a heavenly being.
   **(E)** The lady has bedecked herself with flowers.

3. In the context of the poem, what is "relish"?

   **(A)** Condiment
   **(B)** Enjoyment
   **(C)** A food stuff
   **(D)** Magical potion
   **(E)** Faery poison

4. When the poet writes "manna dew," he is using what type of literary device?

   **(A)** Metaphor
   **(B)** Cacophony
   **(C)** Apostrophe
   **(D)** Hyperbole
   **(E)** Allusion

5. How does setting reinforce the meaning and the mood of the poem?

   **(A)** The knight's gambol in the woods creates a sense of playfulness.
   **(B)** Autumn suggests decay and decline.
   **(C)** Pale knights, princes, and kings imply death.
   **(D)** Flowers, woods, and herbs create a sense of nature, and thus a romantic mood.
   **(E)** Warriors and knights are soldiers, and the implication is violence.

**6.** How do the people in the knight's dream relate to his present condition?

   **(A)** The people are earlier victims of the lady and demonstrate his condition as a new victim.
   **(B)** They represent the end of the chivalric hierarchy.
   **(C)** The people represent rejected suitors for the lady's hand.
   **(D)** They are her guardians.
   **(E)** They are foils for the knight by contrasting with his youth and vigor.

**7.** Why is the knight "alone and pale"?

   **(A)** The knight is terrified by his experiences in the woods.
   **(B)** He is dead.
   **(C)** He is heartbroken because the lady rejected him.
   **(D)** The knight is shocked by the lady's cruelty.
   **(E)** He believes that he has seen ghosts.

**8.** This selection is an example of which two kinds of poetry?

   **(A)** Narrative and ballad
   **(B)** Elegy and lyric
   **(C)** Romantic and narrative
   **(D)** Ballad and elegy
   **(E)** Sonnet and lyric

**9.** Stanzas in this poem are

   **(A)** tercets
   **(B)** couplets
   **(C)** quatrains
   **(D)** septets
   **(E)** cinquains

**10.** The meter of the poem is

   **(A)** iambic pentameter
   **(B)** iambic tetrameter
   **(C)** iambic trimeter
   **(D)** alternating iambic pentameter and tetrameter
   **(E)** alternating iambic tetrameter and iambic trimeter

**11.** What is indicated by the change in person between stanzas 4–6 and 7–9?

   **(A)** The speaker of the poem changes.
   **(B)** The switch foreshadows doom.
   **(C)** The lady's point of view is intriguing.
   **(D)** Humans need to believe in the occult world and mythical beings.
   **(E)** The change indicates that control has switched from the knight to the lady.

**12.** The repetitions in the first, second, and final stanzas serve what purpose?

   **(A)** The repeating phrases indicate that the knight understands his predicament.
   **(B)** They serve no actual purpose.
   **(C)** The repetitions add to the musicality.
   **(D)** They are examples of symbolism.
   **(E)** They are the refrain.

# ANSWER KEY AND EXPLANATIONS

| | | | | |
|---|---|---|---|---|
| 1. A | 4. E | 7. B | 9. C | 11. E |
| 2. D | 5. B | 8. A | 10. E | 12. A |
| 3. D | 6. A | | | |

1. **The correct answer is (A).** This is a surprisingly difficult question because all the answers, except the correct one, have some words similar to those in the poem. Magic, choice (B); dreams, choice (C); medieval people, choice (D); and beauty, choice (E); all appear directly or indirectly in the piece. The key is to recognize that a "theme" question is asking for a response that is pertinent to all elements of a poem. The only response that meets that criterion is choice (A).

2. **The correct answer is (D).** First, notice that this is a "not" question. That means that all the answers will be *true* except for the *correct* one. A quick scan of the poem shows that there are references to her beauty, choice (A); long hair, choice (B); singing, choice (C); and flowers, choice (E). The only answer that is *not true* is the *correct* one, choice (D).

3. **The correct answer is (D).** The first thing to do is to find the reference. It is in the first line of the seventh stanza. If it is not immediately apparent that the answer is a magical potion, then try substituting the answers to eliminate those that do not fit the lines or image. Although relish is a condiment, food products, choices (A) and (C), are not suitable for the image that Keats is creating. Enjoyment, choice (B), does not fit the line if you substitute the answer in the line. The author is not trying to kill the speaker, choice (E).

4. **The correct answer is (E).** This is a reference to a literary and religious fact (food from heaven) that you would be expected to know; hence, it is an allusion. Metaphor, choice (A), states that something is something else. Cacophony, choice (B), is a harsh or dissonant sound. Apostrophe, choice (C), is directly addressing an imaginary, dead, or absent person. Hyperbole, choice (D), is exaggeration for humor.

5. **The correct answer is (B).** To select the correct answer, you need to bring together two items. First, you know that the poem has a somber, as opposed to a cheerful, mood. Second, the last two lines of the second stanza define the setting as autumn ("harvest's done"). The first piece of information eliminates choices (A) and (D). The second piece eliminates choices (C) and (E) because they do not mention the setting. The only response remaining is choice (B).

6. **The correct answer is (A).** The simplest way to address this question is to review the section of the poem dealing with the dream. Beginning with the ninth stanza, the speaker describes his dream. You will quickly see that choice (A) is the only one of the five possibilities that reflects the thoughts of the closing stanzas. Choice (B) is irrelevant to the poem. There is no indication that the lady rejected the other people, choice (C), but rather that she treated them as she has treated the speaker. Choices (D) and (E) contradict the poem.

7. **The correct answer is (B).** At no time does Keats say outright that the knight is dead, and yet it is important for you to recognize that is what the author is saying. He does so by references to the knight's being alone and pale. Do not get tripped up because you gave only a cursory look at the poetry selections. If you did so in this case, it would be easy to select one of the other answers, because each has some relation to Keats' wording, but not his meaning.

8.  **The correct answer is (A).** In this selection, the poem is a type of narrative called a ballad. A ballad is a long narrative poem covering a single dramatic episode. An elegy is a formal poem focusing on death or mortality, and a lyric is a melodious, imaginative poem, usually short and personal, choice (B). This poem is about death, but it is not formal, rather it is fanciful. Romantic, choice (C), is a description of a style but not a type. Only part of choice (D) is correct, ballad, while none of choice (E) is correct.

9.  **The correct answer is (C).** Again, this question involves literary terms that should be familiar to you. Some of these terms may require that you review your literature textbooks. This poem has four-line stanzas called quatrains. A tercet, choice (A), is three lines. A couplet, choice (B), is two lines. A septet, choice (D), is seven lines. A cinquain is five lines.

10. **The correct answer is (E).** This is the third consecutive question about literary elements. You do not need to remember the meaning of *iambic* (one unstressed syllable followed by one stressed syllable) to answer this question since all choices include it. The lines are of different lengths, so that eliminates the first three choices, which indicate every line in the poem is one length. From your knowledge of Latin prefixes, recall that *tri-* means three, *tetra-* means four, and *penta-* means five. The lines have three and four beats, so that eliminates choice (D).

11. **The correct answer is (E).** Stanzas 4–6 explain what the knight did. In stanzas 7–9 the lady begins to act. The speaker does change in this poem, but that switch occurs between stanzas 3 and 4, so choice (A) is incorrect. Doom is foreshadowed throughout the poem, so choice (B) is incorrect. The lady's viewpoint is not presented, choice (C), because she never functions as speaker. Choice (D) is an incorrect reading of the poem.

12. **The correct answer is (A).** Make an educated guess on this question. Eliminate choice (B) because a question would not be posed if there were no purpose. Eliminate choices (D) and (E) since there is little symbolism and no refrain in the poem. The antecedent of *I* in the final stanzas is the knight who recognizes in the final lines what has happened. Choice (C) is irrelevant.

## EXERCISE 2

**Directions:** This section consists of selections of literature and questions on their content, style, and form. After you have read each passage, choose the answer that best answers the question.

**QUESTIONS 1 THROUGH 10 REFER TO THE FOLLOWING POEM. READ THE POEM CAREFULLY AND THEN CHOOSE THE ANSWERS TO THE QUESTIONS.**

**The Chambered Nautilus**

Line   This is the ship of pearl, which, poets feign,
      Sails the unshadowed main—
      The venturous bark that flings
On the sweet summer wind its purpled wings
5    In gulfs enchanted, where the Siren sings,
      And coral reefs lie bare,
Where the cold sea-maids rise to sun their streaming hair.

    Its webs of living gauze no more unfurl;
      Wrecked is the ship of pearl!
10     And every chambered cell,
Where its dim dreaming life was wont to dwell,
As the frail tenant shaped his growing shell,
      Before thee lies revealed—
Its irised ceiling rent, its sunless crypt unsealed!

15   Year after year beheld the silent toil
      That spread his lustrous coil;
      Still, as the spiral grew,
He left the past year's dwelling for the new,
Stole with soft step its shining archway through,
20     Built up its idle door,
Stretched in his last-found home, and knew the old no more.

Thanks for the heavenly message brought by thee,
      Child of the wandering sea,
      Cast from her lap, forlorn!
25   From thy dead lips a clearer note is born
Than ever Triton blew from wreathèd horn!
      While on mine ear it rings,
Through the deep caves of thought I hear a voice that sings:

Build thee more stately mansions, O my soul,
30     As the swift seasons roll!
      Leave thy low-vaulted past!
Let each new temple, nobler than the last,
Shut thee from heaven with a dome more vast,
      Till thou at length art free,
35   Leaving thine outgrown shell by life's unresting sea!
                —Oliver Wendell Holmes

1. What message does the speaker take from the shell?

   **(A)** The sea is a beautiful place.
   **(B)** Strive to live in a manner that makes tomorrow better than to-day.
   **(C)** Birth, death, and rebirth is the cycle of life.
   **(D)** A nautilus can circumnavigate the globe.
   **(E)** People need to protect themselves from the problems of the world.

2. What does the word "bark" (line 3) mean?

   **(A)** Flotsam
   **(B)** Sea foam
   **(C)** The sound of surf, similar to a dog's cry
   **(D)** Jetsam
   **(E)** A type of boat

3. What does the speaker imagine when he sees the shell?

   **(A)** The voice of God speaking to him
   **(B)** The creature's slow death
   **(C)** The marvels of nature
   **(D)** The oceans of the world
   **(E)** Places where the nautilus lived

4. What is it about the chambered nautilus that makes it appropriate for this poem's message?

   **(A)** The sea creature has died.
   **(B)** The clearly defined chambers mark the progress of the animal's growth.
   **(C)** The nautilus is indigenous to oceans near the poet's home in Massachusetts.
   **(D)** The nautilus was highly prized for its beautiful shell.
   **(E)** As a scientist, as well as a writer, Holmes was particularly interested in marine life.

5. Based upon the author's words, which of the following is the best description of the shape of the chambered nautilus?

   **(A)** Elongated tube
   **(B)** Irregular
   **(C)** Oblong
   **(D)** Spherical
   **(E)** Flat

6. How does Holmes compare the growth of the nautilus to the development of human beings?

   **(A)** The nautilus creates a new chamber every year; humans do not.
   **(B)** The voice tells the speaker to build more mansions.
   **(C)** People's souls should outgrow their constraints and expand until completely free.
   **(D)** The death of any of God's creatures, in this case the nautilus, is as important a loss as the death of a person.
   **(E)** Even in death, the nautilus speaks to the soul.

7. Oliver Wendell Holmes would agree with which of the following statements?

   **(A)** It is important to keep growing throughout life.
   **(B)** Study and appreciate creatures from nature.
   **(C)** Build greater and more elegant personal edifices.
   **(D)** Listen to the inner voice represented by the shell.
   **(E)** Love all God's creations, including human beings.

8. Which of the following is not true regarding the meter of the first stanza?

   (A) The stanza is composed in iambic pentameter.
   (B) The first line includes a trochee.
   (C) Lines 4 and 5 are composed in iambic pentameter.
   (D) Line 6 is composed in iambic trimeter.
   (E) Line 7 is composed in iambic hexameter.

9. What figure of speech is found in this line from the second stanza: "As the frail tenant shaped his growing shell"?

   (A) Simile
   (B) Metaphor
   (C) Hyperbole
   (D) Oxymoron
   (E) Personification

10. What are the two classical allusions found in this poem?

    (A) A Jules Verne ship and a Greek sea god
    (B) Holy scripture and enchanting sea nymphs
    (C) A rainbow and the sun god
    (D) A Greek god of the sea and Roman architecture
    (E) Enchanting sea nymphs and a Greek sea god

## ANSWER KEY AND EXPLANATIONS

| | | | | |
|---|---|---|---|---|
| 1. B | 3. E | 5. D | 7. A | 9. E |
| 2. E | 4. B | 6. C | 8. A | 10. E |

1. **The correct answer is (B).** Themes or messages are often contained in the first or last stanzas of lyric poetry. In the last stanza of this poem, the lines express the point of striving for continued improvement day to day. Choices (A) and (C) may be true, but they are not relevant. Choices (D) and (E) may or may not be true, but they are also irrelevant.

2. **The correct answer is (E).** Do not get caught choosing a simple definition like a dog's cry, choice (C). If you read above and below the line, you would see a parallel reference to a ship and a reference to purple wings, possibly sails. Then try eliminating answers by substituting the choices until you can select one that makes sense. Flotsam, choice (A), is the wreckage of a ship or odds and ends. Jetsam, choice (D), is equipment or cargo tossed overboard when a boat is in danger. Choice (B) might be correct, but foam does not have wings.

3. **The correct answer is (E).** The answer to this question is found in the first stanza. For the casual reader, all of the answers appear to have some relation to the subject of the poem. A careful reading will show you that only choice (E) is actually addressed by the poet.

4. **The correct answer is (B).** An understanding of the theme of the poem that you were asked about in question 1 will quickly lead you to the correct answer to this question. Some of the answers have elements that are true, but Holmes selected this shell because its various compartments make his point that we should strive to improve.

5. **The correct answer is (D).** You could use your knowledge of marine life and the appearance of a chambered nautilus to answer this question. Or you could check the poem (line 17) for the direct answer.

6. **The correct answer is (C).** This question has similarities with questions 1 and 4. An understanding of the poem's theme will direct you to the correct answer. Note that this is true even if you do not recall the specific reference in the question (lines 34–35). The only response consistent with the theme is choice (C). Choices (A) and (D) are not relevant. Choice (B) is too literal a reading, and choice (E) is too interpretative.

7. **The correct answer is (A).** The need to understand a poem's message is reinforced in this question. Holmes is speaking of the continuous growth of an individual throughout the individual's life. None of the remaining responses is closely allied with the poem's theme.

8. **The correct answer is (A).** Questions such as this test your ability to apply literary terms and conventions. In this case, the author uses iambic pentameter through much of his work.

9. **The correct answer is (E).** Holmes asks the reader to picture the actions of the chambered nautilus as if it were human. This is personification. A simile, choice (A), compares items using *as* or *like*. A metaphor, choice (B), states that something is something else. Hyperbole, choice (C), is the use of exaggeration to create humor. Oxymoron, choice (D), uses contradictory words or phrases.

10. **The correct answer is (E).** The author alludes to Sirens, who are sea nymphs, and Triton, a Greek sea god. These are both classical allusions. Do not get caught by choice (A). Jules Verne's ship, the *Nautilus*, is an allusion, but would not be considered a *classical* allusion. The Bible, choice (B), is not mentioned in the poem, nor is a rainbow or a sun god, choice (C). None of choice (D) is included.

## EXERCISE 3

**Directions:** This section consists of selections of literature and questions on their content, style, and form. After you have read each passage, choose the answer that best answers the question.

**QUESTIONS 1 THROUGH 10 REFER TO THE FOLLOWING POEM. READ THE POEM CAREFULLY AND THEN CHOOSE THE ANSWERS TO THE QUESTIONS.**

### The First Snowfall

Line   The snow had begun in the gloaming
      And busily all the night
  Had been heaping field highway
      With a silence deep and white.

5   Every pine and fir and hemlock
      Wore ermine too dear for an earl.
  And the poorest twig on the elm tree
      Was ridges inch deep with pearl.

  From shed new-roofed with Carrara*
10      Came Chanticleer's muffled crow,
  The stiff rails softened to swan's-down,
      And still fluttered down the snow.

  I stood and watched by the window
      The noiseless work of the sky,
15   And the sudden flurries of snowbirds,
      Like brown leaves whirling by.

  I thought of a mound in sweet Auburn**
      Where a little headstone stood;
  How the flakes were folding it gently,
20      As did robins the babes in the woods.

  Up spoke our own little Mabel,
      Saying, "Father, who makes it snow?"
  And I told of the good All-Father
      Who cares for us here below.

25   Again I looked at the snowfall,
      And thought of the leaden sky
  That arched o'er our first great sorrow,
      When that mound was heaped so high.

———
* white marble
** a cemetery in Cambridge, Massachusetts

I remembered the gradual patience
30      That fell from that cloud like snow,
Flake by flake, healing and hiding
      That scar that renewed our woe.

And again to the child I whispered,
      "The snow that husheth all,
35   Darling, the merciful Father
      Alone can make it fall!"

Then, with eyes that saw not, I kissed her;
      And she, kissing back, could not know
That my kiss was given to her sister,
40      Folded close under deepening snow.

—James Russell Lowell

1. How could the tone of this poem be characterized?

   (A) Great sadness and anger
   (B) Sadness mingled with hope
   (C) Familial love
   (D) Depression that is close to insanity
   (E) Anxiety combined with fear

2. Which of the following is not true about the setting of this poem?

   (A) It is winter.
   (B) It is morning.
   (C) A graveyard is evoked.
   (D) A funeral is beginning.
   (E) It is snowing.

3. It is evident from the poem that the speaker

   (A) loves both his daughters
   (B) dislikes the bad weather
   (C) is cold and unfeeling
   (D) has lost his wife
   (E) blames God for the tragedy

4. Which of the following best illustrates the theme of "The First Snowfall"?

   (A) Winter brings death and sadness.
   (B) A natural event, such as snow, can remind us of sorrowful events but can also help to heal.
   (C) The world is full of sadness for human beings who are not afraid to feel their emotions.
   (D) Children should understand the important role God takes in the world.
   (E) Natural things such as elms and robins are loved as much as human beings by God.

5. Of what does the snow make the speaker think?

   (A) The coming of spring
   (B) God
   (C) His daughter's death
   (D) The love he feels for his family
   (E) The glory of nature

6. What is the purpose of these lines from the fifth stanza: "I thought of a mound in sweet Auburn/Where a little headstone stood"?

   **(A)** They establish the setting.
   **(B)** They imply the speaker's sorrow regarding his daughter's death without stating it directly.
   **(C)** They suggest the coldness of the day.
   **(D)** They offer the poet's concept of life after death.
   **(E)** They imply that God is the creator of all earthly events.

7. What type of poem is "The First Snowfall"?

   **(A)** A narrative
   **(B)** An ode
   **(C)** An elegy
   **(D)** A lyric
   **(E)** A sonnet

8. What type of rhyme is found in the following line: "Folded close under deepening snow"?

   **(A)** Internal rhyme
   **(B)** Masculine rhyme
   **(C)** Feminine rhyme
   **(D)** Consonance
   **(E)** Assonance

9. What is the meaning of the word "gloaming" in the first line of the poem?

   **(A)** Autumn
   **(B)** Dusk
   **(C)** Increasing cold
   **(D)** First light
   **(E)** Wind

10. What is the purpose of the transition in the fourth stanza?

    **(A)** It changes the focus from the outer world to the speaker's inner self.
    **(B)** It establishes the tone and mood of the poem.
    **(C)** It puts forth the poet's belief that God is the source of all healing.
    **(D)** The lines establish the beauty of nature.
    **(E)** The device is required in romantic poetry.

exercises

## ANSWER KEY AND EXPLANATIONS

| | | | | |
|---|---|---|---|---|
| 1. B | 3. A | 5. C | 7. D | 9. B |
| 2. D | 4. B | 6. B | 8. E | 10. A |

1.  **The correct answer is (B).** The answer is the choice that best defines the tone and that is the most complete. The poem is sad, choices (A) and (B), but not angry, choice (A), fearful, choice (E), or out of control, choice (D). Familial love, choice (C), is certainly present in the poem, but is only part of the answer. Only choice (B) includes both sadness and the positive aspects of the poem.

2.  **The correct answer is (D).** The answer hinges on the *not* in the question. It is snowing, so logically it is winter, choices (A) and (E). Lines 1 and 2 imply that the snow began the evening before, and line 10 reinforces this by mentioning the rooster crowing, so choice (B) is true. Although a funeral has taken place, it is over, the grave is covered, and snow has gathered around the tombstone, choice (C).

3.  **The correct answer is (A).** Eliminating choices works well here. The speaker seems to enjoy the snow; at least he does not mind it, choice (B). The speaker is obviously full of emotion, so choice (C) is incorrect. No wife is mentioned, choice (D). The hope expressed in stanza 8 is not consistent with blaming God, choice (E).

4.  **The correct answer is (B).** Choice (A) is simply incorrect in the context of the poem. Choice (C) is too broad; this is a very personal poem. Choices (D) and (E) are illogical because they are not supported by the facts.

5.  **The correct answer is (C).** This is a straightforward comprehension question. Spring, choice (A), and the glory of nature, choice (E), are irrelevant to the poem. God, choice (B), and familial love, choice (D), are too broad.

6.  **The correct answer is (B).** While this question seems to be about a detail, it also addresses the theme. Only choice (B) reflects the purpose of the poem. The speaker is saddened by his daughter's death; the grave serves to remind him of that tragedy.

7.  **The correct answer is (D).** The poem is highly personal, melodious, and filled with imagery. It does not tell a story, choice (A). It is neither long nor full of praise for a person, choice (B). While the poem is about death, it is not formal, choice (C). Choice (E) does not have the format of a sonnet—14 lines.

8.  **The correct answer is (E).** The repetition of the vowel sound "O" should point you to the correct answer. The words do not rhyme so choices (A), (B), and (C) are incorrect. Consonance is the repetition of a consonant sound, choice (D).

9.  **The correct answer is (B).** If the answer did not come readily, you could have substituted the choices in the line. Also, line 2 provides a clue with the word *night*. Autumn, choice (A), and first light, choice (D), do not make sense with "night." Choices (C) and (E) might be correct choices, but in context, the time of day makes better sense than a climate characteristic.

10. **The correct answer is (A).** This question is similar to question 11 of "La Belle Dame Sans Merci." Elimination of choices helps. Several of the choices are true about the poem, but not about the stanza. The tone and mood are established in the first stanzas, choice (B). The poet's belief about God's power to heal occurs at the end, choice (C). The final two choices are irrelevant to the work.

## EXERCISE 4

**Directions:** This section consists of selections of literature and questions on their content, style, and form. After you have read each passage, choose the answer that best answers the question and mark the space on the answer sheet.

**QUESTIONS 1 THROUGH 10 REFER TO THE FOLLOWING POEM. READ THE POEM CAREFULLY AND THEN CHOOSE THE ANSWERS TO THE QUESTIONS.**

**Sonnet 55**

Line  Not marble, nor the gilded monuments
Of princes shall outlive this powerful rhyme;
But you shall shine more bright in these contents
Than unswept stone, besmeared with sluttish time.
5  When wasteful war shall statues overturn,
And broils root out the work of masonry,
Nor Mars his sword nor war's quick fire shall burn
The living record of your memory.
'Gainst death and all-oblivious enmity
10  Shall you pace forth; your praise shall still find room
Even in the eyes of all posterity
That wear this world out to the ending doom.
So, till the judgment that yourself arise,
You live in this, and dwell in lovers' eyes.

—William Shakespeare

1.  Who or what is the speaker of this poem?

   **(A)**  William Shakespeare
   **(B)**  A friend of the poet
   **(C)**  The writer's lover
   **(D)**  A lover and a poet
   **(E)**  "You"

2.  To whom is the poem spoken?

   **(A)**  An idealized friend or lover of the speaker
   **(B)**  A beautiful but coy woman
   **(C)**  The reader
   **(D)**  Queen Elizabeth I
   **(E)**  The dark lady

3.  Which of the following best describes the theme of the poem?

   **(A)**  War is wasteful and destructive.
   **(B)**  Poetry and the memory of the person about whom this poem is written will outlast material things.
   **(C)**  Poetry can never be a destructive force.
   **(D)**  Memory lives on.
   **(E)**  A poet can overcome death.

4.  Which of the following best identifies the subject of "Sonnet 55"?

   **(A)**  Time and war
   **(B)**  The memory of the speaker's beloved
   **(C)**  The immortality of lovers
   **(D)**  Death and love
   **(E)**  The "all-oblivious enmity"

5. All but one of the following are mentioned as powers of destruction in the poem. Which one is not mentioned?

   (A) Unfeeling nature
   (B) Time
   (C) Death
   (D) War
   (E) Malevolent forgetfulness

6. The poet alludes to which of the following in the poem?

   (A) The god of war and the goddess of love
   (B) The apocalypse and Elizabeth
   (C) Judgment Day and the god of war
   (D) The goddess of love and Judgment Day
   (E) The apocalypse and the goddess of love

7. What is "the living record of your memory" (line 8)?

   (A) Poetry, specifically "Sonnet 55"
   (B) The will of Shakespeare's beloved
   (C) Ending doom
   (D) A Renaissance journal
   (E) The beloved's diary

8. To what does the phrase "the ending doom" (line 12) refer?

   (A) A deep, hidden meaning
   (B) This powerful poem
   (C) The apocalypse described in the Bible
   (D) The poet's fear of death
   (E) War and destruction

9. What does the poet mean by "sluttish time" (line 4)?

   (A) Time is wasteful.
   (B) With the end of time come all kinds of horrors.
   (C) Time ruins everything eventually.
   (D) Time is an immoral woman.
   (E) Time is indiscriminate and wanton when it comes to destruction.

10. In the couplet, the speaker argues which of the following?

   (A) The god of war brings doom.
   (B) The beloved will live on in the sonnet and in lovers' eyes.
   (C) Time is the ultimate destroyer.
   (D) Poetry is important.
   (E) He will rise again on Judgment Day.

## ANSWER KEY AND EXPLANATIONS

| | | | | |
|---|---|---|---|---|
| 1. D | 3. B | 5. A | 7. A | 9. E |
| 2. A | 4. B | 6. C | 8. C | 10. B |

1. **The correct answer is (D).** Never assume that the speaker is the poet, so eliminate choice (A). Choices (B), (C), and (E) actually refer to the person addressed by the speaker.

2. **The correct answer is (A).** Upon a casual reading, several choices may seem like good possibilities. Choices (B), (D), and (E) are not supported by evidence in the poem. Unless every reader was living during the Elizabethan period, choice (C) is illogical.

3. **The correct answer is (B).** A paraphrase gives you this answer. The speaker states that the poem and the memory of the lover will survive longer than buildings and other material things. War, choice (A); time, choice (D); and death, choice (E); cannot stifle poetry. These ideas support the theme expressed in choice (B). Choice (C) is illogical.

4. **The correct answer is (B).** Consistency in answers makes this an easy question. This question is very close to question 2. Choice (E) presents lines from the poem that have little to do with the subject. Choices (A), (C), and (D) are too broad.

5. **The correct answer is (A).** A quick look at the poem gives you this answer. Time is in line 4, death in line 9, war and the god of war in line 7, and malevolent forgetfulness is in the meaning of "all-oblivious enmity" in line 9.

6. **The correct answer is (C).** Both parts of the choice must be correct to make the choice the proper one. There is no mention of the goddess of love, choices (A), (D), and (E), or Elizabeth, choice (B), in the poem. Judgment Day, choice (C), is in line 13 and Mars, the god of war, is in line 7.

7. **The correct answer is (A).** If you read the poem carefully, you will realize that the speaker says nothing will "outlive this powerful rhyme" in line 2. The lines cited in the question restate this idea. Question 1 already established that Shakespeare is not the speaker, so choice (B) is incorrect. Choice (C) is illogical in context, and choices (D) and (E) are not mentioned in the poem.

8. **The correct answer is (C).** This is a question that tests your knowledge of culture. Religion strongly influenced Renaissance England. Most people believed that there would be an end of the world and a Judgment Day. In this context, the other choices are simply incorrect. In addition, choices (D) and (E) have been ruled out by the poet as possible ends to her memory.

9. **The correct answer is (E).** This is difficult because several of the choices make sense. You must pick the one that most accurately defines the imagery—soiled or dirtied by careless time. Choice (D) is too literal a reading of "sluttish time." Choices (A), (B), and (C) are true, but not for the meaning of the words in question.

10. **The correct answer is (B).** Again, if you look for consistency in your answers, you know that the speaker's point is that this poem will outlive many material things. Choices (A) and (C) are not addressed in these two lines. Choice (D) may be true, but is not the point of the poem. Choice (E) is irrelevant.

## EXERCISE 5

**Directions:** This section consists of selections of literature and questions on their content, style, and form. After you have read each passage, choose the answer that best answers the question.

**QUESTIONS 1 THROUGH 11 REFER TO THE FOLLOWING POEM. READ THE POEM CAREFULLY AND THEN CHOOSE THE ANSWERS TO THE QUESTIONS.**

### Hampton Beach

Line The sunlight glitters keen and bright,
    Where, miles away
Lies stretching to my dazzled sight
A luminous belt, a misty light,
5    Beyond the dark pine bluffs and wastes of sandy gray.

The tremulous shadow of the sea!
    Against its ground
Of silvery light, rock, hill, and tree,
Still as a picture, clear and free,
10    With varying outline mark the coast for miles around.

On-on-we tread with loose-flung rein
    Our seaward way,
Through dark-green fields and blossoming grain,
Where the wild brier-rose skirts the lane,
15    And bends above our heads the flowering locust spray.

Ha! like a kind hand on my brow
    Comes this fresh breeze,
Cooling its dull and feverish glow,
While through my being seems to flow
20    The breath of a new life, the healing of the seas!

Now rest we, where this grassy mound
    His feet hath set
In the great waters, which have bound
His granite ankles greenly round
25    With long and tangled moss, and weeds with cool spray wet.

Good-bye to pain and care! I take
    Mine ease today:
Here where these sunny waters break,
And ripples this keen breeze, I shake
30    All burdens from the heart, all weary thoughts away.

I draw a freer breath, I seem
    Like all I see—
Waves in the sun, the white-winged gleam
Of sea birds in the slanting beam
35    And far-off sails which flit before the south wind free.

So when time's veil shall fall asunder,
　　The soul may know
No fearful change, nor sudden wonder,
Nor sink the weight of mystery under,
40　　　But with the upward rise, and with the vastness grow.

And all we shrink from now may seem
　　No new revealing;
Familiar as our childhood's stream,
Or pleasant memory of a dream,
45　　　The loved and cherished past upon the new life stealing.

Serene and mild the untried light
　　May have its dawning:
And, as in summer's northern night
The evening and the dawn unite,
50　　　The sunset hues of time blend with the soul's new morning.

I sit alone; in foam and spray
　　Wave after wave
Breaks on the rocks which, stern and gray,
Shoulder the broken tide away,
55　　　Or murmurs hoarse and strong through mossy cleft and cave.

What heed I of the dusty land
　　And noisy town?
I see the mighty deep expand
From its white line of glimmering sand
60　　　To where the blue of heaven on bluer waves shuts down!

In listless quietude of mind,
　　I yield to all
The change of cloud and wave and wind;
And passive on the flood reclined,
65　　　I wander with the waves, and with them rise and fall.

But look, thou dreamer! wave and shore
　　In shadow lie;
The night-wind warns me back once more
To where, my native hilltops o'er,
70　　　Bends like an arch of fire the glowing sunset sky.

So then, beach, bluff, and wave, farewell!
　　I bear with me
No token stone nor glittering shell,
But long and oft shall memory tell
75　　　Of this brief thoughtful hour of musing by the sea.

　　　　　　　　　　　—John Greenleaf Whittier

1. The phrase "tremulous shadow of the sea" is an example of

   (A) alliteration
   (B) metaphor
   (C) synecdoche
   (D) onomatopoeia
   (E) visual imagery

2. Which of the following is not reflected in the poem?

   (A) The warmth and simplicity of rural New England
   (B) The beauty and majesty of the shore
   (C) The quieting power of the ocean
   (D) The speaker's love for nature
   (E) The need for all people to have time to reflect

3. In the fifth stanza, what type of figure of speech does Whittier use?

   (A) Simile
   (B) Hyperbole
   (C) Conceit
   (D) Personification
   (E) Metaphor

4. What does the speaker mean when he says that he seems like the wave, sea birds, and far-off sails?

   (A) He is far from home.
   (B) He feels free.
   (C) His life is over-burdened, and he must escape.
   (D) He must bear the burden of separation from his loved ones.
   (E) He is playing "hooky" from his job.

5. Which of the following best identifies the rhyme scheme of this poem?

   (A) *abaab* and *cdccd*
   (B) *abbab* and *cddcd*
   (C) *abccb* and *deffe*
   (D) *abcab* and *defde*
   (E) A and B

6. What is Whittier describing when he writes, "when time's veil shall fall asunder" (line 36)?

   (A) Sunset
   (B) The freshness and innocence of a bride in her wedding gown
   (C) Death
   (D) The sun shining through clouds
   (E) Discarding his burdens

7. Why has the speaker no need of "token stone nor glittering shell" (line 73)?

   (A) His memory of the day will last.
   (B) He believes in protecting the environment.
   (C) He does not care for material things.
   (D) He will not take things that do not belong to him.
   (E) The speaker does not need souvenirs of the beach.

8. In the fourth stanza, the predominant images appeal to which of the senses?

   (A) Sight
   (B) Sound
   (C) Touch
   (D) Taste
   (E) Smell

9. Which of the following best explains the change in focus in the sixth stanza?

   (A) The speaker ceases straight description and begins to present his inner feelings.
   (B) The pronoun usage changes.
   (C) The imagery becomes much more vivid.
   (D) The reader recognizes the allegory presented.
   (E) Sentences are written in the active voice.

10. What type of rhyme does the poet use in the tenth stanza when he uses "dawning" and "morning"?

    **(A)** Half rhyme
    **(B)** Feminine rhyme
    **(C)** Masculine rhyme
    **(D)** Assonance
    **(E)** Consonance

11. What does the word "luminous" mean in line 4?

    **(A)** Complaining
    **(B)** Trembling
    **(C)** Into pieces or parts
    **(D)** Light, easy to carry
    **(E)** Shining

## ANSWER KEY AND EXPLANATIONS

| | | | | |
|---|---|---|---|---|
| 1. E | 4. B | 6. C | 8. C | 10. B |
| 2. A | 5. A | 7. A | 9. A | 11. E |
| 3. D | | | | |

1. **The correct answer is (E).** An understanding of the terms in this question will quickly lead you to the correct response, visual imagery. Alliteration, choice (A), is the repetition of consonant sounds in a series. Metaphor, choice (B), states that something is something else. Synecdoche, choice (C), is a figure of speech in which a part of something is used to represent a whole. Onomatopoeia, choice (D), is the use of words that sound like what they mean.

2. **The correct answer is (A).** You need to recognize that this is a *not* question. You are looking for the one answer that is *untrue* and that will be the correct answer. Choice (A) does not reflect the content of the poem; therefore, it is the correct response.

3. **The correct answer is (D).** The reference to "ankles" in the fifth stanza suggests a human characteristic given to an inanimate object—personification. Simile, choice (A), uses *like* or *as* to compare two or more items. Hyperbole, choice (B), exaggerates for comic effect. Conceit, choice (C), is an extended or unusual metaphor. Metaphor, choice (E), states that something is something else.

4. **The correct answer is (B).** This is a variation on a theme or main-idea question. All the choices seem like possibilities, but only choice (B) is broad enough to represent a theme of the poem. The other choices represent details of the poem. There are also two clues to help you. The stanza begins with the speaker drawing a "freer breath" and ends with "which flit before the south wind free."

5. **The correct answer is (A).** The simplest way to find the correct answer is to test the responses. For example, does *abbab* fit the first stanza? No, that eliminates both choices (B) and (E). Continue through the balance of the answers, and you will find that only choice (A) fits.

6. **The correct answer is (C).** For this question, it is helpful to find the reference. It is in the eighth stanza. Notice the word *so*. It indicates a type of transition. Here, the word marks a counterpoint to the freedom portrayed in the previous stanza. The reference in the question is to something opposite of freedom, and in this poem that is an allusion to death. Choice (A) is not mentioned in the poem, and choices (B) and (E) are too literal of an interpretation of the image. Choice (D) is simply incorrect.

7. **The correct answer is (A).** The reference can be found in the final stanza. A reading of this section shows that the speaker will often remember his experiences at the beach. He therefore has no need of items to assist his recall. Choice (E) does not explain an answer but restates the question. Choices (B), (C), and (D) are illogical; they do not relate to the content of the poem.

8. **The correct answer is (C).** The author's images in the fourth stanza ("kind hand on my brow," "cooling," "through my being seems to flow," "breath," "healing") relate to touch/feel.

9. **The correct answer is (A).** The poet shifts the focus from description of what the speaker sees to relaying the inner thoughts and feelings of the speaker. Do not be fooled into thinking that the pronoun changes from third person to first because the content changes from description to personal feelings, choice (B). The content of the images changes, but the vividness remains the same, choice (C). The entire poem is predominantly active voice, so choice (E) is incorrect, as is choice (D). There is no allegory.

10. **The correct answer is (B).** In a feminine rhyme, the accented syllable is followed by an unaccented syllable. Choice (A) (also called slant, off, or near rhyme) is used for surprise by interrupting a regular rhyme. Masculine rhyme, choice (C), is the last syllable of a line. Assonance, choice (D), is the repetition of vowel sounds between different consonants, while consonance, choice (E), is the repetition of identical consonant sounds before and after different vowel sounds.

11. **The correct answer is (E).** Recognize that this is a question of definition. If you did not know that *luminous* means *shining,* substitute the possible answers in context and eliminate those that do not make sense. The word *light* is a clue. A complaining light, choice (A), and an easy-to-carry light, choice (D), do not make sense. Trembling, choice (B), might describe a belt of light, but choice (E) is a better answer. Choice (C) does not fit the context.

## SUMMING IT UP

- Remember that the language of poems is compact and economical, with every word of a poem carrying part of the impact and the meaning.

- If possible, read a poem four times. The first two times you read a poem, read it sentence by sentence, not line by line. After you read the poem a second time, highlight words, phrases, and sentences that seem significant, but do not spend a lot of time at this. During your last read, you should paraphrase the poem. Again, in a test situation, you cannot take the time to write out your paraphrase, but you can "write" it in your mind.

- Use the footnotes. They may help you understand an archaic word or explain a difficult reference.

- Identify the conventions of poetry used in the selection. Determine how the poet uses literary devices and figurative language.

- When reading a poem to find an answer, read the phrases around the reference.

- Answer questions in the order you wish. If you are not confident, skip difficult questions, and answer the easier ones first.

# About the "9" Essay

## OVERVIEW

- Practice plan
- Basic information about the essay section
- Good writing
- Planning and writing each essay: practical advice
- Summing it up

Actually, this title is misleading because, as you read in *Scoring the AP English Literature & Composition Test,* page 6, you do not need three "9" essays to get a "5" for your composite score. You do need to believe that you will understand what the essay questions will ask you and that you will write clear and coherent essays in the time allotted. Now is the time to plan and practice, so you will have the self-confidence to excel, not panic.

Chapters 6, 7, and 9 will help you to understand what the essay questions ask and how to answer each specific type of question. This chapter lays out some basic information about the essay portion of the test and about good writing in general.

## PRACTICE PLAN

In Chapters 6, 7, and 9 you will explore the different types of essays on the AP test, and you will have ample opportunities to practice writing sample essays. The *Free Response* and *Open Essay Guides* will help you plan, pace, and write your essays. Use the rubric and scoring guide to pinpoint your weaknesses and to improve as you write each subsequent essay.

Use the *Practice Test 1: Diagnostic* and the other *Practice Tests* as tools to improve your writing, too. As you write, practice the techniques described in this chapter and in Chapters 6, 7, and 9, and the tips in the *Free Response* and *Open Essay Guides*. Be sure to stay within the 40-minute time limit for each.

chapter 5

Then turn to the *Answer Key and Explanations* section after each test. Compare each essay with the list of suggested points that you might have developed in that essay. Score your essay with the *Self-Evaluation Rubric*. Ask a reliable friend, an AP classmate, or a teacher to holistically evaluate your essay. Where are you weak? What can you improve? Take several of the points from the list and rework your essay with those points, strengthening the weak areas.

Reevaluate your essay. Again compare the points you made with the ones we suggest. Did our suggestions help you to better understand what the question is asking? Is your rewritten essay more tightly focused on the question and more clearly developed as a result of incorporating some of our points? Still need work on your weak points? How much did you improve?

Now, stop. Do not keep working on the same essay to polish it to perfection. You won't have that opportunity during the test. The purpose of reworking your essay is to help you pinpoint what the question is really asking and how you can best answer it with a clear, coherent, and unified essay. Keep in mind what you learned on your first try and go on to the next essay.

## BASIC INFORMATION ABOUT THE ESSAY SECTION

NOTE

See
Chapters 6–10.

1. Section II of the exam has three parts: an essay question on a prose selection, an essay question on a poetry selection, and an open essay on a given topic.

2. You will have 2 hours to write the three essays. The College Board suggests you allot approximately 40 minutes to each essay.

3. Each essay is scored from 0 to 9, with 9 being the highest.

4. Each of your essays will be read by a different reader with knowledge of the literary work that you discuss.

5. Each essay counts for one third of your total essay score. The open essay counts for no more and no less than the other two essays.

6. The essays together account for 55 percent of your final composite score.

What does all this mean? It means that you need to do some planning and practicing.

1, 2     If you have 2 hours—120 minutes—to write all three essays, you cannot spend 90 minutes on one and 15 minutes apiece on the other two. When you practice, take 5 minutes to read each question and selection and to plan what you will say. Use the 35 minutes remaining to write your essay.

3, 5,     Because no single essay counts for more than the others, you don't have to worry
and 6    about doing an outstanding job on the open essay question. However, you do have to do a good job on all three.

Skim the three questions and then put them in the order in which you want to answer them. Begin with the easiest, then move to the next hardest, and finally, write the most difficult. That probably means leaving the open essay question for last.

**4** Because your three essays will be read by three different people, you don't have to worry that one weaker essay will pull down the scores for the other two essays. Instead, you can be confident that your clear, coherent, unified—and neatly written—essays will brighten each grader's pile of vague, incoherent, fragmented, and illegible essays.

Neatness does not count, but it does matter. You cannot expect a reader faced with hundreds of papers to score to take time to puzzle over your handwriting. Write as neatly as you can. If your cursive style is tiny and cramped or large and ill-defined, try printing. You will not have time for much revision, but if you do revise, do it neatly and clearly.

**NOTE**
You will be given scratch paper, but you must take a pen with you to write the essays. Be safe: take at least two.

## GOOD WRITING

You may have to plan and write your essays in 40 minutes, but the characteristics of these essays are no different from those of any good writing: unity, coherence, and adequate development.

First, who is your audience? Second, what is your purpose? Third, what is the appropriate tone?

### Audience

You have an audience of one—a College Board–trained reader who teaches high school or college English and who will be reading hundreds of similar papers. She or he has knowledge of the literary work you have written about and will have a scoring guide or rubric to aid in evaluating your paper. He or she will score your essay holistically; that is, there is no single score for things like grammar and punctuation. The reader will consider every aspect of writing for its impact on the overall impression of your essay. (Our rubric singles out the various descriptors so you can pinpoint your weaknesses to work on and increase your overall score.)

### Purpose

Your purpose is to get a score of 5 or better. To do that, you need to write a unified, coherent, and consistent essay that answers the question. A well-written essay that misses the point of the question will not get you a good score. That is why you need to read Chapters 6, 7, and 9.

## Tone

Your tone is the reflection of your attitude toward the subject of the essay. A writer's tone, for example, may be lighthearted (as in the last sentence in the paragraph numbered 4 on the previous page), brusque, or serious.

The safest tone to adopt is formal and subjective, since you are being asked for your opinion. You do not want to be stuffy and pretentious by using phrases such as "one understands" or "we can surmise." On the other hand, do not be too casual either by writing things like "you know what I mean." Most students, however, err on the side of "faux" erudition, using big words and convoluted constructions. When in doubt, write what you mean simply and directly.

**NOTE**

Remember to use present tense in writing about literature.

How do you develop the proper tone? Through style. Your style should be your own natural style that you use for school essays. That means:

- Using proper grammar and punctuation.

- Choosing words that convey your meaning in an interesting rather than a pedestrian or vague way: "The author created a dynamic personality in Tom Jones" versus "The main character is interesting."

- Avoiding the use of several words when one will do: "There are a number of aspects to the character that are dynamic such as . . ." versus "Jones is both a rascal and . . ."

- Avoiding hackneyed phrases and clichés such as "The protagonist was on cloud nine" versus "The protagonist's demeanor grew ecstatic."

Your style adds interest to the paper. Interesting words and phrasing as much as a unique point of view about a subject can make a paper interesting to read.

## Unity and Coherence

Unity is another word for clarity. A unified paper is one that is clearly developed. Each paragraph has a topic sentence, and every sentence in the paragraph relates to every other sentence and adds to the development of the topic sentence.

In the same way, each paragraph relates to every other, and every paragraph supports the overall thesis. This means, of course, that you need a thesis to develop. Chapters 6, 7, and 9 will help you with developing thesis statements that answer the essay questions.

Remember that your thesis statement contains the central idea that you have developed from brainstorming ideas to answer the essay question. As the *Harbrace College Handbook,* that venerable college English manual, states: "[Your thesis statement] is basically a claim statement, that is, it indicates what you claim to be true, interesting, or valuable about your subject."

Although you can place your thesis statement anywhere in your essay, it is probably safest to put it in the first paragraph, even as the first sentence, so you can refer to it as you write to be sure that everything you are writing develops and supports it. Putting the thesis first also gets you started writing.

## Adequate Development

What is "adequate development"? You have 5 minutes to read and plan and 35 minutes to develop your ideas—neatly. Using the five-paragraph structure will give you a format to work with: a one-paragraph introduction, a three-paragraph middle, and a one-paragraph ending. Your middle section may be more than three paragraphs, but this format gives you direction. The *Free Response* and *Open Essay Guides* will help you with planning and pacing, as well as writing, your essays.

# PLANNING AND WRITING EACH ESSAY: PRACTICAL ADVICE

Once you have decided which question to answer first:

- Read the question again carefully and then the selection, if it is not a free response question.

- Restate to yourself what the question is asking.

- Do not take time to outline, but make a list by brainstorming all the ideas that come to mind as you read.

- Create a thesis from the ideas you generated.

- Turn this brainstorm into an informal working plan by numbering the items that you want to include in your essay in the order in which you want to include them. Do not be afraid to cross out some that no longer apply now that you have a thesis.

- Begin writing your first paragraph by stating the thesis clearly. Take a full 5 minutes to be sure that you are writing a clearly stated and interesting introduction.

- Once you have written the first paragraph, read it to be sure that your ideas are logically following each other and supporting the thesis.

- Write a transition into the second paragraph. Check your list of ideas.

- Keep writing until you have used all the RELEVANT ideas on your list. If a new idea comes from the flow of your writing, use it if it fits.

- Use transitions.

- Allow time to write a solid concluding paragraph. There are several ways to approach the conclusion: rephrasing the thesis, summarizing the main points, or

**NOTE**

Use the scratch paper you are given to jot down your quick list.

**NOTE**

Depending on how large your handwriting is in relation to the amount of essay paper you are given, use every other line. It will make revision easier and your essays easier to read.

referring in some way back to your opening paragraph. Do not leave the reader wondering, "so what?"

- Pace yourself so that you have at least 3 minutes to reread your essay for proofreading and revision. Cross out any irrelevant ideas or words and make any additions. If you have been following your informal plan to develop your thesis, this time should be spent making sure your grammar and mechanics are correct and your handwriting is legible.

A clear, well-organized, coherent, and interesting essay will attract the attention of the reader and serve your purpose.

## SUMMING IT UP

- Section II of the exam has three parts: an essay question on a prose selection, an essay question on a poetry selection, and an open essay on a given topic.

- You will have 2 hours to write the three essays. The College Board suggests approximately 40 minutes for each essay.

- Each essay is scored from 0 to 9, with 9 as the highest.

- Each of your essays will be read by a different reader with knowledge of the literary work that you discuss.

- The essays together count for 55 percent of your final composite score.

- No single essay counts for more than the others.

- To get a score of 5 or better, you need to write a unified, coherent, and consistent essay that answers the question.

- The safest tone to adopt is formal and subjective, since you are being asked for your opinion. Remember to use present tense in writing about literature.

- Remember that your thesis statement contains the central idea that you have developed from brainstorming ideas to answer the essay question.

- Review the chapter's *Planning and Writing Each Essay: Practical Advice*.

# About the Free Response Essay on Prose

## OVERVIEW

- What will you be asked to do?
- What will you need to do?
- Reading the material
- Writing the essay about a prose selection
- Practicing
- Analyzing prose
- Sample essay on prose
- Suggestions for sample essay on prose
- Self-evaluation rubric for the Advanced Placement essays
- Summing it up

Section II of the Advanced Placement Literature and Composition Test asks you to write three essays, one about a prose passage, another about a poetry selection, and a third about a piece of literature of your own choice. Because of the time limits of the AP test and because you probably have not seen the literature that you will be asked to write about, these will be difficult essays to tackle. But if you follow the recommendations in Chapter 5 about good writing in general, and in this chapter and Chapters 7 and 9 about writing the different types of essays in particular, you will be surprised at how prepared you feel, and actually are, going into the test.

## WHAT WILL YOU BE ASKED TO DO?

The question for the prose essay will require you to analyze the passage, either directly or indirectly, for certain traits. When you are analyzing prose, always begin with the theme or meaning of the passage and how the writer uses certain elements or the whole selection to help you, the reader, understand the message. Read the chart, *Analyzing Prose,* on pp. 132–133, for the different elements that you should consider in analyzing a prose selection to get the most out of it.

## WHAT WILL YOU NEED TO DO?

The first thing you will need to do when you begin Section II is to decide the order in which you want to answer the questions. Just as you can choose the order in which to answer the selections in Section I, you can choose the order in which to write your essays. Scan the questions and passages and prioritize them.

First, choose the question and passage that are easiest for you, and work your way up to the most difficult. That often means doing the open essay last. Remember that all three essays are worth the same amount—approximately 18 percentage points apiece—so you will not earn any bonus points by writing the most difficult essay first, and you may tire yourself out.

When you are ready to answer the prose question, you must read the question and passage several times.

## READING THE MATERIAL

The mistake that students often make is writing an essay about something other than the question they are asked to answer. It may be a fabulous "9" essay in all other ways, but if it does not answer the question, it will earn you a low score.

- First, identify the type of essay question you are being asked to answer. Is it asking you for interpretation, synthesis, comparison, and/or evaluation of the selection?

- Underline the important points or key words in the question. If you are being asked to compare elements in two given passages, what are those elements? (The prose essay question may involve two passages.) Underline *compare* and the required elements. Are you being asked to explain how the writer's use of a motif affects the mood? Underline *explain, motif,* and *mood.* You now know that one of the things you will need to look for as you read is a motif.

- Restate the question to yourself—paraphrase it—to be sure you understand what you are being asked to do.

- Once you know what you will need to write about, you are ready to read the selection, and you will need to read it several times. Remember, you have about 5 minutes to read and plan, but the selections are short. Follow these steps to get the most out of each reading:

- Regardless of what the question is asking, you need to determine the theme or meaning of the piece first. In order to talk about elements of the selection, you need to know what the piece is about.

- The first time you read, skim the passage.

- The second time, read carefully.

**NOTE**

You will be given paper for your essay, and you will be able to use your test booklet for scratch paper.

- Be aware of language and diction, character, tone, the writer's intentions and purpose, the selection's impact, and special techniques.

- As you read, underline words and sentences that seem significant and that you might want to quote in your essay. Jot down notes. However, do not spend a lot of time doing this.

## WRITING THE ESSAY ABOUT A PROSE SELECTION

- After you have completed your reading, take a few minutes to plan what you will write. Brainstorm or list ideas and thoughts, but do not outline. Outlining wastes time. What you want to do is analyze the passage. List how each literary element enhances the communication in the passage. Make another list of examples and supporting evidence from the passage. Review anything you underlined in the passage to include in the lists.

- Check through your notes and lists and develop your thesis.

- Organize your ideas and begin writing. Use the suggestions listed in *Planning and Writing Each Essay: Practical Advice* in Chapter 5 and the *Free Response Guides*.

- Periodically reread your introductory paragraph to be sure you stay on track to prove your thesis. Do more than summarize. Include your insights, reactions, and emotions.

- Be sure to include examples from the selection to support your points. However, don't try to use copious quotations to fill up the sheets. You don't need to use complete sentences; you can use ellipses.

- Write an effective concluding paragraph. Restate your thesis and summarize how your essay supports it.

- Plan your time so you can proofread and revise your essay.

The chart *Analyzing Prose* on pp. 132–133 suggests questions to ask yourself to help you analyze literary elements to find the meaning in what you read. Use this chart to prepare the practice essays in this chapter. Try it for the essays you have to write about prose selections in school, too, and see how much easier it is to organize and develop your thoughts.

## PRACTICING

The following question and selection are very similar to those that you will find on the actual AP Literature & Composition Test. Apply the suggestions and strategies you have just learned as you read and write about the excerpt from *Civil Disobedience*. Then, check your essay by reading the suggested points of discussion that follow. Evaluate yourself by using the *Self-Evaluation Rubric* on p. 151.

**TIP**

If you developed an Idea Bank of words and phrases to describe literary works, draw on it to help you develop your thesis. See Chapter 11, p. 250.

**NOTE**

Don't forget to use transitions between ideas and paragraphs.

**ALERT!**

Time yourself as you plan and write your practice essays. That way you will become comfortable with the time limits on the actual AP test.

# ANALYZING PROSE

**Mode of Discourse**

1. What type of prose is it—fiction, exposition, persuasion, description, narrative, drama?
2. Are points developed by definitions, examples, facts, events, or quotations and citations?

**Author**

1. Who is the author?
2. What do you know about the writer and/or the time period in which the passage was written?

**Title**

1. What does the title tell you?
2. What does it suggest about the subject or the theme (meaning) of the passage?

**Subject**

1. What is the subject of the passage?
2. What is this selection about?

**Setting**

1. Where and when does the action in the selection take place?
2. What details does the writer use to create the setting?
3. Does the setting create a mood or feeling?
4. Is the setting a symbol for an important idea that the writer wants to convey?
5. Does the setting play a role in the central conflict?

**Point of View**

1. Is the passage told from the first person or from the third person point of view?
2. Is the narrator limited or omniscient?
3. What effect does the point of view have on the way you experience the selection?

**Central Conflict**

1. In what struggle is the protagonist involved?
2. Is the central conflict internal, within the main character's mind, or external, with another character, society, or nature?
3. How is the conflict resolved?

**Plot or Course of Events**
1. What events take place in the passage?
2. Does the piece have an introduction?
3. If so, what does the reader learn in the introduction?
4. What is the inciting incident?
5. What happens during the development?
6. When does the climax occur?
7. What events mark the resolution?
8. Does the selection have a denouement?
9. Are there special plot devices, such as a surprise ending, foreshadowing, or flashbacks?
10. If there is suspense, how does the writer create it?

**Characterization**
1. Who is the protagonist?
2. Who are the other major and minor characters?
3. Is there conflict among characters?
4. How does the writer reveal each of the characters?
5. Which characters change and which are flat?

**Literary Devices and Figures of Speech**
1. Does the writer make use of devices such as euphony or alliteration?
2. Does the passage contain any examples of figurative language, such as hyperbole, metaphor, or simile?
3. Is there symbolism? What is it?

**Theme or Thesis**
1. What is the theme or central idea of the selection?
2. How is the theme conveyed?

**Style**
1. Are there denotative words, connotative words, abstract words, or inclusive words?
2. What is the tone?
3. What kinds of sentence structure are present?
4. How is the passage organized? What type of structure does the writer use?

**NOTE:** These questions are general. You will need to adapt them to the type of prose you are reading. Some questions are more appropriate for fiction, while others work better with nonfiction. By using them throughout this chapter, you will become so familiar with the questions that you will know automatically which ones to use with each prose passage on the test.

# SAMPLE ESSAY ON PROSE

*SUGGESTED TIME—40 MINUTES*

**NOTE**

When you practice, limit yourself to 40 minutes—5 minutes to read and plan and 35 minutes to write—so you will become comfortable with writing on demand.

**Directions:** Read the following passage carefully. Determine Thoreau's central point. Write a well-organized essay that explains how Thoreau developed and supported his core argument or theme. Consider such literary elements as diction, imagery, tone, theme, and style.

## From *Civil Disobedience*

Line I heartily accept the motto, "That government is best which governs least"; and I should like to see it acted up to more rapidly and systematically. Carried out, it finally amounts to this, which also I believe: "That government is best which governs not at all"; and when men are prepared for it, that will be the kind of government which
5 they will have. Government is at best but an expedient; but most governments are usually, and all governments are sometimes, inexpedient. The objections which have been brought against a standing army, and they are many and weighty, and deserve to prevail, may also at last be brought against a standing government. The standing army is only an arm of the standing government. The government itself, which is only
10 the mode which the people have chosen to execute their will, is equally liable to be abused and perverted before the people can act through it. Witness the present Mexican war, the work of comparatively a few individuals using the standing government as their tool; for in the outset, the people would not have consented to this measure.

15     This American government—what is it but a tradition, though a recent one, endeavoring to transmit itself unimpaired to posterity, but each instant losing some of its integrity? It has not the vitality and force of a single living man; for a single man can bend it to his will. It is a sort of wooden gun to the people themselves; and, if ever they should use it in earnest as a real one against each other, it will surely split. But
20 it is not the less necessary for this; for the people must have some complicated machinery or other, and hear its din, to satisfy that idea of government which they have. Governments show thus how successfully men can be imposed on, even impose on themselves, for their own advantage. It is excellent, we must all allow; yet this government never of itself furthered any enterprise, but by the alacrity with which it
25 got out of its way. *It* does not keep the country free. *It* does not settle the West. *It* does not educate. The character inherent in the American people has done all that has been accomplished; and it would have done somewhat more, if the government had not sometimes got in its way. For government is an expedient by which men would fain succeed in letting one another alone; and, as has been said, when it is most expedient,
30 the governed are most let alone by it. Trade and commerce, if they were not made of India rubber, would never manage to bounce over the obstacles which legislators are continually putting in their way; and, if one were to judge these men wholly by the effects of their actions, and not partly by their intentions, they would deserve to be classed and punished with those mischievous persons who put obstructions on
35 the railroads.

But, to speak practically and as a citizen, unlike those who call themselves no-government men, I ask for, not at once no government, but *at once* a better government. Let every man make known what kind of government would command his respect, and that will be one step toward obtaining it. . . .

—Henry David Thoreau

Before you turn the page and read our suggestions for an essay on this selection, score your essay using the *Self-Evalution Rubric* on p. 151.

## SUGGESTIONS FOR SAMPLE ESSAY ON PROSE

The following points are ones you might have chosen to include in your essay on a passage from *Civil Disobedience*. Consider them as you perform your self-evaluation. You will notice that we discuss elements of literature that are not called for in the essay question. However, by identifying the author, naming the type of literature, and writing the title, you have a place to begin and an opportunity to include information to increase your score.

### Mode of Discourse

This selection is a persuasive essay, a piece of nonfiction. While you were not asked about this point directly in the question, by being specific about what type of literature you read, you appear knowledgeable about English literature.

### Author

Henry David Thoreau lived in the mid-1800s. A Transcendentalist, he put his beliefs into practice by living simply at Walden Pond. His work has inspired others, not only writers but also environmentalists, politicians, and social reformers. Transcendentalists believed in human potential. They felt people were united in a universal soul.

Of course, you cannot find this in the selection, but you might remember some of this, or even more, from your American literature or U.S. history classes. The information may help you understand the selection better and may impress the grader. Remember those multiple-choice questions that tested your cultural knowledge? Facts that you remember and can apply effectively to your essays add points.

### Title

The selection is excerpted from *Civil Disobedience*. That title reveals a great deal about the subject—disobeying the government—and the theme—the best government is the least government. Thoreau wrote this work after spending a night in jail because he refused to pay taxes in protest of slavery and the Mexican War, the war mentioned in the excerpt.

### Subject

The subject is government. Thoreau discusses what type of government is the best and explains what he considers to be the failure of the government in his day.

Yes, this does seem somewhat repetitious. You do not need to repeat information when you take the AP test. But here you are practicing, so think about each literary element even if you find you cover the same ground.

## Literary Devices and Figures of Speech

Thoreau uses the metaphor of a wooden gun for the government. He also compares commerce and trade to rubber, able to bounce over obstructions that the government puts in their path. According to Thoreau, government legislators are similar to individuals who put items on railroad tracks to derail trains and should be punished as those offenders are.

If you quoted any of the lines that contained the imagery, give yourself a higher score. Underlining these images in the selection itself as you read will save you time when you start to write. You will not have to hunt back through the selection.

## Theme or Thesis

Thoreau's idea is that government should do as little as possible. While he would prefer no government, he recognizes that some government must exist. He believes the U.S. government has failed because it has imposed the will of a few, the legislators and the President, upon the majority.

## Style

By contemporary standards, Thoreau's diction is sophisticated and his sentence structure complex. His use of first person plural pronouns establishes an "us against them" relationship. While the tone is sincere and persuasive, there is a lightness and humor to it. The images of the wooden gun, the bouncing rubber, and the punishment of obstructive legislators are amusing. It is somewhat difficult to identify the organization of an excerpt. However, this one does appear to be organized in order of importance. He builds up to his strongest point. In addition, each paragraph develops to a high point in the final sentences.

You most probably could add even more about the style. Be sure to quote directly from the passage to support your position. Remember, your answer can be different or unusual as long as you give logical reasons and offer reasonable support.

## Your Style

You have just read some important points that you might have included in your essay. Now, review your introductory paragraph. If it seems a little dry, consider trying one of these types of openings to punch it up: more forceful or vivid language, a quotation, a rhetorical question, an anecdote, or perhaps one of Thoreau's images. Whatever you add has to relate to your thesis.

Look at your concluding paragraph. A simple summary of your major points creates an effective conclusion. You can also end an essay with a relevant quote. A specific suggestion works well in a persuasive essay. If you have organized your writing around a problem/solution, consider a vivid image of the consequences.

**TIP**

If you have not already started an Idea Bank, see Chapter 11 for information on how to get a head start on developing an effective vocabulary for your essays.

**NOTE**

See "Practice Plan for Studying for the AP English Literature & Composition Test" p. 17.

Once you have evaluated your essay with the *Self-Evaluation Rubric* on p. 151 and reviewed our points, you may choose to revise your essay using the points suggested here. However, do not spend a great deal of time trying to make it perfect. Revise it simply to see how adding some of our points may make it stronger. Whether you revise or not, ask a classmate or your teacher to evaluate your essay using the *Self-Evaluation Rubric* on p. 151. How does your own evaluation match with a more objective view? Keep the differences in mind as you write and score more free response essays.

Now that you have a sense of the logic involved in acing the prose essay question of Section II, try the first two exercises on prose. Study the points for evaluation and use the *Self-Evaluation Rubric*. If you are still unsure about writing essays about prose, continue with the last two exercises. Use the *Free Response Guide* for at least the first two exercises, so you can learn by using the planning and pacing steps.

# EXERCISE 1

*SUGGESTED TIME—40 MINUTES*

**Directions:** Read the following passage carefully. Then write an essay discussing the ways in which Dickens develops the two characters portrayed in this excerpt. Pay particular note to the different literary devices that the author uses in his characterizations. Consider such literary elements as style, imagery, narrative pace, and point of view.

### From *Great Expectations*

Line  "Hold your noise!" cried a terrible voice, as a man started up from among the graves at the side of the church porch. "Keep still, you little devil, or I'll cut your throat!"

A fearful man, all in coarse grey, with a great iron on his leg. A man with no hat, and with broken shoes, and with an old rag tied round his head. A man who had been
5  soaked in water, and smothered in mud, and lamed by stones, and cut by flints, and stung by nettles, and torn by briars; who limped, and shivered, and glared and growled; and whose teeth chattered in his head as he seized me by the chin.

"Oh! Don't cut my throat, sir," I pleaded in terror. "Pray don't do it, sir."

"Tell us your name!" said the man. "Quick!"
10  "Pip, sir."

"Once more," said the man, staring at me. "Give it mouth!"

"Pip. Pip, Sir."

"Show us where you live," said the man. "Point out the place!"

I pointed to where our village lay, on the flat in-shore among the alder-trees and
15  pollards, a mile or more from the church.

The man, after looking at me for a moment, turned me upside down, and emptied my pockets. There was nothing in them but a piece of bread. When the church came to itself—for he was so sudden and strong that he made it go head over heels before me, and I saw the steeple under my feet—when the church came to itself, I say, I was
20  seated on a high tombstone, trembling, while he ate the bread ravenously.

"You young dog," said the man, licking his lips, "what fat cheeks you ha'got."

I believe they were fat, though I was at that time undersized, for my years, and not strong.

"Darn me if I couldn't eat 'em," said the man, with a threatening shake of his head,
25  "and if I han't half a mind to't!"

I earnestly expressed my hope that he wouldn't, and held tighter to the tombstone on which he had put me; partly, to keep myself from crying.

"Now lookee here!" said the man. "Where's your mother?"

"There, sir!" said I.
30  He started, made a short run, and stopped and looked over his shoulder.

"There, sir!" I timidly explained. "Also Georgiana. That's my mother."

"Oh!" said he, coming back. "And is that your father alonger your mother?"

"Yes, sir," said I; "him too; late of this parish."

"Ha!" he muttered then, considering.
35  "Who d'ye live with—supposin' you're kindly let to live, which I han't made up mind about?"

"My sister, sir—Mrs. Joe Gargery—wife of Joe Gargery, the blacksmith, sir."

"Blacksmith, eh?" said he, and looked down at his leg.

40 After darkly looking at his leg and at me several times, he came closer to my tombstone, took me by both arms, and tilted me back as far as he could hold me; so that his eyes looked most powerfully down into mine, and mine looked most helplessly up into his.

"Now lookee here," he said, "the question being whether you're to be let to live. You know what a file is?"

45 "Yes, sir."

"And you know what wittles is?"

"Yes, sir."

After each question he tilted me over a little more, so as to give me a greater sense of helplessness and danger.

50 "You get me a file." He tilted me again. "And you get me wittles." He tilted me again. "You bring 'em both to me." He tilted me again. "Or I'll have your heart and liver out." He tilted me again.

I was dreadfully frightened, and so giddy that I clung to him with both hands, and said, "If you would kindly please to let me keep upright, sir, perhaps I shouldn't be 55 sick, and perhaps I could attend more."

He gave me a most tremendous dip and toll, so that the church jumped over its own weather-cock. Then, he held me by the arms in an upright position on the top of the stone, and went on in these fearful terms:

"You bring me, tomorrow morning early, that file and them wittles. You bring the lot 60 to me, at that old Battery over yonder. You do it, and you never dare to make a sign concerning your having seen such a person as me or any person sumever, and you shall be let to live . . ."

—Charles Dickens

Use the *Self-Evaluation Rubric* on p. 151 to help you assess your progress in writing the free response essays on prose.

# SUGGESTIONS FOR EXERCISE 1

You might have chosen to include the following points in your essay on the passage from *Great Expectations.* Consider them as you do your self-evaluation. Did you understand what the question was asking you? Strengthen your essay using points from this list.

## Background Information

- Mode: fiction; an excerpt from a novel
- Author: Charles Dickens, one of the Victorians' most popular writers; saw the novel as a means of creating social reform
- Title: means the expectation of inheriting money
- Subject: an initial meeting between a child and a very frightening man

## Point of View

- First person narrative style
- Immediacy and sense of reality; reader experiences Pip's upset and fright
- Dialogue establishes the social class of the characters; adds to the sense of Pip's experience

## Characterization

- The protagonist, Pip
- An apparent antagonist revealed in a local graveyard
- Conflict between the two since the "fearful man" threatens Pip with bodily injury and death
- Virtually all revealed through Dickens's precise dialogue

## Literary Devices and Figures of Speech

- Strong visual images developed with precise words
- Examples: Pip turned upside down and righted again; description of the fearful man

## Style

- Rapid narrative pace through short phrases and sentences of the dialogue
- Contrasts with the longer, more complex sentences of the explication
- Precise words and the vernacular move the plot along
- Examples: "ate the bread ravenously"; "dreadfully frightened"

## EXERCISE 2

*SUGGESTED TIME—40 MINUTES*

**Directions:** As a goal for his work, James Boswell stated: "to write, not his panegyrick, which must be all praise, but his Life; which, great and good as he was, must not be supposed to be entirely perfect . . . in every picture there should be shade and light." Read the following passage carefully. Write an essay discussing Boswell's success or failure in achieving his goal. Consider such literary elements as diction, point of view, and tone.

### From "Feelings" in *The Life of Samuel Johnson*

Line [Said Johnson:] "Pity is not natural to man. Children are always cruel. Savages are always cruel. Pity is acquired and improved by the cultivation of reason. We may have uneasy sensations from seeing a creature in distress, without pity; for we have not pity unless we wish to relieve them. When I am on my way to dine with a friend, and
5    finding it late, have bid the coachman make haste, if I happen to attend when he whips his horses, I may feel unpleasantly that the animals are put to pain, but I do not wish him to desist. No, sir, I wish him to drive on."

Johnson's love of little children, which he discovered upon all occasions, calling them "pretty dears," and giving them sweetmeats, was an undoubted proof of the real
10    humanity and gentleness of his disposition.

His uncommon kindness to his servants, and serious concern, not only for their comfort in this world, but their happiness in the next, was another unquestionable evidence of what all, who were intimately acquainted with him, knew to be true.

Nor would it be just, under this head, to omit the fondness which he showed for
15    animals which he had taken under his protection. I never shall forget the indulgence with which he treated Hodge, his cat; for whom he himself used to go out and buy oysters, lest the servants, having that trouble, should take a dislike to the poor creature. I am, unluckily, one of those who have an antipathy to a cat, so that I am uneasy when in the room with one; and I own I frequently suffered a good deal from
20    the presence of this same Hodge. I recollect him one day scrambling up Dr. Johnson's breast, apparently with much satisfaction, while my friend, smiling and half-whistling, rubbed down his back and pulled him by the tail; and when I observed he was a fine cat, saying, "Why, yes, sir, but I have had cats whom I liked better than this;" and then, as if perceiving Hodge to be out of countenance, adding, "but he is a very fine
25    cat, a very fine cat indeed."

This reminds me of the ludicrous account which he gave Mr. Langton of the despicable state of a young gentleman of good family. "Sir, when I heard of him last, he was running about town shooting cats." And then, in a sort of kindly reverie, he bethought himself of his own favorite cat, and said, "But Hodge shan't be shot; no, no, Hodge
30    shall not be shot."

—James Boswell

Use the *Self-Evaluation Rubric* on p. 151 to help you assess your progress in writing the free response essays on prose.

## SUGGESTIONS FOR EXERCISE 2

You might have chosen to include the following points in your essay on the passage from *The Life of Samuel Johnson*. Consider them as you perform your self-evaluation. Did you understand what the question was asking? Strengthen your essay using points from this list.

### Background Information

- Mode: nonfiction; excerpt from biography
- Author: James Boswell, mid- to late 1700s
- Title: a biography; one of the fullest records of a man's life ever written; character of Johnson revealed
- Subject: attitude toward animals, characterization of Johnson

### Point of View

- First person
- Author is narrator
- Personal knowledge and experience
- Accounts of personal dialogues

### Characterization

- Two characters: Johnson and Boswell
- Boswell: admiration of Johnson, respect, almost idolatry, conscientious record, frank
- Examples: allergy to cats, story of Langton
- Johnson: fondness for animals, kind feelings, humor, idiosyncratic
- Examples: getting oysters himself, thinking Hodge could understand

### Theme or Thesis

- Man is made of contradictory qualities. A man as great as Johnson has quirks and idiosyncrasies just as others do.
- Johnson is a man to be admired.

### Style

- Most biographers usually try to be objective; Boswell is not.
- Diction shows admiration: fondness, indulgence, kindly reverie
- Tone: admiration, respect, approval, amusement
- Sentences: direct quotations from conversation, varied, complex but clear
- Examples: "But Hodge shan't be shot; no, no, Hodge shall not be shot"
- Use of specific details: pulling Hodge's tail, half-whistling
- Organization: anecdotal

## EXERCISE 3

*SUGGESTED TIME—40 MINUTES*

**Directions:** A philosopher, poet, orator, and writer, Ralph Waldo Emerson became the most influential member of the Transcendentalists, a group of Massachusetts intellectuals. Transcendental philosophy advocates responsible individualism. Read the following passage carefully. Discuss how the author's argument espouses Transcendentalist ideas. Consider such literary elements as literary devices, tone, and style.

### From *Self-Reliance*

Line    There is a time in every man's education when he arrives at the conviction that envy
is ignorance; that imitation is suicide; that he must take himself for better, for worse,
as his portion; that though the wide universe is full of good, no kernel of nourishing
corn can come to him but through his toil bestowed on that plot of ground which is

5    given to him to till. The power which resides in him is new in nature, and none but he
knows what that is which he can do, nor does he know until he has tried. Not for
nothing one face, one character, one fact makes much impression on him, and another
none. This sculpture in the memory is not without preestablished harmony. The eye
was placed where one ray should fall, that it might testify of that particular ray. We

10    but half express ourselves, and are ashamed of that divine idea which each of us
represents. It may be safely trusted as proportionate and of good issue, so it be
faithfully imparted, but God will not have his work made manifest by cowards. A man
is relieved and gay when he has put his heart into his work and done his best; but
what he has said or done otherwise, shall give him no peace. It is a deliverance which

15    does not deliver. In the attempt his genius deserts him; no muse befriends; no inven-
tion, no hope.

    Trust thyself: every heart vibrates to that iron string. Accept the place the divine
providence has found for you; the society of your contemporaries, the connection of
events. Great men have always done so and confided themselves childlike to the

20    genius of the age, betraying their perception that the absolutely trustworthy was
stirring at their heart, working through their hands, predominating in all their being.
And we are now men, and must accept in the highest mind the same transcendent
destiny; and not minors and invalids in a protected corner, but guides, redeemers, and
benefactors, obeying the Almighty effort and advancing on Chaos and the Dark. . . .

25    Society everywhere is in conspiracy against the manhood of every one of its members. Society is a joint-stock company in which the members agree for the better
securing of his bread to each shareholder, to surrender the liberty and culture of the
eater. The virtue in most request is conformity. Self-reliance is its aversion. It loves
not realities and creators, but names and customs.

30    Whoso would be a man must be a nonconformist. He who would gather immortal
palms must not be hindered by the name of goodness, but must explore if it be
goodness. Nothing is at last sacred but the integrity of our own mind. Absolve you to
yourself, and you shall have the suffrage of the world. . . .

    A foolish consistency is the hobgoblin of little minds, adored by little statesmen and

35    philosophers and divines. With consistency a great soul has simply nothing to do. He
may as well concern himself with his shadow on the wall. Speak what you think now

in hard words and tomorrow speak what tomorrow thinks in hard words again, though it contradict everything you said today. "Ah, so you shall be sure to be misunderstood?"—Is it so bad, then, to be misunderstood? Pythagoras was misunderstood,
40　and Socrates, and Jesus, and Luther, and Copernicus, and Galileo, and Newton, and every pure and wise spirit that ever took flesh. To be great is to be misunderstood. . . .

　　　　　　　　　　　　　　　　　　　　　　—Ralph Waldo Emerson

Use the *Self-Evaluation Rubric* on p. 151 to help you assess your progress in writing the free response essays on prose.

exercises

## SUGGESTIONS FOR EXERCISE 3

You might have chosen to include the following points in your essay on the passage from *Self-Reliance*. Consider them as you do your self-evaluation. Did you understand what the question was asking? Strengthen your essay using points from this list.

### Basic Information

- Mode: nonfiction, excerpt from a persuasive essay
- Author: Emerson, nineteenth-century Transcendentalist
- Title: suggests people should depend on themselves
- Subject: Emerson's philosophy of individualism

### Point of View

- First person
- Reader addressed directly
- Focuses reader's attention
- Adds intimacy

### Central Conflict and Point of Argument

- Individual versus society's conventions
- Society conspires against self-reliance
- Examples: paragraph 3, "joint-stock company," "bread," "liberty and culture of the eater"

### Literary Devices and Figures of Speech

- Use of analogy: kernel of corn; effort needed to produce corn similar to the effort people must make to reach their potential
- Refers to individuals who made important contributions in fields of mathematics, philosophy, religion, and science
- Pythagoras, Socrates, Jesus, Martin Luther, Copernicus, Newton
- Metaphor: society a stock company, consistency a hobgoblin, immortal palms
- Imagery: "Hearts vibrate to that iron string"

### Themes and Theses

- Responsible individualism
- Faith in human potential
- Resistance to pressure of society
- Obey internal dictates
- Conveyed directly; stated clearly throughout essay

## Style

- Positive denotation for words proposing self-reliance; negative denotation for conformity

- Examples: "nourishing," "harmony," "trust;" "foolish"

- Tone: Heartfelt emotion yet logical, erudite

- Developed point by point; order of importance

- Rhetorical question in concluding paragraph

- Varied sentence structure

## EXERCISE 4

*SUGGESTED TIME—40 MINUTES*

**Directions:** The following selection is from *The Pilgrim's Progress from This World to That Which Is To Come,* the most widely read work produced during the Puritan Age. Read the passage carefully. In an essay, discuss how the author delivers his message. Consider such literary elements as literary type, plot, characters, and setting.

### From "Vanity Fair" in *The Pilgrim's Progress*

Line  [B]ut that which did not a little amuse the merchandisers was that these pilgrims set very light by their wares; they cared not so much as to look upon them; and if they called upon them to buy, they would put their fingers in their ears, and cry, "Turn away mine eyes from beholding vanity," and look upwards, signifying that their trade
5    and traffic was in heaven (Psalms 129:37; Philippians 3:19,20).

One chanced mockingly beholding the carriages of the men, to say unto them "What will ye buy?" But they, looking gravely upon him, said, "We buy the truth" (Proverbs 23:23). At that there was an occasion taken to despise the men the more; some mocking, some taunting, some speaking reproachfully, and some calling upon others to
10   smite them. At last things came to a hubbub and great stir in the fair, insomuch that all order was confounded. Now was word presently brought to the great one of the fair, who quickly came down, and deputed some of his most trusty friends to take these men into examination, about whom the fair was almost overturned. So the men were brought to examination, and they sat upon them, asked them whence they came,
15   whither they went, and what they did there, in such an unusual garb? The men told them that they were pilgrims and strangers in the world, and that they were going to their own country, which was the Heavenly Jerusalem (Hebrews 11:13–16); and that they had given no occasion to the men of the town, nor yet to the merchandisers, thus to abuse them, and to let them on their journey, except it was for that, when one
20   asked them what they would buy, they said they would buy the truth. But they that were appointed to examine them did not believe them to be any other than bedlams and mad, or else such as came to put all things into a confusion in the fair. Therefore they took them and beat them, and besmeared them with dirt, and then put them into the cage, that they might be made a spectacle to all the men of the fair.

—John Bunyan

Use the *Self-Evaluation Rubric* on p. 151 to help you assess your progress in writing the free response essays on prose.

# SUGGESTIONS FOR EXERCISE 4

You might have chosen to include the following points in your essay on the passage from *The Pilgrim's Progress*. Consider them as you do your self-evaluation. Did you understand what the question was asking? Strengthen your essay using points from this list.

## Mode of Discourse

- Fiction; an allegory
- Author: John Bunyan, a nonconformist preacher and religious prisoner in the seventeenth century
- Title: indicative of religious literature; subtitle suggests a sin

## Setting

- At a fair in a land that does not follow Christian teachings; avaricious; land of Vanity from the title
- Everything corrupt or with the potential to corrupt at the fair
- Vivid and concrete details
- Examples: "hubbub," mocking and taunting
- Symbolize worldly delights that can corrupt religious life

## Central Conflict

- Human beings versus human beings
- Christian pilgrims versus corrupt worldly individuals

## Plot or Course of Events

- Pilgrims must go through fair; create stir because of their clothing, speech, and lack of interest in merchandise
- Inciting incident: pilgrims' arrival at fair
- Climax: "only buy the truth"
- Resolution: pilgrims caged, but holding fast to faith
- Suspense built through increasingly hostile acts of townspeople

## Characterization

- Protagonist: the pilgrims
- Conflict grows between protagonists and antagonists, the townspeople
- Character revealed through vivid details, action, and dialogue

## Literary Devices and Figures of Speech

- Entire story an allegory
- Experience at fair an allusion to the temptations of Jesus in wilderness
- Town across road: pilgrims must be tested to prove resolve
- Final sentences alluding to humiliation of Jesus
- The fair is a symbol of everything that can corrupt virtue.

## Theme or Thesis

- Allegory of Christian fortitude and faith
- Clear, unambiguous

## SELF-EVALUATION RUBRIC FOR THE ADVANCED PLACEMENT ESSAYS

| | 8–9 | 6–7 | 5 | 3–4 | 1–2 | 0 |
|---|---|---|---|---|---|---|
| **Overall Impression** | Demonstrates excellent control of the literature and outstanding writing competence; thorough and effective; incisive | Demonstrates good control of the literature and good writing competence; less thorough and incisive than the highest papers | Reveals simplistic thinking and/or immature writing; adequate skills | Incomplete thinking; fails to respond adequately to part or parts of the question; may paraphrase rather than analyze | Unacceptably brief; fails to respond to the question; little clarity | Lacking skill and competence |
| **Understanding of the Text** | Excellent understanding of the text; exhibits perception and clarity; original or unique approach; includes apt and specific references | Good understanding of the text; exhibits perception and clarity; includes specific references | Superficial understanding of the text; elements of literature vague, mechanical, overgeneralized | Misreadings and lack of persuasive evidence from the text; meager and unconvincing treatment of literary elements | Serious misreadings and little supporting evidence from the text; erroneous treatment of literary elements | A response with no more than a reference to the literature; blank response, or one completely off the topic |
| **Organization and Development** | Meticulously organized and thoroughly developed; coherent and unified | Well-organized and developed; coherent and unified | Reasonably organized and developed; mostly coherent and unified | Somewhat organized and developed; some incoherence and lack of unity | Little or no organization and development; incoherent and void of unity | No apparent organization or development; incoherent |
| **Use of Sentences** | Effectively varied and engaging; virtually error free | Varied and interesting; a few errors | Adequately varied; some errors | Somewhat varied and marginally interesting; one or more major errors | Little or no variation; dull and uninteresting; some major errors | Numerous major errors |
| **Word Choice** | Interesting and effective; virtually error free | Generally interesting and effective; a few errors | Occasionally interesting and effective; several errors | Somewhat dull and ordinary; some errors in diction | Mostly dull and conventional; numerous errors | Numerous major errors; extremely immature |
| **Grammar and Usage** | Virtually error free | Occasional minor errors | Several minor errors | Some major errors | Severely flawed; frequent major errors | Extremely flawed |

Rate yourself in each of the categories. Choose the description that most accurately reflects your performance, and enter the numbers on the lines below. Be as honest as possible so you will know what areas need work. Then calculate the average of the six numbers to determine your final score. It is difficult to score yourself objectively, so you may wish to ask a respected friend or teacher to assess your writing for a more accurate reflection of its strengths and weaknesses. On the AP test itself, a reader will rate your essay on a scale of 0 to 9, with 9 being the highest.

Rate each category from 9 (high) to 0 (low).

## Exercise 1

**SELF-EVALUATION**

**Overall Impression** _____
**Understanding of the Text** _____
**Organization and Development** _____
**Use of Sentences** _____
**Word Choice (Diction)** _____
**Grammar and Usage** _____

**TOTAL** _____
Divide by 6 for final score _____

**OBJECTIVE EVALUATION**

**Overall Impression** _____
**Understanding of the Text** _____
**Organization and Development** _____
**Use of Sentences** _____
**Word Choice (Diction)** _____
**Grammar and Usage** _____

**TOTAL** _____
Divide by 6 for final score _____

## Exercise 2

**SELF-EVALUATION**

**Overall Impression** _____
**Understanding of the Text** _____
**Organization and Development** _____
**Use of Sentences** _____
**Word Choice (Diction)** _____
**Grammar and Usage** _____

**TOTAL** _____
Divide by 6 for final score _____

**OBJECTIVE EVALUATION**

**Overall Impression** _____
**Understanding of the Text** _____
**Organization and Development** _____
**Use of Sentences** _____
**Word Choice (Diction)** _____
**Grammar and Usage** _____

**TOTAL** _____
Divide by 6 for final score _____

## Exercise 3

**SELF-EVALUATION**

**Overall Impression** _____
**Understanding of the Text** _____
**Organization and Development** _____
**Use of Sentences** _____
**Word Choice (Diction)** _____
**Grammar and Usage** _____

**TOTAL** _____
Divide by 6 for final score _____

**OBJECTIVE EVALUATION**

**Overall Impression** _____
**Understanding of the Text** _____
**Organization and Development** _____
**Use of Sentences** _____
**Word Choice (Diction)** _____
**Grammar and Usage** _____

**TOTAL** _____
Divide by 6 for final score _____

## Exercise 4

| SELF-EVALUATION | | OBJECTIVE EVALUATION | |
|---|---|---|---|
| **Overall Impression** | _____ | **Overall Impression** | _____ |
| **Understanding of the Text** | _____ | **Understanding of the Text** | _____ |
| **Organization and Development** | _____ | **Organization and Development** | _____ |
| **Use of Sentences** | _____ | **Use of Sentences** | _____ |
| **Word Choice (Diction)** | _____ | **Word Choice (Diction)** | _____ |
| **Grammar and Usage** | _____ | **Grammar and Usage** | _____ |
| **TOTAL** | _____ | **TOTAL** | _____ |
| Divide by 6 for final score | _____ | Divide by 6 for final score | _____ |

## SUMMING IT UP

- The question for the prose essay will require you to analyze the passage, either directly or indirectly, for certain traits.

- When you're analyzing prose, always begin with the theme or meaning of the passage and how the writer uses certain elements or the whole selection to help you understand the message.

- Regardless of what the question is asking, you need to determine the theme or meaning of the piece first.

- Periodically reread your introductory paragraph to be sure you stay on track to prove your thesis.

- Write an effective concluding paragraph. Restate your thesis and summarize how your essay supports it. Include your insights, reactions, and emotions.

# About the Free Response Essay on Poetry

## OVERVIEW

- **Reading the material**

- **Writing the essay about a poetry selection**

- **Analyzing poetry**

- **Practicing**

- **Sample essay on poetry**

- **Suggestions for sample essay on poetry**

- **Self-evaluation rubric for the Advanced Placement essays**

- **Summing it up**

You may feel that poetry is too difficult to understand and that you will never be able to write a good essay about it. One way to reduce your anxiety is to recognize that your response to a poem is no more a matter of right or wrong, correct or incorrect, than your reaction to a popular song. A systematic approach to analyzing and writing about poetry will help you to do well on your essays. Chapter 7 offers you a plan of attack.

A poet, more than any other writer, considers each word very carefully. To elicit the desired response from you, the reader, each word must be exactly right. The resulting poem condenses a complex experience into a short, simple work of literature. When reading a poem, you must be equally careful to identify the tools the poet uses and analyze the ways in which they are used to achieve the total effect.

## chapter 7

## READING THE MATERIAL

As obvious as it sounds, before you begin writing the poetry essay you need to read the question and the poetry. Writing about a poem requires that you understand it. You will have to read the selection(s) more than once. The strategy suggested below is similar to, but not exactly the same as, the strategy for reading the prose that we described in Chapter 6.

- First, read the question and the poetry.

- Second, identify what the question is asking you to do. A question may require you to interpret the poetry, synthesize information, compare elements of the poem or poems, and/or evaluate an aspect of the poem. Are you being asked to compare? Compare what? Are you being asked to explain? Explain what? Underline the important points or key words in the question.

- Restate the question to yourself—paraphrase it—so you know what you are being asked to write about.

Now that you know what you are to write about, read the poetry.

- Read the poem four times.

- The first two times you read the poem, read it sentence by sentence, not line by line. In other words, let the punctuation guide you, not the structure.

- The first time you read the poem, skim it. You are looking for the "layout" of the poem.

- The second time you read the poem, take more time and care. Now deal with obscure language and confusing sentences.

- Be aware of language and diction, poetic devices, style, the writer's intentions and purpose, the selection's impact, and special techniques.

- For the third reading, read the poem aloud in your mind to hear the poem's "music." Evaluate the contribution of the rhythm, rhyme, and sound.

- During your last read, paraphrase the poem. Your paraphrase should reflect what the poem states directly and what it implies.

- As you read, highlight or underline the sentences that strike you as important and that you might want to quote in your essay. Jot down notes. However, do not spend a great deal of time doing this.

**NOTE**

Check "A Quick Review of Literary Terms," p. 253, if you feel you need help identifying literary terms.

# WRITING THE ESSAY ABOUT A POETRY SELECTION

In essence, your essay about poetry will evaluate the effectiveness with which the poet uses the elements of poetry. You will show your understanding of the poem by explaining, interpreting, and even judging it. Consider the organizational pattern suggested here to clarify the parts of your literary essay.

## Introduction

Your introduction should include the title of the poem and the name of the poet as well as the form and genre of the poem. Your introduction should present any background information necessary for understanding your thesis. Most important, the introduction should state clearly the main point you will make. You may wish to list the ideas that you will use to support your thesis. Placing your thesis statement toward the end of your introductory paragraph allows you the possibility of a more interesting opening.

## Body of Your Essay

The body of your essay will explore each of the subtopics of the main point, using one or more paragraphs per subtopic. Use information, including quotations or line citations, from the poetry to support your subtopics. Order your paragraphs and your supporting facts logically. Organizing by order of importance works well for literary essays. Be sure to present material to support your thesis and subtopics effectively and adequately.

## Conclusion

Your conclusion should restate the main point you made in the introduction and summarize your argument. The ending paragraph should explain how your essay supports your thesis. The conclusion should also pull the essay together with a closing remark so the reader is not left wondering why you wrote the essay.

Following this structure will make writing the poetry essay easier by giving you a direction. However, you may be thinking, "Where do I get those subtopics, and how can I understand a poem well enough to have an opinion?" Remember that poems are written concisely and for emotional impact. The chart *Analyzing Poetry* on pp. 158–159 suggests a strategy to help you understand poetry, analyze literary elements, and develop your essay points. Use the questions from the chart to practice writing answers to the exercises about poetry you will find in this chapter. Try it for the essays you have to write in school about poetry, and see how much easier it is to organize and develop your ideas.

**ALERT!**
Be sure to include your personal response to the work, supported by evidence from the poem. That shows the reader that you have read the poem thoughtfully.

# ANALYZING POETRY

### Author
1. Who is the author?
2. What do you know about the writer and/or the time period in which the poem was written?

### Title
1. What does the title tell you?
2. What does the title suggest about the poem?

### Genre
1. Is the poem a lyric, such as an ode, elegy, or sonnet?
   - Does it use musical language to express the emotions of the speaker?
   - Who is the speaker?
   - What audience is being addressed?
   - What is the occasion or situation?
2. Is it a narrative poem—that is, does it tell a story?
   - What plot, characters, settings, and point of view does the story have?
3. Is it a dramatic poem?
   - Is it a monologue or dialogue, or does it use some other dramatic technique?
   - What point of view, characters, setting, and situation does the dramatic work present?

### Form
1. Does the poem have a traditional form or pattern? If so, what is it?
2. What is the stanza form?
3. How many lines does each stanza have? Do all the stanzas have the same number of lines?
4. What are the rhyme scheme and the metrical pattern?
5. If the stanzas are written in a standard form, what is it?
6. Does the poem have a special shape or structure that enhances its meaning?

### Subject
1. What is the subject of the poem?
2. What is this poem about?

### Theme or Thesis
1. What is the theme or central idea of the poem?
2. How is the message conveyed?

### Sensory Images
1. What details appeal to your sense of sight?
2. What details appeal to your sense of hearing?
3. What details appeal to your sense of smell?
4. What details appeal to your sense of taste?
5. What details appeal to your sense of touch?
6. What is the purpose of these sensory images?

**Figurative Language**
1.  Are there any metaphors?
2.  Are there similes?
3.  Are there personifications?
4.  Are there other less common figures of speech? What are they?
5.  What purpose do the figures of speech serve?
6.  Is there symbolism?
7.  What do the symbols stand for?
8.  What is the purpose of the symbolism?
9.  Are there allusions?
10. Is the poem allegorical?

**Sound Devices**
1.  Does the writer make use of alliteration?
2.  Does the writer include assonance or consonance?
3.  Does the poet use onomatopoeia?
4.  Does the poet use any type of rhyme, such as end rhyme, interior rhyme, masculine rhyme, or feminine rhyme? What is it?
5.  Are there any repetitions in words, lines, or stanzas?
6.  Does the poem contain euphony, cacophony, parallel structure, or repetition?
7.  What is the meter? What type and number of metrical feet are in a line?
8.  How does the poem use rhythm?
9.  What purpose do these sound effects serve?

**Opposition**
1.  Are there any contrasts between people or personalities?
2.  Are any places contrasted?
3.  Are other elements contrasted?
4.  What is the effect of the contrast?

**Style**
1.  What is the mood or emotional structure?
2.  Does the emotional structure remain constant or does it change?
3.  What is the tone?
4.  Does the tone stay the same or change?
5.  Does the poet use any special techniques, such as unusual punctuation, capitalization, or spacing?
6.  How does the poet use words? Does the poet use words in unusual ways?
7.  How do connotations of words create figurative or extended meaning?

**NOTE:** Use these questions as you practice planning and writing the essay questions on poetry in this chapter. Take the answers to these questions into account as you develop your theses. Pay particular attention to how the various literary techniques contribute to the impact of the poem. Include your own reactions and feelings in your essays, but support them with specifics from the poem. By using these questions throughout this chapter, you will become so familiar with them that you will automatically turn to them to analyze any poetry you read.

## PRACTICING

The question and selection on p. 161 is very similar to those that you will find on the actual AP examination. Apply the suggestions and strategies as you read and write about the poem "My Heart's in the Highlands" by Robert Burns. Then check your essay by reading the suggested points of discussion that follow. Evaluate yourself by using the *Self-Evaluation Rubric* and scoring tool on pp. 176–178.

# SAMPLE ESSAY ON POETRY

*SUGGESTED TIME—40 MINUTES*

**Directions:** Robert Burns, who wrote the following poem, is considered by some to be Scotland's greatest poet. Although he came from a poor background, he had books available to him. Many of his poems were meant to be sung even though he was tone-deaf. Read the poem carefully, then write an essay discussing how Burns elicits an emotional response from the reader or listener. Consider such elements as speaker, form, imagery, and musicality.

**NOTE**
When you practice, limit yourself to 40 minutes—5 minutes to read and plan and 35 minutes to write—so you will become comfortable with writing on demand.

## My Heart's in the Highlands

Line
> My heart's in the Highlands, my heart is not here,
> My heart's in the Highlands a-chasing the deer,
> A-chasing the wild deer and following the roe–
> My heart's in the Highlands, wherever I go!

5
> Farewell to the Highlands, farewell to the North,
> The birthplace of valor, the country of worth!
> Wherever I wander, wherever I rove,
> The hills of the Highlands forever I love.

> Farewell to the mountains high cover'd with snow,
10
> Farewell to the straths* and green valleys below,
> Farewell to the forests and wild-hanging woods,
> Farewell to the torrents and loud-pouring floods!

> My heart's in the Highlands, my heart is not here,
> My heart's in the Highlands a-chasing the deer,
15
> A-chasing the wild deer and following the roe–
> My heart's in the Highlands, wherever I go!

> —Robert Burns

Before you turn the page and read our suggestions for an essay on this poem, score your essay using the *Self-Evaluation Rubric* on p. 176.

* Wide river valleys

# SUGGESTIONS FOR SAMPLE ESSAY ON POETRY

The following are points you might have chosen to include in your essay on the poem "My Heart's in the Highlands." Consider them as you perform your self-evaluation. You will notice that we discuss elements of poetry that are not called for in the essay question. However, by identifying the author, naming the type of poem, and writing the title, you have a place to begin and you give yourself an opportunity to include information to increase your score.

## Author

Robert Burns, perhaps the greatest poet Scotland ever produced, is known for writing songs about love, friendship, and his country. He often used Scottish dialect in his writing, and his most well known song is "Auld Lang Syne."

Of course, you cannot find this information in the poem. However, you may know much of this from your study of literature. Most probably you have heard someone sing "Auld Lang Syne" on New Year's Eve. Just remembering that Burns wrote songs should help you in analyzing the poem.

## Title

The title of the poem tells you quite a bit. The poet identifies a place that is important to him, and the word *heart* indicates a strong emotional attachment to the Highlands.

## Genre, Speaker, and Audience

The poem is a lyric, in fact, a song, and the musical language expresses the emotions of the speaker. In this poem, you can assume that the speaker and the poet are the same. The speaker has left the Highlands and is living elsewhere. The audience includes all people who hear the song.

## Form

Burns wrote four-line stanzas, called quatrains, with a very simple *aabbccdd* rhyme scheme. The metrical pattern includes an opening iambus followed by two dactyl feet and ends with an accented syllable. Since the dactyl feet prevail, the poem is written in dactylic tetrameter. Poets often vary the meter and feet slightly to avoid a work that sounds like a metronome.

It is all well and good to identify rhyme and meter, but you need to relate it to the question. These elements add to the musicality of the poem and increase the emotional tone. If you consistently related the poetic elements to the question, you wrote to the point.

## Theme or Thesis

"My Heart's in the Highlands" shows love for a place, the Highlands of Scotland. Since love is certainly an emotion, this is a good point to mention. Also, remember that you should present a writer's main point even if the question does not ask about it directly. You want to show that you understand the meaning of what you read.

## Sensory Images

This poem has strong visual elements. Burns writes of wild deer, green valleys, and "wild-hanging woods." In addition, there is an aural image in the line "Farewell to the torrents and loud-pouring floods."

These images convey the poet's love for the region, a love that the audience recognizes. Thus, the sensory images elicit an emotional response.

## Sound Devices

Burns uses repetition to great effect. Not only does he repeat the first stanza as the last, he also repeats words, phrases, and rhymes. By using repetition, the poet makes "My Heart's in the Highlands" sound like a song. Burns also uses the devices to emphasize his ideas. The word *Highlands* is repeated eight times, and *Farewell* is repeated six times. The most repeated phrase, "My Heart's in the Highlands," contains the most important idea in the poem. Repetition creates an emotional response because the reader must acknowledge the importance of the poet's attachment to place. Similarly, the poet uses parallelism, the repetition of the same grammatical form or structure, to convey his message and elicit an emotional response. Parallelism adds to the poem's rhythm. All these repetitions add to the feeling of homesickness and nostalgia in the poem. Many readers will relate to these emotions.

While this poem seems simple, the use of sound devices is most effective. The song-like quality makes the main idea of love of place accessible.

## Opposition

The opposition in this poem is between the Highlands and "here." While you do not know what kind of place "here" is, you imagine that it is quite the opposite of the Highlands.

Why is this relevant to the question? This establishes the sense of sadness and nostalgia, the sense of feeling out of place that most people have felt at some time. Thus, Burns creates impact.

**TIP**

Even if you are not asked directly about the poem's meaning, include it in your essay and relate it to the question.

**TIP**

Don't just identify and give examples of the literary devices you find in a poem. Explain how each adds to the poem's impact.

**NOTE**

You can use the concept of opposition when writing about prose works, too.

## Your Style

To write effectively about poetry, you need to support your points with quotes from the poem. You can also cite lines. Add interest to the development of your thesis through word choice and varying sentence structure.

Some of the things we said about the concluding paragraph in an essay about prose also work for poetry. A simple summary may not be flashy, but if it clearly restates your thesis and the points that support it, it will help the reader see where you have been and why. A relevant quotation from the poem or from another related poem or from a critical work can be a clever way to end your essay, but don't misquote.

**NOTE**

See "Practice Plan for Studying for the AP English Literature & Composition Test," p. 17.

Once you have evaluated your essay with the *Self-Evaluation Rubric* on p. 176 and reviewed our points, you may choose to revise your essay using the points suggested here. However, do not spend a great deal of time trying to make it perfect. Revise it simply to see how adding some of our points may make it stronger. Whether you revise or not, ask a classmate or your teacher to evaluate your essay using the *Self-Evaluation Rubric* on p. 176. How does your own evaluation compare with a more objective view? Keep the differences in mind as you write and score more free response essays on poetry.

Now that you have a sense of the logic involved in acing the poetry essay question of Section II, try *Exercise 1* and *Exercise 2*. Study the points for evaluation and use the *Self-Evaluation Rubric*. If you are still unsure about writing essays on poetry, continue with *Exercise 3* and *Exercise 4*.

## EXERCISE 1

*SUGGESTED TIME–40 MINUTES*

**Directions:** Alfred, Lord Tennyson, wrote this poem after returning from one of his favorite places, Ireland. While he was there, he had been impressed with the sounds of bugles from boatmen. Imagery is often a key element in poetry. Read the following poem carefully. Write an essay discussing the images that Tennyson creates in this poem. Explain the literary methods he uses to paint these images. Consider such elements as figurative language, sensory images, sound devices, and opposition.

### The Splendor Falls

Line   The splendor falls on castle walls
      And snowy summits old in story:
  The long light shakes across the lakes,
      And the wild cataract leaps in glory.
5   Blow, bugle, blow, set the wild echoes flying,
  Blow, bugle; answer, echoes, dying, dying, dying.

     O hark, O hear! how thin and clear,
      And thinner, clearer, farther going!
     O sweet and far from cliff and scar
10      The horns of Elfland faintly blowing!
  Blow, let us hear the purple glens replying:
  Blow, bugle; answer, echoes, dying, dying, dying

     O love, they die in yon rich sky,
      They faint on hill or field or river:
15      Our echoes roll from soul to soul,
      And grow for ever and for ever.
  Blow, bugle, blow, set the wild echoes flying,
  And answer, echoes, answer, dying, dying, dying

         —Alfred, Lord Tennyson

Use the *Self-Evaluation Rubric* on p. 176 to help you assess your progress in writing the free response essays on poetry.

## SUGGESTIONS FOR EXERCISE 1

You might have chosen to include the following points in your essay on the passage from "The Splendor Falls." Consider them as you do your self-evaluation. Strengthen your essay using points from this list.

### Background Information

- Author: Tennyson impressed by sounds of the boatmen in Ireland, a sound he uses in this poem
- Subject: portrait of an image that he has seen and heard

### Theme

- No deep meaning to the poem; expression of love by Tennyson for a special place of beauty

### Sensory Images

- Sound: appeals mostly to the sense of hearing; blowing of the bugles and horns, principal sensory vehicle
- Sight: secondary appeal to sight; image of the castle, cataract, rich sky

### Sound Devices

- Alliteration: One example is "long, light . . . lakes."
- Repetition: "dying, dying, dying"; an interesting twist because it suggests diminishing sound as an echo would fade away
- Internal rhyme: used to good advantage in several places, for example, "shakes . . . lakes"

### Opposition

- Unusual opposition with the permanence of elements such as a castle contrasted with the dying echoes

### Style

- Use of words to convey the sound and feel of the subject of his poem; reader "moves in" and hears the boatmen's horns while taking in a view of the water
- Setting: developed almost like a landscape painting; castle, water, hills, and fields all for the reader to see

## EXERCISE 2

*SUGGESTED TIME—40 MINUTES*

**Directions:** William Shakespeare was such a master of the sonnet form that the terms "Shakespearean sonnet" and "English sonnet" are interchangeable. Read the following poem carefully. Write an essay discussing how the poet uses the sonnet form to convey his love. Consider such elements as speaker, imagery, and poetic devices.

### Sonnet 18

Line  Shall I compare thee to a summer's day?
Thou art more lovely and more temperate:
Rough winds do shake the darling buds of May,
And summer's lease hath all too short a date:
5  Sometime too hot the eye of heaven shines,
And often is his gold complexion dimm'd;
And every fair from fair sometime declines,
By chance or nature's changing course untrimm'd;
But thy eternal summer shall not fade,
10  Nor lose possession of that fair thou owest;
Nor shall Death brag thou wander'st in his shade,
When in eternal lines to time thou growest:
      So long as men can breathe, or eyes can see
      So long lives this, and this gives life to thee.

—William Shakespeare

Use the *Self-Evaluation Rubric* on p. 176 to help you assess your progress in writing the free response essays on poetry.

## SUGGESTIONS FOR EXERCISE 2

You might have chosen to include the following points in your essay on Sonnet 18. Consider them as you do your self-evaluation. Strengthen your essay using points from this list.

### Background Information

- Author: William Shakespeare; Elizabethan period poet and playwright
- Genre: sonnet

### Thesis

- The beloved is nature's eternal summer; the lover's beauty will never fade.
- The sonnet ensures immortality.

### Form

- Speaker: the person who loves the person addressed
- Audience: the beloved, the person addressed
- 14 lines; 3 quatrains, ending couplet; traditional Shakespearean/English sonnet form
  - Each quatrain introduces a new premise or aspect to the comparison between a summer's day and the speaker's beloved.
  - The couplet departs from the comparison to comment on the beloved's immortalization through the sonnet.
  - All are characteristic features of English/Shakespearean sonnets.
- Rhyme scheme: *abab cdcd efefgg*
- Iambic pentameter

### Sensory Images

- Sight: much of the poem, description of sun
- Hearing: "Rough winds do shake the darling buds of May"
- Purpose: to expand on the comparison of summer's day and the beloved

### Figurative Language

- Extended metaphor/conceit: loved one fares better than a summer's day; more lovely, more temperate
- Petrarchan conceits, subject of poem compared to some startling object, often in Elizabethan love poems: summer's day and beloved
- Personification: sun has "gold complexion," death "brags"

### Sound Devices

- Some slight alliteration—chance and changing
- Repetition and parallel structure in couplet: adds emphasis to idea of immortality through the sonnet

# EXERCISE 3

*SUGGESTED TIME—40 MINUTES*

**Directions:** Read the following poem carefully. Write an essay that discusses the allusion to spring and Jesus Christ. Consider such literary elements as rhythm, imagery, form, theme, and tone.

## Spring

Line   Nothing is so beautiful as spring—
      When weeds, in wheels, shoot long and lovely and lush;
      Thrush's eggs look little low heavens, and thrush
  Through the echoing timber does so rinse and wring
5   The ear, it strikes like lightnings to hear him sing;
      The glassy peartree leaves and blooms, they brush
      The descending blue; that blue is all in a rush
  With richness; the racing lambs too have fair their fling.

  What is all this juice and all this joy?
10      A strain of the earth's sweet being in the beginning
  In Eden garden.—Have, get, before it cloy,
      Before it cloud, Christ, lord, and sour with sinning,
  Innocent mind and Mayday in girl and boy,
      Most, O maid's child, thy choice and worthy the winning.

                            —Gerard Manley Hopkins

Use the *Self-Evaluation Rubric* on p. 176 to help you assess your progress in writing the free response essays on poetry.

*exercises*

## SUGGESTIONS FOR EXERCISE 3

You might have chosen to include the following points in your essay on the poem "Spring." Consider them as you perform your self-evaluation. Strengthen your essay by using points from this list.

### Background Information

- Author: Roman Catholic priest; English; religious background relates to theme; lived during the mid-nineteenth century
- Form: sonnet; rhyme scheme: *abbaabba cdcdcd*

### Theme

- Octave: develops the beauty of spring
- Sestet: introduces the author's religious thoughts
- Themes: developed from the combination of the octave and sestet:
  - Nature is innocent and reminds us of our innocence as children.
  - People must be shown religion, that is, Jesus Christ, as a way to keep from sinning.

### Sensory Images

- Octave: descriptions of the sights and sounds of spring
- Examples: thrush's eggs, song of the thrush, racing lambs, pear tree
- Impact: demonstrate beauty of spring

### Figurative Language

- Hopkins uses the term "maid's child" as an allusion to Christ.
- Spring: symbol of beginning of world, Eden

### Sound Devices

- Author noted for his rhythms
- Rising accent beginning in the second line
- Developed the "sprung rhythm" that he uses in this work
- Rhythm: culminates in emphasis on imperative verbs: "have," "get," and "cloy;" directed action commonplace in religious thought at the time

### Style

- Octave: an emotional appeal to natural beauty
- Sestet: statement of religious belief of the poet

## EXERCISE 4

*SUGGESTED TIME—40 MINUTES*

**Directions:** Often writers will address similar subjects, themes, or allusions. In many cases, they view them in the same way, but in others they may approach them quite differently. The following two poems, by William Blake and William Wordsworth, have "London" as their title. In a well-organized essay, contrast and compare these two poems. Consider such literary elements as theme, speaker, diction, imagery, form, and tone.

### London

Line    I wander thro' each charter'd street,
        Near where the charter'd Thames does flow,
        And mark in every face I meet
        Marks of weakness, marks of woe.

5       In every cry of every Man,
        In every Infant's cry of fear,
        In every voice; in every ban,
        The mind-forg'd manacles I hear.

        How the Chimney-sweeper's cry
10      Every black'ning Church appalls,
        And the hapless Soldier's sigh
        Runs in blood down Palace walls.

        But most thro' midnight streets I hear
        How the youthful Harlot's curse
15      Blasts the new born Infant's tear,
        And blights with plagues the Marriage hearse.

                                    —William Blake

**London, 1802**

Line    Milton! thou should'st be living at this hour:
        England hath need of thee: she is a fen
        Of stagnant waters: altar, sword, and pen,
        Fireside, the heroic wealth of hall and bower,
5       Have forfeited their ancient English dower
        Of inward happiness. We are selfish men:
        Oh! raise us up, return to us again;
        And give us manners, virtue, freedom, power.
        Thy soul was like a Star, and dwelt apart:
10      Thou hadst a voice whose sound was like the sea:
        Pure as the naked heavens, majestic, free,
        So didst thou travel on life's common way,
        In cheerful godliness; and yet thy heart
        The lowliest duties on herself did lay.

                                    —William Wordsworth

Use the *Self-Evaluation Rubric* on p. 176 to help you assess your progress in writing the free response essays on poetry.

## SUGGESTIONS FOR EXERCISE 4

You might have chosen to include the following points in your essay comparing the two poems about London. Consider them as you perform your self-evaluation. Strengthen your essay using points from this list.

### Background Information

- Authors: Blake and Wordsworth; both lived in London; Blake was born before Wordsworth.
- Title: both "London;" titles define both the setting and subject

### Genre

- Blake

  - Lyric; strongly emotional; horrified and appalled

  - Author is speaker.

  - Point of view: first person

  - Dramatic poem: speaker is walking through London making observations of its degradation; poem travels somewhere

- Wordsworth

  - Sonnet

  - Speaker: people of England

  - Point of view: first person plural, note the words "We are selfish men"

  - Intellectual approach, much less emotion

  - Dramatic poem: calls upon Milton to resurrect spiritual well-being in England to restore England; appeal to Milton to return to London, bring his life-giving force, return England to spiritual health

### Form

- Blake

  - Four stanzas of four lines: first stanza visualizes degradation; second hears degradation; third a combination; fourth the climax, life itself is poisoned

  - Rhyme scheme: *abab* repeated each stanza

  - Metric pattern: iambic tetrameter

  - Form encourages an emotional accessibility

answers exercises

- Wordsworth

    - Sonnet; not classically Shakespearean in format

    - Rhyme scheme, *abbaabba;* for octave; *abbcac* for sestet

    - Metric pattern: iambic pentameter

    - Form more formal; complements intellectual tone

## Theme or Thesis

- Both authors are addressing the spiritual and physical deterioration of London.

- Blake: city corrupted

- Wordsworth: city a marsh full of stagnant water

## Sensory Images

- Blake

    - Broad appeals to the reader's senses. Sight: "And mark in every face I meet,/Marks of weakness . . . woe", "blood." Sound: cries of men, infants, and chimney sweeps, hears a harlot and manacles

    - The sensory images show the deterioration of the city and the despair of the people.

- Wordsworth

    - Limited appeal to the reader's senses; appeal to intellect

## Figurative Language

- Blake

    - Uses less than Wordsworth

    - Symbolism: "Man," "Infant," "chimney sweep," "Harlot"

- Wordsworth

    - Personification: England is personified as an individual to be helped by Milton.

    - Metaphor: England compared to "stagnant water." Milton compared to a star, the sea, and other elements in the sestet.

    - Simile: soul like star, voice sounds like sea, pure as the naked heavens

    - Adds majesty to Milton

## Sound Devices

- Blake

  - Repetition in the first stanza with "charter'd" and "mark." Gives a sense of urgency. Elsewhere, the word *cry* serves to emphasize the state of mind of the people.

- Wordsworth

  - Assonance: line 3 is an *a* sound

  - Minor alliteration: "soul like a Star"

## Style

- Blake

  - Simpler, more dramatic; appeals to the emotions

- Wordsworth

  - Appeals more to the intellect. Wordsworth uses people's feelings for Milton to inject some amount of emotional response. Blake plays on words; "chartered," "mark;" takes the reader to London

  - Leaves the reader on the outside describing the deterioration, almost as a third party

## SELF-EVALUATION RUBRIC FOR THE ADVANCED PLACEMENT ESSAYS

| | 8–9 | 6–7 | 5 | 3–4 | 1–2 | 0 |
|---|---|---|---|---|---|---|
| **Overall Impression** | Demonstrates excellent control of the literature and outstanding writing competence; thorough and effective; incisive | Demonstrates good control of the literature and good writing competence; less thorough and incisive than the highest papers | Reveals simplistic thinking and/or immature writing; adequate skills | Incomplete thinking; fails to respond adequately to part or parts of the question; may paraphrase rather than analyze | Unacceptably brief; fails to respond to the question; little clarity | Lacking skill and competence |
| **Understanding of the Text** | Excellent understanding of the text; exhibits perception and clarity; original or unique approach; includes apt and specific references | Good understanding of the text; exhibits perception and clarity; includes specific references | Superficial understanding of the text; elements of literature vague, mechanical, overgeneralized | Misreadings and lack of persuasive evidence from the text; meager and unconvincing treatment of literary elements | Serious misreadings and little supporting evidence from the text; erroneous treatment of literary elements | A response with no more than a reference to the literature; blank response, or one completely off the topic |
| **Organization and Development** | Meticulously organized and thoroughly developed; coherent and unified | Well-organized and developed; coherent and unified | Reasonably organized and developed; mostly coherent and unified | Somewhat organized and developed; some incoherence and lack of unity | Little or no organization and development; incoherent and void of unity | No apparent organization or development; incoherent |
| **Use of Sentences** | Effectively varied and engaging; virtually error free | Varied and interesting; a few errors | Adequately varied; some errors | Somewhat varied and marginally interesting; one or more major errors | Little or no variation; dull and uninteresting; some major errors | Numerous major errors |
| **Word Choice** | Interesting and effective; virtually error free | Generally interesting and effective; a few errors | Occasionally interesting and effective; several errors | Somewhat dull and ordinary; some errors in diction | Mostly dull and conventional; numerous errors | Numerous major errors; extremely immature |
| **Grammar and Usage** | Virtually error free | Occasional minor errors | Several minor errors | Some major errors | Severely flawed; frequent major errors | Extremely flawed |

Rate yourself in each of the categories. Choose the description that most accurately reflects your performance, and enter the numbers on the lines below. Be as honest as possible so you will know what areas need work. Then calculate the average of the six numbers to determine your final score. It is difficult to score yourself objectively, so you may wish to ask a respected friend or teacher to assess your writing for a more accurate reflection of its strengths and weaknesses. On the AP test itself, a reader will rate your essay on a scale of 0 to 9, with 9 being the highest.

Rate each category from 9 (high) to 0 (low).

## Exercise 1

**SELF-EVALUATION**

Overall Impression _____
Understanding of the Text _____
Organization and Development _____
Use of Sentences _____
Word Choice (Diction) _____
Grammar and Usage _____

TOTAL _____
    Divide by 6 for final score _____

**OBJECTIVE EVALUATION**

Overall Impression _____
Understanding of the Text _____
Organization and Development _____
Use of Sentences _____
Word Choice (Diction) _____
Grammar and Usage _____

TOTAL _____
    Divide by 6 for final score _____

## Exercise 2

**SELF-EVALUATION**

Overall Impression _____
Understanding of the Text _____
Organization and Development _____
Use of Sentences _____
Word Choice (Diction) _____
Grammar and Usage _____

TOTAL _____
    Divide by 6 for final score _____

**OBJECTIVE EVALUATION**

Overall Impression _____
Understanding of the Text _____
Organization and Development _____
Use of Sentences _____
Word Choice (Diction) _____
Grammar and Usage _____

TOTAL _____
    Divide by 6 for final score _____

## Exercise 3

**SELF-EVALUATION**

Overall Impression _____
Understanding of the Text _____
Organization and Development _____
Use of Sentences _____
Word Choice (Diction) _____
Grammar and Usage _____

TOTAL _____
    Divide by 6 for final score _____

**OBJECTIVE EVALUATION**

Overall Impression _____
Understanding of the Text _____
Organization and Development _____
Use of Sentences _____
Word Choice (Diction) _____
Grammar and Usage _____

TOTAL _____
    Divide by 6 for final score _____

## Exercise 4

| SELF-EVALUATION | | OBJECTIVE EVALUATION | |
|---|---|---|---|
| **Overall Impression** | _____ | **Overall Impression** | _____ |
| **Understanding of the Text** | _____ | **Understanding of the Text** | _____ |
| **Organization and Development** | _____ | **Organization and Development** | _____ |
| **Use of Sentences** | _____ | **Use of Sentences** | _____ |
| **Word Choice (Diction)** | _____ | **Word Choice (Diction)** | _____ |
| **Grammar and Usage** | _____ | **Grammar and Usage** | _____ |
| **TOTAL** | _____ | **TOTAL** | _____ |
| Divide by 6 for final score | _____ | Divide by 6 for final score | _____ |

## SUMMING IT UP

- Recognize that your response to a poem is no more a matter of right or wrong, correct or incorrect, than your reaction to a popular song.

- Restate the question to yourself—paraphrase it—so, you know what you're being asked to write about.

- Your essay about poetry will evaluate the effectiveness with which the poet uses the elements of poetry. You will show your understanding of the poem by explaining, interpreting, and even judging it.

- When reading a poem, you must be careful to identify the tools the poet uses and analyze the ways in which they are used to achieve the total effect.

- Be aware of language and diction, poetic devices, style, the writer's intentions and purpose, the selection's impact, and special techniques.

# Free Response Guides

## OVERVIEW

- Planning and writing your free response essay in 10 easy steps
- Summing it up

## PLANNING AND WRITING YOUR FREE RESPONSE ESSAY IN 10 EASY STEPS

In Chapters 6 and 7, you read information about how to plan, organize, and write the free response essays for the AP English Literature & Composition exam. The following section will help you put those 10 steps into practice as you rewrite the exercise essays. The worksheets in this section will guide you through the step-by-step process for reading the question and selection and then planning, organizing, and writing free response essays.

Each practice sheet lists the steps with plenty of space to complete each one. There are also tips about pacing yourself to make the most efficient and effective use of the 40-minute writing period and reminders to use transitions and incorporate new ideas. You will find practice sheets to help you rewrite the prose free response essays given in Chapter 6 and the poetry free response essays given in Chapter 7.

If you practice the 10 steps as you get ready for the real test, you will learn them as you go. You won't need to sit down and memorize them. The idea behind the practice is to become so familiar with the steps that you will internalize them. On the day of the test, you will use the steps—read the question and the selection and plan, organize, and write your essay—without consciously thinking about the steps. They will just come naturally to you.

A last word of advice: Be sure to read the question carefully. You have to be clear about what you are being asked to write about. A well-written essay about the wrong topic is a *wrong* essay.

chapter 8

## EXERCISE 1—PROSE ESSAY

TIP

Set aside
5 minutes for
Steps 1 through 5.

Follow these steps for rewriting your exercise essay.

### Step 1

Read the question again carefully and then the selection.

### Step 2

Restate to yourself what the question is asking. Jot the key words below. On the real test, use the scratch paper.

_____

_____

_____

### Step 3

Read the selection. Do not take time to outline your ideas. Make a list by brainstorming all the ideas that come to mind as you read. Write your ideas below.

_____

_____

_____

_____

_____

_____

_____

_____

_____

_____

_____

_____

## Step 4

Create a thesis from the ideas you brainstormed.

_____

_____

_____

## Step 5

Turn your brainstorm into an informal working plan by numbering the items that you want to include in your essay in the order in which you want to include them. Do not be afraid to cross out some that no longer fit now that you have a thesis for your essay.

## Step 6

Begin writing your first paragraph by stating your thesis clearly.

_____

_____

_____

_____

_____

_____

_____

_____

_____

_____

**TIP**

Take a full 5 minutes to write this first paragraph. You want to be sure that you are writing a clearly stated and interesting introduction.

## Step 7

Once you have written the first paragraph, read it to be sure that your ideas follow each other logically and support the thesis.

## Step 8

Check your quick list of ideas. Choose the next idea and write a transition into your second paragraph. Now keep writing until you see all the RELEVANT ideas on your quick list.

_____

_____

_____

_____

_____

_____

_____

_____

_____

_____

_____

_____

_____

_____

_____

_____

_____

_____

_____

_____

_____

_____

_____

_____

## Step 9

Allow about 5 minutes to write a solid conclusion. Choose one of these ways to conclude:

- Rephrase your thesis.
- Summarize the main points.
- Refer in some way back to your introductory paragraph.

_____

_____

_____

_____

_____

_____

_____

_____

_____

_____

_____

_____

_____

_____

_____

_____

_____

_____

_____

**TIP**

You should have about 8 minutes of your 40 minutes left. How much time do you have?

## Step 10

Proofread and revise—NEATLY.

- Cross out any irrelevant ideas or words.
- Make any additions, especially transitions.
- Smooth out any awkward sentences.
- Check your grammar and mechanics.

**TIP**

You should have paced yourself so that you have 3 minutes for your final review.

## EXERCISE 2—PROSE ESSAY

**TIP**

Set aside
5 minutes for
Steps 1 through 5.

Follow these steps for rewriting your exercise essay.

### Step 1

Read the question again carefully and then the selection.

### Step 2

Restate to yourself what the question is asking. Jot the key words below. On the real test, use the scratch paper.

_____

_____

_____

### Step 3

Read the selection. Do not take time to outline your ideas. Make a list by brainstorming all the ideas that come to mind as you read. Write your ideas below.

_____

_____

_____

_____

_____

_____

_____

_____

_____

_____

_____

_____

## Step 4

Create a thesis from the ideas you brainstormed.

_____

_____

_____

## Step 5

Turn your brainstorm into an informal working plan by numbering the items that you want to include in your essay in the order in which you want to include them. Do not be afraid to cross out some that no longer fit now that you have a thesis for your essay.

## Step 6

Begin writing your first paragraph by stating your thesis clearly.

_____

_____

_____

_____

_____

_____

_____

_____

_____

_____

_____

**TIP**

Take a full 5 minutes to write this first paragraph. You want to be sure that you are writing a clearly stated and interesting introduction.

## Step 7

Once you have written the first paragraph, read it to be sure that your ideas follow each other logically and support the thesis.

## Step 8

Check your quick list of ideas. Choose the next idea and write a transition into your second paragraph. Now keep writing until you see all the RELEVANT ideas on your quick list.

_____

_____

_____

_____

_____

_____

_____

_____

_____

_____

_____

_____

_____

_____

_____

_____

_____

_____

_____

_____

_____

## Step 9

Allow about 5 minutes to write a solid conclusion. Choose one of these ways to conclude:

- Rephrase your thesis.
- Summarize the main points.
- Refer in some way back to your introductory paragraph.

_____

_____

_____

_____

_____

_____

_____

_____

_____

_____

_____

_____

_____

_____

_____

_____

## Step 10

Proofread and revise—NEATLY.

- Cross out any irrelevant ideas or words.
- Make any additions, especially transitions.
- Smooth out any awkward sentences.
- Check your grammar and mechanics.

**TIP**

You should have about 8 minutes of your 40 minutes left. How much time do you have?

**TIP**

You should have paced yourself so that you have 3 minutes for your final review.

## EXERCISE 3—PROSE ESSAY

TIP

Set aside
5 minutes for
Steps 1 through 5.

Follow these steps for rewriting your exercise essay.

### Step 1

Read the question again carefully and then the selection.

### Step 2

Restate to yourself what the question is asking. Jot the key words below. On the real test, use the scratch paper.

_____

_____

_____

### Step 3

Read the selection. Do not take time to outline your ideas. Make a list by brainstorming all the ideas that come to mind as you read. Write your ideas below.

_____

_____

_____

_____

_____

_____

_____

_____

_____

_____

_____

_____

## Step 4

Create a thesis from the ideas you brainstormed.

_____

_____

_____

## Step 5

Turn your brainstorm into an informal working plan by numbering the items that you want to include in your essay in the order in which you want to include them. Do not be afraid to cross out some that no longer fit now that you have a thesis for your essay.

## Step 6

Begin writing your first paragraph by stating your thesis clearly.

_____

_____

_____

_____

_____

_____

_____

_____

_____

_____

**TIP**

Take a full 5 minutes to write this first paragraph. You want to be sure that you are writing a clearly stated and interesting introduction.

## Step 7

Once you have written the first paragraph, read it to be sure that your ideas follow each other logically and support the thesis.

## Step 8

Check your quick list of ideas. Choose the next idea and write a transition into your second paragraph. Now keep writing until you see all the RELEVANT ideas on your quick list.

_____

_____

_____

_____

_____

_____

_____

_____

_____

_____

_____

_____

_____

_____

_____

_____

_____

_____

_____

## Step 9

Allow about 5 minutes to write a solid conclusion. Choose one of these ways to conclude:

- Rephrase your thesis.
- Summarize the main points.
- Refer in some way back to your introductory paragraph.

_____

_____

_____

_____

_____

_____

_____

_____

_____

_____

_____

_____

_____

_____

_____

_____

## Step 10

Proofread and revise—NEATLY.

- Cross out any irrelevant ideas or words.
- Make any additions, especially transitions.
- Smooth out any awkward sentences.
- Check your grammar and mechanics.

**TIP**

You should have about 8 minutes of your 40 minutes left. How much time do you have?

**TIP**

You should have paced yourself so that you have 3 minutes for your final review.

## EXERCISE 4—PROSE ESSAY

TIP

Set aside
5 minutes for
Steps 1 through 5.

Follow these steps for rewriting your exercise essay.

### Step 1

Read the question again carefully and then the selection.

### Step 2

Restate to yourself what the question is asking. Jot the key words below. On the real test, use the scratch paper.

_____

_____

_____

### Step 3

Read the selection. Do not take time to outline your ideas. Make a list by brainstorming all the ideas that come to mind as you read. Write your ideas below.

_____

_____

_____

_____

_____

_____

_____

_____

_____

_____

_____

_____

## Step 4

Create a thesis from the ideas you brainstormed.

_____

_____

_____

## Step 5

Turn your brainstorm into an informal working plan by numbering the items that you want to include in your essay in the order in which you want to include them. Do not be afraid to cross out some that no longer fit now that you have a thesis for your essay.

## Step 6

Begin writing your first paragraph by stating your thesis clearly.

_____

_____

_____

_____

_____

_____

_____

_____

_____

_____

_____

**TIP**

Take a full 5 minutes to write this first paragraph. You want to be sure that you are writing a clearly stated and interesting introduction.

## Step 7

Once you have written the first paragraph, read it to be sure that your ideas follow each other logically and support the thesis.

TIP

By now you
should be about
10 minutes into
your 40 minutes of
writing time.
Where are you?
You want to
leave 3 minutes
at the end for
proofreading
and revising.

TIP

Don't forget to
use transitions
between your
paragraphs.

TIP

If a new idea
comes from the
flow or your
writing, use it IF IT
FITS THE CONTEXT.

### Step 8

Check your quick list of ideas. Choose the next idea and write a transition into your second paragraph. Now keep writing until you see all the RELEVANT ideas on your quick list.

_____

_____

_____

_____

_____

_____

_____

_____

_____

_____

_____

_____

_____

_____

_____

_____

_____

_____

_____

_____

_____

## Step 9

Allow about 5 minutes to write a solid conclusion. Choose one of these ways to conclude:

- Rephrase your thesis.
- Summarize the main points.
- Refer in some way back to your introductory paragraph.

TIP

You should have about 8 minutes of your 40 minutes left. How much time do you have?

_____

_____

_____

_____

_____

_____

_____

_____

_____

_____

_____

_____

_____

_____

_____

_____

## Step 10

Proofread and revise—NEATLY.

- Cross out any irrelevant ideas or words.
- Make any additions, especially transitions.
- Smooth out any awkward sentences.
- Check your grammar and mechanics.

TIP

You should have paced yourself so that you have 3 minutes for your final review.

## EXERCISE 5—POETRY ESSAY

**TIP**

Set aside
5 minutes for
Steps 1 through 5.

Follow these steps for rewriting your exercise essay.

### Step 1

Read the question again carefully and then the selection.

### Step 2

Restate to yourself what the question is asking. Jot the key words below. On the real test, use the scratch paper.

_____

_____

_____

### Step 3

Read the selection. Do not take time to outline your ideas. Make a list by brainstorming all the ideas that come to mind as you read. Write your ideas below.

_____

_____

_____

_____

_____

_____

_____

_____

_____

_____

_____

## Step 4

Create a thesis from the ideas you brainstormed.

_____

_____

_____

## Step 5

Turn your brainstorm into an informal working plan by numbering the items that you want to include in your essay in the order in which you want to include them. Do not be afraid to cross out some that no longer fit now that you have a thesis for your essay.

## Step 6

Begin writing your first paragraph by stating your thesis clearly.

_____

_____

_____

_____

_____

_____

_____

_____

_____

_____

_____

_____

**TIP**

Take a full 5 minutes to write this first paragraph. You want to be sure that you are writing a clearly stated and interesting introduction.

## Step 7

Once you have written the first paragraph, read it to be sure that your ideas follow each other logically and support the thesis.

TIP

By now you should be about 10 minutes into your 40 minutes of writing time. Where are you? You want to leave 3 minutes at the end for proofreading and revising.

TIP

Don't forget to use transitions between your paragraphs.

TIP

If a new idea comes from the flow or your writing, use it IF IT FITS THE CONTEXT.

## Step 8

Check your quick list of ideas. Choose the next idea and write a transition into your second paragraph. Now keep writing until you see all the RELEVANT ideas on your quick list.

_____

_____

_____

_____

_____

_____

_____

_____

_____

_____

_____

_____

_____

_____

_____

_____

_____

_____

_____

_____

_____

_____

_____

_____

## Step 9

Allow about 5 minutes to write a solid conclusion. Choose one of these ways to conclude:

- Rephrase your thesis.
- Summarize the main points.
- Refer in some way back to your introductory paragraph.

**TIP**

You should have about 8 minutes of your 40 minutes left. How much time do you have?

_____

_____

_____

_____

_____

_____

_____

_____

_____

_____

_____

_____

_____

_____

_____

## Step 10

Proofread and revise—NEATLY.

- Cross out any irrelevant ideas or words.
- Make any additions, especially transitions.
- Smooth out any awkward sentences.
- Check your grammar and mechanics.

**TIP**

You should have paced yourself so that you have 3 minutes for your final review.

## EXERCISE 6—POETRY ESSAY

TIP

Set aside
5 minutes for
Steps 1 through 5.

Follow these steps for rewriting your exercise essay.

### Step 1

Read the question again carefully and then the selection.

### Step 2

Restate to yourself what the question is asking. Jot the key words below. On the real test, use the scratch paper.

_____

_____

_____

### Step 3

Read the selection. Do not take time to outline your ideas. Make a list by brainstorming all the ideas that come to mind as you read. Write your ideas below.

_____

_____

_____

_____

_____

_____

_____

_____

_____

_____

_____

_____

_____

## Step 4

Create a thesis from the ideas you brainstormed.

_____

_____

_____

## Step 5

Turn your brainstorm into an informal working plan by numbering the items that you want to include in your essay in the order in which you want to include them. Do not be afraid to cross out some that no longer fit now that you have a thesis for your essay.

## Step 6

Begin writing your first paragraph by stating your thesis clearly.

_____

_____

_____

_____

_____

_____

_____

_____

_____

_____

_____

_____

**TIP**

Take a full 5 minutes to write this first paragraph. You want to be sure that you are writing a clearly stated and interesting introduction.

## Step 7

Once you have written the first paragraph, read it to be sure that your ideas follow each other logically and support the thesis.

TIP

By now you
should be about
10 minutes into
your 40 minutes of
writing time.
Where are you?
You want to
leave 3 minutes
at the end for
proofreading
and revising.

TIP

Don't forget to
use transitions
between your
paragraphs.

TIP

If a new idea
comes from the
flow or your
writing, use it IF IT
FITS THE CONTEXT.

### Step 8

Check your quick list of ideas. Choose the next idea and write a transition into your second paragraph. Now keep writing until you see all the RELEVANT ideas on your quick list.

_____

_____

_____

_____

_____

_____

_____

_____

_____

_____

_____

_____

_____

_____

_____

_____

_____

_____

_____

_____

_____

_____

_____

## Step 9

Allow about 5 minutes to write a solid conclusion. Choose one of these ways to conclude:

- Rephrase your thesis.
- Summarize the main points.
- Refer in some way back to your introductory paragraph.

_____

_____

_____

_____

_____

_____

_____

_____

_____

_____

_____

_____

_____

_____

_____

## Step 10

Proofread and revise—NEATLY.

- Cross out any irrelevant ideas or words.
- Make any additions, especially transitions.
- Smooth out any awkward sentences.
- Check your grammar and mechanics.

**TIP**

You should have about 8 minutes of your 40 minutes left. How much time do you have?

**TIP**

You should have paced yourself so that you have 3 minutes for your final review.

## EXERCISE 7—POETRY ESSAY

**TIP**

Set aside
5 minutes for
Steps 1 through 5.

Follow these steps for rewriting your exercise essay.

### Step 1

Read the question again carefully and then the selection.

### Step 2

Restate to yourself what the question is asking. Jot the key words below. On the real test, use the scratch paper.

_____

_____

_____

### Step 3

Read the selection. Do not take time to outline your ideas. Make a list by brainstorming all the ideas that come to mind as you read. Write your ideas below.

_____

_____

_____

_____

_____

_____

_____

_____

_____

_____

_____

_____

_____

## Step 4

Create a thesis from the ideas you brainstormed.

_____

_____

_____

## Step 5

Turn your brainstorm into an informal working plan by numbering the items that you want to include in your essay in the order in which you want to include them. Do not be afraid to cross out some that no longer fit now that you have a thesis for your essay.

## Step 6

Begin writing your first paragraph by stating your thesis clearly.

_____

_____

_____

_____

_____

_____

_____

_____

_____

_____

_____

**TIP**

Take a full 5 minutes to write this first paragraph. You want to be sure that you are writing a clearly stated and interesting introduction.

## Step 7

Once you have written the first paragraph, read it to be sure that your ideas follow each other logically and support the thesis.

## Step 8

Check your quick list of ideas. Choose the next idea and write a transition into your second paragraph. Now keep writing until you see all the RELEVANT ideas on your quick list.

_____

_____

_____

_____

_____

_____

_____

_____

_____

_____

_____

_____

_____

_____

_____

_____

_____

_____

_____

_____

## Step 9

Allow about 5 minutes to write a solid conclusion. Choose one of these ways to conclude:

- Rephrase your thesis.
- Summarize the main points.
- Refer in some way back to your introductory paragraph.

_____

_____

_____

_____

_____

_____

_____

_____

_____

_____

_____

_____

_____

_____

_____

_____

## Step 10

Proofread and revise—NEATLY.

- Cross out any irrelevant ideas or words.
- Make any additions, especially transitions.
- Smooth out any awkward sentences.
- Check your grammar and mechanics.

**TIP**

You should have about 8 minutes of your 40 minutes left. How much time do you have?

**TIP**

You should have paced yourself so that you have 3 minutes for your final review.

## EXERCISE 8—POETRY ESSAY

TIP

Set aside
5 minutes for
Steps 1 through 5.

Follow these steps for rewriting your exercise essay.

### Step 1

Read the question again carefully and then the selection.

### Step 2

Restate to yourself what the question is asking. Jot the Key words below. On the real test, use the scratch paper.

_____

_____

_____

### Step 3

Read the selection. Do not take time to outline your ideas. Make a list by brainstorming all the ideas that come to mind as you read. Write your ideas below.

_____

_____

_____

_____

_____

_____

_____

_____

_____

_____

_____

_____

## Step 4

Create a thesis from the ideas you brainstormed.

_____

_____

_____

## Step 5

Turn your brainstorm into an informal working plan by numbering the items that you want to include in your essay in the order in which you want to include them. Do not be afraid to cross out some that no longer fit now that you have a thesis for your essay.

## Step 6

Begin writing your first paragraph by stating your thesis clearly.

_____

_____

_____

_____

_____

_____

_____

_____

_____

_____

**TIP**

Take a full 5 minutes to write this first paragraph. You want to be sure that you are writing a clearly stated and interesting introduction.

## Step 7

Once you have written the first paragraph, read it to be sure that your ideas follow each other logically and support the thesis.

## Step 8

Check your quick list of ideas. Choose the next idea and write a transition into your second paragraph. Now keep writing until you see all the RELEVANT ideas on your quick list.

_____

_____

_____

_____

_____

_____

_____

_____

_____

_____

_____

_____

_____

_____

_____

_____

_____

_____

_____

_____

_____

_____

## Step 9

Allow about 5 minutes to write a solid conclusion. Choose one of these ways to conclude:

- Rephrase your thesis.
- Summarize the main points.
- Refer in some way back to your introductory paragraph.

**TIP**

You should have about 8 minutes of your 40 minutes left. How much time do you have?

_____

_____

_____

_____

_____

_____

_____

_____

_____

_____

_____

_____

_____

_____

_____

## Step 10

Proofread and revise—NEATLY.

- Cross out any irrelevant ideas or words.
- Make any additions, especially transitions.
- Smooth out any awkward sentences.
- Check your grammar and mechanics.

**TIP**

You should have paced yourself so that you have 3 minutes for your final review.

## SUMMING IT UP

- Restate to yourself what the question is really asking.

- While reading the selection, don't take time to outline your ideas. Make a list by brainstorming all the ideas that come to mind as you read.

- Turn your brainstorm into an informal working plan.

- Take a full 5 minutes to write the first paragraph. Make sure your ideas follow each other logically and support the thesis.

- Don't forget to use transitions between your following paragraphs.

- Allow about 5 minutes to write a solid conclusion by rephrasing your thesis, summarizing the main points, or referring back to your introductory paragraph.

- Proofread and revise.

# About the Open Essay

chapter 9

Students often think that the most intimidating part of the AP English Literature & Composition exam is the open essay. However, it does not need to be because it is the one essay that you can plan in advance. Unlike the two free response essays, the open essay question does not give you the literary selection to write about. Instead, the open essay requires you to write about a concept supported by evidence from literature that you choose.

While this may sound more difficult, it can actually be easier. You have the opportunity to write about literature you know and appreciate—and have studied. You do not need to understand and analyze literature you have never seen before the test. You are free to apply what you know about a favorite play or novel to the discussion of the essay question.

## WHAT WILL YOU BE ASKED TO DO?

What are you likely to be asked in the open essay question? The question will ask you to support a critical statement or comment about life as reflected in literature of your choice. The question may relate either to critical theory or to the work's content. Questions may ask about what makes a story tragic, the role that characters play in plot development, the price of suffering, or the effects of society and civilization.

The following are some examples of the two question types that you may be asked to write about:

- Critical Theory

  - Some characters' main purpose is to help the reader understand the story. Discuss such a character, explaining his or her function and how that character helps the reader to understand the plot.

  - Discuss the concept of the tragic flaw. Is it inaccurate to state that some tragic heroes have no flaws yet suffer terribly?

  - Show how the author enlists the reader's sympathy through identification with the protagonist and his or her challenges.

- Content

  - Discuss how a character experiences an insight that reveals something about who he or she is. Describe how that character attempts to change, and evaluate whether that change is believable.

  - Discuss how society forces people into a mold and how they are therefore prevented from experiencing personal fulfillment in their lives.

  - Discuss how a work of literature comments on human values and on what is good and bad in human nature as well as how it suggests an attitude the reader may take toward life and living.

NOTE

Remember to use
present tense
when writing
about literature.

## PREPARING FOR THE OPEN ESSAY

In Chapters 5, 6, and 7, you learned the skills, strategies, and techniques necessary to write good free response essays. Use the same strategies in answering the open essay. To help you, you should prepare two works of literature that you can use as the basis for your open essay. If you thoroughly analyze two works—one novel and one play—so that you know them inside out, you will not have to spend time during the test trying to decide what work to write about and what you know about it. The College Board's *Advanced Placement Course Description* for English suggests that the best way to prepare is to analyze and write about what you analyze. Why not use this writing as the basis for the actual test?

The following suggestions will help you choose effective works:

- Your choices must be novels or plays. The question will indicate what type of literature you may use to exemplify your thesis. Short stories or poetry—except for long poems—are not always acceptable, so don't spend time working them up.

- You need a book that is full of material to write about—complex characters, an involved plot, meaningful themes, elegant language.

- Choose works that you have studied. You have notes about the book. You wrote about it. You participated in discussions. You know it.

- Both the author and the book should be well respected. Stephen King and *Star Wars* books will not impress the evaluators.

- You need to really like and understand the novel or play you choose. Because you love it, you will remember it well. You will write more easily about it because you have personal opinions. Your enthusiasm will show in your essay.

- Plays by Shakespeare are excellent choices. His plays have all the elements necessary for a good essay. Also, since they are plays, they are shorter to reread than many other works.

- Choose works that are very different from each other. If you choose *Macbeth,* your second choice should not be *Hamlet. The Sun Also Rises* or *The House on Mango Street* are better choices. In other words, do not choose two tragic dramas or two contemporary novels.

- Be sensitive to the gender of the main characters and the authors. If possible, choose one work with a female main character and the other with a male main character.

After you have made your choice, reread both works. We suggest using an annotated or critical edition that presents additional information about the work, the style, the themes, the author, and so forth.

- Study your two choices as carefully and completely as you can.

- Review any class notes or papers you may have written about the works.

- Discuss the works with friends and teachers to gain more insights and to clarify your own thinking.

- Learn a little about the authors, their time period, and their styles.

- Jot down quotes that highlight important aspects of the works, such as the theme or the characters. Memorize the lines so you can weave them into your essay.

Your last study step involves writing a first paragraph and a final paragraph. Imagine the question is something like, "How does the writer use the devices of literature to convey the themes?" How do your two works stack up against the question? Which one would be the better work to use to illustrate your essay on thematic development?

Choose one. Use the strategies for brainstorming and developing a thesis in Chapter 5, p. 125. Then write the first paragraph. In the introduction, briefly state your central idea and list the points that you will use to demonstrate the validity of your position. Note any unique facts or background about the work that you think will help the grader to comprehend your ideas. Then write the final paragraph, and conclude by stating the total impression. Restate your thesis and summarize major points in this paragraph.

## EVALUATING LITERATURE

Evaluating literature, which you may be asked to do in Section II of the test, can be the most abstract, philosophical, and difficult writing you will do. Although standards of taste differ, let the following five concepts serve as guides to help you with an evaluation question:

### Truth

While truth is often used to mean "real" when people discuss literature, for the purposes of evaluation, truth implies generality and universality. For example, the dilemma facing Oedipus, in *Oedipus Rex,* that human beings often face difficult or impossible situations that result in great suffering, is as true today as it was 2,500 years ago. Thus, the play measures up to one standard—truth—you can use to evaluate a work of literature.

### Affirmative

Literary characters should be worth caring about no matter how horrid their condition or situation is. Good art is affirmative. Authors may create tragedy or comedy, love or hate, or the heights or depths of human nature, but in good literature, the view is that life is valuable and worthy of respect and dignity. In *Death of a Salesman,* for example, Willie Loman dies, and the message is that it is a loss worth mourning.

### Vitality

Good literature seems to have a life of its own. When you reread great literature, you gain new insights that were not a part of your original experience. As you experience such works as Cervantes's *Don Quixote* or Dickens's *David Copperfield,* you discover new understandings and wisdom.

### Beauty

In literature, beauty results from unity, symmetry, harmony, and proportion. When you recognize the relationship of the parts to the whole, you perceive the beauty of the work. In the eighteenth century, people believed beauty was found where variety existed within order. Pope's couplets serve as an example of this standard of beauty. In the Romantic and post-Romantic periods, the concept of beauty revolved around greater freedom. You can find the results of this idea in James Joyce's stream-of-consciousness narratives and freedom of syntax. While concepts of beauty have changed, unity and proportion are still applicable.

Studies of style, structure, tone, imagery, and point of view are all means of deciding if a work is beautiful. However, excellence in any one of these does not make the entire work beautiful.

## Total Effect

A final way to determine a literary work's worth is to consider its total effect, both as an artistic form and as a vehicle for emotions and impressions. If what you read has merit, you become emotionally involved with the characters. When you are involved with the characters and the characters are involved with evil, your own conscience causes you to wish events had transpired differently. The result—catharsis—is an emotionally draining experience. *Hamlet* is a superb example. In short, a great work may not be perfect, but if the total effect is that it impresses you, flaws become minor. Likewise, excellent technique does not justify a claim of greatness for a work. Unless everything from the plot to the message is balanced, a work cannot claim excellence.

## PRACTICING

The Sample Open Essay on p. 220 is very similar to those that you will find on the actual AP English Literature & Composition Test. Apply these suggestions and strategies as you write about character development. Use one of the two works you have prepared. Then check your essay by reading the suggested points of discussion that follow. Evaluate your essay by using the *Self-Evaluation Rubric* on p. 227.

NOTE

See "Nine-Week Practice Plan for Studying for the AP English Literature & Composition Test," p. 17.

After you finish your evaluation of the sample, try *Exercise 1*. If you still feel you need practice, continue with *Exercise 2*. Alternate the two works you have chosen as the basis for your open essay so you can see how each could fit different kinds of questions. Turn to Chapter 10, *Open Essay Guides*, to learn an efficient process for planning, pacing, and writing your open essay.

# SAMPLE OPEN ESSAY

*SUGGESTED TIME—40 MINUTES*

**Directions:** Authors use many devices to develop their characters. In some situations, they use dialogue and description. In other cases, writers make use of other literary elements to make their characters come alive. Names, nonverbal communication, and small episodes all may tell the reader a great deal about a character's personality.

Using one of the works listed below or a novel, play, or epic of your choice, discuss the ways the author develops characters.

Faulkner, *The Sound and the Fury*

Melville, *Moby Dick*

Dickens, *A Tale of Two Cities*

Fielding, *Tom Jones*

Hugo, *Les Miserables*

Wells, *Invisible Man*

Pasternak, *Dr. Zhivago*

Lawrence, *Sons and Lovers*

Steinbeck, *The Grapes of Wrath*

Swift, *Gulliver's Travels*

Conrad, *Lord Jim*

Heller, *Catch-22*

Walker, *The Color Purple*

Golding, *Lord of the Flies*

Hemingway, *A Farewell to Arms*

Dickens, *Great Expectations*

Brontë, *Wuthering Heights*

Dostoyevsky, *Crime and Punishment*

Cervantes, *Don Quixote*

Before you turn the page and read our suggestions for an essay on this question, score your own essay using the *Self-Evaluation Rubric* on p. 227.

# SUGGESTIONS FOR SAMPLE OPEN ESSAY

You might have chosen to discuss the following points in your essay on character development. Consider them as you perform your self-evaluation. Strengthen your essay by using points from this list.

## Character

- Determine the characters' major traits when analyzing literature.

- What you know about a character is determined by what the author tells.

- Information coming from other characters must be considered carefully. Define the relationship between the character and the informant to understand the information better.

- The words of a character are good indicators of who he or she truly is. However, proceed cautiously because characters, like people in real life, lie, pretend, or disguise themselves.

- Actions speak louder than words. Consider what characters do as well as what they say.

- Characters can be round or fully developed with many realistic characteristics; flat, nonindividual but representative types; dynamic, having the capacity to change; or static, staying the same.

- Take into account who is telling the story. Narrators can influence your perception.

- Protagonists and antagonists deserve most of the attention.

- The protagonist often brings a message from the writer, and that message usually relates to the theme.

- Identifying the protagonist is sometimes difficult, and doing so makes you think about the elements of the work.

- Characters can encounter forces that are other than human. How they react reveals a great deal about them.

- How people cope with economic, social, or political forces reveals character.

- The struggle between the protagonist and the antagonist is crucial to a literary work. How it is resolved gives you insight into the characters and the meaning of the piece.

- You should expect characters who are true to life. Determine if the characters are plausible or if they are mythical. Identify surprising behavior or exaggeration.

- Be sure to relate the characters to the meaning of the work.

**TIP**

Did you recognize this as a content question? Be sure you know what the question is asking you to write about; in this case, it asks you to describe the author's development of character.

## EXERCISE 1

*SUGGESTED TIME—40 MINUTES*

**Directions:** In good literature, writers create a world in which readers experience intensification or alteration in their consciousness about certain aspects of life.

Choose a novel, epic, or play of literary merit and write an essay in which you identify the ways in which it changed your awareness or your views of life. You may wish to discuss this change of state by discussing the setting, the action, and the theme development. Avoid plot summary.

You may select a work from the list below, or you may choose another work of comparable literary merit suitable to the topic.

Dostoyevsky, *The Brothers Karamazov*

Walker, *The Color Purple*

Dickens, *David Copperfield*

Miller, *Death of a Salesman*

Tyler, *Dinner at the Homesick Restaurant*

Austen, *Emma*

Joyce, *Portrait of the Artist as a Young Man*

Fitzgerald, *The Great Gatsby*

Shaw, *Pygmalion*

Austen, *Sense and Sensibility*

Hemingway, *The Sun Also Rises*

Dickens, *Tale of Two Cities*

Brontë, *Wuthering Heights*

Use the *Self-Evaluation Rubric* on p. 227 to help you assess your progress in writing the open essay.

## SUGGESTIONS FOR EXERCISE 1

You might have included the following in your essay on how a work can change a reader's view of life. Consider them in your self-evaluation. Strengthen your essay by using points from this list.

### Setting

- Environment within which the action takes place: geographical location, historical period, seasons, weather, building or room, clothing, work, social circumstances, customs—the elements necessary for creating a sense of time and place

- Purpose of setting:

  - Make work more believable through description

  - Create mood or atmosphere

  - Create conflict: character versus environment

  - Symbolize key concepts

- Reflect character's situation

- Complicate plot

- Highlight the theme

- Add to overall effect of the work

### Action/Plot

- A series of related events moving from a problem to a solution

- Exposition: presentation of characters and situation

- Conflict: source of tension

- Internal conflict: within a character

- External conflict: between two or more characters or a force of nature

- Climax: the turning point

- Resolution: how problem is solved

- Complications: events that stand in the way of resolution

- Foreshadowing: use of hints to suggest what is to come

- Suspense: creation of anxious uncertainty

- Subplot: series of events outside but related to main plot

## Theme

- Central idea of literary work: insight about life or human experience
- Occasionally stated directly
- Usually implied
- Methods of expression

    - Direct statements by unnamed speaker/narrator

    - Direct statements by the persona—first-person narrator

    - Dramatic statements by characters

    - Figurative language

    - Characters who stand for ideas

    - Work itself represents idea

## EXERCISE 2

*SUGGESTED TIME—40 MINUTES*

**Directions:** In some works of literature, the passage from one state to another—in growth, in belief, in understanding, in knowledge—is a terrifying process.

Choose a novel or play of literary merit and write an essay in which you show how such a change in a character is a frightening process and leads to destruction or violent cleansing. You may wish to discuss how the author's use of action, theme, or character development elicits a sympathetic response from the reader. Avoid plot summary.

You may select a work from the list below, or you may choose another work of comparable literary merit suitable to the topic.

Orwell, *1984*

Sophocles, *Antigone*

Morrison, *Beloved*

Dostoyevsky, *Crime and Punishment*

Marlowe, *Doctor Faustus*

Shakespeare, *Hamlet*

Conrad, *Heart of Darkness*

Brontë, *Jane Eyre*

Conrad, *Lord Jim*

Shakespeare, *Macbeth*

Flaubert, *Madame Bovary*

Euripides, *Medea*

Melville, *Moby Dick*

Sophocles, *Oedipus Rex*

Shakespeare, *Othello*

Hemingway, *The Old Man and the Sea*

Crane, *Red Badge of Courage*

Hawthorne, *The Scarlet Letter*

Lee, *To Kill a Mockingbird*

Use the *Self-Evaluation Rubric* on p. 227 to help you assess your progress in writing the open essay.

exercises

## SUGGESTIONS FOR EXERCISE 2

You might have chosen to include the following points in your essay on character change. Consider them as you do your self-evaluation. Strengthen your essay by using points from this list.

### Action/Plot

- A series of related events moving from a problem to a solution
- Exposition presents characters and situation
- Conflict: source of tension
- Internal conflict: within a character
- External conflict: between two or more characters or a force of nature
- Climax: the turning point
- Resolution: how problem is solved
- Complications: events that stand in the way of resolution
- Foreshadowing: use of hints to suggest what is to come

### Theme

- General idea or insight into life revealed in the literature
- Sometimes stated directly, sometimes indirectly
- Symbols representing something other than themselves sometimes suggest theme
- Key statements point to theme
- Makes reader a bit wiser about the human condition

### Characterization

- Direct characterization: telling you directly about a character's personality
- Indirect characterization: revealing personality through descriptions, thoughts, words, and actions
- Round characters: fully developed
- Flat characters: only one or two character traits
- Dynamic characters change; static characters do not change
- Motivation: reason for character's behavior
- Characters convey theme

## SELF-EVALUATION RUBRIC FOR THE ADVANCED PLACEMENT ESSAYS

| | 8–9 | 6–7 | 5 | 3–4 | 1–2 | 0 |
|---|---|---|---|---|---|---|
| **Overall Impression** | Demonstrates excellent control of the literature and outstanding writing competence; thorough and effective; incisive | Demonstrates good control of the literature and good writing competence; less thorough and incisive than the highest papers | Reveals simplistic thinking and/or immature writing; adequate skills | Incomplete thinking; fails to respond adequately to part or parts of the question; may paraphrase rather than analyze | Unacceptably brief; fails to respond to the question; little clarity | Lacking skill and competence |
| **Understanding of the Text** | Excellent understanding of the text; exhibits perception and clarity; original or unique approach; includes apt and specific references | Good understanding of the text; exhibits perception and clarity; includes specific references | Superficial understanding of the text; elements of literature vague, mechanical, overgeneralized | Misreadings and lack of persuasive evidence from the text; meager and unconvincing treatment of literary elements | Serious misreadings and little supporting evidence from the text; erroneous treatment of literary elements | A response with no more than a reference to the literature; blank response, or one completely off the topic |
| **Organization and Development** | Meticulously organized and thoroughly developed; coherent and unified | Well-organized and developed; coherent and unified | Reasonably organized and developed; mostly coherent and unified | Somewhat organized and developed; some incoherence and lack of unity | Little or no organization and development; incoherent and void of unity | No apparent organization or development; incoherent |
| **Use of Sentences** | Effectively varied and engaging; virtually error free | Varied and interesting; a few errors | Adequately varied; some errors | Somewhat varied and marginally interesting; one or more major errors | Little or no variation; dull and uninteresting; some major errors | Numerous major errors |
| **Word Choice** | Interesting and effective; virtually error free | Generally interesting and effective; a few errors | Occasionally interesting and effective; several errors | Somewhat dull and ordinary; some errors in diction | Mostly dull and conventional; numerous errors | Numerous major errors; extremely immature |
| **Grammar and Usage** | Virtually error free | Occasional minor errors | Several minor errors | Some major errors | Severely flawed; frequent major errors | Extremely flawed |

Rate yourself in each of the categories. Choose the description that most accurately reflects your performance, and enter the numbers on the lines below. Be as honest as possible so you will know what areas need work. Then calculate the average of the six numbers to determine your final score. It is difficult to score yourself objectively, so you may wish to ask a respected friend or teacher to assess your writing for a more accurate reflection of its strengths and weaknesses. On the AP test itself, a reader will rate your essay on a scale of 0 to 9, with 9 being the highest.

Rate each category from 9 (high) to 0 (low).

## Exercise 1

**SELF-EVALUATION**

Overall Impression        _____
Understanding of the Text   _____
Organization and Development  _____
Use of Sentences          _____
Word Choice (Diction)     _____
Grammar and Usage         _____

TOTAL                     _____
    Divide by 6 for final score  _____

**OBJECTIVE EVALUATION**

Overall Impression        _____
Understanding of the Text   _____
Organization and Development  _____
Use of Sentences          _____
Word Choice (Diction)     _____
Grammar and Usage         _____

TOTAL                     _____
    Divide by 6 for final score  _____

## Exercise 2

**SELF-EVALUATION**

Overall Impression        _____
Understanding of the Text   _____
Organization and Development  _____
Use of Sentences          _____
Word Choice (Diction)     _____
Grammar and Usage         _____

TOTAL                     _____
    Divide by 6 for final score  _____

**OBJECTIVE EVALUATION**

Overall Impression        _____
Understanding of the Text   _____
Organization and Development  _____
Use of Sentences          _____
Word Choice (Diction)     _____
Grammar and Usage         _____

TOTAL                     _____
    Divide by 6 for final score  _____

# SUMMING IT UP

- The open essay is the one essay that you can plan in advance. The open essay requires you to write about a concept supported by evidence from literature that you choose.

- The question will ask you to support a critical statement or comment about life as reflected in literature of your choice. It may relate either to critical theory or to the work's content.

- Your literature choices must be novels or plays. Short stories or poetry—except for long poems—are not always acceptable.

- You need works that are full of material to write about—complex characters, involved plot, meaningful themes, elegant language.

- Choose works that you have studied since you already have notes about them, wrote about them, and participated in discussions.

- Plays by Shakespeare are excellent choices.

- Choose works that are very different from each other. In other words, do not choose two tragic dramas or two contemporary novels.

- After you've made your choice, reread both works and review your papers.

# Open Essay Guides

## chapter 10

## OVERVIEW

- Planning and writing your open essay in 10 easy steps
- Summing it up

## PLANNING AND WRITING YOUR OPEN ESSAY IN 10 EASY STEPS

Chapter 9 offered you advice about how to get ready for the open essay by preparing two works of literature, for example, a novel and a play. The idea is that if you have learned two works of literature thoroughly, you won't be caught off guard when you have to use examples from a literary work to illustrate and support your thesis.

This chapter offers some additional help for rewriting your open essay. These are 10 practical steps for planning, organizing, and writing the essays. The following section will help you put these 10 steps into practice. The guides in this section will take you through the step-by-step process for planning, organizing, and rewriting your open essay exercises using the works that you have already prepared.

Each guide lists the steps with plenty of space to complete each one. There are also tips about pacing yourself to make the most efficient and effective use of the 40-minute writing period and reminders to use transitions and incorporate new ideas.

If you practice the 10 steps as you get ready for the real test, you will learn them as you go. You won't need to sit down and memorize them. The idea behind the practice is to become so familiar with the steps that you will internalize them. On the day of the test, you will use the steps—read the question and the selection and plan, organize, and write your essay—without consciously thinking about the steps. They will just come naturally to you.

A last word of advice: Be sure to read the question carefully. You have to be clear about what you are being asked to write about. A well-written essay about the wrong topic is the *wrong* essay.

# EXERCISE 1

**TIP**

Set aside
5 minutes for
Steps 1 through 5.

Once you have decided which piece of literature to write about, follow these steps for rewriting your exercise essay.

## Step 1

Read the question again carefully and then the selection.

## Step 2

Restate to yourself what the question is asking. Jot the key words below. On the real test, use the scratch paper.

_____

_____

_____

## Step 3

How do the two works of literature that you prepared for the test stack up against the question? Decide which one is the better work to use to illustrate your essay on the topic. Then make a quick list by brainstorming all the ideas that come to mind from your preparation of the work. Write your ideas below.

_____

_____

_____

_____

_____

_____

_____

_____

_____

_____

_____

## Step 4

Create a thesis from the ideas you brainstormed.

_____

_____

_____

## Step 5

Turn your brainstorm into an informal working plan by numbering the items that you want to include in your essay in the order in which you want to include them. Do not be afraid to cross out some that no longer fit now that you have a thesis for your essay.

## Step 6

Begin writing your first paragraph by stating your thesis clearly. List the points you will use to demonstrate the validity of your position. Note any unique facts or background about the work that you think will help the grader better understand your ideas.

_____

_____

_____

_____

_____

_____

_____

_____

_____

**TIP**

Take a full 5 minutes to write a clearly stated and interesting first paragraph.

## Step 7

Once you have written the first paragraph, read it to be sure that your ideas follow each other logically and support the thesis.

TIP

By now you
should be about
10 minutes into
your 40 minutes of
writing time.
Where are you?
You want to
leave 3 minutes
at the end for
proofreading
and revising.

TIP

Don't forget to
use transitions
between your
paragraphs.

TIP

If a new idea
comes from the
flow or your
writing, use it IF IT
FITS THE CONTEXT.

## Step 8

Check your quick list of ideas. Choose the next idea and write a transition into your second paragraph. Now keep writing until you see all the RELEVANT ideas on your quick list.

_____

_____

_____

_____

_____

_____

_____

_____

_____

_____

_____

_____

_____

_____

_____

_____

_____

_____

_____

_____

_____

_____

_____

_____

_____

## Step 9

Allow about 5 minutes to write a solid conclusion. Choose one of these ways to conclude:

- Rephrase your thesis.
- Summarize the main points.
- Refer in some way back to your introductory paragraph.

**TIP**

You should have about 8 minutes of your 40 minutes left. How much time do you have?

_____

_____

_____

_____

_____

_____

_____

_____

_____

_____

_____

_____

_____

_____

_____

## Step 10

Proofread and revise—NEATLY.

- Cross out any irrelevant ideas or words.
- Make any additions, especially transitions.
- Smooth out any awkward sentences.
- Check your grammar and mechanics.

**TIP**

You should have paced yourself so that you have 3 minutes for your final review.

## EXERCISE 2

**TIP**

Set aside
5 minutes for
Steps 1 through 5.

Once you have decided which piece of literature to write about, follow these steps for rewriting your exercise essay.

### Step 1

Read the question again carefully and then the selection.

### Step 2

Restate to yourself what the question is asking. Jot the key words below. On the real test, use the scratch paper.

_____

_____

_____

### Step 3

How do the two works of literature that you prepared for the test stack up against the question? Decide which one is the better work to use to illustrate your essay on the topic. Then make a quick list by brainstorming all the ideas that come to mind from your preparation of the work. Write your ideas below.

_____

_____

_____

_____

_____

_____

_____

_____

_____

## Step 4

Create a thesis from the ideas you brainstormed.

_____

_____

_____

## Step 5

Turn your brainstorm into an informal working plan by numbering the items that you want to include in your essay in the order in which you want to include them. Do not be afraid to cross out some that no longer fit now that you have a thesis for your essay.

## Step 6

Begin writing your first paragraph by stating your thesis clearly. List the points you will use to demonstrate the validity of your position. Note any unique facts or background about the work that you think will help the grader better understand your ideas.

_____

_____

_____

_____

_____

_____

_____

_____

_____

_____

**TIP**

Take a full 5 minutes to write a clearly stated and interesting first paragraph.

## Step 7

Once you have written the first paragraph, read it to be sure that your ideas follow each other logically and support the thesis.

## Step 8

Check your quick list of ideas. Choose the next idea and write a transition into your second paragraph. Now keep writing until you see all the RELEVANT ideas on your quick list.

_____

_____

_____

_____

_____

_____

_____

_____

_____

_____

_____

_____

_____

_____

_____

_____

_____

_____

_____

_____

_____

## Step 9

Allow about 5 minutes to write a solid conclusion. Choose one of these ways to conclude:

- Rephrase your thesis.
- Summarize the main points.
- Refer in some way back to your introductory paragraph.

_____

_____

_____

_____

_____

_____

_____

_____

_____

_____

_____

_____

_____

_____

_____

_____

_____

_____

**TIP**

You should have about 8 minutes of your 40 minutes left. How much time do you have?

## Step 10

Proofread and revise—NEATLY.

- Cross out any irrelevant ideas or words.
- Make any additions, especially transitions.
- Smooth out any awkward sentences.
- Check your grammar and mechanics.

**TIP**

You should have paced yourself so that you have 3 minutes for your final review.

## SUMMING IT UP

- Be sure to read the question carefully.

- Take a full 5 minutes to write a clearly stated and interesting first paragraph.

- Don't forget to use transitions between your paragraphs.

- If a new idea comes from the flow of your writing, use it if it fits the context.

- Proofread and revise.

# A Quick Review of Grammar *et al.*

## OVERVIEW

- Grammar for the multiple-choice questions
- Some practical advice on writing your essays
- Summing it up

This chapter has two parts: (1) a quick review of parts of speech for the multiple-choice section and (2) a quick overview of the grammar and punctuation that you are most likely to need to write a grammatically correct essay. The second part also offers tips for good writing.

## GRAMMAR FOR THE MULTIPLE-CHOICE QUESTIONS

The grammar questions on the AP English Literature & Composition Test are really disguised comprehension questions. They will ask you to identify one of the parts of speech—nouns, verbs, adjectives, adverbs, prepositions, conjunctions, and interjections—or they will ask you to classify parts of a sentence—subjects, predicates, complements, modifiers, or an antecedent of a word. In answering questions, remember:

- For the subject, look for nouns, pronouns, or word groups (gerunds, participial phrases, or clauses) acting as essential nouns that tell you *who* or *what* the sentence is about.

  > **What I have described in the Frenchman** was merely the result of an excited, or perhaps of a diseased, intelligence.
  > —*The Murders in the Rue Morgue,* Edgar Allan Poe

  Note: The subject will not be stated if the sentence or clause is imperative.

  > "Do talk to me as if I were one," said Lord Warburton.
  > —*Portrait of a Lady,* Henry James

241

- The direct object is a noun, pronoun, or group of words acting as a noun that receives the action of a transitive verb, the person or thing acted upon. To find a direct object, rephrase the sentence by changing it into a *whom* or *what* question.

  I believe that I have omitted **mentioning** that in my first voyage from Boston to Philadelphia, being becalmed off Block Island, our crew employed themselves catching cod and hauled up a great number.

  —*Autobiography of Benjamin Franklin,* Benjamin Franklin

  Rephrased: I have omitted whom or what? The direct object is *mentioning*.

- An indirect object is a noun or pronoun that appears with a direct object and names the person or thing that something is given to or done for.

  Whichever way I turn, O I think you could give **me** my mate back again if you only would

  —"Sea-Drift," Walt Whitman

- A sentence can have both an object and an indirect object.

  Whichever way I turn, O I think you could give **me** my **mate** back again if you only would

  —"Sea-Drift," Walt Whitman

- Verbs express action, occurrence (*appear, become, continue, feel, grow, look, remain, seem, sound,* and *taste*), or state of being (the verb *to be*).

  Ye Angells bright, **pluck** from your Wings a Quill;
  　**Make** me a pen thereof that best **will write**:
  **Lende** me your fancy and Angellick skill
  　To **treate** this Theme, more rich than Rubies bright.

  —"Meditation Sixty: Second Series," Edward Taylor

- Verbs that express occurrence or state of being are called intransitive verbs and have no objects.

  The first time that the sun rose on thine oath
  To love me, I **looked** forward to the moon
  To slacken all those bonds which seemed too soon
  And quickly tied to make a lasting troth.

  —*Sonnets from the Portuguese,* Elizabeth Barrett Browning

  *Looked* is an intransitive verb and, therefore, has no object. *Forward* is an adverb that answers the question "where," and the adverbial phrase "the first time" answers the question "when."

- An antecedent is a noun or words taking the place of nouns for which a pronoun stands.

> No good novel will ever proceed from **a** superficial mind; that seems to me an **axiom** which, for the artist in fiction, will cover all needful moral ground: if the youthful aspirant take **it** to heart **it** will illuminate for him many of the mysteries of "purpose."
>
> —"The Art of Fiction," Henry James

# SOME PRACTICAL ADVICE ON WRITING YOUR ESSAYS

The basic grammar and punctuation we are talking about here will help you with writing. Review the following rules and tips before you write a practice essay, and then evaluate your finished essay against them. As you write your next essay, keep in mind any rules you had trouble with. If necessary, focus on one rule at a time. It is important that you are comfortable with the rules of grammar and punctuation so that, as you write, you don't spend time thinking about where the commas should go.

## Sentence Structure

Good writing has a variety of sentence structures: simple, compound, complex, and compound-complex. Sentence combining is one way to be sure you have a varied sentence pattern that will add interest to your writing. Consider the following examples as possibilities that you have to choose from, and note the correct punctuation for each. All quotations are from Henry Adams's "American Ideals."

### SIMPLE SENTENCE

Of all historical problems, the nature of a national character is the most difficult and the most important.

Ralph Waldo Emerson, a more distinct idealist, was born in 1780.

### COMPOUND SENTENCE

After the downfall of the French republic, they [Americans] had no right to expect a kind word from Europe**, and** during the next twenty years, they rarely received one.

Probably Jefferson came nearest to the mark**, for** he represented the hopes of science as well as the prejudices of Virginia.

### COMPLEX SENTENCE

Lincoln was born in 1809, the moment **when** American character stood in lowest esteem. Jefferson, the literary representative of his class, spoke chiefly for Virginians, and dreaded so greatly his own reputation as a visionary **that** he seldom or never uttered his whole thought.

## COMPOUND–COMPLEX SENTENCES

Benjamin Franklin had raised high the reputation of American printers, **and** the actual President of the United States, **who** signed with Franklin the treaty of peace with Great Britain, was the son of a farmer, and had himself kept a school in his youth.

In the year 1800, Eli Terry, another Connecticut Yankee of the same class, took into his employ two young men **to help** him make wooden clocks, **and** this was the capital **on which** the greatest clock-manufactory in the world began its operation.

## PARALLEL CONSTRUCTION

In addition to using dependent and independent clauses to add variety, try using words, phrases, and clauses in parallel constructions. Parallelism reinforces equal ideas, contributes to ease in reading, and, most important, adds clarity and rhythm to your ideas. The most simple parallelism consists of/employs comparisons and contrasts.

Eli Whitney was **better** educated than Fitch, but had **neither wealth, social influence, nor patron to back his ingenuity.**

Review your own essays and underline sentences that you could combine. Then try combining them on a separate sheet of paper. This is a good exercise to get you accustomed to varying your sentence structures as you write. But do not try for variety for the first time during the real test.

In combining sentences, do not fall prey to run-on sentences, sentence fragments, or comma splices.

- A run-on sentence is a compound or compound-complex sentence in which neither a conjunction nor punctuation separates two or more independent clauses. You can fix a run-on sentence by using (1) a coordinating conjunction if you are writing a compound sentence, (2) a coordinating adverb, (3) a transitional phrase, and/or (4) a semicolon in a complex or compound-complex sentence. The examples are taken, with our apologies, from "Milton" by John Babington Macaulay.

  1. Milton was, like Dante, a statesman and a lover**, and,** like Dante, he had been unfortunate in ambition and in love.

  2. Milton was, like Dante, a statesman and a lover**; moreover,** like Dante, he had been unfortunate in ambition and in love.

  3. Milton was, like Dante, a statesman and a lover**; in addition,** like Dante, he had been unfortunate in ambition and in love.

  4. Milton was, like Dante, a statesman and a lover**;** like Dante, he had been unfortunate in ambition and in love. (**Macaulay's choice**)

Did you notice that these sentences are also examples of both comparison and the use of independent clauses as parallelism?

- A sentence fragment is just that—part of a sentence, a group of words that does not express a complete thought. If it has a verb form—a verbal such as a participle—it may look like a sentence, but it is not a sentence. You can avoid sentence fragments by always making sure that:

1.  The verb is a verb—not a participial form (-ing or -ed) without its auxiliary (some form of *have* or *be*) or an infinitive (*to* plus a verb).

2.  There is a subject. If there is none, add one or attach the fragment to a sentence.

3.  You remove any incorrectly used subordinating conjunctions, or you combine the fragment so it becomes a sentence.

    a.  Such as it was. When, on the eve of great events, he [Milton] returned from his travels, in the prime of health and manly beauty. Loaded with literary distinctions, and glowing with patriotic hopes. . . .

    b.  Such as it was. When, on the eve of great events, he [Milton] returned from his travels, in the prime of health and manly beauty, **loaded** with literary distinctions, and glowing with patriotic hopes. . . .

    c.  Such as it was. When, on the eve of great events, he [Milton] returned from his travels, in the prime of health and manly beauty. **He was** loaded with literary distinctions, and glowing with patriotic hopes. . . .

    d.  Such as it was **when**, on the eve of great events, he [Milton] returned from his travels, in the prime of health and manly beauty, **loaded** with literary distinctions, and glowing with patriotic hopes. . . . (**Macaulay's choice**)

| CONJUNCTIVE ADVERBS | | TRANSITIONAL PHRASES |
| --- | --- | --- |
| also | meanwhile | after all |
| anyhow | moreover | as a consequence |
| anyway | nevertheless | as a result |
| besides | next | at any rate |
| consequently | nonetheless | at the same time |
| finally | now | by the way |
| furthermore | otherwise | even so |
| hence | similarly | for example |
| however | still | in addition |
| incidentally | then | in fact |
| indeed | therefore | in other words |
| likewise | thus | in the second place |
| | | on the contrary |
| | | on the other hand |

- Comma splices occur when two or more independent clauses are joined by a comma (1) when some other punctuation or (2) a coordinating or (3) subordinating conjunction should have been used.

Euripedes attempted to carry the reform further, it was a task beyond his powers, perhaps beyond any powers.

1.  Euripedes attempted to carry the reform further; it was a task beyond his powers, perhaps beyond any powers. (**Macauly's choice**)

2.  Euripedes attempted to carry the reform further, **but** it was a task beyond his powers, perhaps beyond any powers.

3.  **While** Euripedes attempted to carry the reform further, the task was beyond his powers, perhaps beyond any powers.

| COORDINATING CONJUNCTIONS | SUBORDINATING CONJUNCTIONS | |
|---|---|---|
| and | after | no matter how |
| but | although | now that |
| or | as far as | once |
| for | as soon as | provided that |
| nor | as if | since |
| so | as though | so that |
| yet | because | supposing that |
| | before | than |
| | even if | though |
| | even though | till, until |
| | how | unless |
| | if | when, whenever |
| | inasmuch as | where, wherever |
| | in case that | whether |
| | insofar as | while |
| | in that | why |

**RELATIVE PRONOUNS**
(used to introduce subordinate
clauses that function as nouns)

| | |
|---|---|
| that | who, whoever |
| what | whom, whomever |
| which | whose |

You can also use subordinate conjunctions, conjunctive adverbs, and transitional phrases to link ideas between sentences and even paragraphs.

**Now** let us compare with the exact detail . . .

**Once more,** compare . . .

We venture to say, **on the contrary,** . . .

—"Milton," Thomas Babington Macaulay

## Grammar and Punctuation

What do you need to know about grammar and punctuation for the AP English Literature & Composition Test? Enough to be able to write and punctuate grammatically correct sentences. (This, by the way, is a sentence fragment. In your own writing, an occasional sentence fragment works, but do not take the chance in your essays. The reader may not understand that you wrote a sentence fragment for a purpose and not as a mistake.)

If you find any of the rules in the following brief review unfamiliar, go back to your English composition text and review the appropriate section in more depth. Do some of the practice exercises the text undoubtedly has. The following examples are taken from Henry James's "The Art of Fiction."

**NOTE**
Concentrate on those rules that you are most likely to need for your own writing.

### USE COMMAS

- After each word, phrase, or clause in a series

  Art lives **upon discussion, upon experiment, upon curiosity, upon variety of attempt, upon the exchange of views, and the comparison of standpoints** . . .

  **Discussion, suggestion, formulation,** these things are fertilizing when they are frank and sincere.

- Before a coordinating conjunction that links parts of a compound sentence or links independent clauses in a compound-complex sentence

  Humanity is immense, **and** reality has myriad forms.

  The subject-matter of fiction is stored up likewise in documents and records, **and** if it will not give itself away, as they say in California, it must speak with assurance . . .

- To set off introductory phrases and clauses

  **In a digression, a parenthesis, or an aside,** he [Anthony Trollope] concedes to the reader that he and this trusting friend are only "making believe."

  **If experience consists of impressions,** it may be said that impressions are experience . . .

- To set off nonrestrictive and other parenthetical expressions, that is, adjective clauses and phrases that provide additional, nonessential information and that can be omitted without changing the thought of the sentence

  . . . the analogy between the art of the painter and the art of the novelist is, **so far as I am able to see,** complete.

The reality of Don Quixote or of Mr. Micawber is a very delicate shade; it is a reality so colored by the author's vision that, **vivid as it may be,** one would hesitate to propose it as a model . . .

- To set off a nonrestrictive appositive, a word or phrase that provides additional nonessential information about a noun or pronoun

Henry James, **the brother of William James,** was . . .

The essay "The Art of Fiction," **part of a larger work,** was one of . . .

## USE SEMICOLONS

- To separate parts of a compound sentence when there is no conjunction, and thus avoid a run-on sentence

Milton was, like Dante, a statesman and a lover; like Dante, he had been unfortunate in ambition and in love. (Macaulay's choice)

- To separate a transitional word or phrase from the preceding clause when the word or phrase introduces a new independent clause, thus avoiding a run-on sentence

Milton was, like Dante, a statesman and a lover; **in addition,** like Dante, he had been unfortunate in ambition and in love.

## USE COLONS

- To introduce a formal list of items or a long quotation; do not use colons between a verb and its object or after *such as*. To use a colon, you need to have a list that it sets off.

The following five writers exemplify realism in the twentieth century:

NOT

The five writers who best exemplify realism are:

## SOME MISCELLANEOUS *DO'S* AND *DON'TS*:

- Don't overuse dashes. Dashes should be used (1) to show a break in thought, (2) to set off a parenthetical element for emphasis or clarity, or (3) to set off an introductory list or series. The use of dashes often marks the work of a writer with little to say, one who does not have command of the conventions of English, or an individual who does not know how to develop ideas clearly. Use dashes in your essays with restraint.

- If you are mentioning by title the name of a book or play, underline it, since you cannot italicize it.

- If you are mentioning the name of a poem, a chapter title, or a short story, enclose it in quotation marks.

- Place commas inside quotation marks, but place colons and semicolons outside the quotation marks.

- Question marks should be placed inside quotation marks if they are part of the quotation and outside if they are not.

- Discuss literary works using the present tense.

- Don't confuse *its* and *it's*. Ask yourself if the sentence makes sense when you use the words *it is* (The dog shook *it is* tail). If not, then use *its*. If so, then use *it's*. (*It is* a Yorkshire terrier.) Try the same strategy for *your* and *you're,* and *their* and *they're*.

## Diction

Word choice speaks volumes about you. (That phrase is a cliché that would be best to avoid.) The following are some *Do's* and *Don'ts* to consider in your writing (this is a formal list, so a colon is the correct punctuation):

- Your essays are formal, so do not use slang or colloquialisms such as (this is not a formal list, so a colon is not correct punctuation) *awesome, totally, clueless.*

- Do not use nonstandard English.

- Be sure you know the difference between each of the following (another formal list):

| | |
|---|---|
| accept, except | fewer, less |
| affect, effect | good, well |
| allusion, illusion | if, whether |
| among, between | imply, infer |
| can, may | may be, maybe |
| compare with, compare to | media, medium |
| different from, different than | sensuous, sensual |
| explicit, implicit | that, which |
| farther, further | |

- Use

    *but that,* not *but what*
    *because of,* not *due to*
    *because,* not *on account of*
    rarely, hardly ever, *not* rarely ever
    kind, kind of a, *not* sort, sort of

NOTE

Having this list in
mind will keep
you from having
writer's block
during the test.

## DEVELOP AN IDEA BANK

Before you begin practicing for the essay section of the test, brainstorm all the words and phrases you can think of to describe a literary work. Divide the list by fiction, nonfiction, poetry, and drama, and then make categories under each. You might do the exercise with a friend, and then share lists to gather as many words as you can. Use this as your idea bank and your word bank and consult it before you begin each practice essay. Here is a start on your list.

| DRAMA | DICTION | STYLE |
|---|---|---|
| denouement | verbose | convoluted |
| rising action | wordy | elegant |
| mood | flowery | precise |

## SUMMING IT UP

- The grammar questions will ask you to identify one of the parts of speech:

  - Nouns

  - Verbs

  - Adjectives

  - Adverbs

  - Prepositions

  - Conjunctions

  - Interjections

- The grammar questions will ask you to classify parts of a sentence:

  - Subjects

  - Predicates

  - Complements

  - Modifiers

  - Antecedent

- Review grammar rules and tips.

- Develop an idea bank.

# A Quick Review of Literary Terms

You will find a few questions on the multiple-choice section of the test that ask you to identify literary types and devices. Do not memorize the following list, but as you read novels, poems, plays, short stories, and essays, see if you can pick out examples.

**accent:** the stressed portion of a word

**allegory:** an extended narrative in prose or verse in which characters, events, and settings represent abstract qualities and in which the writer intends a second meaning to be read beneath the surface story; the underlying meaning may be moral, religious, political, social, or satiric

**alliteration:** the repetition of consonant sounds at the beginning of words that are close to one another; for example, "beautiful blossoms blooming between the bushes"

**allusion:** a reference to another work or famous figure assumed to be well known enough to be recognized by the reader

**anachronism:** an event, object, custom, person, or thing that is out of order in time; some anachronisms are unintentional, such as when an actor performing Shakespeare forgets to take off his watch; others are deliberately used to achieve a humorous or satiric effect, such as the sustained anachronism of Mark Twain's *A Connecticut Yankee in King Arthur's Court*

**analogy:** a comparison of two similar but different things, usually to clarify an action or a relationship, such as comparing the work of a heart to that of a pump

**anecdote:** a short, simple narrative of an incident

**aphorism:** a short, often witty statement of a principle or a truth about life

**apostrophe:** the device of calling out to an imaginary, dead, or absent person, or to a place, thing, or personified abstraction either to begin a poem or to make a dramatic break in thought somewhere within the poem (usually in poetry but sometimes in prose)

**aside:** a brief speech or comment that an actor makes to the audience, supposedly without being heard by the other actors on stage; often used for melodramatic or comedic effect

**assonance:** the repetition of vowel sounds between different consonants, such as in *neigh/fade*

**ballad:** a long narrative poem that presents a single dramatic episode, which is often tragic or violent; the two types of ballads are:

- **folk ballad:** one of the earliest forms of literature, a folk ballad was usually sung and was passed down orally from singer to singer; its author (if a single author) is generally unknown, and its form and melody often changed according to a singer's preference

- **literary ballad:** also called an art ballad, this is a ballad that imitates the form and spirit of the folk ballad, but is more polished and uses a higher level of poetic diction

**blank verse:** poetry written in unrhymed iambic pentameter; a favorite form used by Shakespeare

**burlesque:** broad parody; whereas a parody will imitate and exaggerate a specific work, such as *Romeo and Juliet,* a burlesque will take an entire style or form, such as pastoral poetry, and exaggerate it into ridiculousness

**cacophony:** harsh, awkward, or dissonant sounds used deliberately in poetry or prose; the opposite of euphony

**caricature:** descriptive writing that greatly exaggerates a specific feature of appearance or a facet of personality

**catharsis:** the emotional release that an audience member experiences as a result of watching a tragedy

**chorus:** in Greek drama, a group of characters who comments on the action taking place on stage

**classicism:** the principles and styles admired in the classics of Greek and Roman literature, such as objectivity, sensibility, restraint, and formality

**colloquialism:** a word or phrase used in everyday conversation and informal writing that is sometimes inappropriate in formal writing

**conceit:** an elaborate **figure of speech** in which two seemingly dissimilar things or situations are compared

**consonance:** the repetition of identical consonant sounds before and after different vowel sounds, as in *boost/best*; can also be seen within several compound words, such as *fulfill* and *ping-pong*

**conundrum:** a riddle whose answer is or involves a pun; may also be a paradox or difficult problem

**description:** the picturing in words of something or someone through detailed observation of color, motion, sound, taste, smell, and touch; one of the four **modes of discourse**

**diction:** word choice; also called **syntax**

**discourse:** spoken or written language, including literary works; the four traditionally classified **modes of discourse** are **description, exposition, narration,** and **persuasion**

**dissonance:** the grating of sounds that are harsh or do not go together

**elegy:** a formal poem focusing on death or mortality, usually beginning with the recent death of a particular person

**end rhyme:** a rhyme that comes at the end of lines of poetry; for example:

> Her voice, soft and lovely when she *sings,*
> Came to me last night in a *dream.*
> In my head her voice still *rings,*
> How pleasant last night must *seem.*

**epic:** a long narrative poem about a serious or profound subject in a dignified style; usually featuring heroic characters and deeds important in legends; two famous examples include the *Iliad* and the *Odyssey,* both written by the Greek poet Homer

**epigram:** a concise, witty saying in poetry or prose that either stands alone or is part of a larger work; may also refer to a short poem of this type

**euphony:** a succession of harmonious sounds used in poetry or prose; the opposite of **cacophony**

**exemplum:** a brief tale used in medieval times to illustrate a sermon or teach a lesson

**exposition:** the immediate revelation to the audience of the setting and other background information necessary for understanding the plot; also, explanation; one of the four **modes of discourse**

**farce:** a light, dramatic composition characterized by broad satirical comedy and a highly improbable plot

**figurative language:** language that contains **figures of speech** such as similes and metaphors in order to create associations that are imaginative rather than literal

**figures of speech:** expressions such as similes, metaphors, and personifications that make imaginative, rather than literal, comparisons or associations

**foil:** a character who, by contrast, highlights the characteristics of another character

**folklore:** traditional stories, songs, dances, and customs that are preserved among a people; folklore usually precedes literature, being passed down orally between generations until recorded by scholars

**foot:** the combination of stressed and unstressed syllables that makes up the basic rhythmic unit of a line of poetry; common poetic feet include:

- **anapest:** two unstressed followed by one stressed syllable, as in in-ter-*rupt*

- **dactyl:** one stressed followed by two unstressed syllables, as in *beau*-ti-ful

- **iamb:** one unstressed followed by one stressed syllable, as in dis-*turb*

- **spondee:** two successive stressed syllables, as in *hodge-podge*

- **trochee:** one stressed followed by one unstressed syllable, as in *in*-jure and *con*-stant

**foreshadowing:** the use of a hint or clue to suggest a larger event that occurs later in the work

**free verse:** poetry that is written without a regular meter, usually without rhyme

**genre:** a type of literary work, such as a novel or poem; there are also subgenres, such as science fiction novel and sonnet, within the larger genres

**gothic:** referring to a type of novel that emerged in the eighteenth century that uses mystery, suspense, and sensational and supernatural occurrences to evoke terror

**hubris:** the excessive pride or ambition that leads a tragic hero to disregard warnings of impending doom, eventually causing his or her downfall

**humor:** anything that causes laughter or amusement; up until the end of the Renaissance, humor meant a person's temperament

**hyperbole:** deliberate exaggeration in order to create **humor** or emphasis

**idyll:** a short descriptive narrative, usually a poem, about an idealized country life; also called a **pastoral**

**imagery:** words or phrases that use a collection of images to appeal to one or more of the five senses in order to create a mental picture

**interior monologue:** writing that records the conversation that occurs inside a character's head

**internal rhyme:** a rhyme occurring within a line of poetry, as in Edgar Allan Poe's "The Raven":

> Once upon a midnight *dreary,* while I pondered,
>> weak and *weary,*
> Over many a quaint and curious volume of forgotten lore,
> While I nodded, nearly *napping,* suddenly there came
>> a *tapping,*
> As of some one gently *rapping, rapping* at my chamber door.

**inversion:** reversing the customary order of elements in a sentence or phrase; used effectively in many cases, such as posing a question: "Are you going to the store?" Often used ineffectively in poetry, making it seem artifical and stilted, "to the hounds she rode, with her flags behind her streaming"

**irony:** a situation or statement in which the actual outcome or meaning is opposite to what was expected

**loose sentence:** a sentence that is grammatically complete before its end, such as "Thalia played the violin with an intensity never before seen in a high school music class"; the sentence is grammatically complete with the word *violin*

**lyric:** a type of melodious, imaginative, and subjective poetry that is usually short and personal, expressing the thoughts and feelings of a single speaker rather than telling a story

**metaphor:** a figure of speech in which one thing is referred to as another; for example, "my love is a fragile flower"

**meter:** the repetition of a regular rhythmic unit in a line of poetry; meters found in poetry include:

- **monometer:** one foot (rare)
- **dimeter:** two feet (rare)
- **trimeter:** three feet
- **tetrameter:** four feet
- **pentameter:** five feet
- **hexameter:** six feet
- **heptameter:** seven feet (rare)

**metonymy:** a **figure of speech** that uses the name of an object, person, or idea to represent something with which it is associated, such as using "the crown" to refer to a monarch

**mode:** the method or form of a literary work; a manner in which a work of literature is written

**mood:** similar to **tone,** mood is the primary emotional attitude of a work

**myth:** one story in a system of narratives set in a complete imaginary world that once served to explain the origin of life, religious beliefs, and the forces of nature as supernatural occurrences

**narration:** the telling of a story in fiction, nonfiction, poetry, or drama; one of the four **modes of discourse**

**naturalism:** a literary movement that grew out of realism in France, the United States, and England in the late nineteenth and early twentieth centuries; it portrays humans as having no free will, being driven by the natural forces of heredity, environment, and animalistic urges over which they have no control

**objectivity:** an impersonal presentation of events and characters

**ode:** a long lyric poem, usually serious and elevated in tone; often written to praise someone or something

**onomatopoeia:** the use of words that sound like what they mean, such as *hiss* and *boom*

**oxymoron:** a **figure of speech** composed of contradictory words or phrases, such as "wise fool"

**parable:** a short tale that teaches a moral; similar to but shorter than an **allegory**

**paradox:** a statement that seems to contradict itself but that turns out to have a rational meaning, as in this quotation from Henry David Thoreau: "I never found the companion that was so companionable as solitude."

**parallelism:** the technique of arranging words, phrases, clauses, or larger structures by placing them side to side and making them similar in form

**parody:** a work that ridicules the style of another work by imitating and exaggerating its elements

**pastoral:** a poem about idealized rural life, or shepherds, or both; also called an **idyll**

**periodic sentence:** a sentence that is not grammatically complete until its last phrase, such as, "Despite Glenn's hatred of his sister's laziness and noisy eating habits, he still cared for her."

**personification:** the attribution of human qualities to a nonhuman or an inanimate object

**persuasion:** one of the four **modes of discourse**; language intended to convince through appeals to reason or emotion; also called **argument**

**Petrarchan sonnet:** one of the most important types of **sonnets,** composed of an octave with an *abba abba* rhyme scheme, and ending in a sestet with a *cde cde* rhyme scheme; also called an Italian sonnet

**point of view:** the perspective from which a story is presented; common points of view include:

- **first person narrator:** a narrator, referred to as "I," who is a character in the story and relates the actions through his or her own perspective, also revealing his or her own thoughts

- **stream of consciousness narrator:** like a first person narrator, but instead placing the reader inside the character's head, making the reader privy to the continuous, chaotic flow of disconnected, half-formed thoughts and impressions as they flow through the character's consciousness

- **omniscient narrator:** a third person narrator, referred to as "he," "she," or "they," who is able to see into each character's mind and understands all the action

- **limited omniscient narrator:** a third person narrator who only reports the thoughts of one character, and generally only what that one character sees

- **objective narrator:** a third person narrator who only reports what would be visible to a camera; thoughts and feelings are only revealed if a character speaks of them

**protagonist:** the main character of a literary work

**realism:** a nineteenth-century literary movement in Europe and the United States that stressed accuracy in the portrayal of life, focusing on characters with whom middle-class readers could easily identify; in direct contrast with **romanticism**

**refrain:** a line or group of lines that is periodically repeated throughout a poem

**regionalism:** an element in literature that conveys a realistic portrayal of a specific geographic locale, using the locale and its influences as a major part of the plot

**rhyme:** a similarity of accented sounds between two words, such as *sad / mad;* rhymes can be masculine or feminine:

- **masculine:** the rhyme sound is the last syllable of a line, i.e., *profound / bound*

- **feminine:** the accented syllable is followed by an unaccented syllable, i.e., *banding / landing*

**romanticism:** a literary, artistic, and philosophical movement that began in the eighteenth century as a reaction against neoclassicism; the focal points of the movement are imagination, emotion, and freedom, stressing subjectivity, individuality, the love and worship of nature, and a fascination with the past

**sarcasm:** harsh, caustic personal remarks to or about someone; less subtle than **irony**

**simile:** a **figure of speech** that uses *like, as,* or *as if* to make a direct comparison between two essentially different objects, actions, or qualities; for example, "the sky looked like an artist's canvas"

**soliloquy:** a speech spoken by a character alone on stage, giving the impression that the audience is listening to the character's thoughts; perhaps the most famous example is Hamlet's speech beginning "To be, or not to be"

**sonnet:** a fourteen-line **lyric** poem in **iambic pentameter**

**speaker:** the voice of a poem; an author may speak as himself or herself or as a fictitious character

**stanza:** a group of lines in the formal pattern of a poem; types of stanzas include:

- **couplet:** the simplest stanza, consisting of two rhymed lines

- **tercet:** three lines, usually having the same rhyme

- **quatrain:** four lines

- **cinquain:** five lines

- **sestet:** six lines

- **octave:** eight lines

**stereotype:** a character who represents a trait that is usually attributed to a particular social or racial group and lacks individuality

**stock character:** a standard character who may be **stereotyped,** such as the miser or the fool, or universally recognized, like the hard-boiled private eye in detective stories

**style:** an author's characteristic manner of expression

**subjectivity:** a personal presentation of events and characters, influenced by the author's feelings and opinions

**suspension of disbelief:** the demand made of a theater audience to provide some details with their imagination and to accept the limitations of reality and staging; also, the acceptance of the incidents of the plot by a reader or audience

**symbolism:** the use of symbols, or anything that is meant to be taken both literally and as representative of a higher and more complex significance

**synecdoche:** a **figure of speech** in which a part of something is used to represent a whole, such as using "boards" to mean "a stage" or "wheels" to mean "a car"

**syntax:** word choice or **diction**

**theme:** the central idea or "message" of a literary work

**tone:** the characteristic emotion or attitude of an author toward the characters, subject, and audience

**tragic flaw:** the one weakness that causes the downfall of the hero in a tragedy

**villanelle:** a lyric poem consisting of five tercets and a final quatrain

**voice:** the way a written work conveys an author's attitude

# PART IV
## THREE PRACTICE TESTS

# ANSWER SHEET PRACTICE TEST 2

## SECTION I

1. Ⓐ Ⓑ Ⓒ Ⓓ Ⓔ
2. Ⓐ Ⓑ Ⓒ Ⓓ Ⓔ
3. Ⓐ Ⓑ Ⓒ Ⓓ Ⓔ
4. Ⓐ Ⓑ Ⓒ Ⓓ Ⓔ
5. Ⓐ Ⓑ Ⓒ Ⓓ Ⓔ
6. Ⓐ Ⓑ Ⓒ Ⓓ Ⓔ
7. Ⓐ Ⓑ Ⓒ Ⓓ Ⓔ
8. Ⓐ Ⓑ Ⓒ Ⓓ Ⓔ
9. Ⓐ Ⓑ Ⓒ Ⓓ Ⓔ
10. Ⓐ Ⓑ Ⓒ Ⓓ Ⓔ
11. Ⓐ Ⓑ Ⓒ Ⓓ Ⓔ
12. Ⓐ Ⓑ Ⓒ Ⓓ Ⓔ
13. Ⓐ Ⓑ Ⓒ Ⓓ Ⓔ
14. Ⓐ Ⓑ Ⓒ Ⓓ Ⓔ
15. Ⓐ Ⓑ Ⓒ Ⓓ Ⓔ
16. Ⓐ Ⓑ Ⓒ Ⓓ Ⓔ
17. Ⓐ Ⓑ Ⓒ Ⓓ Ⓔ

18. Ⓐ Ⓑ Ⓒ Ⓓ Ⓔ
19. Ⓐ Ⓑ Ⓒ Ⓓ Ⓔ
20. Ⓐ Ⓑ Ⓒ Ⓓ Ⓔ
21. Ⓐ Ⓑ Ⓒ Ⓓ Ⓔ
22. Ⓐ Ⓑ Ⓒ Ⓓ Ⓔ
23. Ⓐ Ⓑ Ⓒ Ⓓ Ⓔ
24. Ⓐ Ⓑ Ⓒ Ⓓ Ⓔ
25. Ⓐ Ⓑ Ⓒ Ⓓ Ⓔ
26. Ⓐ Ⓑ Ⓒ Ⓓ Ⓔ
27. Ⓐ Ⓑ Ⓒ Ⓓ Ⓔ
28. Ⓐ Ⓑ Ⓒ Ⓓ Ⓔ
29. Ⓐ Ⓑ Ⓒ Ⓓ Ⓔ
30. Ⓐ Ⓑ Ⓒ Ⓓ Ⓔ
31. Ⓐ Ⓑ Ⓒ Ⓓ Ⓔ
32. Ⓐ Ⓑ Ⓒ Ⓓ Ⓔ
33. Ⓐ Ⓑ Ⓒ Ⓓ Ⓔ
34. Ⓐ Ⓑ Ⓒ Ⓓ Ⓔ

35. Ⓐ Ⓑ Ⓒ Ⓓ Ⓔ
36. Ⓐ Ⓑ Ⓒ Ⓓ Ⓔ
37. Ⓐ Ⓑ Ⓒ Ⓓ Ⓔ
38. Ⓐ Ⓑ Ⓒ Ⓓ Ⓔ
39. Ⓐ Ⓑ Ⓒ Ⓓ Ⓔ
40. Ⓐ Ⓑ Ⓒ Ⓓ Ⓔ
41. Ⓐ Ⓑ Ⓒ Ⓓ Ⓔ
42. Ⓐ Ⓑ Ⓒ Ⓓ Ⓔ
43. Ⓐ Ⓑ Ⓒ Ⓓ Ⓔ
44. Ⓐ Ⓑ Ⓒ Ⓓ Ⓔ
45. Ⓐ Ⓑ Ⓒ Ⓓ Ⓔ
46. Ⓐ Ⓑ Ⓒ Ⓓ Ⓔ
47. Ⓐ Ⓑ Ⓒ Ⓓ Ⓔ
48. Ⓐ Ⓑ Ⓒ Ⓓ Ⓔ
49. Ⓐ Ⓑ Ⓒ Ⓓ Ⓔ
50. Ⓐ Ⓑ Ⓒ Ⓓ Ⓔ

answer sheet

## SECTION II

### Essay Question 1

_____

_____

_____

_____

_____

_____

_____

_____

_____

_____

_____

_____

_____

_____

_____

_____

_____

_____

_____

_____

_____

_____

_____

_____

_____

answer sheet

**Essay Question 2**

_____

_____

_____

_____

_____

_____

_____

_____

_____

_____

_____

_____

_____

_____

_____

_____

_____

_____

_____

_____

_____

_____

_____

_____

_____

answer sheet

**Essay Question 3**

answer sheet

# Practice Test 2

## SECTION I

*50 QUESTIONS • 60 MINUTES*

> **Directions:** This section consists of selections of literature and questions on their content, style, and form. After you have read each passage, choose the answer that best answers the question and mark the space on the answer sheet.

**QUESTIONS 1 THROUGH 15 REFER TO THE FOLLOWING SELECTION THAT WAS WRITTEN IN 1780 WHEN BENJAMIN FRANKLIN WAS RESTRICTED TO HIS HOUSE DURING AN ATTACK OF GOUT. READ THE PASSAGE CAREFULLY AND THEN CHOOSE THE ANSWERS TO THE QUESTIONS.**

**From "Dialogue Between Franklin and the Gout"**

Line

**Franklin.** How can you so cruelly sport with my torments?

**Gout.** Sport! I am very serious. I have here a list of offenses against your own health distinctly written and can justify every stroke inflicted on you.

5 **Franklin.** Read it, then.

**Gout.** It is too long a detail, but I will briefly mention some particulars.

**Franklin.** Proceed. I am all attention.

**Gout.** Do you remember how often you have promised yourself,
10 the following morning, a walk in the grove of Boulogne, in the garden de la Muette, or in your own garden, and have violated your promise, alleging, at one time, it was too cold, at another, too warm, too wind, too moist, or what else you pleased, when in truth it was too nothing but
15 your insuperable love of ease?

**Franklin.** That I confess may have happened occasionally, probably ten times in a year.

**Gout.** Your confession is very far short of the truth. The gross amount is one hundred and ninety-nine times.

20 **Franklin.** Is it possible?

**Gout.** So possible, that it is fact. You may rely on the accuracy of my statement. You know M. Brillon's gardens and what fine walks they contain, you know the handsome flight of a hundred steps which lead from the terrace above to the

273

25    lawn below. You have been in the practice of visiting this amiable family twice a week, after dinner, and it is a maxim of your own that "a man may take as much exercise in walking a mile up and down stairs as in ten on level ground." What an opportunity was here for you to have had exercise in both these ways! Did you embrace it, and how often?

30   **Franklin.**  I cannot immediately answer that question.

      **Gout.**  I will do it for you: not once.

  **Franklin.**  Not once?

      **Gout.**  Even so. During the summer you went there at six o'clock. You found the charming lady with her lovely children and friends eager to walk with you and entertain you with their agreeable conversation, and what has been your choice? Why to sit on the terrace, satisfying yourself with the fine prospect and passing your eye over the beauties of the garden below, without taking one step to descend and walk about in them. On the contrary, you call for tea and the chessboard, and lo! You are occupied in your seat till nine o'clock, and that besides two hours' play after dinner; and then, instead of walking home, which would have bestirred you a little, you step into your carriage. How absurd to suppose that all this carelessness can be reconcilable with health without my interposition!

  **Franklin.**  I am convinced now of the justness of poor Richard's remark that "Our debts and our sins are always greater than we think for."

      **Gout.**  So it is. You philosophers are sages in your maxims and fools in your conduct.

  **Franklin.**  But do you charge among my crimes that I return in a carriage from M. Brillon's?

50       **Gout.**  Certainly, for, having been seated all the while, you cannot object the fatigue of the day and cannot want therefore the relief of a carriage.

  **Franklin.**  What then would you have me do with my carriage?

      **Gout.**  Burn it if you choose, you would at least get heat out of it once in this way; or, if you dislike that proposal, here's another for you: observe the poor peasants who work in the vineyard and grounds about the villages of Passy, Auteuil, Chaillot, etc., you may find every day among these deserving creatures four or five old men and women bent and perhaps crippled by weight of years and too long and too great labor. After a most fatiguing day these people have to trudge a mile or two to their smoky huts. Order your coachman to set them down. This is an act that will be good for your soul; and, at the same time, after your visit to the Brillons', if you return on foot, that will be good for your body.

  **Franklin.**  Ah! How tiresome you are!

      **Gout.**  Well, then, to my office, it should not be forgotten that I am your physician. There . . .

65   **Franklin.**  Oh! Oh!—for Heaven's sake leave me! And I promise faithfully never more to play at chess but to take exercise daily and live temperately.

      **Gout.**  I know you too well. You promise fair, but, after a few months of good health, you will return to your old habits; your fine promises will be forgotten like the forms of last year's clouds. Let us then finish the account, and I will go. But I leave you with an assurance of visiting you again at a proper time and place, for my object is your good, and you are sensible now that I am your *real friend.*

—Benjamin Franklin

1. Which of the following best summarizes the theme of this excerpt?

   (A) A statement on the health of wealthy individuals
   (B) A delineation of the reasons to exercise
   (C) A fanciful discussion between a man and his disease
   (D) A lamentation of a man who is hurting
   (E) A dialogue for a morality play

2. What is the literary process that gives Gout voice?

   (A) Alliteration
   (B) Metaphor
   (C) Allegory
   (D) Personification
   (E) Simile

3. What is the tone of the dialogue?

   (A) Clinical, scientific
   (B) Reasoned, yet humorous
   (C) Formal and structured
   (D) Silly and frivolous
   (E) Objective

4. When Franklin acknowledges the justness of the statement "Our debts and our sins are always greater than we think for," (lines 44–45) which of the following is he confirming?

   (A) We believe that many of our debts are too great.
   (B) We believe that we should not have any debts.
   (C) We believe that our debts and our sins are always smaller than they turn out to be.
   (D) We believe that committing a sin should not create a debt that we must pay.
   (E) We believe that others do not have to pay as heavily for their sins.

5. The eighteenth century was called the Age of Reason. How does this dialogue reflect this?

   (A) Gout attempts to reason with Franklin.
   (B) Franklin accepts scientific reasoning.
   (C) The passage requires intuitive thought development on the part of the reader.
   (D) The concern for health is a "reasonable" interest.
   (E) Dialogue was a popular literary form in the 1700s.

6. Which of the following is the best characterization of Gout's reaction to Franklin's statement that Gout is sporting with him?

   (A) Indignant
   (B) Pleased
   (C) Chastised
   (D) Contrite
   (E) Oblivious

7. From this dialogue, what assumption can be made about what Franklin advocates?

   (A) Walking when in a foreign country
   (B) Helping the poor and less fortunate
   (C) Reasonable and responsible behavior on the part of the individual
   (D) Involvement in the health practices of others
   (E) Limiting time spent playing games

8. Why does Gout count as one of Franklin's crimes that he rode home in his carriage from M. Brillon's?

   (A) Franklin sat on the terrace looking at the garden.
   (B) Franklin did not let the peasants from the village of Passy ride with him.
   (C) Franklin played chess for two hours after dinner.
   (D) Franklin sat all day and so could not be tired.
   (E) Franklin walked a mile up and down the stairs.

9. Gout's attitude toward Franklin is best identified as

   (A) disgusted
   (B) conciliatory
   (C) superficial
   (D) stern
   (E) pedantic

10. Why does the author elect to express his ideas through a dialogue between Gout and Franklin?

    (A) It allows clarity between Gout's thoughts and Franklin's reaction.
    (B) It makes it easier for Franklin to dispute the misinterpretation of Gout.
    (C) The author's only purpose was to be light-hearted.
    (D) It challenges the reader to take the side of Gout or Franklin.
    (E) It leaves ambiguity as to the motives of Gout and Franklin.

11. Which of the following statements most accurately characterizes the interests of Franklin?

    (A) He likes walking in the gardens.
    (B) He enjoys being with friends.
    (C) He likes to be outdoors in the sun.
    (D) He enjoys a sedentary lifestyle.
    (E) He puts his work second to pleasure.

12. What does the sentence in line 30, "I cannot immediately answer that question," say about Franklin's state of mind?

    (A) He is argumentative.
    (B) He is forgetful.
    (C) He is feeling guilty.
    (D) He is not being serious.
    (E) He is tired of the discussion.

13. How does the dialogue reflect the eighteenth century's interest in science?

    (A) The mention of gardens
    (B) Recognition that walking is important exercise
    (C) Use of scientific reasons for medical conditions
    (D) Use of scientific language
    (E) Inclusion of quotations from an important scientific work

14. What is Franklin the author suggesting by Gout's statement "So it is. You philosophers are sages in your maxims and fools in your conduct." (lines 46–47)?

    (A) Philosophers are ignorant.
    (B) Wise people are infallible.
    (C) People can make wise statements and take unwise actions.
    (D) Intelligent comments are not always used.
    (E) People can make ill-considered statements.

15. Which of the following identifies the best reason why Franklin the author suggests that Franklin the character give his carriage to the peasants?

    (A) Franklin needs to show regret for his failures.
    (B) The suggestion contrasts with Franklin's lifestyle.
    (C) The peasants are not able to walk as well as Franklin after they have been working.
    (D) Franklin is not happy with his lifestyle.
    (E) The workers suggested it to Franklin.

QUESTIONS 16 THROUGH 26 REFER TO THE FOLLOWING SELECTION FROM *HENRY V.* READ THE PASSAGE CAREFULLY AND THEN CHOOSE THE ANSWERS TO THE QUESTIONS.

**From *Henry V***

Line  This day is called the Feast of Crispian.
He that outlives this day and comes safe home
Will stand a tip-toe when this day is named
And rouse him at the name of Crispian.
5    He that shall live this day and see old age
Will yearly on the vigil feast his neighbours
And say, "Tomorrow is Saint Crispian."
Then will he strip his sleeve and show his scars
And say, "These wounds I had on Crispian's day."
10   Old men forget; yet all shall be forgot
But he'll remember, with advantages
What feats he did that day. Then shall our names,
Familiar in his mouth as household words—
Harry the king, Bedford and Exeter,
15   Warwick and Talbot, Salisbury and Gloucester—
Be in their flowing cups freshly remembered.
This story shall the good man teach his son,
And Crispin Crispian shall ne'er go by
From this day to the ending of the world
20   But we in it shall be rememberèd,
We few, we happy few, we band of brothers,
For he today that sheds his blood with me
Shall be my brother; be he ne'er so vile,
This day shall gentle his condition.
25   And gentlemen in England now abed
Shall think themselves accursed they were not here,
And hold their manhoods cheap whiles any speaks
That fought with us upon Saint Crispin's day.

—William Shakespeare

**16.** Which of the following is true of this excerpt?

 **(A)** It is an example of free verse.
 **(B)** It is an epic.
 **(C)** It is an example of blank verse.
 **(D)** It is an example of lyric poetry.
 **(E)** It is an example of a sonnet.

**17.** What is the meter used in this speech?

 **(A)** Trochaic tetrameter
 **(B)** Dactyllic hexameter
 **(C)** Iambic hexameter
 **(D)** Iambic pentameter
 **(E)** Dactyllic pentameter

**18.** What does the word "advantages" mean in line 11?

 **(A)** Help from others in telling the story
 **(B)** Exaggerations and additions in retelling the day's events
 **(C)** Benefits
 **(D)** Help from others on the day of the battle
 **(E)** Preference

**GO ON TO THE NEXT PAGE**

19. What is the meaning of the phrase "be he ne'er so vile,/This day shall gentle his condition"?

    **(A)** If a man is feeling low, then he can look back on what he did this day and feel braver, more worthy.
    **(B)** It is a bitter time, but it will be better.
    **(C)** There is little chance of winning, so accept defeat with grace.
    **(D)** There is always ugliness, but a man can find something good in every situation.
    **(E)** Victory is illusive, but a man can always count on his brothers.

20. Other parts of this play are unmetered. Why would Shakespeare choose to use meter for this section?

    **(A)** To make the phrases read more smoothly
    **(B)** To increase the pace of the action
    **(C)** To give a lyrical quality to the acting
    **(D)** To create a vehicle for theatrical declamation
    **(E)** To highlight the king's more erudite speech

21. What does the king say will happen to those people who are with him on Saint Crispin's Day?

    **(A)** They will perish in battle.
    **(B)** They will conquer their enemies.
    **(C)** They will be long remembered.
    **(D)** They will all become noblemen.
    **(E)** They will return to their previous lives.

22. What is the purpose of this speech?

    **(A)** To strengthen his political ties
    **(B)** To excite his troops
    **(C)** To place fear in the hearts of his enemies
    **(D)** To praise his friends
    **(E)** To honor Saint Crispin

23. Which of the following best summarizes the meaning conveyed in lines 25–26?

    **(A)** Englishmen will always look on Saint Crispin's Day with pride.
    **(B)** Saint Crispin's Day will always be a day of celebration in England.
    **(C)** Some Englishmen do not celebrate Saint Crispin's Day.
    **(D)** Englishmen will regret not fighting with the king on this particular Saint Crispin's Day.
    **(E)** There are some cowardly Englishmen who did not join the king in this fight.

24. What word describes the tone of this excerpt?

    **(A)** Mournful
    **(B)** Solemn
    **(C)** Inspiring
    **(D)** Stentorian
    **(E)** Veiled

25. Why did the king say that some would wish to show their scars?

    **(A)** To garner sympathy for their wounds
    **(B)** To prove they were at the battle on Saint Crispin's Day
    **(C)** As a symbol of their courage
    **(D)** As a symbol of their nobility
    **(E)** As a tradition of Saint Crispin's Day

26. The reference to "we" in line 21 is to whom?

    **(A)** The king's entourage
    **(B)** The nobility of England
    **(C)** The participating soldiers
    **(D)** The celebrants
    **(E)** All Englishmen

QUESTIONS 27 THROUGH 37 REFER TO THE FOLLOWING POEM. READ THE PASSAGE CAREFULLY AND THEN CHOOSE THE ANSWERS TO THE QUESTIONS.

**The Tide Rises, The Tide Falls**

Line   The tide rises, the tide falls,
    The twilight darkens, the curlew calls;
    Along the sea sands damp and brown
    The traveler hastens toward the town,
5       And the tide rises, the tide falls.

    Darkness settles on roofs and walls.
    But the sea, the sea in the darkness calls;
    The little waves, with their soft, white hands,
    Efface the footprints in the sands,
10       And the tide rises, the tide falls.

    The morning breaks; the steeds in their stalls
    Stamp and neigh, as the hostler calls;
    The day returns, but nevermore
    Returns the traveler to the shore,
15       And the tide rises, the tide falls.

—Henry Wadsworth Longfellow

**27.** The stanza length of "The Tide Rises, The Tide Falls" is which of the following?

(A) Tercet
(B) Quatrain
(C) Cinquain
(D) Sestet
(E) Octave

**28.** What does the rising and falling of the tide represent?

(A) The comings and goings of a traveler
(B) Life cycle
(C) Lunar phases
(D) Emotional highs and lows
(E) Triviality of life

**29.** What does the author portray with the image of darkness in the first stanza?

(A) Closure of day
(B) Silence
(C) Ominous portent
(D) Softening of sounds
(E) Arrival of the traveler

**30.** What does the poem suggest about the relationship between humanity and nature?

(A) Humanity and nature are in harmony.
(B) Humanity destroys nature.
(C) Humanity is transitory, nature eternal.
(D) Humanity will survive despite the challenges of nature.
(E) Humanity is dependent upon nature.

**31.** All of the following are true about the effect of the refrain, or repeated line, EXCEPT

(A) It reflects the comings and goings of the traveler.
(B) It breaks the passage between thoughts.
(C) It provides continuity.
(D) It emphasizes the change in image in the last stanza.
(E) It reflects the tide's motion.

**GO ON TO THE NEXT PAGE**

**32.** What detail of the setting in the first stanza suggests that the traveler is nearing death?

    **(A)** The call of the curlew
    **(B)** The darkening sky
    **(C)** The tidal movement
    **(D)** The traveler
    **(E)** The brown sands

**33.** What is the effect of the "little waves" in lines 8–9?

    **(A)** They show the transitory nature of humanity.
    **(B)** They establish poetic rhythm.
    **(C)** They clear the scene for a new life.
    **(D)** They create a soft image.
    **(E)** They mirror the motion of the tides.

**34.** What is the meaning of the word "hostler" in line 12?

    **(A)** A herald
    **(B)** A servant
    **(C)** A groom
    **(D)** A page
    **(E)** A mule

**35.** How does the rhythm of the refrain contribute to the meaning of the poem?

    **(A)** The repetition is similar to the traveler's movements.
    **(B)** It makes no contribution.
    **(C)** It mirrors the rise and fall of the tide.
    **(D)** It suggests continuity.
    **(E)** It suggests an uncertain pattern.

**36.** What type of figure of speech is found in line 8?

    **(A)** Metaphor
    **(B)** Simile
    **(C)** Alliteration
    **(D)** Oxymoron
    **(E)** Personification

**37.** What does the last stanza suggest about the author's view of death?

    **(A)** Death is a cold finality.
    **(B)** Life goes on after the death of an individual.
    **(C)** Sadness is the ultimate experience of an individual.
    **(D)** No one escapes the fear of death.
    **(E)** Nature recycles life.

**QUESTIONS 38 THROUGH 50 REFER TO THE FOLLOWING SELECTION BY WALT WHITMAN. READ THE PASSAGE CAREFULLY AND THEN CHOOSE THE ANSWERS TO THE QUESTIONS.**

**From "Preface" to the 1855 Edition of *Leaves of Grass***

Line   America does not repel the past or what it has produced under its forms or amid other politics or the idea of castes or the old religions . . . accepts the lesson with calmness . . . is not so impatient as has been supposed that the slough still sticks to opinions and manners and literature while the life which served its requirements has passed
5      into the new life of the new forms . . . perceives that the corpse is slowly borne from the eating and sleeping rooms of the house . . . perceives that it waits a little while in the door . . . that it was fittest for its days . . . that its action has descended to the stalwart and well-shaped heir who approaches . . . and that he shall be fittest for his days.
10         The Americans of all nations at any time upon the earth have probably the fullest poetical nature. The United States themselves are essentially the greatest poem. In the history of the earth hitherto the largest and most stirring appear tame and orderly to their ampler largeness and stir. Here at last is something in the doings of man that corresponds with the broadcast doings of the day and night. Here is not
15     merely a nation but a teeming nation of nations. Here is action untied from strings necessarily blind to particulars and details magnificently moving in vast masses. Here is the hospitality which forever indicates heroes. . . . Here are the roughs and beards and space and ruggedness and nonchalance that the soul loves. Here the performance disdaining the trivial unapproached in the tremendous audacity of its crowds and
20     groupings and the push of its perspective spreads with crampless and flowing breadth and showers its prolific and splendid extravagance. One sees it must indeed own the riches of the summer and winter, and need never bankrupt while corn grows from the ground or orchards drop apples or the bays contain fish or men beget children upon women. . . .

—Walt Whitman

**38.** Which of the following is the best statement of the theme of this passage?

(A) A portrait of the beauty of the United States

(B) A forecast of the future of poetry in the United States

(C) A merging of new and old literary styles

(D) A discussion of the resources and poetry of the United States

(E) A poetic definition of the United States

**39.** In line 5, what does the word "corpse" refer to?

(A) Old forms of poetry

(B) The past

(C) Slough

(D) Older opinions and manners

(E) Current politics

**40.** How does Whitman suggest that the past and present are linked?

(A) The past nourishes and educates the present.

(B) The past complicates the present.

(C) In the present, the past is viewed differently.

(D) The present is merely a mirror image of the past.

(E) The present can only be seen in the context of the past.

**GO ON TO THE NEXT PAGE**

**41.** Which of the following statements does not reflect Whitman's ideas about the United States?

   **(A)** It is larger than most other countries.

   **(B)** The population is more literate than that of other nations.

   **(C)** The people of the United States have built a unique nation.

   **(D)** It is a county of vast riches in people and nature.

   **(E)** It is a country in transition.

**42.** When Whitman wrote "perceives that the corpse is slowly borne from the eating and sleeping rooms of the house," (lines 5–6) he used what type of literary device?

   **(A)** Personification

   **(B)** Meter

   **(C)** Oxymoron

   **(D)** Conceit

   **(E)** Metaphor

**43.** Which is the best interpretation of Whitman's statement "The United States themselves are essentially the greatest poem." in line 11?

   **(A)** The greatest volume of good poetry is from the United States.

   **(B)** The nation's vibrancy, beauty, and diversity are poetic.

   **(C)** The people of the nation are poetic.

   **(D)** The United States is the leader in finding new forms of poetry.

   **(E)** U.S. literature has poetry at its root.

**44.** The sentence "Here are the roughs and beards and space and ruggedness and nonchalance that the soul loves." (lines 17–18) is intended as

   **(A)** A challenge presented to humanity

   **(B)** Symbolic of emotional highs and lows

   **(C)** A metaphor for the American landscape, physical and cultural

   **(D)** A contrast between something easy and something difficult

   **(E)** The style and dress at the time of writing

**45.** Which of the following words would best characterize the United States according to Whitman?

   **(A)** Rigid

   **(B)** Malleable

   **(C)** Anti-intellectual

   **(D)** Exuberant

   **(E)** Enshrining the past

**46.** What does Whitman mean when he comments that the United States "is not merely a nation but a teeming nation of nations" (lines 14–15)?

   **(A)** New Americans have increased the population tremendously.

   **(B)** The nation's resources can support a large population.

   **(C)** People come to the United States to make their fortunes.

   **(D)** Native Americans represent nations within a nation.

   **(E)** The United States is a culturally diverse nation.

**47.** The repetition of the word "Here" and the sentences following in the second paragraph are an example of

   **(A)** parallelism

   **(B)** free verse

   **(C)** artistic license

   **(D)** redundancy

   **(E)** romantic language

**48.** In the second paragraph, Whitman uses the word "Here" to begin numerous sentences. What effect does that create?

**(A)** A ponderous feeling
**(B)** A sense of predictability
**(C)** Formality
**(D)** Exuberance
**(E)** A musical, poetic feeling

**49.** The compound verb in the sentence beginning "Here the performance . . ." (lines 18–21) is

**(A)** push and spreads
**(B)** unapproached and showers
**(C)** unapproached and disdaining
**(D)** spreads and showers
**(E)** crowds and showers

**50.** What is Whitman saying in the sentence "Here at last is something in the doings of man that corresponds with the broadcast doings of the day and night." (lines 13–14)?

**(A)** The people of the United States follow a pattern like day becomes night.
**(B)** The nation's actions are unpredictable.
**(C)** The influence of the United States spreads as widely as day and night.
**(D)** Man meets his challenges on a day-to-day basis.
**(E)** Man has found a place in the United States where his actions are compatible with nature.

**S T O P**   If you finish before time is called, you may check your work on this section only. Do not turn to any other section in the test.

# SECTION II

*3 QUESTIONS • 2 HOURS*

> **Directions:** *Jane Eyre* is a grim and passionate novel of an orphan girl who becomes a governess as an adult. This passage from the first chapter creates the feeling of constraint and imprisonment of the main character. Write a well-organized essay in which you discuss the ways by which the author creates this feeling. Be sure to consider such literary elements as diction, imagery, structure, and point of view.

## Essay Question 1

*SUGGESTED TIME—40 MINUTES*

### From *Jane Eyre*

Line    There was no possibility of taking a walk that day. We had been wandering, indeed, in the leafless shrubbery an hour in the morning; but since dinner (Mrs. Reed, when there was no company, dined early) the cold winter wind had brought with it clouds so somber and a rain so penetrating, that further outdoor exercise was now out of the
5    question.

I was glad of it: I never liked long walks, especially on chilly afternoons: dreadful to me was the coming home in the raw twilight, saddened by chidings of Bessie, the nurse, and humbled by the consciousness of my physical inferiority to Liza, John, and Georgiana Reed.

10    The said Eliza, John, and Georgiana were now clustered round their mamma in the drawing room: she lay reclined on the sofa by the fireside, and with her darlings about her (for the time neither quarreling nor crying) looked perfectly happy. Me, she had dispensed from joining the group; saying, "She regretted to be under the necessity of keeping me at a distance; but that until she heard from Bessie and could discover by
15    her own observation that I was endeavoring in good earnest to acquire a more sociable and childlike disposition, a more attractive and sprightly manner—something lighter, franker, more natural, as it were—she really must exclude me from privileges intended only for contented, happy, little children."

"What does Bessie say I have done?" I asked.

20    "Jane, I don't like cavilers [people who find fault or criticize] or questioners; besides, there is something truly forbidding in a child taking up her elders in that manner. Be seated somewhere; and until you can speak pleasantly, remain silent."

A small breakfast room adjoined the drawing room. I slipped in there. It contained a bookcase: I soon possessed myself of a volume, taking care that it should be one
25    stored with pictures. I mounted into the window seat: gathering up my feet, I sat cross-legged like a Turk; and having drawn the red moreen [sturdy fabric, often embossed] curtain nearly closed, I was shrined in double retirement.

Folds of scarlet drapery shut in my view to the right hand; to the left were the clear panes of glass, protecting, but not separating me from the drear November day. At
30    intervals, while turning over the leaves of my book, I studied the aspect of that winter afternoon. Afar, it offered a pale blank of mist and cloud; near, a scene of wet lawn and storm-beat shrub, with ceaseless rain sweeping away wildly before a long and lamentable blast.

—Charlotte Brontë

**Directions:** Read the following poem carefully. Write a well-organized essay that examines how the poet's style conveys her meaning. Consider form, word choice, stanza length and format, length and arrangement of lines, and literary devices.

## Essay Question 2

*SUGGESTED TIME—40 MINUTES*

### The Soul selects her own Society

Line  The Soul selects her own Society—
Then—shuts the Door—
To her divine Majority—
Present no more—

5  Unmoved—she notes the Chariots–pausing—
At her low Gate—
Unmoved—an Emperor be kneeling
Upon her Mat—

I've known her—from an ample nation—
10  Choose One—
Then—close the Valves of her attention—
Like Stone

—Emily Dickinson

**Directions:** In good literature, writers create a consistent mood, and readers experience intensification or alteration in their consciousness of certain aspects of life as a result.

Choose a novel, epic, or play of literary merit and write an essay in which you discuss the mood of the work and identify ways in which the story intensified your consciousness of certain aspects of life or changed your views about certain of life's aspects. You may wish to discuss this change of state through the action, theme, or character development. Avoid plot summary.

You may select a work from the list below, or you may choose another work of comparable literary merit suitable to the topic.

## Essay Question 3

### *SUGGESTED TIME—40 MINUTES*

Dostoyevsky, *The Brothers Karamazov*

Walker, *The Color Purple*

Dickens, *David Copperfield*

Miller, *Death of a Salesman*

Tyler, *Dinner at the Homesick Restaurant*

Joyce, *Dubliners*

Austen, *Emma*

Fitzgerald, *The Great Gatsby*

Shaw, *Pygmalion*

Austen, *Sense and Sensibility*

Hemingway, *The Sun Also Rises*

Dickens, *A Tale of Two Cities*

Brontë, *Wuthering Heights*

**S T O P**    If you finish before time is called, you may check your work on this section only. Do not turn to any other section in the test.

# ANSWER KEY AND EXPLANATIONS

## Section I

| | | | | |
|---|---|---|---|---|
| 1. C | 11. D | 21. C | 31. E | 41. B |
| 2. D | 12. C | 22. B | 32. B | 42. E |
| 3. B | 13. C | 23. D | 33. C | 43. B |
| 4. C | 14. C | 24. C | 34. C | 44. C |
| 5. A | 15. B | 25. B | 35. C | 45. B |
| 6. A | 16. C | 26. C | 36. E | 46. E |
| 7. C | 17. D | 27. C | 37. B | 47. A |
| 8. D | 18. B | 28. B | 38. E | 48. D |
| 9. D | 19. A | 29. C | 39. B | 49. D |
| 10. A | 20. E | 30. C | 40. A | 50. C |

1. **The correct answer is (C).** Each of the choices has a small element of correctness. The characters do make comments about health, choice (A), and some discussion about exercise takes place, choice (B). Franklin does mention the pain of the gout attack, choice (D). Dialogue occurs, although not suited to a morality play, choice (E). However, because the question asks for the theme of the passage, only choice (C) is correct.

2. **The correct answer is (D).** An alliteration is the repetition of an initial consonant sound, choice (A). A metaphor is a figure of speech in which one thing is spoken of as though it were something else, choice (B). An allegory is a literary work with two or more levels of meaning, one of which is literal and others symbolic, choice (C). A simile is a figure of speech that compares two unlike things by using words such as *like* or *as*, choice (E). None of these applies to the selection. Allowing the disease to speak is personification, the giving of human characteristics to nonhuman things, choice (D).

3. **The correct answer is (B).** Choices (A), (C), and (E), but not choice (D), seem reasonable, but only choice (B) includes both elements of the tone—the humor and the reasoned presentation of medical information given.

4. **The correct answer is (C).** Franklin is lamenting the thought that people's debts and sins are always greater than people imagine them to be. Choice (A) restates part of the maxim, while choices (B), (D), and (E) are not accurate restatements.

5. **The correct answer is (A).** Choice (E) may be an interesting fact but does not relate to the content of the selection—nor does choice (C). Choice (D) relates somewhat, but it does not include any reference to the characters. While Franklin may accept scientific reasoning, choice (B) is not the more accurate restatement of the development of the passage. Choice (A) is the more accurate restatement of what occurs in the selection.

6. **The correct answer is (A).** Gout states that he is very serious and can justify every action (lines 2–4). He is indignant, or righteously angry, choice (A), and is not pleased, choice (B), or feeling chastised, choice (C), or contrite, choice (D). Gout certainly is not oblivious, choice (E), but very concerned about Franklin's health.

7. **The correct answer is (C).** On the surface, all the choices seem correct because each is mentioned in the selection. However, choices (A), (B), (D), and (E) are specific details that support Franklin's point that reasonable and responsible behavior cures gout—choice (C).

8. **The correct answer is (D).** Once you eliminate choice (E), which is simply incorrect, you can approach the question either as a straightforward comprehension question if you know what lines 50–51 mean, or you can try eliminating choices. Choices (A) and (C) are true, but do not answer the question. Choice (B) is not true because Franklin the character has not considered offering the peasants a ride. This leaves choice (D).

9. **The correct answer is (D).** The choice in determining the correct answer is between choices (D) and (E) because the other choices do not express the tone of Gout's comments. If Gout were disgusted, choice (A), he would not bother trying to reason with Franklin. There is no conciliation in his tone, choice (B), nor are his arguments superficial, choice (C). Gout is not dealing with trivial ideas in a narrow bookish manner, so choice (D) is the correct descriptor.

10. **The correct answer is (A).** Choice (B) is incorrect because Gout is not misinterpreting Franklin the character's actions; Franklin agrees with Gout. The topic is serious— Franklin the character agrees with Gout—so Franklin the author's purpose is more than to write some light-hearted prose, choice (C). The theme is developed in such a way as to make Gout's argument more persuasive, thus eliminating choice (D) as untrue. Choice (E) is inaccurate because the motives are clearly developed. Choice (A) is the best answer in that the use of dialogue permits Franklin the writer to focus on Gout's comments and easily refute Franklin the character's defense.

11. **The correct answer is (D).** The key here is to notice that the word *interests* is plural. Franklin does enjoy being with friends, choice (B), but that is only one interest. He says he likes walking in the gardens, choice (A), but does not act as if he does. There is no information in the selection to support choice (C). Knowing Franklin as a historical figure would indicate that choice (E) is incorrect. Therefore, the statement that best characterizes what we do know about Franklin from the selection is that he enjoys those things—interests—that do not require him to do anything more than sit, choice (D).

12. **The correct answer is (C).** Franklin will not answer because he knows he did not follow his own advice. At this point in the dialogue, he is not arguing with Gout nor is there any sign that he has tired of the conversation, so choices (A) and (E) are incorrect. Franklin has not shown himself to be forgetful, thus eliminating choice (B). While the tone of the passage is amusing, the Franklin of the dialogue is serious, thus eliminating choice (D).

13. **The correct answer is (C).** Use of scientific explanations, rather than superstitions or religious beliefs, for medical conditions was a discovery of the eighteenth century. Question 5 gave you a clue in stating that the passage was written during the Age of Reason. Neither choice (D) nor choice (E) is true of the selection. Choice (A) is irrelevant, and while choice (B) is true, choice (C) is a better overall statement.

14. **The correct answer is (C).** The statement contrasts two sets of circumstances. The correct answer must have two sets of answers as well. Only choice (C) fulfills the requirement (sages/fools; wise statements/unwise actions). Choices (A), (B), (D), and (E) all deal with single concepts.

15. **The correct answer is (B).** Choice (C) may be true, but it was not mentioned. Franklin the character is not unhappy with his lifestyle, making choice (D) untrue. Choice (E) is not true because Gout suggests it. Choice (A) may be true, but the contrast in lifestyles, choice (B), is the issue raised by Franklin the author through Gout.

16. **The correct answer is (C).** Blank verse is poetry written in unrhymed iambic pentameter. As you have undoubtedly learned, Shakespeare often employed iambic pentameter in plays and poetry. While choices (A), (B), (D), and (E) are legitimate forms of poetry, their requirements are not met in this speech. Free verse, choice (A), has no regular rhyme scheme or metrical pattern, while this excerpt has meter. An epic, choice (B), is a long poem written on a heroic theme such as the *Iliad,* while this is a speech. A lyric, choice (D), explores the poet's emotions and interest in the natural world. A sonnet, choice (E), may be written in iambic pentameter, but it is only fourteen lines.

17. **The correct answer is (D).** If you figured out the answer to question 16, this one should have been easy. If you did not remember that blank verse is written in iambic pentameter, you could have figured it out by scanning the lines. Iambic pentameter has five stressed syllables, with the stress on the second syllable. Choices (A), (B), (C), and (E) are simply incorrect.

18. **The correct answer is (B).** You need to read the word in context. Choice (A) is incorrect because the line begins by saying that the speaker will remember; nowhere does the passage say that the speaker will need help from others for the retelling. Choices (C) and (E) do not make sense if they are substituted for *advantages*. Choice (D) does not relate to the statement, which leaves choice (B). The mention of "flowing cups" (line 16) indicates that the speaker is drinking, which often leads to boasting and exaggerations of actions.

19. **The correct answer is (A).** There is no indication in the passage that these are bad times, choice (B); on the contrary, Henry paints the forthcoming battle as glorious. For the same reason, choice (C) is incorrect. The second part of choice (E) is accurate in terms of the passage, but the first part is not stated in the passage. Choice (D) may seem like a good choice because it is a broad statement, but it does not reflect the meaning of the lines, which relate directly to this particular battle.

20. **The correct answer is (E).** The strong meter of this passage adds to its power. This is not a smooth or lyrical passage, so choices (A) and (C) can be eliminated. Meter in this passage does not increase pace; if anything, it slows the passage down, so choice (B) is incorrect. Choice (D) is not correct because there is no erudite language in the passage.

21. **The correct answer is (C).** This is a straight comprehension question. Henry's entire speech is about the glory that the soldiers will earn by fighting in this battle. He states that all the soldiers will be remembered for years to come. While all those who hear the speech may wish that choices (B) and (E) come true, neither sentiment is raised in the speech. Choice (A) makes no sense in a speech meant to encourage the soldiers. Choice (D) may be figuratively true, but not literally and does not restate Henry's words.

22. **The correct answer is (B).** What else would a commander do before a battle but stir up his troops and encourage them to fight well? Only choice (C) is a possible alternative choice, but there is no indication that the enemy is within hearing distance.

23. **The correct answer is (D).** Choosing the correct answer requires a careful reading of the lines in question. The king clearly says that the men sleeping in England the night of the speech will feel cursed that they were not present at the battle. Choices (A), (B), and (C) have little or no relationship to the king's words. You may wonder about choice (E), but the last two lines state that those who did not fight may feel guilty or even cowardly that they did not fight, but the king does not say they are cowards.

24. **The correct answer is (C).** The reasoning necessary to answer this question is similar to that required for question 22. Since you know that the audience for this speech is the troops and the king wants to inspire his soldiers to fight well, the tone logically must be rousing. Choices (A), (B), (D), and (E) do not fit the purpose of the speech.

25. **The correct answer is (B).** At first glance, there seem to be several logical possibilities, but you can eliminate choice (A) because garnering sympathy is not consistent with a rousing speech. Choice (E) can also be eliminated because no tradition has yet been established. When the king speaks of nobility, he is speaking symbolically, so choice (D) might be a possibility. However, like courage, the point of choice (C), nobility is implicit in fighting the Saint Crispin's day battle, so choice (B) is the best choice.

26. **The correct answer is (C).** The implied antecedent of *we* is those who are to fight the battle. While some of the soldiers are noblemen or members of his entourage, the king is addressing all his troops. Therefore, the answer cannot be choices (A) or (B). The celebration has not begun, so choice (D) can be eliminated. All Englishmen cannot be referred to as "We few," thus choice (E) is incorrect.

27. **The correct answer is (C).** If you have studied Latin or a Romance language, you might be able to figure this answer out from the root words of the stanza forms. The tercet, choice (A), has three lines per stanza. The quatrain, choice (B), has four lines. The correct answer, the cinquain, has five lines. The sestet, choice (D), has six, and the octave, choice (E), has eight.

28. **The correct answer is (B).** Choice (A) is too literal an interpretation. The poem does not mention the moon, so choice (C) is inappropriate. Choice (D) can be eliminated because emotions are not a part of the poem. Choice (E) contradicts the sense of the poem.

29. **The correct answer is (C).** Both choices (A) and (E) are too literal an interpretation. Since a bird is heard, silence seems out of place, choice (B). Choice (D) does not make much sense. The darkness suggests death, hence, an ominous portent.

30. **The correct answer is (C).** To answer this one correctly, you must understand the entire poem. Longfellow is saying that humans, symbolized by the traveler, come and go, but the rhythms of nature, the tides, remain forever. Humans are mortal; nature is eternal. Only choice (C) applies. Choices (A), (B), (D), and (E) are not accurate restatements of Longfellow's theme.

31. **The correct answer is (E).** The refrain repeats in a predictable pattern. What in this poem has a continuing, predictable motion? The tide. Therefore, the tide's motion is the correct answer. Choices (A), (B), (C), and (D) might apply partially, but choice (E) is the most accurate.

32. **The correct answer is (B).** This question is related to question 29. If you understood that the image of darkness represents something ominous, then it is not too much of a leap to understand that darkness is foreshadowing death, especially since day comes in the last stanza and the traveler is no more. Choice (D) is incorrect because the traveler is the one who is dying so he cannot foreshadow his own death.

33. **The correct answer is (C).** This question tests reading comprehension and understanding of figurative language. The poet writes that the waves erase footprints in the sand, which suggests clearing the scene for new life as morning brings a new day. Choices (A), (B), (D), and (E) are not so clear an expression of the meaning of the image.

34. **The correct answer is (C).** If you do not know the word, try figuring it out from context. According to the poem, the hostler works with horses. Heralds and pages, choices (A) and (D), did not work in stables, and there is nothing to indicate the poem is set in the Middle Ages or Renaissance anyway. A servant, choice (B), might work in the stable, but the word *groom* is more specific. A mule is not a human being, so it is obviously the wrong choice, choice (E).

35. **The correct answer is (C).** This answer is similar to that of question 31 but asks you to dig deeper into the poem. If you hear the poem in your mind, you will notice that the refrain rises and falls in rhythm, just as the tide rises and falls. The refrain reinforces in rhythm the meaning of the words. There is a continuity to the rise and fall of the tide, choice (D), but choice (C) is a clearer statement of the interaction between the refrain and the rhythm. Choices (A), (B), and (E) are incorrect because the traveler's movements are not repeated, choice (A); the rhythm makes a contribution, choice (B); and the pattern is regular, choice (E).

36. **The correct answer is (E).** Personification gives human qualities to nonhuman things. In the line in question, the waves have hands. Certainly that is giving waves a human aspect. While choices (A), (B), (C), and (D) are all figures of speech, only choice (E) applies to the line. Metaphor equates something with something else, choice (A), while a simile uses *as* or *like,* choice (B). Alliteration is the repetition of initial consonant sounds, choice (C), and an oxymoron combines opposite or contradictory terms, choice (D).

37. **The correct answer is (B).** The poet says in the last stanza that the morning comes, the horses are still alive, and the tide rises and falls even though the traveler does not return. You know that the traveler has died, yet other life continues. Death is not presented as cold, choice (A), and sadness is not a part of the poem, choice (C). According to the poem, death is not feared, choice (D), but a natural part of the life cycle. Choice (E) has nothing to do with the poem.

38. **The correct answer is (E).** While the passage does touch on the beauty of the United States, that is not the main focus, so choice (A) can be eliminated. Nothing really is said about poetry as literature, so choice (B) is incorrect. The past and the present are discussed but not in terms of literature, so choice (C) cannot be the answer. Choice (D) has virtually nothing to do with the passage. That leaves choice (E).

00. **The correct answer is (D).** There is no mention of poetry in the paragraph, eliminating choice (A). *Slough,* choice (C) means literally the skin of a snake that is cast off; figuratively, it means a layer that is cast off. You might not know that, but from the context you could at least figure out that slough was something extraneous—maybe like fuzz—that stuck to something else. It would not seem important enough to be a corpse. Choice (D) is related to choice (C). Line 2 mentions politics but in the context of creating the past. Choices (C), (D), and (E) all relate in some way to the past, choice (B).

40. **The correct answer is (A).** Whitman suggests that America accepts the lesson of the past with calmness. The past informs and educates the present. Choice (E) has a subtle implication that the past is always present, while Whitman suggests that the past nurtures the present for a time and then leaves. Choices (B), (C), and (D) are incorrect restatements of the passage's theme.

41. **The correct answer is (B).** Using the process of elimination, choice (A) is wrong because the writer states plainly that the United States is large. Choices (C) and (D) contradict Whitman's assertions that diversity makes the nation unique. Certainly, the United States is a nation that is changing, so choice (E) is not the answer. That leaves, choice (B), and nowhere does the writer speak of Americans' ability to read.

42. **The correct answer is (E).** When Whitman writes about the past, he calls it a corpse. Personification, choice (A), gives human characteristics to nonhuman things, including concepts, but in this instance, metaphor is a more accurate identification of how Whitman uses the figure of speech in context. The passage is prose, so choice (B) is incorrect. Oxymoron, choice (C), combines two contradictory ideas and is wrong in context. A conceit, choice (D), is an extended metaphor comparing two or more ideas and is, therefore, incorrect.

43. **The correct answer is (B).** The poet states that the nation is a poem. The only answer that indicates the same thing is choice (B), that the nation is poetic. While choices (A), (C), (D), and (E) mention poetry, they do not indicate that it is the United States itself that is the poem.

44. **The correct answer is (C).** This is a difficult question. By logically examining the choices you can see that choice (E) is too simplistic. Humanity is not Whitman's subject, choice (A), nor are emotions, choice (B). A contrast is possible, but not between easy and difficult, choice (D), which does not relate to the passage. That leaves the physical and cultural landscape.

45. **The correct answer is (B).** To choose the right answer here is really an issue of vocabulary. If you do not know what choice (B) means, choices (A) and (E) can be eliminated because they contradict what Whitman says about the United States. He does not mention education, so eliminate choice (C). Whitman's tone in the passage is one of exuberance, choice (D), but he does not characterize the nation that way. That leaves choice (B), which means that something is not rigid and can be changed and molded.

46. **The correct answer is (E).** Whitman stresses the diversity of the United States that he finds positive. While aspects of choices (A), (B), (C), and (D) may be true, they are not points that Whitman makes in this selection.

47. **The correct answer is (A).** This selection cannot be free verse, choice (B)—even if that is Whitman's poetic style—since the passage is prose. Artistic license, choice (C), has no meaning in terms of the repetition. The language is anything but romantic, choice (E). While the repetition may be redundant, choice (D), the writer uses it purposely to create unity and a sense of rhythm, which better fits the definition of parallelism.

48. **The correct answer is (D).** The tone of this paragraph is neither ponderous, choice (A), nor formal, choice (C), but joyous. The repetition of the word *Here* helps develop that tone. One might argue that the repetition is stylistically poetic, choice (E); however, the passage is strong and powerful, not musical. Choice (B) is not an accurate reading of the paragraph.

49. **The correct answer is (D).** This is a very complex sentence, but you can eliminate choices (A), (B), and (C) because a compound verb has the same tenses for both or all verbs. *Crowds* and *showers,* choice (E), could be nouns or verbs, but in this sentence, *crowds* is a noun, the object of the preposition *of.*

50. **The correct answer is (C).** Choice (E) may sound important but has no relationship to the passage. Choice (A) is too simplistic. Choices (B) and (D) may be true, but do not relate to the passage.

## Section II

### SUGGESTIONS FOR ESSAY QUESTION 1

The following are points you might have chosen to include in your essay on the passage from *Jane Eyre*. Consider them as you do your self-evaluation. Revise your essay using points from this list that will strengthen it.

### *Form or Mode*
- Excerpt from a novel
- Romantic period because of treatment of children and experiences of women

### *Theme*
- For the passage, a dream of freedom in a grim world by escaping into books

### *Characters*
- Constrained and imprisoned main character (Jane)
- Hypocritical antagonist (Mrs. Reed)
- Vicious or at least unkind antagonists—the children

### *Dialogue*
- Spotlights Jane's untenable situation
- "Jane, I don't like cavilers or questioners: besides, there is something truly forbidding in a child taking up her elders in that manner."

### *Conflict*
- Human being against human being
- One person, Jane, in conflict with all other characters in this passage
- Conflict not of Jane's doing

### *Setting*
- Cold winter wind
- Somber clouds
- Penetrating rain
- Dreary household

### *Point of View*
- First person—from the point of view of the victim; only her side of the story is known

### Diction

- Long, complex sentences: "Afar, it offered a pale blank of mist and cloud; near, a scene of wet lawn and storm-beat shrub, with ceaseless rain sweeping away wildly before a long and lamentable blast."

## SUGGESTIONS FOR ESSAY QUESTION 2

The following are points that you might have chosen to include in your essay on "The Soul selects her own Society." Consider them as you complete your self-evaluation. Revise your essay using points from this list that will strengthen it.

### Type and Form

- Lyric
- Three quatrains
- Varied line length
- Brevity of lines
- Short stanzas

### Mechanics

- Unconventional punctuation, especially the dash
- Unconventional capitalization; many nouns capitalized

### Rhythm

- Rhythm mostly iambic
- Frequent variations

### Rhyme

- Lines 2 and 4 of each stanza rhyme
- Slanted, or partial rhyme—rhythms in which the final sound is similar but not identical

### Word Choice

- Simple, short words
- Concrete

### Figurative Language

- Metaphor of the soul as a woman in a house
- Simile "Like Stone"

### Imagery

- Divine Majority: people to whom she reveals herself
- The speaker's soul
- Third stanza: soul's society only one individual

### Theme

- Self examination: know thyself
- The soul chooses whom to befriend and love
- Wealth and power unimportant in the choice

## SUGGESTIONS FOR ESSAY QUESTION 3

The following are points about tone you might have chosen to discuss in your essay on the mood and alteration of consciousness produced by literature. Consider them as you do your self-evaluation. Revise your essay using points from this list that will strengthen it.

### Tone

- Attitude implied by the author toward the subject and the audience
- Conveyed through word choice and details
- Author's intent and comments
- Consider the feeling the story leaves you with
- Irony—contrast between what is and what seems to be
- Verbal irony—speaker says one thing but means another, usually the opposite
- Dramatic irony—audience has information the characters do not
- Use of style to establish mood and tone

### Style

- Language appropriate to the purpose of the work
- Contribution of language to impact
- Sentence length and structure
- Figures of speech
- Metaphor—comparison of two essentially unlike things
- Metonymy—use of closely related ideas for the idea itself
- Word choice
- Allusions
- Dialogue
- Sensory details

## SELF-EVALUATION RUBRIC FOR THE ADVANCED PLACEMENT ESSAYS

| | 8–9 | 6–7 | 5 | 3–4 | 1–2 | 0 |
|---|---|---|---|---|---|---|
| **Overall Impression** | Demonstrates excellent control of the literature and outstanding writing competence; thorough and effective; incisive | Demonstrates good control of the literature and good writing competence; less thorough and incisive than the highest papers | Reveals simplistic thinking and/or immature writing; adequate skills | Incomplete thinking; fails to respond adequately to part or parts of the question; may paraphrase rather than analyze | Unacceptably brief; fails to respond to the question; little clarity | Lacking skill and competence |
| **Understanding of the Text** | Excellent understanding of the text; exhibits perception and clarity; original or unique approach; includes apt and specific references | Good understanding of the text; exhibits perception and clarity; includes specific references | Superficial understanding of the text; elements of literature vague, mechanical, overgeneralized | Misreadings and lack of persuasive evidence from the text; meager and unconvincing treatment of literary elements | Serious misreadings and little supporting evidence from the text; erroneous treatment of literary elements | A response with no more than a reference to the literature; blank response, or one completely off the topic |
| **Organization and Development** | Meticulously organized and thoroughly developed; coherent and unified | Well-organized and developed; coherent and unified | Reasonably organized and developed; mostly coherent and unified | Somewhat organized and developed; some incoherence and lack of unity | Little or no organization and development; incoherent and void of unity | No apparent organization or development; incoherent |
| **Use of Sentences** | Effectively varied and engaging; virtually error free | Varied and interesting; a few errors | Adequately varied; some errors | Somewhat varied and marginally interesting; one or more major errors | Little or no variation; dull and uninteresting; some major errors | Numerous major errors |
| **Word Choice** | Interesting and effective; virtually error free | Generally interesting and effective; a few errors | Occasionally interesting and effective; several errors | Somewhat dull and ordinary; some errors in diction | Mostly dull and conventional; numerous errors | Numerous major errors; extremely immature |
| **Grammar and Usage** | Virtually error free | Occasional minor errors | Several minor errors | Some major errors | Severely flawed; frequent major errors | Extremely flawed |

Rate yourself in each of the categories. Choose the description that most accurately reflects your performance, and enter the numbers on the lines below. Be as honest as possible so you will know what areas need work. Then calculate the average of the six numbers to determine your final score. It is difficult to score yourself objectively, so you may wish to ask a respected friend or teacher to assess your writing for a more accurate reflection of its strengths and weaknesses. On the AP test itself, a reader will rate your essay on a scale of 0 to 9, with 9 being the highest.

Rate each category from 9 (high) to 0 (low).

## Essay Question 1

**SELF-EVALUATION**

- Overall Impression ____
- Understanding of the Text ____
- Organization and Development ____
- Use of Sentences ____
- Word Choice (Diction) ____
- Grammar and Usage ____

TOTAL ____
    Divide by 6 for final score ____

**OBJECTIVE EVALUATION**

- Overall Impression ____
- Understanding of the Text ____
- Organization and Development ____
- Use of Sentences ____
- Word Choice (Diction) ____
- Grammar and Usage ____

TOTAL ____
    Divide by 6 for final score ____

## Essay Question 2

**SELF-EVALUATION**

- Overall Impression ____
- Understanding of the Text ____
- Organization and Development ____
- Use of Sentences ____
- Word Choice (Diction) ____
- Grammar and Usage ____

TOTAL ____
    Divide by 6 for final score ____

**OBJECTIVE EVALUATION**

- Overall Impression ____
- Understanding of the Text ____
- Organization and Development ____
- Use of Sentences ____
- Word Choice (Diction) ____
- Grammar and Usage ____

TOTAL ____
    Divide by 6 for final score ____

## Essay Question 3

**SELF-EVALUATION**

- Overall Impression ____
- Understanding of the Text ____
- Organization and Development ____
- Use of Sentences ____
- Word Choice (Diction) ____
- Grammar and Usage ____

TOTAL ____
    Divide by 6 for final score ____

**OBJECTIVE EVALUATION**

- Overall Impression ____
- Understanding of the Text ____
- Organization and Development ____
- Use of Sentences ____
- Word Choice (Diction) ____
- Grammar and Usage ____

TOTAL ____
    Divide by 6 for final score ____

# ANSWER SHEET PRACTICE TEST 3

## SECTION I

1. Ⓐ Ⓑ Ⓒ Ⓓ Ⓔ
2. Ⓐ Ⓑ Ⓒ Ⓓ Ⓔ
3. Ⓐ Ⓑ Ⓒ Ⓓ Ⓔ
4. Ⓐ Ⓑ Ⓒ Ⓓ Ⓔ
5. Ⓐ Ⓑ Ⓒ Ⓓ Ⓔ
6. Ⓐ Ⓑ Ⓒ Ⓓ Ⓔ
7. Ⓐ Ⓑ Ⓒ Ⓓ Ⓔ
8. Ⓐ Ⓑ Ⓒ Ⓓ Ⓔ
9. Ⓐ Ⓑ Ⓒ Ⓓ Ⓔ
10. Ⓐ Ⓑ Ⓒ Ⓓ Ⓔ
11. Ⓐ Ⓑ Ⓒ Ⓓ Ⓔ
12. Ⓐ Ⓑ Ⓒ Ⓓ Ⓔ
13. Ⓐ Ⓑ Ⓒ Ⓓ Ⓔ
14. Ⓐ Ⓑ Ⓒ Ⓓ Ⓔ
15. Ⓐ Ⓑ Ⓒ Ⓓ Ⓔ
16. Ⓐ Ⓑ Ⓒ Ⓓ Ⓔ
17. Ⓐ Ⓑ Ⓒ Ⓓ Ⓔ

18. Ⓐ Ⓑ Ⓒ Ⓓ Ⓔ
19. Ⓐ Ⓑ Ⓒ Ⓓ Ⓔ
20. Ⓐ Ⓑ Ⓒ Ⓓ Ⓔ
21. Ⓐ Ⓑ Ⓒ Ⓓ Ⓔ
22. Ⓐ Ⓑ Ⓒ Ⓓ Ⓔ
23. Ⓐ Ⓑ Ⓒ Ⓓ Ⓔ
24. Ⓐ Ⓑ Ⓒ Ⓓ Ⓔ
25. Ⓐ Ⓑ Ⓒ Ⓓ Ⓔ
26. Ⓐ Ⓑ Ⓒ Ⓓ Ⓔ
27. Ⓐ Ⓑ Ⓒ Ⓓ Ⓔ
28. Ⓐ Ⓑ Ⓒ Ⓓ Ⓔ
29. Ⓐ Ⓑ Ⓒ Ⓓ Ⓔ
30. Ⓐ Ⓑ Ⓒ Ⓓ Ⓔ
31. Ⓐ Ⓑ Ⓒ Ⓓ Ⓔ
32. Ⓐ Ⓑ Ⓒ Ⓓ Ⓔ
33. Ⓐ Ⓑ Ⓒ Ⓓ Ⓔ
34. Ⓐ Ⓑ Ⓒ Ⓓ Ⓔ

35. Ⓐ Ⓑ Ⓒ Ⓓ Ⓔ
36. Ⓐ Ⓑ Ⓒ Ⓓ Ⓔ
37. Ⓐ Ⓑ Ⓒ Ⓓ Ⓔ
38. Ⓐ Ⓑ Ⓒ Ⓓ Ⓔ
39. Ⓐ Ⓑ Ⓒ Ⓓ Ⓔ
40. Ⓐ Ⓑ Ⓒ Ⓓ Ⓔ
41. Ⓐ Ⓑ Ⓒ Ⓓ Ⓔ
42. Ⓐ Ⓑ Ⓒ Ⓓ Ⓔ
43. Ⓐ Ⓑ Ⓒ Ⓓ Ⓔ
44. Ⓐ Ⓑ Ⓒ Ⓓ Ⓔ
45. Ⓐ Ⓑ Ⓒ Ⓓ Ⓔ
46. Ⓐ Ⓑ Ⓒ Ⓓ Ⓔ
47. Ⓐ Ⓑ Ⓒ Ⓓ Ⓔ
48. Ⓐ Ⓑ Ⓒ Ⓓ Ⓔ
49. Ⓐ Ⓑ Ⓒ Ⓓ Ⓔ
50. Ⓐ Ⓑ Ⓒ Ⓓ Ⓔ

answer sheet

## SECTION II

**Essay Question 1**

_____

_____

_____

_____

_____

_____

_____

_____

_____

_____

_____

_____

_____

_____

_____

_____

_____

_____

_____

_____

_____

answer sheet

**Essay Question 2**

_____

_____

_____

_____

_____

_____

_____

_____

_____

_____

_____

_____

_____

_____

_____

_____

_____

_____

_____

_____

_____

answer sheet

**Essay Question 3**

_____

_____

_____

_____

_____

_____

_____

_____

_____

_____

_____

_____

_____

_____

_____

_____

_____

_____

_____

_____

_____

_____

_____

_____

answer sheet

# Practice Test 3

## SECTION I

*50 QUESTIONS • 60 MINUTES*

**Directions:** This section consists of selections of literature and questions on their content, style, and form. After you have read each passage, choose the answer that best answers the question and mark the space on the answer sheet.

**QUESTIONS 1 THROUGH 9 REFER TO THE FOLLOWING POEM. READ THE PASSAGE CAREFULLY AND THEN CHOOSE THE ANSWERS TO THE QUESTIONS.**

### The Lamb

Line     Little lamb, who made thee?
          Dost thou know who made thee?
    Gave thee life, and bid thee feed,
    By the stream and o'er the mead;
5    Gave thee clothing of delight,
    Softest clothing, woolly, bright;
    Gave thee such a tender voice,
    Making all the vales rejoice?
          Little Lamb, who made thee?
10   Dost thou know who made thee?

          Little Lamb, I'll tell thee,
          Little Lamb, I'll tell thee.
    His is callèd by thy name,
    For He calls Himself a Lamb.
15   He is meek, and He is mild;
    He became a little child.
    I a child, and thou a lamb,
    We are callèd by His name.
          Little Lamb, God bless thee!
20   Little Lamb, God bless thee!

               —William Blake

1. What is the theme of this poem?

    (A) The lamb and the speaker are alone in the world.
    (B) All creatures face uncertain futures.
    (C) Animals provide joy to human-kind.
    (D) All creatures in the world are one with God.
    (E) God created animals to meet the needs of humanity.

2. How does the speaker identify himself in the second stanza?

    (A) As a child and a Christian
    (B) As a meek and mild individual
    (C) As a lamb
    (D) As a seeker of truth
    (E) As a simple unnamed person

3. One could assume from this poem that the poet was concerned with which of the following?

    (A) Simple everyday life
    (B) Social injustice
    (C) Animal husbandry
    (D) The beauty of nature
    (E) Faith and the heavenly realm

4. Why would Blake choose to use so many monosyllabic words in this poem?

    (A) Less complicated to rhyme
    (B) To give a quick rhythm to the poem
    (C) To create a childlike, innocent mood
    (D) To mirror the movement of the young animal and the child
    (E) To give an uplifting feel to the poem

5. How would Blake characterize the creator imagined in this poem?

    (A) Demanding and forgiving
    (B) Quiet and remote
    (C) Friendly and understanding
    (D) Gentle and compassionate
    (E) Protective and wise

6. What two things does the lamb symbolize?

    (A) Creation and rebirth
    (B) Innocence and longing
    (C) Shyness and inquisitiveness
    (D) Spring and rebirth
    (E) Innocence and Christ

7. What is the best way to characterize this poem?

    (A) A childlike fantasy
    (B) A summary of a religious belief (creed)
    (C) Complex
    (D) Unsentimental
    (E) Didactic

8. What device does Blake use to create the poem's mood?

    (A) Simile
    (B) Repetition
    (C) Alliteration
    (D) Conceit
    (E) Onomatopoeia

9. What are the dominant literary devices in the poem?

    (A) Allusion and simile
    (B) Personification and caricature
    (C) Apostrophe and metaphor
    (D) Allegory and apostrophe
    (E) Pastoral and metaphor

**QUESTIONS 10 THROUGH 24 REFER TO THE FOLLOWING SELECTION. READ THE PASSAGE CAREFULLY AND THEN CHOOSE THE ANSWERS TO THE QUESTIONS.**

**From *Roughing It***

Line  It was always very cold on that lake shore* in the night, but we had plenty of blankets and were warm enough. We never moved a muscle all night, but waked at early dawn in the original positions, and got up at once, thoroughly refreshed, free from soreness, and brim full of friskiness. There is no end of wholesome medicine in such
5     an experience. That morning we could have whipped ten such people as we were the day before—sick ones at any rate. But the world is slow, and people will go to "water cures" and "movement cures" and to foreign lands for health. Three months of camp life on Lake Tahoe would restore an Egyptian mummy to his pristine vigor, and give him an appetite like an alligator. I do not mean the oldest and driest mummies, of
10    course, but the fresher ones. The air up there in the clouds is very pure and fine, bracing and delicious. And why shouldn't it be?—it is the same the angels breathe. I think that hardly any amount of fatigue can be gathered together that a man cannot sleep off in one night on the sand by its side. Not under a roof, but under the sky; it seldom or never rains there in the summertime. I know a man who went there to die.
15    But he made a failure of it. He was a skeleton when he came, and could barely stand. He had no appetite, and did nothing but read tracts and reflect on the future. Three months later he was sleeping out of doors regularly, eating all he could hold, three times a day, and chasing game over the mountains three thousand feet high for recreation. And he was a skeleton no longer, but weighed part of a ton. This is no
20    fancy sketch, but the truth. His disease was consumption. I confidently commend his experience to other skeletons.

—Mark Twain

_____
* Lake Tahoe on the California Nevada border.

10. What is the tone of the passage?

   (A) Witty
   (B) Serious, scientific
   (C) Insightful
   (D) Argumentative
   (E) Questioning, curious

11. Which of the following is the best statement of the theme of this passage?

   (A) Lake Tahoe is beautiful.
   (B) Going to Lake Tahoe can be helpful.
   (C) The air and water quality of Lake Tahoe are outstanding.
   (D) Lake Tahoe and its environs have recuperative powers.
   (E) It is important to keep Lake Tahoe pristine.

12. This selection can be classified as a(n)

   (A) expository essay
   (B) dramatic dialogue
   (C) exaggerated anecdote
   (D) modern myth
   (E) persuasive essay

13. The writer's purpose in this selection is to

   (A) amuse and entertain his audience
   (B) inform the audience about Lake Tahoe
   (C) teach about the environment
   (D) advocate a national park system through interesting readers in natural wonders
   (E) subtly suggest a healthy lifestyle

**GO ON TO THE NEXT PAGE**

14. What is the setting of this selection?

    (A) The Appalachian mountains in the mid-1800s
    (B) The West in the late twentieth century
    (C) The high deserts of the Southwest in the late 1700s
    (D) The mountains of the West in the mid-1800s
    (E) The Finger Lakes region of New York at the turn of the century

15. Which of the following is the best characterization of Mark Twain's diction?

    (A) He uses a great deal of folksy language.
    (B) Twain's diction is erudite.
    (C) His style is very sophisticated.
    (D) He is somewhat careless and irresponsible in his word choices.
    (E) The passage is structured and static.

16. This passage from *Roughing It* could be considered an example of

    (A) romanticism
    (B) realism
    (C) naturalism
    (D) classicism
    (E) regionalism

17. When Twain writes "But the world is slow" in line 6 he is saying

    (A) people lack energy
    (B) it takes time to communicate
    (C) people take time to learn
    (D) it takes a long time to get to a new place
    (E) there is little that is new

18. All of the following assessments of Twain's style are true as evidenced in this selection EXCEPT

    (A) Twain's genius is essentially western
    (B) Twain was a folklorist
    (C) Twain was a naturalist who concentrated on form
    (D) Twain had a relaxed style
    (E) Twain piles detail on detail

19. When Twain writes "I think that hardly any amount of fatigue can be gathered together that a man cannot sleep off in one night on the sand by its side," (lines 11–13) he is saying that the speaker thinks that

    (A) people never get enough sleep
    (B) many people sleep too much
    (C) sand forms a relaxing bed
    (D) anyone can get fully rested at Lake Tahoe
    (E) sands at Lake Tahoe have medicinal qualities

20. The words "bracing" and "delicious" (line 11) suggest that the air is

    (A) cold and tasteful
    (B) supportive and tasty
    (C) invigorating and enjoyable
    (D) refreshing and supportive
    (E) invigorating and refreshing

21. Based on the passage, what conclusion can be drawn about Mark Twain's feelings toward the locale?

    (A) He finds it amusing.
    (B) He enjoys the Mississippi River more.
    (C) He likes it.
    (D) He feels it lacks the depth of the East.
    (E) He wishes it were warmer.

22. When Twain states the air is what "angels breathe," (line 11) he is alluding to what aspect of the environment?

    (A) The cold
    (B) The moisture
    (C) The heavenly scent from the pines
    (D) The altitude
    (E) The perfection of the heavens

**23.** Which of the following does not apply to Twain's style in this selection?

(A) He uses specific details to create a sense of realism.

(B) He captures the local color.

(C) The speaker seems to be an ordinary person, the common man.

(D) The language has the flavor and rhythms of common speech.

(E) The style imitates Shakespearean sentence structure.

**24.** The reference to the "Egyptian mummy" in line 8 is an example of

(A) parody

(B) personification

(C) hyperbole

(D) metaphor

(E) humor

practice test

**QUESTIONS 25 THROUGH 35 REFER TO THE FOLLOWING SELECTION. READ THE POEM CAREFULLY AND THEN CHOOSE THE ANSWERS TO THE QUESTIONS.**

**Fueled**

Line   Fueled
     by a million
     man-made
     wings of fire—
5    the rocket tore a tunnel
     through the sky—
     and everybody cheered.
     Fueled
     only by a thought from God—
10   the seedling
     urged its way
     through the thicknesses of black—
     and as it pierced
     the heavy ceiling of the soil—
15   and launched itself
     up into outer space—
     no
     one
     even
20   clapped.

—Marcie Hans

**25.** What question is the writer posing throughout this poem?

    **(A)** Does life begin with the growth of a single plant or an explosion like a rocket engine?
    **(B)** Does a plant have the same power as a rocket?
    **(C)** Are the greatest miracles in life the inventions and achievements of individuals or do they come from nature?
    **(D)** How does a rocket contribute to the life of a single plant?
    **(E)** Why don't people care as much about plants as outer space?

**26.** This poem is constructed around a(n)

    **(A)** metaphor
    **(B)** conundrum
    **(C)** argument
    **(D)** question
    **(E)** contrast

**27.** To what does the phrase "a million man-made wings of fire" (lines 2–4) refer?

    **(A)** A large flight of aircraft
    **(B)** The burning of tremendous amounts of fuel
    **(C)** Sun reflecting off a skyscraper
    **(D)** The people cheering the rocket taking off
    **(E)** A huge flock of birds flying at sunset

**28.** What is the meaning of the phrase "Fueled only by a thought from God" (lines 8–9)?

    **(A)** A single thought from the mind of God is as powerful as man-made technology.
    **(B)** Humanity is directed by God.
    **(C)** God controls everything in the universe.
    **(D)** Humanity is of little consequence in nature.
    **(E)** Thoughts are all-powerful.

29. What does "outer space" refer to in line 16?

(A) The rocket's final resting place
(B) The domain of God
(C) The goal of the rocket
(D) The seedling has grown upward through the ground and entered the open air.
(E) The seedling's place of origin

30. What symbolizes life in this poem?

(A) Wings of fire
(B) The rocket
(C) The seedling
(D) Outer space
(E) A thought of God

31. What two objects are in parallelism?

(A) Sky and outer space
(B) Rocket and seedling
(C) Wings and tunnel
(D) Seedling and tunnel
(E) Fire and sky

32. The phrase "the rocket tore a tunnel through the sky" (lines 5–6) is an example of what type of figurative language?

(A) Alliteration
(B) Allegory
(C) Onomatopoeia
(D) Personification
(E) Metaphor

33. Which of the following best expresses the meaning of the last four lines of the poem?

(A) No one follows the teachings of God.
(B) The seedling is one of God's creations.
(C) No one notices what a thought from God has achieved in the seedling.
(D) A rocket is more important than a seedling.
(E) Humanity is like a seedling to God.

34. What does the title of the poem have to do with a symbol of life?

(A) Rockets need fuel.
(B) Humankind needs spiritual and physical fuel.
(C) Seedlings need fuel to grow.
(D) All things need fuel to grow.
(E) God is the fuel of humankind.

35. Which of the following most closely represents the poet's attitude toward the two accomplishments?

(A) The poet feels that human technological achievements approach those of nature.
(B) Hans sees birth and life as miraculous as any scientific or engineering advance.
(C) The cycles of nature are God-given.
(D) When scientists developed rockets, they were playing God.
(E) Science is a metaphor for religion.

QUESTIONS 36 THROUGH 50 REFER TO THE FOLLOWING LETTER FROM SAMUEL JOHNSON TO LORD CHESTERFIELD. AFTER THE PUBLICATION OF SAMUEL JOHNSON'S *DICTIONARY OF THE ENGLISH LANGUAGE,* LORD CHESTERFIELD WROTE TWO ARTICLES PRAISING THE WORK. EARLIER, CHESTERFIELD HAD IGNORED TWO REQUESTS FROM JOHNSON FOR FINANCIAL ASSISTANCE TO PRODUCE THE DICTIONARY. READ THE PASSAGE CAREFULLY AND THEN CHOOSE THE ANSWERS TO THE QUESTIONS.

### "Letter to Lord Chesterfield"

Line To the Right Honorable
The Earl of Chesterfield

February 7, 1755

My Lord:

5      I have been lately informed by the proprietor of the *World* that two papers in which my *Dictionary* is recommended to the public were written by your Lordship. To be so distinguished is an honor which, being very little accustomed to favors from the great, I know not well how to receive, or in what terms to acknowledge.

When upon some slight encouragement I first visited your Lordship, I was overpow-
10    ered like the rest of mankind by the enchantment of your address,[1] and could not forbear to wish that I might boast myself "*Le vainqueur du vainqueur de la terre*"[2]; that I might obtain that regard for which I saw the world contending, but I found my attendance so little encouraged that neither pride nor modesty would suffer me to continue it. When I had once addressed your Lordship in public, I had exhausted all
15    the art of pleasing which a retired and uncourtly scholar can possess. I had done all that I could; and no man is well pleased to have his all neglected, be it ever so little.

Seven years, my Lord, have now passed since I waited in your outward rooms or was repulsed from your door, during which time I have been pushing on my work through difficulties of which it is useless to complain and have brought it at last to the
20    verge of publication without one act of assistance, one word of encouragement, or one smile of favor. Such treatment I did not expect, for I never had a patron before.

The shepherd in Virgil grew at last acquainted with love, and found him a native of the rocks (Virgil's shepherd complains that love must have been born among jagged rocks). Is not a patron, my Lord, one who looks with unconcern on a man struggling
25    for life in the water and when he has reached ground encumbers him with help? The notice which you have been pleased to take of my labors, had it been early, had been kind; but it has been delayed till I am indifferent and cannot enjoy it, till I am solitary and cannot impart it, till I am known and do not want it.

I hope it is no very cynical asperity not to confess obligation where no benefit has
30    been received, or to be unwilling that the public should consider me as owing that to a patron which Providence has enabled me to do for myself.

Having carried on my work thus far with so little obligation to any favorer of learning, I shall not be disappointed though I should conclude it, if less be possible, with less; for I have been long wakened from that dream of hope, in which I once
35    boasted myself with so much exultation, my Lord.

Your Lordship's most humble,
Most obedient servant,
Samuel Johnson

_____
[1] conversation
[2] "the conqueror of the earth"

36. What was the purpose of this letter?

    **(A)** To ask for a financial settlement now that the dictionary was completed

    **(B)** To thank Chesterfield for his two glowing reviews

    **(C)** To express his disapproval of Chesterfield's misleading praise for his work

    **(D)** To inquire if Chesterfield might fund a second edition

    **(E)** To castigate the earl in front of all England

37. What tone is expressed in this letter?

    **(A)** Subtly stated anger and resentment

    **(B)** Grateful thanks

    **(C)** Condescending superiority

    **(D)** Obsequious fawning

    **(E)** Vicious coldness

38. Johnson writes "When upon some slight encouragement I first visited your Lordship, I was overpowered like the rest of mankind by the enchantment of your address, and could not forbear to wish that I might boast myself *'Le vainqueur du vainqueur de la terre'*; that I might obtain that regard for which I saw the world contending . . ." (lines 9–12). What stylistic device does he employ?

    **(A)** Allusion
    **(B)** Exemplum
    **(C)** Parallelism
    **(D)** Figurative language
    **(E)** Overstatement

39. In the fifth paragraph Johnson implies that Lord Chesterfield may have conveyed misinformation in his articles. What might Chesterfield have suggested?

    **(A)** The earl may have hinted that he had encouraged and supported Johnson throughout his years of working on the dictionary.

    **(B)** Chesterfield might have suggested that he inspired Johnson to begin the dictionary.

    **(C)** The earl might have implied that he provided Johnson with a house, servants, food, drink, and all other necessities of life.

    **(D)** Chesterfield might have implied that he himself contributed to the dictionary.

    **(E)** The earl might have implied that Johnson could not have completed the work without Chesterfield's help and monetary assistance.

40. Which of the following is an example of allusion?

    **(A)** "Is not a patron, my Lord, one who looks with unconcern on a man struggling for life in the water and when he has reached ground encumbers him with help?"

    **(B)** "I have been long wakened from that dream of hope, in which I once boasted myself with so much exultation, my Lord."

    **(C)** "I have been lately informed by the proprietor of the *World* that two papers in which my *Dictionary* is recommended to the public were written by your Lordship."

    **(D)** "The shepherd in Virgil grew at last acquainted with love, and found him a native of the rocks."

    **(E)** "Your lordship's most humble, Most obedient servant, Samuel Johnson"

**GO ON TO THE NEXT PAGE**

41. Samuel Johnson would have you believe which of the following about himself?

    (A) He is a sycophant.
    (B) He is indebted to Lord Chesterfield.
    (C) He no longer needs Lord Chesterfield's help.
    (D) He never sought assistance from a patron.
    (E) Lord Chesterfield is a man of unquestioning largess.

42. Samuel Johnson's expression "the enchantment of your address" (line 10) is

    (A) witty
    (B) argumentative
    (C) metaphorical
    (D) symbolic
    (E) sarcastic

43. Which phrase best describes Johnson's feelings as expressed in the passage?

    (A) "being very little accustomed to favors from the great"
    (B) "neither pride nor modesty would suffer me to continue"
    (C) "retired and uncourtly scholar"
    (D) "Such treatment I did not expect"
    (E) "long wakened from that dream of hope, in which I once boasted myself with so much exultation"

44. With which of these statements would Samuel Johnson agree?

    (A) No one likes one's work to be ignored.
    (B) One should never forget the little people.
    (C) Samuel Johnson had done everything he could to get the earl's attention.
    (D) Samuel Johnson had never done anything great before his dictionary.
    (E) No one can be happy doing only little things.

45. The closing of the letter can best be interpreted as

    (A) obsequious
    (B) facetious
    (C) punctilious
    (D) ironic
    (E) obligatory

46. What stylistic device can be found in the sentence, "Seven years, my Lord, have now passed since I waited in your outward rooms or was repulsed from your door, during which time I have been pushing on my work through difficulties of which it is useless to complain and have brought it at last to the verge of publication without one act of assistance; one word of encouragement, or one smile of favor." (lines 17–21)?

    (A) Parallelism
    (B) Overstatement
    (C) Allusion
    (D) Imagery
    (E) Quotation

47. Which of the following is not true of Johnson's diction?

    (A) Clear
    (B) Correct
    (C) Effective
    (D) Simple
    (E) Too formal for today's tastes

48. What is the feeling that Samuel Johnson conveys in the phrase "till I am known and do not want it"? (line 28)

    (A) People know who I am, and I do not need anyone's money.
    (B) I do not feel that you are a supporter of me.
    (C) Now that I am well known, I do not need your assistance.
    (D) He does not want anyone to help him publish his dictionary.
    (E) There are very few people who will spend time helping others.

49. The word "favorer" in line 32 refers to

    (A) student
    (B) teacher
    (C) audience
    (D) patron
    (E) adulator

50. Which of the following assessments does not accurately characterize the overall impression created by the selection?

    (A) Punctilious in courtesy
    (B) Faultless in manners
    (C) Ironic
    (D) Indignant
    (E) Forthright

**STOP** If you finish before time is called, you may check your work on this section only. Do not turn to any other section in the test.

# SECTION II

*3 QUESTIONS • 2 HOURS*

**Directions:** The following two poems treat historical subject matter. Read the poems carefully. Then write a well-organized essay explaining why one poem is more effective than the other in communicating its message. Consider such elements as rhythm, rhyme, diction, imagery, and purpose.

## Essay Question 1

*SUGGESTED TIME—40 MINUTES*

### Old Ironsides

Line  Ay, tear her tattered ensign down!
            Long has it waved on high,
      And many an eye has danced to see
            That banner in the sky;
5     Beneath it rung the battle shout,
            And burst the cannons roar;
      The meteor of the ocean air
            Shall sweep the clouds no more.

      Her deck, once red with heroes' blood,
10          Where knelt the vanquished foe,
      When winds were hurrying o'er the flood,
            And waves were white below,
      No more shall feel the victor's tread,
            Or know the conquered knee;—
15    The harpies of the shore shall pluck
            The eagle of the sea!

      Oh, better that her shattered bulk
            Should sink beneath the wave;
      Her thunders shook the mighty deep,
20          And there should be her grave;
      Nail to the mast her holy flag,
            Set every threadbare sail,
      And give her to the god of storms,
            The lightning and the gale!

                              —Oliver Wendell Holmes

**Douglass**

Line   Ah, Douglass, we have fall'n on evil days,
       Such days as thou, not even thou didst know,
       When thee, the eyes of that harsh long ago
    Saw, salient, at the cross of devious ways,
5     And all the country heard thee with amaze,
       Not ended then, the passionate ebb and flow,
       The awful tide that battled to and fro;
    We ride amid a tempest of dispraise.

    Now, when the waves of swift dissension swarm,
10       And Honour, the strong pilot, lieth stark,
    Oh, for thy voice high-sounding o'er the storm,
       For thy strong arm to guide the shivering bark,
    The blast-defying power of thy form,
       To give us comfort through the lonely dark.

              —Paul Laurence Dunbar

practice test

**GO ON TO THE NEXT PAGE** ➡

**Directions:** Read the passage below carefully. Write a well-organized essay that discusses the author's use of the resources of language to inspire his audience to combat injustice in the world.

## Essay Question 2

*SUGGESTED TIME—40 MINUTES*

**"Address to the Graduating Class"**
**University High School**
**Oxford, Mississippi, May 28, 1951**

Line　　Years ago, before any of you were born, a wise Frenchman said, "If youth knew; if age could." We all know what he meant: that when you are young, you have the power to do anything, but you don't know what to do. Then, when you have got old and experience and observation have taught you answers, you are tired, frightened; you don't
5　　care, you want to be left alone as long as you yourself are safe; you no longer have the capacity or the will to grieve over any wrongs but your own.

　　So you young men and women in this room tonight, and in thousands of other rooms like this one about the earth today, have the power to change the world, rid it forever of war and injustice and suffering, provided you know how, know what to do.
10　　And so according to the old Frenchman, since you can't know what to do because you are young, then anyone standing here with a head full of white hair, should be able to tell you.

　　But maybe this one is not as old and wise as his white hairs pretend or claim. Because he can't give you a glib answer or pattern either. But he can tell you this, because he believes this. What threatens us today is fear. Not the atom bomb, nor
15　　even fear of it, because if the bomb fell on Oxford tonight, all it could do would be to kill us, which is nothing, since in doing that, it will have robbed itself of its only power over us: which is fear of it, the being afraid of it. Our danger is not that. Our danger is the forces in the world today which are trying to use man's fear to rob him of his individuality, his soul, trying to reduce him to an unthinking mass by fear and
20　　bribery—giving him free food which he has not earned, easy and valueless money which he has not worked for; the economies or ideologies or political systems, communist or socialist or democratic, whatever they wish to call themselves, the tyrants and the politicians, American or European or Asiatic, whatever they call themselves, who would reduce man to one obedient mass for their own aggrandizement and power, or
25　　because they themselves are baffled and afraid, afraid of, or incapable of, believing in man's capacity for courage and endurance and sacrifice.

　　That is what we must resist, if we are to change the world for man's peace and security. It is not men in the mass who can and will save Man. It is Man himself, created in the image of God so that he shall have the power and the will to choose
30　　right from wrong, and so be able to save himself because he is worth saving;—Man, the individual, men and women, who will refuse always to be tricked or frightened or bribed into surrendering, not just the right but the duty too, to choose between justice and injustice, courage and cowardice, sacrifice and greed, pity and self;—who will believe always not only in the right of man to be free of injustice and rapacity and
35　　deception, but the duty and responsibility of man to see that justice and truth and pity and compassion are done.

　　So, never be afraid. Never be afraid to raise your voice for honesty and truth and compassion, against injustice and lying and greed. If you, not just you in this room

40 tonight, but in all the thousands of other rooms like this one about the world today and tomorrow and next week, will do this, not as a class or classes, but as individuals, men and women, you will change the earth; in one generation all the Napoleons and Hitlers and Caesars and Mussolinis and Stalins and all the other tyrants who want power and aggrandizement, and the simple politicians and time-servers who them-

45 selves are merely baffled or ignorant or afraid, who have used, or are using, or hope to use, man's fear and greed for man's enslavement, will have vanished from the face of it.

—William Faulkner

practice test

**Directions:** In some works of literature, violent external action sometimes reveals and explores the complex personalities of characters. In other works, characters reveal themselves more through inward psychological processes.

Choose a novel or play of literary merit and write an essay in which you show how either external action or mental processes reveals the personalities of the characters. You may wish to discuss how the action, theme, or mood and tone affect characters' internal processes or the external action. Avoid plot summary.

You may select a work from the list below, or you may choose another work of comparable literary merit suitable to the topic.

## Essay Question 3

***SUGGESTED TIME—40 MINUTES***

Faulkner, *Absalom, Absalom*

Faulkner, *As I Lay Dying*

Huxley, *Brave New World*

Heller, *Catch-22*

Dostoyevsky, *Crime and Punishment*

Walker, *The Color Purple*

Austen, *Emma*

Hemingway, *A Farewell to Arms*

Dickens, *Great Expectations*

Shakespeare, *Hamlet*

Shakespeare, *Henry V*

Wolfe, *Look Homeward, Angel*

Golding, *Lord of the Flies*

Melville, *Moby-Dick*

Joyce, *Portrait of the Artist as a Young Man*

Hardy, *The Return of the Native*

Rhys, *Wide Sargasso Sea*

**S T O P**   If you finish before time is called, you may check your work on this section only. Do not turn to any other section in the test.

# ANSWER KEY AND EXPLANATIONS

## Section I

| | | | | |
|---|---|---|---|---|
| 1. D | 11. D | 21. C | 31. B | 41. C |
| 2. A | 12. C | 22. D | 32. D | 42. E |
| 3. E | 13. A | 23. E | 33. C | 43. B |
| 4. C | 14. D | 24. C | 34. D | 44. A |
| 5. D | 15. A | 25. C | 35. B | 45. D |
| 6. E | 16. E | 26. E | 36. C | 46. A |
| 7. E | 17. C | 27. B | 37. A | 47. D |
| 8. B | 18. C | 28. A | 38. E | 48. C |
| 9. C | 19. D | 29. D | 39. A | 49. D |
| 10. A | 20. C | 30. C | 40. D | 50. E |

1. **The correct answer is (D).** Blake creates two characters in this poem—the speaker and a lamb. The speaker draws a parallel between both the lamb and the speaker and their relationship with God. The answer that is consistent with this is choice (D). Choice (E) mentions God, but the poem does not say that animals were created to satisfy humankind's needs. Choices (A), (B), and (C) do not mention God at all.

2. **The correct answer is (A).** The speaker says in the second stanza "I a child," thereby identifying the speaker as a child. The speaker goes on to say, "We are callèd by His name." A clue in this sentence is the capital "H" in the word *His*. This tells you that it is a reference to God, or, as in this case, Jesus Christ. Choice (C) is clearly incorrect, while choices (B), (D), and (E) do not relate to the poem.

3. **The correct answer is (E).** This question is most easily answered through the process of elimination. Choices (A) and (E) are possibilities, but choices (B), (C), and (D) are not discussed, so they can be eliminated. While the setting of the poem is simple, choice (A) is only loosely associated with the topic. Choice (E), which touches on the religious aspect of the poem, is the most accurate response to the question.

4. **The correct answer is (C).** The two principal characters are children of their species. To reinforce this concept, Blake has chosen a word pattern that is childlike and simple. Such a speech scheme would tend to be monosyllabic. Choices (B) and (E) are not consistent with the theme of the poem. Choice (D) is not true, and while choice (A) may be true, the best response in the context of the poem is choice (C).

5. **The correct answer is (D).** The speaker states that God is mild and meek, synonyms for compassionate, and calls Himself a lamb, which is characterized in literature as a soft, gentle animal. There is nothing in the poem that describes God as choices (A), (B), (C), or (E).

6. **The correct answer is (E).** Experience outside this poem helps you to respond to this question. Children and lambs are often portrayed as symbols of innocence, which eliminates all answers except choices (B) and (E). There is no mention of longing in the poem, so choice (B) can be eliminated. The poem states that God calls himself the "Lamb of God," and in Christian religion, this is more specifically a reference to Jesus Christ.

7. **The correct answer is (E).** The content and development of the poem are not consistent with choices (A), (B), (C), or (D). It is not a fantasy, a statement of religious belief, or complex. It is sentimental in the sense of exhibiting tender or gentle feelings. This leaves choice (E), and if you know anything about Blake, you will know that many of his poems are didactic, or instructional, in tone and intent.

8. **The correct answer is (B).** For reasons similar to those discussed in question 4 about monosyllabic word choice, Blake repeated words to develop the simple, childlike quality he wanted in the poem. None of the other choices is represented in the poem. A simile uses *like* or *as* to compare two things, choice (A). Alliteration is a repetition of initial consonant sounds, choice (C). A conceit is an extended metaphor or comparison that states that something *is* something else, choice (D). Onomatopoeia is a word that sounds like what it means, choice (E).

9. **The correct answer is (C).** In this question you have to match two items to find the correct answer. An allusion, choice (A), is a reference to a famous person or to another work; there is no such reference, so choice (A) is incorrect because if half the answer is wrong, the whole answer is wrong. In personification, choice (B), human qualities are given to a nonhuman object. The use of the word *voice* in reference to the lamb may be personification, but there is nothing about the poem that is a caricature, an exaggerated verbal portrait of someone, so choice (B) can be eliminated. An allegory, choice (D), is a story in which each part has some larger symbolic meaning, and apostrophe, choice (E), is directly addressing a person or thing, absent or present; the latter may be true of the poem, but the poem is not an allegory, so choice (D) can be eliminated. The setting of a pastoral, choice (E), is nature and often the subject is shepherds, but there are no shepherds, literal or figurative, in this poem. Even though the lamb is used as a metaphor for God, choice (E) is incorrect because the poem is not a pastoral. By working through the answers, you can see that two items are correct and are paired in choice (C), apostrophe and metaphor.

10. **The correct answer is (A).** The tone of the passage could not be considered serious or deep. Any answer with that sense would be incorrect, so choices (B), (C), and (D) can be eliminated. Humor and wit are more evident in the writing than questioning or curiosity, choice (E), so choice (A) is the better response.

11. **The correct answer is (D).** Each of the five answers has an element of Twain's commentary in them; therefore, you must look for the response that best matches or sums up the main idea. Much of the selection links Lake Tahoe to improving health. Choice (D) is the only choice that recognizes the recuperative powers of the area. Choices (A) and (E) focus more on the scenic beauty, and choices (B) and (C) touch on aspects of the area that might be helpful to good health and support, choice (D).

12. **The correct answer is (C).** This selection should not be viewed as a serious piece of writing, and any response that suggests that view is incorrect. That includes choices (A), (B), and (E). Of the two remaining answers, the passage is an anecdote, a short narrative, rather than a myth, a story once believed to be true, choice (D).

13. **The correct answer is (A).** The speaker is not a teacher or an advocate, so choices (B), (C), and (D) can be eliminated. Choice (E) suggests a more indirect approach, but there is nothing subtle about the speaker; he tells his audience what they should do. The simple answer, to amuse and entertain, is the best response.

14. **The correct answer is (D).** The possible correct answers can quickly be reduced by two, choices (A) and (E), because the excerpt states that Lake Tahoe is on the California-Nevada border. The locale is not set in a desert, so that eliminates choice (C). Mark Twain wrote in the 1800s, eliminating choice (B), and the lake is in the mountains. This identifies choice (D) as the correct answer.

15. **The correct answer is (A).** Twain's diction could not be called erudite, choice (B), and his style is not sophisticated, choice (C). Although he chooses words of common speech, he does so with care, choice (D), to paint vivid images. The passage is dynamic rather than static, so choice (E) can be eliminated. Examples like "brim full of friskiness" (line 4) support choice (A) as the correct answer.

16. **The correct answer is (E).** This is not a romantic passage, choice (A); it does not express great emotion or devotion even though nature is featured prominently. Considering the amount of exaggeration, it certainly is not realistic, choice (B). Neither is it an example of naturalism or classicism, choices (C) and (D), in subject matter. The focus of this passage is clearly on a specific area of the country. This type of advocacy for a territory is known as regionalism.

17. **The correct answer is (C).** It is important to put the question in context. The phrase represents a transition from Twain's listing of health benefits at Lake Tahoe to other approaches that were then in vogue. The reference to slowness shows that the author was indicating that it will take time for people to learn about something new and change. Choices (A) and (E) have no relationship to the content. On a quick reading, you might think that choice (D) could be correct, but choice (D) relates to real movement. In that context, the author is not speaking about literal movement. Choice (B) might seem correct, but the author is implying that people have to change their ways; he does not say how they will learn about new things.

18. **The correct answer is (C).** Choices (A), (B), and (E) are fairly obviously the wrong answers; the selection is set in the West, choice (A); his subject matter is more folklore than classical, choice (B); and he uses several stories to make his point when one might do, choice (E). Do not confuse the term "naturalist," choice (C), as a literary movement with an environmentalist; Twain was not a naturalist, and the form of his writing was not of concern to him (or he would not have used so many details and folksy language). Twain's relaxed style carries the reader along, choice (D).

19. **The correct answer is (D).** The question is asking about sleep, the topic of the sentence. The items to note in reading the sentence are the antecedent of *its* (Lake Tahoe) and the recuperative powers of the lake. These elements identify choice (D) as the answer. Choices (A), (B), and (C) do not mention the lake, while choice (E) does not mention sleep.

20. **The correct answer is (C).** While delicious may mean tasty, it does not mean tasteful, so you can eliminate choice (A). Both sets of words in choices (D) and (E) mean "bracing," so they can be eliminated. Although "bracing" can mean supportive, choice (B), invigorating is a better meaning in the context of air, and delicious when referring to the senses means enjoyable, choice (C).

21. **The correct answer is (C).** The identification of the answer requires that you make an inference about the author's feelings. It is clear from Twain's comments that he has a positive feeling for the area. Only choices (A) and (C) have this connotation, but Twain writes about incidents that supposedly occurred in the area that were amusing. It is not the area that is amusing to him, choice (A). This leaves choice (C) as the answer. Choices (B) and (D) are distractors that bear no relation to the selection, while choice (E) might seem correct if you focus on Twain's comment about the "bracing air."

22. **The correct answer is (D).** Taken with the phrase "the air up there in the clouds," the reference to angels points directly to height as an element in the answer. Since angels are said to be "up" in the heavens, choice (D) is the answer. Choices (C) and (E) may distract you, but the question asks about the environment—in the mountains. Choices (A) and (B) do not relate to angels.

23. **The correct answer is (E).** If you did not readily see that Twain does not use classical Shakespearean sentence structure, try the process of elimination. The author uses both specific details, choice (A), and local color, choice (B), to make his points. The speaker is also an ordinary person using common speech, choices (C) and (D).

24. **The correct answer is (C).** A parody takes another work as its subject and exaggerates it to the point of making it ridiculous. There is no other work involved, so choice (A) is incorrect, as is choice (D) because the mummy is not standing for anything else. There is no personification of the mummy, thus eliminating choice (B). The choice then is between hyperbole and humor. Although the reference may be humorous, choice (E), it is plainly an exaggeration.

25. **The correct answer is (C).** Choices (D) and (E) do not recognize the proper relationship between the seedling and the rocket. Choices (A), (B), and (C) have varying degrees of association between the two elements of the poem. However, the beginning of life and equivalent power do not follow the theme as closely as questioning what is the greatest miracle in life.

26. **The correct answer is (E).** The poet contrasts human beings' reactions to the lift-off of a rocket with the growth of a seedling. While there is an implied question in the poem, choice (D), the selection is not built around it. A metaphor states that something *is* something else, which has no relation to the devices in the poem, choice (A), nor is the poem a conundrum, or riddle, choice (B). There is no argument to support choice (C).

27. **The correct answer is (B).** The author creates an image of a rocket that is flying on man-made fire. The pictures created in choices (C), (D), and (E) do not match Hans's image. Choice (A) has some of the proper characteristics, but the author refers to a rocket, not an aircraft.

28. **The correct answer is (A).** Choice (B) is incorrect because there is no mention of people in relation to God as force. Choice (D) has nothing to do with the poem, and it is not all thoughts as implied in choice (E) that are all-powerful, only God's. Choice (C) may be implied in the poem, but is not stated, while choice (A) is the better restatement of the poem's theme.

29. **The correct answer is (D).** Marcie Hans is clear in lines 10–16 that she is describing the seedling taking root and poking through the soil toward the sky. The world outside the soil is "outer space" for the seedling. Choices (A), (B), (C), and (E) do not capture this concept.

30. **The correct answer is (C).** Because the two central objects in the poem are the rocket and the seedling, one must symbolize life. Since a seedling is made by God and a rocket by man, choice (C) is the correct response. Choices (A), (D), and (E) are not central images.

**31. The correct answer is (B).** Once again the question revolves around identification of the core elements of the poem. These are the rocket and the seedling. This time they are identified as the two elements of the parallel construction. The parallel element for sky is soil, not outer space, so choice (A) is incorrect. The wings of fire propelled the rocket through the tunnel, so wings and tunnel are not parallel, but in a cause-and-effect relationship, choice (C). Likewise, the seedling is the actor while the tunnel is the recipient of the actions of the rocket, so choice (D) is incorrect. Fire and sky, choice (E), are in a similar relationship to choice (C).

**32. The correct answer is (D).** The quotation demonstrates personification by giving an inanimate object human characteristics—the ability to tear. There is no repetition of initial consonants in the poem, so choice (A) is incorrect. This is not a story whose parts have symbolic meanings, choice (B). Neither the word *rocket* nor any other word in the phrase sounds like what it does, thus eliminating choice (C). A metaphor, choice (E), states that something *is* something else; there is no example of this.

**33. The correct answer is (C).** In the lines just preceding those cited in the question, Hans has said that the seedling has just broken out of its soil birthplace. Unlike the rocket, no one has noticed the seedling's accomplishment. Earlier, it was established that a mere thought from God powered the seedling. Choice (A) has nothing to do with the poem. The poem implies exactly the opposite of choice (D). Nowhere does the poem equate humans with the seedling, explicitly or implicitly, eliminating choice (E). While choice (B) is true, choice (C) more closely reflects the poem's content.

**34. The correct answer is (D).** Once again, you should look to both of the central images, the rocket and the seedling. In parallel construction, both the rocket and seedling would require fuel. The only answer that includes them both is choice (D).

**35. The correct answer is (B).** Three of the choices, (A), (D), and (E), can be eliminated because they do not follow the key points of the poem. Deciding between choices (B) and (C) is more difficult; however, the reference to the "cycles of nature" could only have relevance for the seedling. Choice (B) covers both the rocket and the seedling.

**36. The correct answer is (C).** Choices (A), (B), and (D) do not correctly recognize the subject of Johnson's letter. Choice (E) has identified the correct tone of the writing, but a letter is for an audience of one, not all of England.

**37. The correct answer is (A).** Johnson's disapproval of Lord Chesterfield is clear in this passage; therefore, choices (B) and (D) are incorrect. Of the remaining possibilities, you need to identify the best response. Choice (A), subtle anger and resentment, is the best reflection of the tone of the letter. Johnson may be cool to the earl, but there are no vicious remarks in the letter, choice (E), nor is he condescending, choice (C).

**38. The correct answer is (E).** An overstatement is an intentional exaggeration, choice (E). Allusion is an indirect reference to historical or fictional characters, places, or events that a writer assumes you will recognize, choice (A). An exemplum is a brief tale or anecdote used to illustrate a moral lesson, choice (B). Parallelism shows that words, phrases, or other structures are comparable in content and importance by placing them side by side and making them similar in form, choice (C). Figurative language is an expression intended to be interpreted imaginatively, choice (D).

**39.    The correct answer is (A).** This is a difficult question because all of the answers are true to a certain degree. Because you are being asked to make an assumption based on the tone and content of the letter, the best approach is to choose the most general answer. Choice (A) is the most general and conveys what Johnson had hoped to receive from Chesterfield when he went to call on him. Since you cannot read what Chesterfield wrote, you cannot know if the details in choices (B) or (C) or the implications in choices (D) and (E) are correct.

**40.    The correct answer is (D).** Allusion is an indirect reference to historical or fictional characters, places, or events that a writer assumes you will recognize. In choice (D), Virgil's shepherd is an allusion to a classical Roman work. None of the other quotations has such a reference.

**41.    The correct answer is (C).** The best approach for this is the process of elimination. Johnson is neither a sycophant, or he would not have written the letter, choice (A), nor is he indebted to Lord Chesterfield, or he would have no reason to write this letter, choice (B). He did seek assistance from the earl, who refused to become Johnson's patron, so choice (D) is incorrect. Lord Chesterfield could not be called generous from Johnson's experience, choice (E). The remaining answer, that Johnson no longer needs the earl's help, is the correct response.

**42.    The correct answer is (E).** Johnson does not find anything in his experience with Lord Chesterfield to be witty about, choice (A). Sarcasm is the better of the two terms to explain the courteous word with an underlying pejorative intent. A metaphor states that something *is* something else, while a symbol represents an idea or a concept, choices (C) and (D), neither of which applies, nor does argumentative, choice (B).

**43.    The correct answer is (B).** All the responses relate to Johnson's feelings, but the one that best exemplifies them, based on the tone, style, and diction, is choice (B). Johnson is a proud and independent man who knows the value of the work he set out to accomplish with the *Dictionary*.

**44.    The correct answer is (A).** In the last sentence of paragraph two Johnson says, "I had done all that I could; and no man is well pleased to have his all neglected, be it ever so little." In other words, no one likes to have what he or she has done, no matter how small, ignored. Choice (B) may be true, but it is not the major argument of the letter, while choice (E) has nothing to do with the selection. You cannot know from the selection whether choice (D) is true or not.

**45.    The correct answer is (D).** Obsequious, choice (A), means fawning or an overly anxious willingness to serve. This contradicts the point of the letter. Facetious, choice (B), means joking, and there is nothing lighthearted about this letter. The question asks for the best interpretation, and while the wording of the closing may be obligatory, choice (E), and Johnson is punctilious (very careful about observing ceremony and tradition) in using it, choice (C), he is using it as one last jab of irony, choice (D).

**46.    The correct answer is (A).** Parallelism is a technique of showing that words, phrases, or other structures are comparable in content and importance by placing them side by side and making them similar in form. The many conjunctions and prepositions in this passage are a clue that the lines have parallel structure. Overstatement, choice (B), is an exaggeration but to a lesser degree than hyperbole. Allusion, choice (C), is a reference to a famous person or to another work. Imagery, choice (D), refers to figures of speech in general, and Johnson is saying what he said, not quoting it, choice (E).

**47.    The correct answer is (D).** Process of elimination guides you to the answer. Johnson's writing is clear, correct, and effective, and his diction is difficult for readers today, choices (A), (B), (C), and (E). However, you cannot call this letter simple.

48.  **The correct answer is (C).** In the context of the last sentence of the fourth paragraph, Johnson is chastising Lord Chesterfield for making his comments about Johnson's work so late that they did not help Johnson. In light of that, the best response is choice (C). Choice (A) is too specific in that it says money when Johnson had been looking for support in addition to money. Choice (B) is too simplistic. Choices (D) and (E) do not reflect the context of the phrase.

49.  **The correct answer is (D).** In the context of the letter, the only answer that can be correct is choice (D). Johnson is saying that he has worked all this time without any help. He has made no reference in the letter to students, choice (A); teachers, choice (B); or an audience, choice (C). Choice (E) is a distractor because a patron is an admirer of the person assisted, but an adulator is one who admires another to excess.

50.  **The correct answer is (E).** Although you should have not chosen "punctilious" in question 45 as the best answer, it does characterize Johnson's letter and, therefore, should not be chosen here either, choice (A). The letter does observe the formalities of the period, choice (B), and in its use of irony, choice (C), it shows Johnson's indignation, choice (D). However, because he uses irony, it is not completely forthright, choice (E).

## Section II

### SUGGESTIONS FOR ESSAY QUESTION 1

The following are points you might have chosen to include in your essay contrasting "Old Ironsides" and "Douglass." Consider them as you do your self-evaluation. Revise your essay using points from the list to strengthen it.

|  | "Old Ironsides" | "Douglass" |
|---|---|---|
| **Type** | Mostly iambic feet; alternating lines of trimeter and tetrameter; patriotic | Shakespearean sonnet; form conveys sense of dignity |
| **Themes** | Promoting an important cause; save the battleship *Constitution* from demolition | People's need for Douglass's guidance and comfort; developed in the sestet |
| **Speaker** | A patriot who would rather see the ship scuttled than demolished | A despairing African American |
| **Tone** | Patriotic; rousing | Despair; formality |
| **Figurative Language** | "Ironsides:" symbol of patriotism and heroism; eagle: national symbol | Assonance: "Saw, salient, at the cross of devious ways," "waves of swift dissension swarm" |
| **Imagery** | Patriotic: "red with heroes' blood," "eagle of the sea" | To bring out feeling of troubled times: "We ride amid a tempest of dispraise." "Waves of swift dissension" |
| **Diction and Poetic Devices** | Meter encourages oral presentation | Thee and thy; formal, dignified |

### SUGGESTIONS FOR ESSAY QUESTION 2

The following are points you might have chosen to include in your essay on Faulkner's speech to the graduating class. Consider them as you do your self-evaluation. Revise your essay using points from the list to strengthen it.

#### *Form or Mode*

- Prose; a speech
- Persuasive

#### *Theme*

- Individuals can and must choose to change the world for the better.
- "It is man himself, created in the image of God so that he shall have the power and the will to choose right from wrong, and so be able to save himself because he is worth saving."

### Characters

- Faulkner, the speaker
- Audience, the graduating students

### Conflict

- Good versus evil

### Content/Important Points

- Beginning quotation
- Youth has power to rid world of war and injustice
- Fear danger in world
- Danger in those who use human fear to control humankind
- Right and duty to choose justice, courage, sacrifice, compassion
- If people choose right actions, tyrants will disappear

### Setting

- Speech given at graduation
- Contemporary times—the bomb

### Point of View

- First person

### Diction/Syntax/Style

- Offers no proof to support opening quotation; abandons point in third paragraph
- Speaking directly to students; use of second person, *you*
- Long, complex sentences
- Much parallel construction: "giving him free food which he has not earned, easy and valueless money which he has not worked for"
- Cadence ministerial, almost musical
- Word choice sophisticated, but comprehensible: "glib," "baffled," "aggrandizement"

### SUGGESTIONS FOR ESSAY QUESTION 3

The following are points about plot and characterization that you might have chosen to discuss in your essay on character development in literature. Consider them as you do your self-evaluation. Revise your essay using points from the list to strengthen it.

### Action/Plot

- A series of related events moving from a problem to a solution
- Exposition of characters and situation
- Conflict, source of tension
- Internal conflict within a character
- External conflict between two or more characters or a force of nature
- Climax, the turning point
- Resolution, how problem is solved
- Complications, events that stand in the way of resolution
- Foreshadowing, use of hints to suggest what is to come

### Characterization

- Direct characterization, directly telling about a character's personality
- Indirect characterization, revealing personality through descriptions, thoughts, words, and actions
- Round characters, fully developed
- Flat characters, only one or two character traits
- Dynamic characters change
- Static characters do not change
- Motivation, reason for character's behavior
- Characters convey theme
- Focus on protagonists and antagonists
- A message from the writer usually relating to the theme through the protagonist
- Identifying the protagonist sometimes difficult and not always necessary
- Great deal of revelation about characters in reaction to forces that are other than human
- Character revealed by how people cope with economic, social, or political world
- The struggle between the protagonist and the antagonist crucial to a literary work
- Resolution: insight into the characters and the meaning of the piece

## SELF-EVALUATION RUBRIC FOR THE ADVANCED PLACEMENT ESSAYS

| | 8–9 | 6–7 | 5 | 3–4 | 1–2 | 0 |
|---|---|---|---|---|---|---|
| **Overall Impression** | Demonstrates excellent control of the literature and outstanding writing competence; thorough and effective; incisive | Demonstrates good control of the literature and good writing competence; less thorough and incisive than the highest papers | Reveals simplistic thinking and/or immature writing; adequate skills | Incomplete thinking; fails to respond adequately to part or parts of the question; may paraphrase rather than analyze | Unacceptably brief; fails to respond to the question; little clarity | Lacking skill and competence |
| **Understanding of the Text** | Excellent understanding of the text; exhibits perception and clarity; original or unique approach; includes apt and specific references | Good understanding of the text; exhibits perception and clarity; includes specific references | Superficial understanding of the text; elements of literature vague, mechanical, overgeneralized | Misreadings and lack of persuasive evidence from the text; meager and unconvincing treatment of literary elements | Serious misreadings and little supporting evidence from the text; erroneous treatment of literary elements | A response with no more than a reference to the literature; blank response, or one completely off the topic |
| **Organization and Development** | Meticulously organized and thoroughly developed; coherent and unified | Well-organized and developed; coherent and unified | Reasonably organized and developed; mostly coherent and unified | Somewhat organized and developed; some incoherence and lack of unity | Little or no organization and development; incoherent and void of unity | No apparent organization or development; incoherent |
| **Use of Sentences** | Effectively varied and engaging; virtually error free | Varied and interesting; a few errors | Adequately varied; some errors | Somewhat varied and marginally interesting; one or more major errors | Little or no variation; dull and uninteresting; some major errors | Numerous major errors |
| **Word Choice** | Interesting and effective; virtually error free | Generally interesting and effective; a few errors | Occasionally interesting and effective; several errors | Somewhat dull and ordinary; some errors in diction | Mostly dull and conventional; numerous errors | Numerous major errors; extremely immature |
| **Grammar and Usage** | Virtually error free | Occasional minor errors | Several minor errors | Some major errors | Severely flawed; frequent major errors | Extremely flawed |

Rate yourself in each of the categories. Choose the description that most accurately reflects your performance, and enter the numbers on the lines below. Be as honest as possible so you will know what areas need work. Then calculate the average of the six numbers to determine your final score. It is difficult to score yourself objectively, so you may wish to ask a respected friend or teacher to assess your writing for a more accurate reflection of its strengths and weaknesses. On the AP test itself, a reader will rate your essay on a scale of 0 to 9, with 9 being the highest.

Rate each category from 9 (high) to 0 (low).

# Essay Question 1

**SELF-EVALUATION**

Overall Impression _____
Understanding of the Text _____
Organization and Development _____
Use of Sentences _____
Word Choice (Diction) _____
Grammar and Usage _____

TOTAL _____
Divide by 6 for final score _____

**OBJECTIVE EVALUATION**

Overall Impression _____
Understanding of the Text _____
Organization and Development _____
Use of Sentences _____
Word Choice (Diction) _____
Grammar and Usage _____

TOTAL _____
Divide by 6 for final score _____

# Essay Question 2

**SELF-EVALUATION**

Overall Impression _____
Understanding of the Text _____
Organization and Development _____
Use of Sentences _____
Word Choice (Diction) _____
Grammar and Usage _____

TOTAL _____
Divide by 6 for final score _____

**OBJECTIVE EVALUATION**

Overall Impression _____
Understanding of the Text _____
Organization and Development _____
Use of Sentences _____
Word Choice (Diction) _____
Grammar and Usage _____

TOTAL _____
Divide by 6 for final score _____

# Essay Question 3

**SELF-EVALUATION**

Overall Impression _____
Understanding of the Text _____
Organization and Development _____
Use of Sentences _____
Word Choice (Diction) _____
Grammar and Usage _____

TOTAL _____
Divide by 6 for final score _____

**OBJECTIVE EVALUATION**

Overall Impression _____
Understanding of the Text _____
Organization and Development _____
Use of Sentences _____
Word Choice (Diction) _____
Grammar and Usage _____

TOTAL _____
Divide by 6 for final score _____

# ANSWER SHEET PRACTICE TEST 4

## SECTION I

1. Ⓐ Ⓑ Ⓒ Ⓓ Ⓔ
2. Ⓐ Ⓑ Ⓒ Ⓓ Ⓔ
3. Ⓐ Ⓑ Ⓒ Ⓓ Ⓔ
4. Ⓐ Ⓑ Ⓒ Ⓓ Ⓔ
5. Ⓐ Ⓑ Ⓒ Ⓓ Ⓔ
6. Ⓐ Ⓑ Ⓒ Ⓓ Ⓔ
7. Ⓐ Ⓑ Ⓒ Ⓓ Ⓔ
8. Ⓐ Ⓑ Ⓒ Ⓓ Ⓔ
9. Ⓐ Ⓑ Ⓒ Ⓓ Ⓔ
10. Ⓐ Ⓑ Ⓒ Ⓓ Ⓔ
11. Ⓐ Ⓑ Ⓒ Ⓓ Ⓔ
12. Ⓐ Ⓑ Ⓒ Ⓓ Ⓔ
13. Ⓐ Ⓑ Ⓒ Ⓓ Ⓔ
14. Ⓐ Ⓑ Ⓒ Ⓓ Ⓔ
15. Ⓐ Ⓑ Ⓒ Ⓓ Ⓔ
16. Ⓐ Ⓑ Ⓒ Ⓓ Ⓔ
17. Ⓐ Ⓑ Ⓒ Ⓓ Ⓔ

18. Ⓐ Ⓑ Ⓒ Ⓓ Ⓔ
19. Ⓐ Ⓑ Ⓒ Ⓓ Ⓔ
20. Ⓐ Ⓑ Ⓒ Ⓓ Ⓔ
21. Ⓐ Ⓑ Ⓒ Ⓓ Ⓔ
22. Ⓐ Ⓑ Ⓒ Ⓓ Ⓔ
23. Ⓐ Ⓑ Ⓒ Ⓓ Ⓔ
24. Ⓐ Ⓑ Ⓒ Ⓓ Ⓔ
25. Ⓐ Ⓑ Ⓒ Ⓓ Ⓔ
26. Ⓐ Ⓑ Ⓒ Ⓓ Ⓔ
27. Ⓐ Ⓑ Ⓒ Ⓓ Ⓔ
28. Ⓐ Ⓑ Ⓒ Ⓓ Ⓔ
29. Ⓐ Ⓑ Ⓒ Ⓓ Ⓔ
30. Ⓐ Ⓑ Ⓒ Ⓓ Ⓔ
31. Ⓐ Ⓑ Ⓒ Ⓓ Ⓔ
32. Ⓐ Ⓑ Ⓒ Ⓓ Ⓔ
33. Ⓐ Ⓑ Ⓒ Ⓓ Ⓔ
34. Ⓐ Ⓑ Ⓒ Ⓓ Ⓔ

35. Ⓐ Ⓑ Ⓒ Ⓓ Ⓔ
36. Ⓐ Ⓑ Ⓒ Ⓓ Ⓔ
37. Ⓐ Ⓑ Ⓒ Ⓓ Ⓔ
38. Ⓐ Ⓑ Ⓒ Ⓓ Ⓔ
39. Ⓐ Ⓑ Ⓒ Ⓓ Ⓔ
40. Ⓐ Ⓑ Ⓒ Ⓓ Ⓔ
41. Ⓐ Ⓑ Ⓒ Ⓓ Ⓔ
42. Ⓐ Ⓑ Ⓒ Ⓓ Ⓔ
43. Ⓐ Ⓑ Ⓒ Ⓓ Ⓔ
44. Ⓐ Ⓑ Ⓒ Ⓓ Ⓔ
45. Ⓐ Ⓑ Ⓒ Ⓓ Ⓔ
46. Ⓐ Ⓑ Ⓒ Ⓓ Ⓔ
47. Ⓐ Ⓑ Ⓒ Ⓓ Ⓔ
48. Ⓐ Ⓑ Ⓒ Ⓓ Ⓔ
49. Ⓐ Ⓑ Ⓒ Ⓓ Ⓔ
50. Ⓐ Ⓑ Ⓒ Ⓓ Ⓔ

answer sheet

## SECTION II

## Essay Question 1

_____

_____

_____

_____

_____

_____

_____

_____

_____

_____

_____

_____

_____

_____

_____

_____

_____

_____

_____

_____

answer sheet

**Essay Question 2**

_____

_____

_____

_____

_____

_____

_____

_____

_____

_____

_____

_____

_____

_____

_____

_____

_____

_____

_____

_____

_____

_____

_____

_____

_____

answer sheet

**Essay Question 3**

_____

_____

_____

_____

_____

_____

_____

_____

_____

_____

_____

_____

_____

_____

_____

_____

_____

_____

_____

_____

_____

_____

_____

answer sheet

# Practice Test 4

## SECTION I

*50 QUESTIONS • 60 MINUTES*

> **Directions:** This section consists of selections of literature and questions on their content, style, and form. After you have read each passage, choose the answer that best answers the question and mark the space on the answer sheet.

**QUESTIONS 1 THROUGH 13 REFER TO THE FOLLOWING SELECTION. IN THIS EXCERPT FROM *MY BONDAGE AND MY FREEDOM* BY FREDERICK DOUGLASS, THE AUTHOR SPEAKS ABOUT HIS YOUTH AS A SLAVE. READ THE PASSAGE CAREFULLY AND THEN CHOOSE THE CORRECT ANSWERS TO THE QUESTIONS.**

### From *My Bondage and My Freedom*

Line  When I was about thirteen years old, and had succeeded in learning to
read, every increase of knowledge, especially respecting the free states,
added something to the almost intolerable burden of the thought—
"I am a slave fore life." To my bondage I saw no end, it was a terrible
5  reality, and I shall never be able to tell how sadly that thought chafed
my young spirit. Fortunately, or unfortunately, about this time in my
life, I had made enough money to buy what was then a very popular
schoolbook, the *Columbian Orator.* I bought this addition to my library,
of Mr. Knight, on Thames street Fell's Point, Baltimore, and paid him
10  fifty cents for it. I was first led to buy this book, by hearing some little
boys say they were going to learn some little pieces out of it for the
Exhibition. This volume was, indeed, a rich treasure, and every
opportunity afforded me, for a time, was spent in diligently perusing it.
. . . The dialogue and the speeches were all redolent of the principles of
15  liberty; and poured floods of light on the nature and character of
slavery. As I read, behold! The very discontent so graphically predicted
by Master Hugh, had already come upon me. I was no longer the
light-hearted, gleesome boy, full of mirth and play, as when I landed
first at Baltimore. Knowledge had come. . . . This knowledge opened
20  my eyes to the horrible pit, and revealed the teeth of the frightful
dragon that was ready to pounce upon me, but it opened no way for my
escape. I have often wished myself a beast, or a bird—anything, rather

than a slave. I was wretched and gloomy. Beyond my ability to describe. I was too
thoughtful to be happy. It was this everlasting thinking which distressed and tor-
25 mented me; and yet there was no getting rid of the subject of my thoughts. All nature
was redolent of it. Once awakened by the silver trump* of knowledge, my spirit was
roused to eternal wakefulness. Liberty! The inestimable birthright of every man, had,
for me, converted every object into an asserter of this great right. It was heard in
every sound, and beheld in every object. It was ever present, to torment me with a
30 sense of my wretched condition. The more beautiful and charming were the smiles of
nature, the more horrible and desolate was my condition. I saw nothing without
seeing it. I do not exaggerate, when I say, that it looked from every star, smiled in
every calm, breathed in every wind, and moved in every storm.

—Frederick Douglass

---

\* trumpet

1. This passage is primarily concerned
with

    (A) the importance of reading for
    Frederick Douglass
    (B) Douglass's conclusion that
    slavery is intolerable
    (C) the author's experiences at the
    hands of white boys
    (D) the writer's knowledge of the
    Constitution of the United
    States
    (E) the reasons why he was no
    longer a happy youngster

2. Which of the following describes the
tone of the passage?

    (A) Light and humorous
    (B) Ironic
    (C) Academic
    (D) Sincere and powerful
    (E) Angry and violent

3. This passage is an example of a(n)

    (A) slave narrative
    (B) picaresque novel
    (C) biography
    (D) historical text
    (E) secondary source

4. The style of this excerpt can best be
described as

    (A) elaborate, complex, and circum-
    spect
    (B) poetic
    (C) plain, forceful, and direct
    (D) obscure and difficult
    (E) Elizabethan

5. According to the author, why is
education incompatible with slavery?

    (A) The system keeps slaves from
    living in harmony with their
    souls.
    (B) Education makes slaves dissat-
    isfied with their position.
    (C) Slaves learn about the Constitu-
    tion and the Bill of Rights.
    (D) Education makes slaves danger-
    ous to their owners.
    (E) Owners do not want slaves
    wasting work time reading and
    learning.

6. What effect does reading the *Columbian Orator* have upon young Douglass?

   (A) He decides to buy the book for fifty cents.
   (B) Douglass decides to enter the Exhibition and compete against white boys.
   (C) The book increases his longing for freedom.
   (D) He discovers that he is a victim of an oppressive system.
   (E) He develops a plan to escape north.

7. Which of the following is not an accurate analysis of this passage?

   (A) Douglass's descriptions are straightforward.
   (B) The author offers little interpretation of the significance of events.
   (C) The passage is factual.
   (D) The author employs many literary allusions.
   (E) Douglass allows readers to draw their own conclusions.

8. When Douglass writes, "This knowledge opened my eyes to the horrible pit, and revealed the teeth of the frightful dragon that was ready to pounce upon me," (lines 19–21) he was referring to

   (A) Mr. Hugh, his owner
   (B) the effects of education
   (C) the *Columbian Orator*
   (D) the institution of slavery
   (E) events that had happened to him

9. What structure does Douglass employ in the following sentence: "The more beautiful and charming were the smiles of nature, the more horrible and desolate was my condition." (lines 30–31)?

   (A) Metaphor
   (B) Parallelism
   (C) Exaggeration
   (D) Eloquence
   (E) Cacophony

10. In the sentence "It was this everlasting thinking which distressed and tormented me; and yet there was no getting rid of the subject of my thoughts," (lines 24–25) the word "thinking" is which of the following?

    (A) A participle
    (B) A verb
    (C) An infinitive
    (D) An adverbial phrase
    (E) A gerund

11. What significant change does Douglass describe in the lines "As I read, behold! The very discontent so graphically predicted by Master Hugh, had already come upon me." (lines 16–17)?

    (A) The young Douglass came to the conclusion that slavery was wrong.
    (B) Douglass decided he would pursue higher education.
    (C) The writer decided he would act lighthearted and mirthful while planning his escape.
    (D) His spirit awakened.
    (E) Douglass found his soul.

12. The words "Liberty! The inestimable birthright of every man" (line 27) probably refer to which document?

    (A) Bill of Rights
    (B) Declaration of Independence
    (C) U.S. Constitution
    (D) Magna Carta
    (E) Articles of Confederation

13. Douglass uses the word "redolent" twice (line 14 and line 26). What does the word mean?

    (A) Filled with
    (B) Sweet-smelling
    (C) Evocative of
    (D) Excessive
    (E) Exuding

**GO ON TO THE NEXT PAGE** →

QUESTIONS 14 THROUGH 25 REFER TO THE FOLLOWING POEM. READ THE PASSAGE
CAREFULLY AND THEN CHOOSE THE ANSWERS TO THE QUESTIONS.

## Sonnet 29

Line   When in disgrace with fortune and men's eyes,
       I all alone beweep my outcast state,
       And trouble deaf heaven with my bootless cries,
       And look upon myself and curse my fate,
5      Wishing me like to one more rich in hope,
       Featured like him, like him with friends possessed,
       Desiring this man's art, and that man's scope,
       With what I most enjoy contented least.
       Yet in these thoughts myself almost despising,
10     Haply I think on thee, and then my state,
       Like to the lark at break of day arising
       From sullen earth, sings hymns at heaven's gate;
            For thy sweet love remembered such wealth brings
            That then I scorn to change my state with kings.

—William Shakespeare

**14.** This sonnet is concerned with

   **(A)** the misfortunes that plague
        everyone
   **(B)** the beauty of a new morning
   **(C)** how the thought of the speaker's
        beloved can change one's mood
   **(D)** the speaker's envy of other
        peoples' lives
   **(E)** the resentment that heaven has
        given the speaker a poor lot
        in life

**15.** Which of the following choices best describes the mood of lines 1 through 8?

   **(A)** Joy
   **(B)** Anger
   **(C)** Resignation
   **(D)** Frustration
   **(E)** Self-pity

**16.** What is the tone of the last six lines?

   **(A)** Despair
   **(B)** Elation
   **(C)** Heartache
   **(D)** Confidence
   **(E)** Calmness

**17.** The first two quatrains express
distinct but related thoughts. What
are they?

   **(A)** The first quatrain expresses the
        speaker's extreme dissatisfac-
        tion with himself; the second,
        envy of others' happier lives.
   **(B)** The first quatrain expresses the
        speaker's dissatisfaction, and
        the second presents a solution.
   **(C)** The first quatrain shows that
        the speaker is very religious,
        and the second expresses his
        contentment with life.
   **(D)** The first quatrain shows how
        envious of others the speaker is,
        and the second, his love of
        nature and beauty.
   **(E)** The first quatrain speaks of his
        dissatisfaction and envy, and
        the second tells of his beloved.

18. What is the meaning of the phrase "trouble deaf heaven" in line 3?

    (A) The heavens are in turmoil.
    (B) People are deaf to the will of God.
    (C) God's will falls on deaf ears.
    (D) Troubled times are not heard in heaven.
    (E) One prays, but God does not hear.

19. Which lines summarize the theme of the sonnet?

    (A) The final couplet
    (B) The first quatrain
    (C) The second quatrain
    (D) Lines 10 through 12
    (E) Lines 2 through 8

20. What does the poet mean when he writes "that man's scope"?

    (A) The man has made a profit in business.
    (B) By chance, the man has made a fortune.
    (C) The man is strong and handsome.
    (D) The man is very intelligent.
    (E) The man owns a rare astronomical instrument.

21. The comparison of the speaker to a lark (lines 11–12) is appropriate because a lark

    (A) flies upward the way the speaker's mood improves
    (B) rises up to heaven
    (C) is fragile like a person's ego
    (D) is a symbol of goodwill
    (E) sings its song as it sees the new day break

22. In lines 4 through 7, the speaker explains that he envies all of the following aspects of others EXCEPT

    (A) hopefulness
    (B) having many friends
    (C) skill as an equestrian
    (D) a handsome appearance
    (E) intellectual ability

23. What rhyming words represent the *d*'s in the rhyme scheme?

    (A) Eyes, cries
    (B) Brings, kings
    (C) Hope, scope
    (D) State, gate
    (E) Possessed, least

24. This sonnet is organized like a Petrarchan sonnet because

    (A) it consists of three quatrains and a couplet
    (B) an unhappy situation is presented in the octave and a response and solution occurs in the sestet
    (C) it has the rhyme scheme of *abab, cdcd, efef, gg*
    (D) it is written in iambic pentameter
    (E) the solution is presented in the final couplet

25. Which of the following best summarizes the meaning of the first line of the sonnet?

    (A) It is a time of good luck in dealing with other people.
    (B) It is a time of despair.
    (C) It is a time of change.
    (D) It is a time when everyone is watching what the speaker is doing.
    (E) It is a time of sorrow because the speaker's wealth is gone.

**GO ON TO THE NEXT PAGE**

QUESTIONS 26 THROUGH 40 REFER TO THE FOLLOWING SELECTION FROM *POLITICS AND THE ENGLISH LANGUAGE* BY GEORGE ORWELL. ORWELL EXPRESSES A CONCERN FOR THE ENGLISH LANGUAGE AND THE MANIPULATION OF LANGUAGE IN THE MODERN WORLD. READ THE PASSAGE CAREFULLY AND THEN CHOOSE THE ANSWERS TO THE QUESTIONS.

### From *Politics and the English Language*

Line  Most people who bother with the matter at all would admit that the English language is in a bad way, but it is generally assumed that we cannot by conscious action do anything about it. Our civilization is decadent and our language—so the argument runs—must inevitably share in the general collapse. It follows that any struggle
5  against the abuse of language is a sentimental archaism, like preferring candles to electric light or hansom cabs to aeroplanes. Underneath this lies the half-conscious belief that language is a natural growth and not an instrument which we shape for our own purposes. . . .

The defense of the English language implies more than this, and perhaps it is best
10  to start by saying what it does *not* imply.

To begin with it has nothing to do with archaism, with salvaging of obsolete words and turns of speech, or with the setting up of a "standard English" which must never be departed from. On the contrary, it is especially concerned with the scrapping of every word or idiom which has out worn its usefulness. It has nothing to do with
15  correct grammar and syntax, which are of no importance so long as one makes one's meaning clear, or with the avoidance of Americanisms, or with having what is called a "good prose style." On the other hand it is not concerned with fake simplicity and the attempt to make written English colloquial. Nor does it even imply in every case preferring the Saxon word to the Latin one, though it does imply using the fewest and
20  the shortest words that will cover one's meaning. What is above all needed is to let the meaning choose the word, and not the other way about. In prose, the worst thing one can do with words is to surrender to them. When you think of a concrete object, you think wordless, and then, if you want to describe the thing you have been visualizing you probably hunt about till you find the exact words that seem to fit it. When you
25  think of something abstract you are more inclined to use words from the start, and unless you make a conscious effort to prevent it, the existing dialect will come rushing in and do the job for you, at the expense of blurring or even changing your meaning. Probably it is better to put off using words as long as possible and get one's meaning as clear as one can through pictures or sensations. Afterwards one can choose—not
30  simply *accept*—the phrases that will best cover the meaning, and then switch round and decide what impression one's words are likely to make on another person. This last effort of the mind cuts out all stale or mixed images, all prefabricated phrases, needless repetitions, and humbug and vagueness generally. But one can often be in doubt about the effect of a word or a phrase, and one needs rules that one can rely on
35  when instinct fails. I think the following rules will cover most cases:

   (i)   Never use a metaphor, simile, or other figure of speech which you are used to seeing in print.

   (ii)   Never use a long word where a short one will do.

   (iii)   If it is possible to cut a word out, always cut it out.

40   (iv)   Never use the passive where you can use the active.

   (v)   Never use a foreign phrase, a scientific word, or a jargon word if you can think of an everyday English equivalent.

   (vi)   Break any of these rules sooner than say anything outright barbarous.

These rules sound elementary, and so they are, but they demand a deep change in
45  attitude in anyone who has grown used to writing in the style now fashionable. One

could keep all of them and still write bad English, but one could not write the kind of stuff that I quoted in those five specimens at the beginning of this article.

50    I have not here been considering the literary use of language, but merely language as an instrument of expressing and not for concealing or preventing thought. . . . One can at least change one's own habits, and from time to time one can even, if one jeers loudly enough, send some worn-out and useless phrase—some *jackboot, Achilles' heel, hotbed, melting pot, acid test, veritable inferno* or other lump of verbal refuse—into the dustbin where it belongs.

—George Orwell

**26.** The chief topic of this selection is

(A)  poor use of English
(B)  diction
(C)  chauvinistic disregard for foreign words and phrases
(D)  grammar and mechanics
(E)  scientific language and jargon

**27.** This passage is primarily concerned with

(A)  the meanings of words
(B)  the rules of syntax and structure in the English language
(C)  the use of colloquialisms in the English language
(D)  some rules to be used for better writing
(E)  integration of scientific and foreign words into the English language

**28.** Which of the following best expresses one of the author's goals?

(A)  To expand the use of the English language
(B)  To introduce new grammar rules
(C)  To teach creative writing
(D)  To find new means of expression
(E)  To simplify word use and sentence structure

**29.** The author advocates which of the following actions?

(A)  Using simplicity to make English colloquial
(B)  The use of detailed descriptive phrasing
(C)  Simple direct word selection
(D)  The use of common idioms
(E)  The occasional use of foreign phrases to add interest

**30.** The general tone of this passage is

(A)  subtly humorous
(B)  serious and persuasive
(C)  ironic
(D)  satirical
(E)  dramatic and portentous

**31.** The word "Americanisms" in line 16 refers to

(A)  terms found in American English
(B)  uniquely American pronunciation
(C)  incorrect spelling
(D)  American literature
(E)  hybrid sentence structure

**32.** George Orwell would agree with which of the following statements?

(A)  You can break the rules whenever you want.
(B)  You should never break the rules.
(C)  You can break the rules if the writing makes better sense.
(D)  You can break the rules early in a document if you are consistent.
(E)  Rules are useful conventions.

**33.** In the third paragraph, the author identifies what situation under which rules are necessary?

(A)  When vagueness is required
(B)  When one's sense of what is good fails
(C)  When there are no guidelines
(D)  Whenever one is writing informally
(E)  Rules are never required.

**GO ON TO THE NEXT PAGE**

34. What does the author think will happen if his rules are followed?

   (A) Anything written will be good.
   (B) Writing will be easier to read.
   (C) More people will read.
   (D) Writing will be as good as possible.
   (E) More people will write.

35. Which of the following best summarizes what the author is saying in the last sentence of the excerpt?

   (A) He is listing some of his favorite phrases.
   (B) He is describing a house cleaning.
   (C) He is promoting his idea of reducing the amount of trite phrases.
   (D) He is advocating a return to traditional English.
   (E) He does not like today's authors.

36. What is the best paraphrase for the following sentence: "What is above all needed is to let the meaning choose the word, and not the other way about." (lines 20–21)?

   (A) Definitions of words should change depending on context.
   (B) A writer's meaning should determine word choice.
   (C) Words should always have the same meaning no matter how they are used.
   (D) A universal English system should be used.
   (E) The shortest and fewest words should be used.

37. According to Orwell's rules, why would he object to the following sentence: "The rich treasury of our language might go down the drain"?

   (A) Never use a metaphor, simile, or other figure of speech that you are used to seeing in print.
   (B) Never use a long word where a short one will do.
   (C) If it is possible to cut a word out, always cut it out.
   (D) Never use the passive where you can use the active.
   (E) Never use a foreign phrase, a scientific word, or a jargon word if you can think of an everyday English equivalent.

38. In the third paragraph, Orwell first uses the pronoun "one" and then switches to the pronoun "you." What is the effect of that change?

   (A) By so doing, he spotlights poor syntax.
   (B) By using "you," he relates more directly to the reader.
   (C) He is following his own advice to simplify.
   (D) He is using an everyday English equivalent.
   (E) He is using standard English.

39. This sentence from the third paragraph, "In prose, the worst thing one can do with words is to surrender to them." (lines 21–22) contains which of the following?

   (A) Simile
   (B) Metaphor
   (C) Personification
   (D) Onomatopoeia
   (E) Alliteration

40. Which of the following is the best explanation of the author's rationale for saying grammar and syntax are not important?

   (A) Grammar and syntax rules are too strict.
   (B) Grammar and syntax are never a major problem.
   (C) Grammar and syntax are not so important as long as the meaning is clear.
   (D) Grammar and syntax rules are too lax.
   (E) Grammar and syntax are not universally understood.

QUESTIONS 41 THROUGH 50 REFER TO THE FOLLOWING POEM. READ THE PASSAGE
CAREFULLY AND THEN CHOOSE THE ANSWERS TO THE QUESTIONS.

**Huswifery**

Line   Make me, O Lord, Thy spinning wheel complete,
       Thy holy word my distaff[1] make for me.
       Make mine affections Thy swift flyers[2] neat
       And make my soul Thy holy spoole to be.
5      My conversation make to be Thy reel
       And reel the yarn thereon spun of Thy wheel.

       Make me Thy loom then, knit therein this twine;
       And make Thy holy spirit, Lord, wind quills[3];
       Then weave the web Thyself. The yarn is fine.
10     Thine ordinances[4] make my fulling mills.
       Then dye the same in heavenly colors choice,
       All pinked with varnished flowers of paradise.

       Then clothe therewith mine understanding, will,
       Affections, judgment, conscience, memory
15     My words, and actions, that their shine may fill
       My ways with glory and Thee glorify.
       Then mine apparel shall display before Ye
       That I am clothed in holy robes for glory.

                                    —Edward Taylor

_____
[1] Staff on which flax or wool is wound for spinning.
[2] Part of spinning wheel that twists fibers into yarn.
[3] Spindles or bobbins that hold yarn once it is spun.
[4] Sacraments.

**41.** To whom is this poem addressed?

   **(A)** The speaker's master
   **(B)** God
   **(C)** The speaker's husband
   **(D)** The speaker's soul
   **(E)** The head of the Puritan church

**42.** With which of the following is this
poem primarily concerned?

   **(A)** Becoming a devoted servant of
God and praising God
   **(B)** Weaving the finest threads of
prayer
   **(C)** Developing skill as a Christian
   **(D)** Gaining God's approval
   **(E)** Becoming an excellent house-
keeper for God's sake

**43.** What does the poem suggest about
the speaker's attitude toward God?

   **(A)** Believes God is an aloof, distant
being
   **(B)** Finds God's essence in work
   **(C)** Will gain God's approval by
making holy garments
   **(D)** Desires to be an instrument of
God
   **(E)** Finds God in familiar objects

**44.** On a figurative level, what process
does the poet describe?

   **(A)** How to achieve salvation
   **(B)** How to spin yarn, make it into
cloth, and dye it
   **(C)** How to dye cloth the colors of
heaven
   **(D)** How to glorify God
   **(E)** How to gain glory from God

**GO ON TO THE NEXT PAGE**

**45.** What comparison does the poet develop?

(A) Housework with the search for God

(B) Spinning with making robes of glory

(C) Spinning with gaining salvation

(D) Affection and conscience with working for salvation

(E) Spinning wheel with the word of the Bible

**46.** What is the best restatement of lines 13–16?

(A) All my thoughts and actions will glorify God if I am holy enough.

(B) A holy cloth will cover all that I think, do, and say, and my goodness will shine brightly for the glory of God.

(C) Cover all my thoughts, words, and deeds with holiness so that they may radiate goodness and glorify God.

(D) Cover all my thoughts, words, and deeds with the cloth of holiness so that all that I do may radiate goodness and give glory to God.

(E) My understanding, will, affections, judgment, conscience, memory, words, and actions will reflect the brightness of God.

**47.** What is the tone of lines 17–18?

(A) Submission

(B) Resignation

(C) Joy

(D) Solemnity

(E) Piety

**48.** This poem utilizes what figure of speech?

(A) Simile

(B) Metaphor

(C) Oxymoron

(D) Hyperbole

(E) Conceit

**49.** What does the comparison Taylor uses suggest about his beliefs concerning the relationship between God and the world?

(A) Souls will be saved through good works.

(B) God is active and involved in the daily affairs of human beings.

(C) Honest work is a way to salvation.

(D) Through making beautiful things for God and the church, people will find grace.

(E) Only through work can people understand God's will.

**50.** The majority of sentences in this poem are

(A) declarative

(B) compound–complex

(C) interrogatory

(D) imperative

(E) run-on

**STOP**    If you finish before time is called, you may check your work on this section only. Do not turn to any other section in the test.

# SECTION II

*3 QUESTIONS 2 HOURS*

> **Directions:** The following two poems, written by women, are about forces of nature. Read the two poems carefully. Then write a well-organized essay. Consider such elements as speaker, diction, imagery, form, and tone.

## Essay Question 1

*SUGGESTED TIME—40 MINUTES*

**The Wind—
tapped like a tired Man**

Line    The Wind—tapped like a tired Man
        And like a Host—"Come in"
        I boldly answered—entered then
        My Residence within

5       A rapid—footless Guest—
        To offer whom a Chair
        Were as impossible as hand
        A Sofa to the Air—

        No Bone had he to bind Him—
10      His speech was like the Push
        Of numerous Humming Birds at once
        From a superior Bush—

        His Countenance—a Billow—
        His Fingers, as He passed
15      Let go a music—as of tunes
        Blown tremulous in Glass—

        He visited—still flitting—
        Then like a timid man
        Again, He tapped—twas flurriedly—
20      And I became alone

                            —Emily Dickinson

**GO ON TO THE NEXT PAGE** ➔

**July Storm**

Line   Like a tall woman walking across the hayfield,
    The rain came slowly, dressed in crystal and
        the sun,
    Rustling along the ground. She stopped at our
5         apple tree

    Only a whispering moment, then swept
        darkening skirts over the lake
    And so serenely climbed the wooded hills.
    Was the rainbow a ribbon that she wore?
10    We never wondered. It seemed a part of her
        brightness
    And the way she moved lightly but with
        assurance over the earth.

—Elizabeth Coatsworth

**Directions:** Read the following work carefully. Then write a well-organized essay in which you discuss how the selection uses humor to comment on human nature and human conduct. Consider such literary elements as diction, narrative pace, satire, and point of view.

## Essay Question 2

*SUGGESTED TIME—40 MINUTES*

### Advice to Little Girls

Line  Good little girls ought not to make mouths at their teachers for every trifling offense. This retaliation should only be resorted to under peculiarly aggravated circumstances.

If you have nothing but a rag-doll stuffed with sawdust, while one of your more fortunate little playmates has a costly China one, you should treat her with a show of
5     kindness nevertheless. And you ought not to attempt to make a forcible swap with her unless your conscience would justify you in it, and you know you are able to do it.

You ought never to take your little brother's "chewing-gum" away from him by main force; it is better to rope him in with the promise of the first two dollars and a half you find floating down the river on a grindstone. In the artless simplicity natural to
10    his time of life, he will regard it as a perfectly fair transaction. In all ages of the world this eminently plausible fiction has lured the obtuse infant to financial ruin and disaster.

If at any time you find it necessary to correct your brother, do not correct him with mud—never, on any account, throw mud at him, because it will spoil his clothes. It is
15    better to scald him a little, for then you obtain desirable results. You secure his immediate attention to the lessons you are inculcating, and at the same time your hot water will have a tendency to move impurities from his person, and possibly the skin, in spots.

If your mother tells you to do a thing, it is wrong to reply that you won't. It is
20    better and more becoming to intimate that you will do as she bids you, and then afterward act quietly in the matter according to the dictates of your best judgment.

You should ever bear in mind that it is to your kind parents that you are indebted for your food, and your nice bed, and for your beautiful clothes, and for the privilege of staying home from school when you let on that you are sick. Therefore you ought to
25    respect their little prejudices, and humor their little foibles until they get to crowding you too much.

Good little girls always show marked deference for the aged. You ought never to "sass" old people unless they "sass" you first.

—Mark Twain

**Directions:** Through literature, readers encounter experiences that may not occur in their own lives. This enlarges and enriches their experience.

Choose a novel or play of literary merit and write an essay in which you show how a novel, epic poem, or a drama that you read provides the reader with enriching vicarious experience. You may wish to discuss how the author created this vicarious experience through action, theme, or character development. Avoid plot summary.

You may select a work from the list below, or you may choose another work of comparable literary merit suitable to the topic.

## Essay Question 3

### *SUGGESTED TIME—40 MINUTES*

Orwell, *Animal Farm*

Morrison, *Beloved*

*Beowulf*

Vonnegut, *Cat's Cradle*

Heller, *Catch-22*

Chekhov, *The Cherry Orchard*

Steinbeck, *The Grapes of Wrath*

Fitzgerald, *The Great Gatsby*

Homer, *The Iliad*

Orwell, *1984*

Homer, *The Odyssey*

Kesey, *One Flew Over the Cuckoo's Nest*

Austen, *Pride and Prejudice*

Wolfe, *The Right Stuff*

Camus, *The Stranger*

Shakespeare, *The Tempest*

Shakespeare, *Twelfth Night*

**STOP**    If you finish before time is called, you may check your work on this section only. Do not turn to any other section in the test.

## ANSWER KEY AND EXPLANATIONS

### Section I

| | | | | |
|---|---|---|---|---|
| 1. B | 11. A | 21. A | 31. A | 41. B |
| 2. D | 12. B | 22. C | 32. C | 42. A |
| 3. A | 13. C | 23. E | 33. B | 43. D |
| 4. C | 14. C | 24. B | 34. B | 44. A |
| 5. B | 15. E | 25. B | 35. C | 45. C |
| 6. C | 16. B | 26. B | 36. B | 46. C |
| 7. D | 17. A | 27. D | 37. A | 47. C |
| 8. D | 18. E | 28. E | 38. B | 48. E |
| 9. B | 19. A | 29. C | 39. C | 49. B |
| 10. E | 20. D | 30. B | 40. C | 50. D |

1. **The correct answer is (B).** While both choices (A) and (E) are mentioned in the selection, they only support the main idea—that slavery is intolerable—they do not restate it. While white children are mentioned in the passage, Douglass does not describe experiences with them, so choice (C) is incorrect. Choice (D) is wrong because there is no mention of the Constitution.

2. **The correct answer is (D).** The question is easily answered by working through the choices and eliminating wrong ones. There is nothing amusing, ironic, or academic in this passage; thus, choices (A), (B), and (C) can be eliminated. While the writer has every right to be angry, he does not express that emotion in this passage, eliminating choice (E). Certainly, the passage is both powerful and sincere, which is choice (D).

3. **The correct answer is (A).** If you know who Frederick Douglass is, you will know that his autobiographies are considered classic examples of the slave narrative genre. If you do not know who he is, then you will have to work your way through the choices. A picaresque novel, choice (B), is a fictional account of the adventures of a vagabond or rogue, which does not fit the life described here. Since Douglass wrote this, evidenced by the use of the first-person pronouns, it cannot be a biography, choice (C), nor can it be a textbook, choice (D). The same logic eliminates choice (E), since a secondary source is a work written about another person or another time.

4. **The correct answer is (C).** If you correctly answered the question about tone, this one should have been easy. The style is plain, easy to understand, and eloquent in its simplicity. There are no tortured sentences, choices (A) and (D), or Shakespearean phrases, choice (E). While the writer does use some figurative language, the effect is not poetic, choice (B).

5. **The correct answer is (B).** On first glance, choice (A) seems as if it might have some validity; however, there is little mention of spiritual aspects in the passage. Likewise, choice (D) has possibilities, but the writer does not talk about dangers to owners, only the debilitating effects on those enslaved. Choice (C) is wrong because Douglass does not discuss the Constitution or the Bill of Rights. The issues in choice (E) do not appear in the selection.

6.  **The correct answer is (C).** This is a comprehension question. Douglass states that the book created discontent with his status of slave. You might feel that choice (D) is correct, but be aware that the writer already knew that he was a slave. The question asks about something that happened after Douglass bought the book, so choice (A) is incorrect since it states how much he paid for the book. Neither choice (B) nor choice (E) is mentioned in the selection.

7.  **The correct answer is (D).** There are no literary allusions in the passage. An allusion is a passing reference to people, places, or events that readers will recognize. The writer does refer obliquely to the Declaration of Independence once, but that hardly qualifies as many allusions, and it is not a literary allusion but a political allusion in any case. If you got question 4 correct, you will know that Douglass's descriptions are straightforward, choice (A). Because choice (B) is an accurate description of the selection, so then is choice (E). The passage is also factual in nature, recounting what Douglass did and felt, choice (C).

8.  **The correct answer is (D).** Here, the writer is using figurative language to emphasize the horror of slavery. He likens slavery to a dragon's lair. To answer this, you need to figure out to what the "this" in "this knowledge" refers. It would be unlikely that Douglass was referring to a person with this phrase, eliminating choice (A). The closest reference is the contents of the volume he was reading, but not the volume itself, *Columbian Orator,* choice (C). The contents relate to the value of liberty to illuminate the ills of slavery, choice (D). Choice (E) is too broad, and choice (B) is not relevant to the context.

9.  **The correct answer is (B).** Structure refers to the design or arrangement of parts in a work of literature. Parallelism, choice (B), creates a symmetrical arrangement, in this case, of clauses. Metaphors compare two unlike things, so choice (A) does not apply. Exaggeration is overstatement usually for the purpose of creating humor or horror, neither of which is the case in this passage, choice (C). While the selection is eloquent, choice (D), eloquence is not a recognized structure. Cacophony, choice (E), is a literary device, not a structure, that creates harsh sound.

10. **The correct answer is (E).** A gerund is a verb form ending in *–ing* that functions as a noun. *Thinking,* in this sentence, functions as a predicate nominative or noun. A participle, choice (A), may also end in *–ing* (or *–ed*), but functions as an adjective, not a noun. A verb, choice (B), is the predicate in a sentence, the action word. An infinitive, choice (C), is almost always made up of *to* plus a verb. An adverbial phrase, choice (D), modifies a verb or an adjective. None of these applies to the word *thinking.*

11. **The correct answer is (A).** This question tests your comprehension. The lines you are asked about record Douglass's recognition that slavery is intolerable. The writer can no longer be happy in his state of bondage. Choice (B) does not relate to anything in the selection. The words *gleesome* and *mirth* are used in the selection, but there is no mention of escape, choice (C). Choices (D) and (E) would require a metaphorical interpretation that you are not asked to make.

12. **The correct answer is (B).** This is similar to a cultural question you might find on the test. You might know that a nineteenth-century book of orations that contains speeches "redolent of the principles of liberty" (line 14) would most probably contain the opening lines of the Declaration of Independence that speak of "man's" inalienable rights to life, liberty, and the pursuit of happiness. However, the phrase quoted in the question paraphrases this idea. There are no clues to any of the other documents listed among the choices (A), (C), (D), or (E).

13. **The correct answer is (C).** *Redolent* does mean sweet-smelling, choice (B), as well as evocative, choice (C), but in context, choice (C) is the correct answer. Choice (A) might seem to fit with the speeches, but nature is not filled with liberty. Choices (D) and (E) are distractors.

14. **The correct answer is (C).** In the first line of the poem, Shakespeare identifies a character who is out of luck and not well respected by his peers. In line 10, the poet introduces the one individual who can bring joy to the life of the speaker. The speaker can experience this emotional change through the mere thought of the beloved. None of the other ideas fits the sentiment or the content of the poem. The speaker is neither resentful nor envious, choices (D) and (E). The poem is not about the morning, choice (B), nor other people's misfortunes, choice (A).

15. **The correct answer is (E).** The first eight lines of the sonnet delineate all the negative things that the speaker has experienced or feels. He feels, for example, that he has appealed for help, and no one has responded. His list of negative feelings about himself shows self-pity, choice (E), rather than passive submission, choice (C). There is no expression of great anger, choice (B), or of having been thwarted, choice (D). The feeling is more one of whining. Choice (A), joy, is found in the final six lines.

16. **The correct answer is (B).** In contrast with the first eight lines, the last six lines are uplifting. Shakespeare has his character express his joy at the simple thought of thinking about his loved one. The tone is the opposite of despair, choice (A), and heartache, choice (C); neither confidence, choice (D), nor calmness, choice (E), is an accurate description of the positive feeling.

17. **The correct answer is (A).** The second line of the first quatrain makes a clear reference to the speaker's view of himself. He pities himself because he believes no one cares about him. The first line of the second quatrain shifts to his view of others. Choice (B) may seem as though it might be correct, but it misreads the second quatrain. The word *desiring* (line 7) is a clue to the speaker's attitude in this quatrain so envy, choice (A), is a more accurate answer. Choice (C) does not reflect the content, nor does choice (D). You might be fooled into choosing choice (E) unless you check the poem before answering. The beloved is not in these eight lines.

18. **The correct answer is (E).** The word *deaf* is the key to this answer. Shakespeare's speaker is lamenting the fact that his cries are falling on deaf ears in heaven. He is praying, but God is not listening to him. This is another example of self-pity. Choices (A), (B), and (D) do not reflect the content of the sonnet. Heaven (God) is the one being appealed to, not the one giving directions, so choice (C) is wrong.

19. **The correct answer is (A).** The final couplet tells the reader that no matter how bad things have been for the speaker, because of his beloved, he would not trade his position for a king's. The first and second quatrains, choices (B) and (C), only list the speaker's problems. The other line possibilities, choices (D) and (E), are only parts of the theme—supporting details.

20. **The correct answer is (D).** This phrase is contained in the second quatrain where Shakespeare has the speaker enumerating the qualities that others have that the speaker would like to have. This eliminates choice (E) since it refers to an object. The word *scope* is better associated with a person's mind than his fortune, choices (A) and (B), or appearance, choice (C). That makes the correct answer choice (D). Choices (A) and (B) could confuse you since the only difference in the idea is the phrase *by chance* in choice (B).

21.  **The correct answer is (A).** Shakespeare wants to create an exhilarating mood. The lark provides that vehicle because as a bird its flight toward heaven is uplifting. In addition, the lark has a beautiful song, a characteristic that in literature elicits joy in the hearer. Choices (B) and (E) are only partially correct. They are in a sense supporting details that help to create the overall image of the lark in the sonnet. Neither choice (C) nor choice (D) is an accurate reading of the content.

22.  **The correct answer is (C).** This question is best approached by eliminating all the right answers. Check each phrase to see if it is in the quatrain: hopefulness = "rich in hope," choice (A); many friends = "like him with friends possessed," choice (B); handsome appearance = "featured like him," choice (D); and intellectual ability = "that man's scope," choice (E). The phrase that is not in the quatrain is choice (C) and the correct response.

23.  **The correct answer is (E).** The rhyme scheme of this sonnet, as is true of all Shakespearean sonnets, is *ab, ab, cd, cd*. Following that rhyme scheme, the correct answer has the words *possessed* and *least* as "*d*'s."

24.  **The correct answer is (B).** A Petrarchan sonnet has specified characteristics. The most important of these is that it proposes an unhappy situation in the first eight lines, and suggests a solution in the last six lines. None of the other answers applies.

25.  **The correct answer is (B).** The line has a negative feeling because of the word *disgrace;* therefore, any answer, such as choices (A), (C), or (D), with a positive or neutral connotation should be eliminated. Of the remaining two answers, choice (B) reflects the sense of the expression "disgrace with fortune [read as luck, not wealth] and men's eyes." Choice (E) takes a literal reading of the line as wealth, and is, therefore, incorrect.

26.  **The correct answer is (B).** Because all of these answers are touched on in this passage, the answer that covers the broadest portion of the selection is the correct response. Diction deals with the choice of words in written or spoken language, and, therefore, choice (B) is the most encompassing of the available responses.

27.  **The correct answer is (D).** The question asks for the primary concern of the passage. The author discusses all of these answers at some point in his writings, but he spends most of his time listing and discussing some rules for better writing.

28.  **The correct answer is (E).** The best approach for this question is to work through the answers, eliminating the incorrect ones. Orwell does not propose the expanded use of the English language, the introduction of new grammar rules, or the teaching of creative writing, choices (A), (B), and (C). He may imply a search for new means of expression, choice (D), but he clearly states a predilection for word and sentence simplification, choice (E).

29.  **The correct answer is (C).** Orwell states that he is an advocate of simple direct word selection. Each of the remaining four responses is counter to his fundamental thesis of simplicity.

30.  **The correct answer is (B).** The question asks the reader to determine the feel or tone of the excerpt. The passage cannot be viewed as humorous, choice (A); ironic, choice (C); satirical, choice (D); or dramatic, choice (E). Orwell is quite serious in his concern for language, and his essay is meant to be persuasive, choice (B).

31. **The correct answer is (A).** In the context of this work, Orwell is speaking in defense of the English language. He lists a series of items that he is not defending, and one of these is "Americanisms." In this context he was writing about expressions and usage that are uniquely American, but not American pronunciations, choice (B), or literature, choice (D). Choices (C) and (E) are not relevant to the content.

32. **The correct answer is (C).** The author lists six rules that he believes will improve writing. The last of these states "Break any of these rules sooner than say anything outright barbarous." That rule is consistent with choice (C). He does not advocate irresponsible or unreasoned breaking of the rules, choices (A) and (D), nor does he advocate rigid adherence to rules, choice (B). Choice (E) is a statement of opinion that Orwell would probably agree with, but it is not the most accurate restatement of the essay. Be careful of such distractors that seem to be reasonable answers; check to make sure they most accurately reflect the content.

33. **The correct answer is (B).** In the third paragraph, Orwell says, "But one can often be in doubt about the effect of a word or a phrase, and one needs rules that one can rely on when instinct fails." None of the other responses reflects Orwell's statement.

34. **The correct answer is (B).** In the last sentence of the third paragraph, the author expresses the sentiment that these rules will not make bad writing good, the opposite of choice (A). On the other hand, good writing does employ these rules. Choices (B) and (D) are similar. The difference is that components other than following the rules are needed to make writing "as good as possible," choice (D). Regardless of the other components, writing will be "easier to follow" if the writer follows the rules. Choice (C) is irrelevant to the passage.

35. **The correct answer is (C).** Orwell lists some phrases that were popular at the time he wrote this article. He suggests that they be thrown in the trashcan. Choice (A) is the opposite of what Orwell is saying. Choice (B) would be correct only if you were asked a question about metaphor. Orwell may be advocating choice (D) at some point in the essay, but the question asks what Orwell is saying in the last sentence, and choice (C) restates his idea. Choice (E) is irrelevant to the sentence.

36. **The correct answer is (B).** The author is stating that what a writer intends to say should determine his word selection. The chosen words should not alter the writer's meaning. Choices (A) and (C) incorrectly deal with the definitions of words. Orwell does not address the responses contained in choices (D) and (E) in the lines cited.

37. **The correct answer is (A).** In the sentence given, there is figurative language that is a cliché, "go down the drain." Orwell would also object to the redundant phrase "rich treasury." However, there is no response that deals with redundancy. Choice (C) deals with wordiness, not redundancy. The given sentence has no long words, choice (B); is not in the passive voice, choice (D); and contains no foreign phrases, scientific words, or jargon, choice (E). A cliché is not jargon.

38. **The correct answer is (B).** At first, you might think that several of these are possible answers. Remember that the writer states that it is acceptable to break rules if the meaning becomes clearer by doing so. Orwell wants the reader to pay close attention here, so he addresses the audience directly. The other responses do not make sense in the context.

39. **The correct answer is (C).** The definition of personification is a figure of speech in which inanimate objects or abstractions are endowed with human characteristics. In this sentence, *words* is given a human characteristic that suggests that a person can surrender to them. A simile uses *like* or *as* for comparison, choice (A), while a metaphor states that something is something else, choice (B). Words that sound like their meanings are examples of onomatopoeia, choice (D), and words in a series that repeat initial consonant sounds are examples of alliteration, choice (E).

40. **The correct answer is (C).** The readers of your essays may not agree with Orwell, but he states in the third paragraph, "It has nothing to do with correct grammar and syntax, which are of no importance so long as one makes one's meaning clear . . ." The context does not support choices (A), (D), or (E). Choice (B) is only half right. The statement from Orwell has the qualifier "so long as one's meaning is clear," thus eliminating choice (B).

41. **The correct answer is (B).** The speaker in Taylor's poem is asking to be formed and developed by something greater than the speaker. The answer that clearly reflects that relationship is God, choice (B). The use of the word *Lord* in line 1 is an additional indication that the speaker is addressing God. Choices (A) and (C) are incorrect on that basis and because they attempt to read the poem literally. The speaker's soul is the speaker, so choice (D) is incorrect. Choice (E) is a distractor to confuse you. Taylor was a Puritan minister, but any religious poem would more likely be addressed to a spiritual being than to a human, even a church dignitary.

42. **The correct answer is (A).** The poem concerns the relationship between the speaker and God. The lack of a reference to God excludes choice (B). The speaker is asking God to construct him as a spinning wheel creates yarn that becomes cloth, which makes choice (A) the better answer than choice (E). In choice (A), the speaker will follow God's words and praise God, while in choice (E) the speaker will do something—become an excellent housekeeper—for God's sake. There is no mention of asking for God's approval, choice (D), and choice (C) is not an accurate reading of the emotional level of the poem.

43. **The correct answer is (D).** In stanza 1, the speaker is asking to be formed by God as a spinning wheel makes yarn. In stanza 2, the speaker is asking to be made into a loom that weaves cloth. The speaker is asking God to take charge of his life. God is not seen as aloof, but personal to the speaker, making choice (A) incorrect. Although the conceit revolves around labor and familiar objects, it does not indicate that they are a way to God, eliminating choices (B) and (E). Choice (C) is a distractor for anyone who reads the lines literally.

44. **The correct answer is (A).** The metaphor that Taylor uses is the spinning and weaving of yarn into cloth, which stands for being molded and formed by God and being open to God's grace. Choice (B) is a description of the metaphor, but not what it represents. Choice (C) is one part of the process. Choices (D) and (E) are partial readings of the final three lines.

45. **The correct answer is (C).** Taylor, through the speaker in this poem, develops a parallel between the cloth-making process and a man's being formed and molded by God. Choice (C) best states this theme by comparing cloth-making with gaining salvation. Choices (A) and (E) are not relevant to the imagery of the poem. Choice (B) is too literal an interpretation. Affection and conscience, choice (D), are part of gaining salvation, not a comparison.

46. **The correct answer is (C).** Choice (A) is incorrect because there is no qualifier in the poem; the speaker assumes that he will be holy once God has formed him. Choice (B) is too literal a reading of the word *clothe*, as is choice (D). Choice (E) states a passive reflection of God's glory rather than an active affirmation, which the lines indicate with the phrase "may fill / My ways with glory and Thee glorify."

47. **The correct answer is (C).** The speaker exults that once he has received God's grace—been molded and formed by God—he will glorify God. Submission, choice (A), and resignation, choice (B), are too passive; solemnity, choice (D), and piety, choice (E), are too restrained.

48. **The correct answer is (E).** A conceit is a fanciful poetic image, especially an elaborate or exaggerated comparison. The comparison of spinning cloth with God's grace meets this definition. A simile, choice (A), uses *like* or *as* for a comparison while a metaphor, choice (B), states that something is something else but not in an elaborate or fanciful way. Oxymoron, choice (C), combines opposite or contradictory terms. Hyperbole, choice (D), is exaggeration.

49. **The correct answer is (B).** As a Puritan, Taylor believed that God's grace is granted, not earned through works, which he expresses in the poem, making choices (A), (C), and (D) incorrect. Taylor's speaker is not trying to understand God's will through the cloth-making process, so choice (E) is incorrect.

50. **The correct answer is (D).** An imperative sentence directly addresses someone and requests or orders that the person do something. There are only two declarative sentences, choice (A), sentences that make statements, in the poem (lines 9 and 17–18). There is one compound-complex sentence, choice (B), lines 3–4, and no questions, choice (C). Although the sentences are convoluted, there are no run-on sentences, choice (E).

## Section II

### SUGGESTIONS FOR ESSAY QUESTION 1

The following are points that you might have chosen to include in your essay comparing "The Wind—tapped like a tired Man" by Emily Dickinson and "July Storm" by Elizabeth Coatsworth. Consider them as you do your self-evaluation. Revise your essay using points from the list to strengthen it.

|  | "The Wind—tapped like a tired Man" | "July Storm" |
|---|---|---|
| **Type** | Lyric; quatrains; *abcb* rhyme scheme | Free verse |
| **Themes** | Delighting in nature | Delighting in nature |
| **Speaker** | Host is the speaker; Wind is the guest | The observers of the rain |
| **Tone** | Playful, childlike, pleasant | Gentle |
| **Figurative Language** | Extended metaphor of the wind as a man; also a personification since wind has human qualities | Extended simile comparing the rainstorm to a tall woman; personify aspects of nature to show changing weather |
| **Imagery** | Visual and sound images; for example, "footless guest"; "Again, He tapped—twas flurriedly—" | Strong visual images: "dressed in crystal and sun" "swept darkening skirts over the lake"; auditory images: "whispering moment" "Rustling along the ground" |
| **Musical Devices** | Assonance, for example, the *i* sounds | Consonance in the many *s* sounds, like the sound of rain |

### SUGGESTIONS FOR ESSAY QUESTION 2

The following are points you might have chosen to include in your essay on Mark Twain's "Advice to Little Girls." Consider them as you do your self-evaluation. Revise your essay using points from the list to strengthen it.

#### *Form or Mode*

- Humorous essay

#### *Theme*

- Facetious advice telling girls how to behave

### Characters
- Narrator, Mark Twain
- Addressing girls in general

### Dialogue
- No specific dialogue
- Chatty and familiar style

### Conflict
- Girls versus convention

### Plot
- No real plot
- Basically advice on how girls can actually do what they want while appearing to be ever so proper

### Setting
- Mid-1800s, probably around 1865

### Point of View
- Written to the second person

### Diction
- Very informal
- Much humor
- "And you ought not to attempt to make a forcible swap with her unless your conscience would justify you in it, and you know you are able to do it."
- Tone: tongue in cheek
- Folksy language

## SUGGESTIONS FOR ESSAY QUESTION 3

The following are points about action, theme, and character you might have chosen to discuss in your essay on vicarious experience in literature. Consider them as you do your self-evaluation. Revise your essay using points from the list to strengthen it.

### Action/Plot
- A series of related events moving from a problem to a solution
- Exposition presents characters and situation
- Conflict, source of tension

- Internal conflict within a character
- External conflict between two or more characters or a force of nature
- Climax, the turning point
- Resolution, how problem is solved
- Complications, events that stand in the way of resolution
- Foreshadowing, use of hints to suggest what is to come

### Theme
- General idea or insight into life revealed in the literature
- Sometimes stated directly; sometimes indirectly
- Symbols representing something other than themselves sometimes suggest theme.
- Key statements point to theme
- Makes reader a bit wiser about the human condition

### Characterization
- Direct characterization, directly telling you about a character's personality
- Indirect characterization, revealing personality through descriptions, thoughts, words, and actions
- Round characters, fully developed
- Flat characters, only one or two character traits
- Dynamic characters change
- Static characters do not change
- Motivation, reason for character's behavior
- Characters convey theme

## SELF-EVALUATION RUBRIC FOR THE ADVANCED PLACEMENT ESSAYS

| | 8–9 | 6–7 | 5 | 3–4 | 1–2 | 0 |
|---|---|---|---|---|---|---|
| **Overall Impression** | Demonstrates excellent control of the literature and outstanding writing competence; thorough and effective; incisive | Demonstrates good control of the literature and good writing competence; less thorough and incisive than the highest papers | Reveals simplistic thinking and/or immature writing; adequate skills | Incomplete thinking; fails to respond adequately to part or parts of the question; may paraphrase rather than analyze | Unacceptably brief; fails to respond to the question; little clarity | Lacking skill and competence |
| **Understanding of the Text** | Excellent understanding of the text; exhibits perception and clarity; original or unique approach; includes apt and specific references | Good understanding of the text; exhibits perception and clarity; includes specific references | Superficial understanding of the text; elements of literature vague, mechanical, overgeneralized | Misreadings and lack of persuasive evidence from the text; meager and unconvincing treatment of literary elements | Serious misreadings and little supporting evidence from the text; erroneous treatment of literary elements | A response with no more than a reference to the literature; blank response, or one completely off the topic |
| **Organization and Development** | Meticulously organized and thoroughly developed; coherent and unified | Well-organized and developed; coherent and unified | Reasonably organized and developed; mostly coherent and unified | Somewhat organized and developed; some incoherence and lack of unity | Little or no organization and development; incoherent and void of unity | No apparent organization or development; incoherent |
| **Use of Sentences** | Effectively varied and engaging; virtually error free | Varied and interesting; a few errors | Adequately varied; some errors | Somewhat varied and marginally interesting; one or more major errors | Little or no variation; dull and uninteresting; some major errors | Numerous major errors |
| **Word Choice** | Interesting and effective; virtually error free | Generally interesting and effective; a few errors | Occasionally interesting and effective; several errors | Somewhat dull and ordinary; some errors in diction | Mostly dull and conventional; numerous errors | Numerous major errors; extremely immature |
| **Grammar and Usage** | Virtually error free | Occasional minor errors | Several minor errors | Some major errors | Severely flawed; frequent major errors | Extremely flawed |

Rate yourself in each of the categories. Choose the description that most accurately reflects your performance, and enter the numbers on the lines below. Be as honest as possible so you will know what areas need work. Then calculate the average of the six numbers to determine your final score. It is difficult to score yourself objectively, so you may wish to ask a respected friend or teacher to assess your writing for a more accurate reflection of its strengths and weaknesses. On the AP test itself, a reader will rate your essay on a scale of 0 to 9, with 9 being the highest.

Rate each category from 9 (high) to 0 (low).

## Essay Question 1

**SELF-EVALUATION**
Overall Impression \_\_\_\_
Understanding of the Text \_\_\_\_
Organization and Development \_\_\_\_
Use of Sentences \_\_\_\_
Word Choice (Diction) \_\_\_\_
Grammar and Usage \_\_\_\_

TOTAL \_\_\_\_
    Divide by 6 for final score \_\_\_\_

**OBJECTIVE EVALUATION**
Overall Impression \_\_\_\_
Understanding of the Text \_\_\_\_
Organization and Development \_\_\_\_
Use of Sentences \_\_\_\_
Word Choice (Diction) \_\_\_\_
Grammar and Usage \_\_\_\_

TOTAL \_\_\_\_
    Divide by 6 for final score \_\_\_\_

## Essay Question 2

**SELF-EVALUATION**
Overall Impression \_\_\_\_
Understanding of the Text \_\_\_\_
Organization and Development \_\_\_\_
Use of Sentences \_\_\_\_
Word Choice (Diction) \_\_\_\_
Grammar and Usage \_\_\_\_

TOTAL \_\_\_\_
    Divide by 6 for final score \_\_\_\_

**OBJECTIVE EVALUATION**
Overall Impression \_\_\_\_
Understanding of the Text \_\_\_\_
Organization and Development \_\_\_\_
Use of Sentences \_\_\_\_
Word Choice (Diction) \_\_\_\_
Grammar and Usage \_\_\_\_

TOTAL \_\_\_\_
    Divide by 6 for final score \_\_\_\_

## Essay Question 3

**SELF-EVALUATION**
Overall Impression \_\_\_\_
Understanding of the Text \_\_\_\_
Organization and Development \_\_\_\_
Use of Sentences \_\_\_\_
Word Choice (Diction) \_\_\_\_
Grammar and Usage \_\_\_\_

TOTAL \_\_\_\_
    Divide by 6 for final score \_\_\_\_

**OBJECTIVE EVALUATION**
Overall Impression \_\_\_\_
Understanding of the Text \_\_\_\_
Organization and Development \_\_\_\_
Use of Sentences \_\_\_\_
Word Choice (Diction) \_\_\_\_
Grammar and Usage \_\_\_\_

TOTAL \_\_\_\_
    Divide by 6 for final score \_\_\_\_

# APPENDIX

College-by-College Guide to AP Credit
and Placement

# College-by-College Guide to AP Credit and Placement

For the past two decades, national and international participation in the AP Program has grown steadily. Colleges and universities routinely award credit for AP exam scores of 3, 4, or 5, depending on the exam taken. The following chart indicates the score required for AP credit, how many credits are granted, what courses are waived based on those credits, and other policy stipulations at more than 400 selective colleges and universities.

Use this chart to discover just how valuable a good score on the AP English Literature & Composition Test can be!

appendix

| School Name | Required Score | Credits Granted | Course Waived | Stipulations |
|---|---|---|---|---|
| Agnes Scott College (GA) | 4–5 | 4 | ENG 110 | Students who score 4–5 on both English exams get 8 hours and fulfill the literature distribution in addition to the Specific 1 standard. |
| Albany College of Pharmacy of Union University (NY) | 4–5 | | | |
| Albertson College of Idaho (ID) | 3–5 | | | |
| Albion College (MI) | 4 | | ENGL 151 & WCE | |
| Albright College (PA) | 4–5 | | | |
| Allegheny College (PA) | 4–5 | | | |
| Alma College (MI) | 3 | | ENG 180(4) | |
| American University (DC) | 4–5 | 6 | LIT 120G & LIT 125G | |
| Auburn University (AL) | 4–5 | 3 | ENGL 1100 | |
| Augustana College (SD) | 4–5 | | | |
| Austin College (TX) | 4–5 | | English Elective | |
| Azusa Pacific University (CA) | 3–4 | 3 | Freshman Writing Seminar or Lang/Lit core | |
| | 5 | 6 | Freshman Writing Seminar and Lang/ Lit core | If score is a 5 in both English Language and English Literature, student receives 9 units of credit - ENGL110, ENGL111, 3 units non-GS elective. |
| Baldwin-Wallace College (OH) | 3–5 | 3 | ENG LIT | |
| Bard College (NY) | 5 | | | |
| Bates College (ME) | 4–5 | | 1 Unspecified | |
| Baylor University (TX) | 4 | | ENGL 1302 | For the minimum score: 4, plus ACT English 29+, or SAT Verbal/Critical Reading 670+. |
| Belmont University (TN) | 4–5 | | ENG 1010 | If you want to take both English Lang & Comp and English Lit & Comp then you need a 4 on both tests, which will give you 3 hours of general elective credit and exemption from ENG 1010. |
| Beloit College (WI) | 4–5 | 4 | | Credit will be granted once a student matriculates to Beloit College and provides official score reports to the Registrar's Office. |

| School Name | Required Score | Credits Granted | Course Waived | Stipulations |
|---|---|---|---|---|
| Benedictine University (IL) | 3 | 3 | RHET 101 | |
| Bentley College (MA) | 4–5 | | | High school graduates who have taken the AP exams may be awarded credit for scores of 4 or 5, on any subject test. |
| Berea College (KY) | 3–5 | | | |
| Bernard M. Baruch College of the City University of New York (NY) | 4–5 | | | |
| Birmingham-Southern College (AL) | 5 | | EH 200 | |
| Boston College (MA) | 4–5 | | | |
| Boston University (MA) | 4–5 | | Any two from EN 141, EN 142, & EN 143 | |
| Bowdoin College (ME) | 4–5 | | | |
| Bradley University (IL) | 3–5 | 3 | ENG 115 | |
| Brandeis University (MA) | 4–5 | | | |
| Brigham Young University (UT) | 3–5 | 6 | ENGL 115 | |
| Bryan College (TN) | 3–5 | | | |
| Bryn Mawr College (PA) | 5 | | | |
| Bucknell University (PA) | 4–5 | | | Credit is awarded for only 1 English AP exam. |
| Butler University (IN) | 4–5 | 3 | ID 103 | |
| Calvin College (MI) | 4 | 3 | English elective | |
| | 5 | 6 | ENGL 101 & English elective | |
| Canisius College (NY) | 3 | 3 | Free elective | |
| | 4–5 | 6 | ENG 102 and 1 Free elective | If Honors student, 2 Free electives. |
| Carleton College (MN) | 4–5 | 6 | | Score of 5: Part I of Writing Requirement fulfilled. |
| Carnegie Mellon University (PA) | 4–5 | | | |
| Carroll College (MT) | 3–5 | | | |
| Carson-Newman College (TN) | 4–5 | | | |
| Case Western Reserve University (OH) | 4–5 | 3 | ENGL 200 | |
| Cedarville University (OH) | 3 | 0 | None | |
| | 4–5 | 3 | LIT 2300 | |
| Central College (IA) | 3–5 | | | |

| School Name | Required Score | Credits Granted | Course Waived | Stipulations |
|---|---|---|---|---|
| Centre College (KY) | 4–5 | | | |
| Chapman University (CA) | 4 | 3 | ENG 103 | |
| Christendom College (VA) | 4–5 | | | |
| Christian Brothers University (TN) | 4–5 | | | |
| Clarkson University (NY) | 4–5 | | LF 200 | |
| Clark University (MA) | 4–5 | | | |
| Clemson University (SC) | 3–4 | 3 | ENGL 101 | |
| | 5 | 6 | ENGL 101 & ENGL 103 | |
| Coe College (IA) | 4–5 | | | |
| Colby College (ME) | 4–5 | | | |
| Colgate University (NY) | 4–5 | | | |
| College of Charleston (SC) | 3 | 3 | ENGL 101 | 3 = ENGL 101, 4 or 5 = ENGL 101 & 102 |
| | 4–5 | 6 | ENGL 101 & ENGL 102 | 3 = ENGL 101, 4 or 5 = ENGL 101 & 102 |
| The College of New Jersey (NJ) | 4–5 | | Liberal Learning, Literary Arts Requirement | Student with a minimum score of 4 in any AP History or English receives waiver of WRI 102 Academic Writing. |
| College of Saint Benedict (MN) | 3 | | ENGL 133 | |
| | 4–5 | 4 | ENGL 133 | |
| The College of St. Scholastica (MN) | 4–5 | 4 | ENG 1115 | |
| College of the Atlantic (ME) | 4–5 | | | |
| College of the Holy Cross (MA) | 4–5 | | | |
| The College of William and Mary (VA) | 4–5 | 3 | Writing 101 | A score of 4 or 5 on the English Literature and Composition examination is awarded 3 hours of credit equivalent to English 201 and exemption from Writing 101. |
| The College of Wooster (OH) | 4–5 | | | |
| Colorado Christian University (CO) | 3–5 | | | |
| The Colorado College (CO) | 5 | | | |
| Colorado School of Mines (CO) | 4–5 | 3 | Humanities | |
| Colorado State University (CO) | 4 | 3 | E CC 140 | |
| | 5 | 6 | E CC 140 & COCC 150 | |
| Columbia College (NY) | 5 | 3 | No exemption | |

| School Name | Required Score | Credits Granted | Course Waived | Stipulations |
|---|---|---|---|---|
| Columbia University, The Fu Foundation School of Engineering and Applied Science (NY) | 5 | 3 | No exemption | |
| Concordia College (MN) | 4 | | ENG 222E | |
| Connecticut College (CT) | 4–5 | | | |
| Converse College (SC) | 3 | 3 | | Students who score 3 in English will be placed in English 290 (Advanced Composition) and will receive the AP credit only upon successful completion of English 290. |
| | 4–5 | 6 | | |
| Cornell College (IA) | 4–5 | | | |
| Cornerstone University (MI) | 4–5 | 7 | ENG 113 & ENG 223 | Credit will not be granted for both English Lang & Comp and English Lit & Comp. |
| Covenant College (GA) | 4 | 3 | ENG 114 | |
| Creighton University (NE) | 4 | 6 | ENG 000—elective credit | |
| Dartmouth College (NH) | 5 | | | |
| Davidson College (NC) | 4–5 | | ENG 110 | |
| Denison University (OH) | 4–5 | | FYS 101 | |
| DePauw University (IN) | 4–5 | 4 | ENG 155 | |
| Dickinson College (PA) | 4–5 | | ENGL LIT | Although students receive credit for ENGL LIT, this credit does NOT fulfill the Writing Intensive requirement. The AP course can count as ENGL 101 for the English major. |
| Dominican University (IL) | 3–5 | 6 | ENGL 101 & LA Requirement | |
| Drake University (IA) | 3 | 6 | ENG 1 + Lit | |
| Drew University (NJ) | 4–5 | 4 | ENGL 1 | English Comp only. |
| Drexel University (PA) | 4–5 | | | |
| Drury University (MO) | 3–5 | 3 | Elective only | |
| Duke University (NC) | 4–5 | | ENGL 20 | |
| Duquesne University (PA) | 4 | 3 | ENGL 102 | |
| Earlham College (IN) | 5 | 6 | | |
| Elizabethtown College (PA) | 3–5 | 3 | EN 104 | |
| Elmira College (NY) | 3 | 3 | 3 GN Culture & Civilization | |

| School Name | Required Score | Credits Granted | Course Waived | Stipulations |
|---|---|---|---|---|
| Elmira College—*continued* | 4 | 6 | 6 GN Culture & Civilization | |
| | 5 | 9 | 6 GN Culture & Civilization | Additional qualifying measures are used to determine the fulfillment of the Freshman writing requirement. Advanced Placement in English will not necessarily fulfill such a requirement. |
| Elon University (NC) | 4–5 | 4 | LIT elective | |
| Embry-Riddle Aeronautical University (AZ) | 3–5 | | | |
| Emerson College (MA) | 4–5 | | WP 101 | A score of 4–5 on both AP Lit & Comp and Lang & Comp will exempt from WP 101 and an additional 100 level literature course. |
| Emory University (GA) | 4–5 | 4 | | In the case of two AP results for individual language examinations (i.e., English Literature and English Language), credit may be awarded for either examination but not for both. |
| Erskine College (SC) | 4–5 | | | |
| Eugene Lang College The New School for Liberal Arts (NY) | 4–5 | | | |
| Fairfield University (CT) | 4–5 | 3 | EN 11 | |
| Florida Institute of Technology (FL) | 4–5 | 3 | Writing about Literature | |
| Florida International University (FL) | 3 | 3 | ENC 1101 | |
| | 4–5 | 6 | ENC 1101 & ENC 1102 | |
| Florida State University (FL) | 3 | 3 | ENC 1101 | |
| | 4–5 | 6 | ENC 1101 & 1102 or ENC 1101 & LIT 1005 | LIT 1005 if the student has already received credit for ENC 1102 through another exam. |
| Fordham University (NY) | 3–5 | | | Currently, a grade of 3 will be accepted as elective credit. However, grades of 4 or 5 may be applied toward the core curriculum. |
| Franciscan University of Steubenville (OH) | 4–5 | | | |
| Franklin and Marshall College (PA) | 4–5 | | General elective | |

| School Name | Required Score | Credits Granted | Course Waived | Stipulations |
|---|---|---|---|---|
| Furman University (SC) | 4–5 | | ENGL 12 | Scores of 4 or 5 on both tests (English Lit & Comp and English Lang & Comp) earn credit for English 12 and English General Credit. |
| George Fox University (OR) | 3 | 3 | LITR 100 | |
| | 4–5 | 6 | WRIT 110 & LITR 100 | |
| Georgetown College (KY) | 3–5 | 3–6 | | |
| Georgetown University (DC) | 4–5 | 3 | | If a student takes both tests, then the higher score is used because credit is awarded only once for both tests. No credit for a score of 3. |
| The George Washington University (DC) | 4 | 3 | ENGL 52 | |
| | 5 | 6 | ENGL 51 & ENGL 52 | |
| Georgia Institute of Technology (GA) | 4–5 | 3 | ENGL 1101 | |
| Georgia State University (GA) | 3–5 | | | |
| Gettysburg College (PA) | 4–5 | 4 | | |
| Gonzaga University (WA) | 4 | 3 | Elective | Credits will be awarded that may be used to fulfill the overall credit requirements for graduation but may not be used to fulfill core curriculum or major requirements. |
| | 5 | 3 | ENGL 101 | |
| Gordon College (MA) | 4–5 | | | |
| Goshen College (IN) | 3 | 3 | elective; must take Engl 110 or 204 for Gen Ed | |
| | 4–5 | 3 | Engl 110/Gen Ed | |
| Goucher College (MD) | 4–5 | | | |
| Grinnell College (IA) | 5 | 4 | | |
| Grove City College (PA) | 4–5 | | | |
| Gustavus Adolphus College (MN) | 4–5 | | | |
| Hamilton College (NY) | 4–5 | | | Recipients of scores of 4 or 5 on either or both of the AP examinations in English may place directly into one of several 200-level courses. |

| School Name | Required Score | Credits Granted | Course Waived | Stipulations |
|---|---|---|---|---|
| Hamline University (MN) | 4–5 | | Elective Credit | |
| Hampshire College (MA) | 3–5 | | | |
| Hanover College (IN) | 3–5 | | | |
| Harding University (AR) | 3 | 3 | ENG 111 | |
| Harvard University (MA) | 5 | | No equivalent | Placement in English 10, English 17, or middle-group course. |
| Haverford College (PA) | 4–5 | | | The registrar will award one course credit for an AP score of 5 and one-half course credit for a score of 4. No credit is awarded for scores under 4. |
| Hendrix College (AR) | 4–5 | | One course elective | |
| Hillsdale College (MI) | 3 | 3 | | |
| | 4–5 | 6 | | |
| Hiram College (OH) | 4–5 | | | |
| Hobart and William Smith Colleges (NY) | 4–5 | | | |
| Hope College (MI) | 4–5 | | | |
| Houghton College (NY) | 4–5 | 3 | Principles of Writing | Should a student take both AP English exams, he/she would receive credit for both POW and Lit of West World. |
| Illinois College (IL) | 4–5 | | | |
| Illinois Institute of Technology (IL) | 3 | 3 | HUM 106 | |
| | 4–5 | 6 | HUM 106 & HUM 390 | |
| Illinois Wesleyan University (IL) | 4–5 | | | Credit will be granted and recorded by IWU only after the successful completion of four course units of study in residence. |
| Iowa State University of Science and Technology (IA) | 3–5 | | | |
| Ithaca College (NY) | 3 | 6 | ENG 377–1 & ENG 307–1 | Adv. Placement is granted for only one English exam. |
| James Madison University (VA) | 4–5 | 3 | GWRIT 103 | |
| John Brown University (AR) | 3–5 | | EGL 1023 | |
| John Carroll University (OH) | 4–5 | 6 | EN 111 & EN 112 | |
| Juniata College (PA) | 4–5 | | | |
| Kalamazoo College (MI) | 4–5 | | | |

| School Name | Required Score | Credits Granted | Course Waived | Stipulations |
|---|---|---|---|---|
| Kenyon College (OH) | 4–5 | | ENGL 111Y-112Y or ENGL 103 & 104 | Placement in any 200-level course. |
| Kettering University (MI) | 4–5 | 4 | HUMN 201 | |
| Knox College (IL) | 3 | | ENG 101 | |
| | 4–5 | | ENG 101 & ENG 102 | |
| Lafayette College (PA) | 4–5 | | ENG 110 | Can only receive credit for English 110 once. |
| Lake Forest College (IL) | 4–5 | | | |
| Lawrence Technological University (MI) | 4 | 3 | | Enroll in LLT 1213. If the student earns a "C" or better in the first attempt, he/she should contact the Student Service Center to request credit for COM 1103. |
| | 5 | 3 | COM 1103 | |
| Lawrence University (WI) | 4–5 | | | |
| Lebanon Valley College (PA) | 4–5 | 6 | ENG 111 & ENG 120 | |
| Lehigh University (PA) | 4 | 3 | Freshman English | These students will complete the 6-hour requirement by taking an English course suggested by the department, typically ENGL 11. |
| | 5 | 6 | Freshman English | |
| LeTourneau University (TX) | 4–5 | 3 | Literature Elective | |
| Lewis & Clark College (OR) | 4–5 | | | Placement into English 205 or 206. |
| Linfield College (OR) | 4–5 | | | |
| Lipscomb University (TN) | 3 | 6 | EN 1113 | |
| | 4–5 | 6 | EN 1113 & EN 1123 | |
| Louisiana State University and Agricultural and Mechanical College (LA) | 3 | 3 | ENG 1001 | |
| | 4 | 6 | ENG 1001 & ENG 1002 | |
| | 5 | 9 | ENG 1001, 1002 & 2025 or ENG 2027, 2029 or 2123 | |

| School Name | Required Score | Credits Granted | Course Waived | Stipulations |
|---|---|---|---|---|
| Loyola College in Maryland (MD) | 4–5 | | | |
| Loyola Marymount University (CA) | 4–5 | 3 | ENG 140 | |
| Loyola University Chicago (IL) | 4–5 | 6 | ENGL 105 & ENGL 273 | |
| Luther College (IA) | 4–5 | 4 | | |
| Lycoming College (PA) | 4–5 | 8 | ENGL 106 & ENGL 215 | |
| Lyon College (AR) | 4–5 | | | |
| Macalester College (MN) | 4–5 | | ENGL 125 | AP credit in English may not be included in the minimum number of courses for a major or minor in English. |
| Marist College (NY) | 3–4 | 3 | ENG 911L | |
| | 5 | 6 | ENG 911L & ENG 912L | |
| Marlboro College (VT) | 4–5 | 8 | | |
| Marquette University (WI) | 4 | 3 | ENGL 1 | |
| | 5 | 6 | ENGL 1 & ENGL 2 | |
| Maryville College (TN) | 3–5 | | | |
| Maryville University of Saint Louis (MO) | 3–5 | | | |
| The Master's College and Seminary (CA) | 3–5 | | | |
| McDaniel College (MD) | 4–5 | | | Students may receive advanced placement plus up to 8 hours credit. |
| McGill University (QC) | 4–5 | 6 | | Possible exemption for ENGL 200/201/202/203. Contact the Dept. of English |
| McKendree College (IL) | 3–5 | 3 | None | |
| Mercer University (GA) | 3–5 | | | |
| Messiah College (PA) | 3–5 | 3 | ENG 218(general education literature requirement) | |
| Miami University (OH) | 4 | 3 | ENG 111 | Then enroll in English 113. |
| | 5 | 6 | ENG 111 & ENG 112 | |
| Michigan State University (MI) | 3 | 0 | WRA 150 | |
| | 4–5 | 4 | WRA 150 | |

| School Name | Required Score | Credits Granted | Course Waived | Stipulations |
|---|---|---|---|---|
| Michigan Technological University (MI) | 4–5 | 3 | UN 1001 | Or 3 credits for UN 2001 if student is already receiving credit UN 1001. |
| Middlebury College (VT) | 4–5 | | | Only one English exam will receive credit; this cannot be used toward the English major. |
| Milligan College (TN) | 4–5 | 6 | HUMN 101W & General elective | |
| Millsaps College (MS) | 4–5 | 6 | Elective credit | The elective credit counts for English majors. |
| Mills College (CA) | 4–5 | | | |
| Mississippi College (MS) | 4–5 | 3 | ENG 212 | |
| Missouri State University (MO) | 4–5 | 3 | ENG electives | |
| Moravian College (PA) | 4–5 | | | |
| Morehouse College (GA) | 4–5 | | | |
| Mount Holyoke College (MA) | 4–5 | 4 | | |
| Mount Saint Vincent University (NS) | 4–5 | | | |
| Muhlenberg College (PA) | 3–5 | | | |
| Murray State University (KY) | 3–4 | 3 | ENG 101 | If you get a score of 3 take ENG 102, if you get a score of 4 take ENG 104. |
| | 5 | 6 | ENG 101 & ENG 102 | |
| New College of Florida (FL) | 4–5 | | | |
| New Jersey Institute of Technology (NJ) | 4–5 | 3 | HSS 101 | |
| New Mexico Institute of Mining and Technology (NM) | 4–5 | 3 | ENGL 111 | Proceed directly into ENGL 112. |
| New York University (NY) | 4–5 | 4 | No course equivalent | |
| North Central College (IL) | 4–5 | 3 | ENG 196 | |
| Northwestern College (IA) | 4–5 | 4 | ENG 220 | |
| Northwestern College (MN) | 3–5 | 4 | LIT 1000 | |
| Northwestern University (IL) | 5 | | 2 English electives | |
| Occidental College (CA) | 4–5 | | | |
| Oglethorpe University (GA) | 3 | 4 | | Essay will be evaluated by English faculty |
| | 4–5 | 4 | Elective credit | |
| Ohio Northern University (OH) | 3 | 4 | ENGL 110 | |

| School Name | Required Score | Credits Granted | Course Waived | Stipulations |
|---|---|---|---|---|
| Ohio Northern University—*continued* | 4 | 8 | ENGL 110 & ENGL 111 | |
| | 5 | 12 | ENGL 110, 111, 204 | |
| The Ohio State University (OH) | 4 | 5 | ENG 110.01 | |
| | 5 | 5 | ENG H110.01 | |
| Ohio Wesleyan University (OH) | 4–5 | | English Literature course | |
| Oklahoma City University (OK) | 4–5 | 3 | ENGL 1213 | |
| Oklahoma State University (OK) | 3 | 3 | ENGL 1113 | |
| | 4–5 | 6 | ENGL 1113 & ENGL 1213 | |
| Pacific Lutheran University (WA) | 4–5 | 4 | Elective | |
| Pacific University (OR) | 4–5 | 3 | | |
| Peabody Conservatory of Music of The Johns Hopkins University (MD) | 4–5 | | | |
| The Pennsylvania State University University Park Campus (PA) | 4–5 | 3 | ENGL 001 | |
| Pepperdine University (CA) | 3–5 | 4 | TENG 100.01 | |
| Pitzer College (CA) | 4–5 | | | |
| Point Loma Nazarene University (CA) | 3 | 3 | | |
| | 4–5 | 6 | | |
| Polytechnic University, Brooklyn Campus (NY) | 4–5 | | EN 1204 | Students who achieve a 4 or 5 on the Literature and Composition exam will receive credit for EN 1204 once they have earned credit for EN 1014. |
| Pomona College (CA) | 4–5 | | | When both have been taken, credit will be given for the Literature exam. |
| Presbyterian College (SC) | 3 | 3 | ENGL 109 | |
| | 4–5 | 6 | ENGL 110 & ENGL 111 | |
| Princeton University (NJ) | 5 | | No course equivalent | AP credit is not awarded for the International English Language AP exam. |
| Providence College (RI) | 4–5 | | | |

| School Name | Required Score | Credits Granted | Course Waived | Stipulations |
|---|---|---|---|---|
| Purdue University (IN) | 4–5 | 3 | ENGL 231 | |
| Queen's University at Kingston (ON) | 4–5 | | | TBA |
| Quincy University (IL) | 4–5 | | | |
| Quinnipiac University (CT) | 4–5 | 3 | EN 102 | |
| Randolph-Macon Woman's College (VA) | 4–5 | | | |
| Reed College (OR) | 4–5 | | | |
| Rensselaer Polytechnic Institute (NY) | 4–5 | 4 | | |
| Rhodes College (TN) | 4–5 | 8 | ENG 151 & one unspecified course | |
| Rice University (TX) | 4–5 | 3 | ENGL 122 | |
| Rochester Institute of Technology (NY) | 3–5 | | | |
| Rollins College (FL) | 4–5 | 4 | Writing Gen Ed | |
| Rose-Hulman Institute of Technology (IN) | 4–5 | 4 | Humanities credit | |
| Rutgers, The State University of New Jersey, Newark (NJ) | 4–5 | | | |
| Rutgers, The State University of New Jersey, New Brunswick/Piscataway (NJ) | 4–5 | | | |
| Saint Francis University (PA) | 3 | | ENG 104 | |
| | 4–5 | | English writing elective & ENG 104 | |
| Saint John's University (MN) | 3 | 0 | ENGL 133 | |
| | 4–5 | 4 | ENGL 133 | |
| Saint Joseph's University (PA) | 4–5 | 3 | ENG 1011 or ENG 1021 | |
| St. Lawrence University (NY) | 4–5 | | ENGL 190 | |
| St. Louis College of Pharmacy (MO) | 3–5 | | | |
| Saint Louis University (MO) | 4–5 | 3 | ENGA 202 | |
| Saint Mary's College (IN) | 4–5 | 6 | ENLT 100 level | |
| Saint Mary's College of California (CA) | 3 | | ENGL 00E | |
| | 4–5 | | ENGL 4 | |

| School Name | Required Score | Credits Granted | Course Waived | Stipulations |
|---|---|---|---|---|
| St. Mary's College of Maryland (MD) | 4–5 | | | |
| St. Norbert College (WI) | 3–5 | | | |
| St. Olaf College (MN) | 5 | | | Credit awarded for only one English AP exam not both Lang/Comp and Lit/Comp |
| Salem College (NC) | 4–5 | | English course credit | 1 English course credit plus placement in English 103. |
| Samford University (AL) | 4–5 | 4 | UCCA 101 | |
| San Diego State University (CA) | 3–5 | 6 | ENGL 220 & Rhetoric & Writing Studies 100 | |
| Santa Clara University (CA) | 4–5 | 4 | | Third Writing requirement for Arts and Sciences and Business students is the course waived. |
| Sarah Lawrence College (NY) | 4–5 | | | |
| Scripps College (CA) | 4–5 | | | |
| Seattle Pacific University (WA) | 3–5 | 5 | Arts & Humanities | |
| Seattle University (WA) | 4–5 | 10 | ENGL 110 & ENGL 120 | Fulfilling English core requirements. A maximum of 10 credits will be granted for English even if two exams are completed. |
| Sewanee: The University of the South (TN) | 4–5 | 4 | | |
| Siena College (NY) | 4–5 | | | |
| Simpson College (IA) | 3–5 | | | |
| Skidmore College (NY) | 4–5 | | | |
| Smith College (MA) | 4–5 | | | |
| Southern Methodist University (TX) | 4 | 3 | ENGL 1301 | |
| | 5 | 6 | ENGL 1301 & ENGL 1302 | |
| Southwest Baptist University (MO) | 3–5 | 3 | ENG 2213 | |
| Southwestern University (TX) | 4–5 | 3–4 | ENG 10-013 | If both, extra hours are given. |
| State University of New York at Binghamton (NY) | 3–5 | 4 | Elective credit | |
| State University of New York at Buffalo (NY) | 3–5 | | | |
| State University of New York College at Geneseo (NY) | 3–4 | 6 | ENGL 1TR (not for major credit) | |

| School Name | Required Score | Credits Granted | Course Waived | Stipulations |
|---|---|---|---|---|
| State University of New York College at Geneseo—*continued* | 5 | 6 | ENGL 142 (for major), ENGL 1TR (not for major credit) | |
| State University of New York College of Environmental Science and Forestry (NY) | 3–5 | | | |
| Stetson University (FL) | 4–5 | 3 | EH 131 | |
| Stevens Institute of Technology (NJ) | 4–5 | 3 | Humanities course | You may receive credit for a spring semester freshman- or sophomore-level humanities course in Group A: Literature/Philosophy as a result of a successful AP exam in English. |
| Stonehill College (MA) | 4–5 | 6 | Two General electives | |
| Stony Brook University, State University of New York (NY) | 3–5 | 3 | None | |
| Susquehanna University (PA) | 4–5 | | | In exceptional cases, the department may also recommend credit for scores of 3. |
| Swarthmore College (PA) | 4–5 | | | May count toward ENGL major. |
| Sweet Briar College (VA) | 4–5 | | | |
| Syracuse University (NY) | 4–5 | 3 | ETS 151 or ETS 152 or 153 or 295 or 296 | |
| Tabor College (KS) | 3–5 | 6 | EN 101 GE Literature | |
| Taylor University (IN) | 4–5 | 3 | ENG 110 | There must be an essay included with a score of at least 4. |
| Tennessee Technological University (TN) | 4–5 | 3 | ENGL 2330 | |
| Texas A&M University (TX) | 3 | 3 | ENGL 104 | |
| | 4–5 | 6 | ENGL 104 & ENGL 203 | |
| Texas Christian University (TX) | 3 | 3 | 10803 | |
| | 4–5 | 6 | 10803,10103 | |
| Texas Tech University (TX) | 3 | 3 | ENGL 1301 | |
| | 4–5 | 6 | ENGL 1301 & ENGL 1302 | |
| Transylvania University (KY) | 4–5 | | | |

| School Name | Required Score | Credits Granted | Course Waived | Stipulations |
|---|---|---|---|---|
| Trinity College (CT) | 4–5 | | | Neither can be counted toward the English major. |
| Trinity University (TX) | 4–5 | 6 | ENGL 2301 & ENGL 2303 | Exempted from ENGL 1302 Writing Workshop with a score of 5 only. |
| Truman State University (MO) | 3–5 | 3 | ENG 111 | |
| Tufts University (MA) | 4 | | | If both tests are taken, only one acceleration credit is awarded to the student. Exemption from the first semester of the College Writing Requirement (placement in English 2 or an equivalent course); one acceleration credit. |
| | 5 | | | If both tests are taken, only one acceleration credit is awarded to the student. Exemption from the College Writing Requirement; one acceleration credit. |
| Tulane University (LA) | 4–5 | 4 | ENGL 101 | |
| Union College (NE) | 3–5 | | | |
| Union College (NY) | 4–5 | | | |
| Union University (TN) | 3–5 | 6 | ENG 111 & ENG 112 | |
| The University of Alabama in Huntsville (AL) | 3 | 3 | EH 101 | |
| | 4–5 | 6 | EH 101 & EH 102 | |
| The University of Arizona (AZ) | 4–5 | 0-3 | | If student completes ENGL 109H with a grade of "C" or better, student will have 3 units from 109H, plus 3 ENGL department elective credits from AP. Without a grade of "C" in 109H, student will not receive AP credit. |
| University of Arkansas (AR) | 3–4 | | ENGL 1013 | |
| | 5 | | ENGL 1013 & ENGL 1023 | |
| University of California, Berkeley (CA) | 3–5 | | | A score of 3 satisfies Entry Level Writing. A score of 4 satisfies Entry Level Writing and the first half of R&C. A score of 5 satisfies Entry Level Writing and both halves of R&C. |

| School Name | Required Score | Credits Granted | Course Waived | Stipulations |
|---|---|---|---|---|
| University of California, Davis (CA) | 3 | 8 | | Maximum credit allowed: 8 units for all English exams. A score of 3, 4, or 5 on the English AP examination satisfies the University of California Entry Level Writing Requirement (formerly known as the Subject A requirement). |
| | 4–5 | 8 | English 1, 3 | |
| University of California, Irvine (CA) | 3 | 8 | Elective credit only | |
| | 4–5 | 8 | | One course toward category IV of the UCI breadth requirement from the English 28 series plus 4 units of elective credit; may not replace English major, minor, or School of Humanities requirements. |
| University of California, Los Angeles (CA) | 3–5 | | | |
| University of California, Riverside (CA) | 3 | 8 | ENGL 001A & elective | Or 8 elective units if the student enrolls in ENGL 001A. |
| | 4–5 | 8 | ENGL 001A & ENGL 001B | |
| University of California, Santa Cruz (CA) | 3–5 | 8 | | Satisfies one "IH" and Entry Level Writing Requirement. AP score of 4 or 5 satisfies "C-1". Maximum of 8 credits granted. |
| University of Central Arkansas (AR) | 3 | | WRTG 1310 | |
| | 4–5 | | WRTG 1310 & WRTG 1320 | |
| University of Colorado at Boulder (CO) | 3 | 3 | ENGL 1500 | |
| | 4–5 | 6 | ENGL 1500 & ENGL 2502 | |
| University of Connecticut (CT) | 4–5 | 4 | ENGL 104 | The AP Examination in English Language or English Literature does not fulfill the University of Connecticut Writing Competency requirement. |
| University of Dallas (TX) | 3–5 | 6 | ENG credit | Only 6 total credits of English awarded for either or both exams. |
| University of Dayton (OH) | 4 | 3 | | One English Exam only. |
| | 5 | 6 | | |
| University of Delaware (DE) | 3 | 3 | ENGL 166 | |

| School Name | Required Score | Credits Granted | Course Waived | Stipulations |
|---|---|---|---|---|
| University of Delaware—*continued* | 4 | 3 | ENGL 200 | |
| | 5 | 6 | ENGL 166 & ENGL 200 | |
| University of Denver (CO) | 3 | 4 | 4 Elective | |
| | 4 | 8 | 4 AHUM/ 4 elective | |
| | 5 | 12 | 4 First Year Writing/4 AHUM/ 4 elective | |
| University of Evansville (IN) | 4–5 | | | |
| University of Florida (FL) | 3 | 3 | AML 2070 | |
| | 4–5 | 6 | AML 2070 & ENL 2022 | |
| University of Georgia (GA) | 3–4 | 3 | ENGL 1101 | |
| | 5 | 6 | ENGL 1101 & ENGL 1102 | |
| University of Illinois at Chicago (IL) | 4–5 | 3 | ENGL 101 | |
| University of Illinois at Urbana–Champaign (IL) | 4–5 | 7 | ENG 103 & Rhetoric 105 & Comp I requirement | |
| The University of Iowa (IA) | 4–5 | 3 | 08G:001 | |
| University of Kansas (KS) | 3 | 0 | ENGL 101 | Placement in ENGL 105 |
| | 4 | 3 | ENGL 105 | Placement in ENGL 205 |
| | 5 | 6 | ENGL 105 & ENGL 205 | |
| University of Kentucky (KY) | 3–5 | 3 | ENG 161 | 3 credit hours for ENG 161 with a grade of CR. Does not satisfy University Writing Requirement. |
| University of Maryland, Baltimore County (MD) | 4–5 | 6 | ENGL 100 & ENGL 210 | |
| University of Maryland, College Park (MD) | 3 | 3 | LL elective | |
| | 4–5 | 6 | LL elective & ENGL 240 | |
| University of Mary Washington (VA) | 3–5 | 3 | ENGL 0205 | |
| University of Miami (FL) | 5 | 6 | ENG 105 & ENG 106 | |

| School Name | Required Score | Credits Granted | Course Waived | Stipulations |
|---|---|---|---|---|
| University of Michigan (MI) | 3–4 | 3 | | Does not satisfy the English Composition or distribution requirements in English. |
| University of Michigan–Dearborn (MI) | 3–4 | | ENGL 231 | |
| | 5 | | ENGL 231 & COMP 105 | |
| University of Minnesota, Morris (MN) | 3–4 | 4 | ENGL 1011 | If Comp/Lang taken also, credits awarded as GER electives. |
| | 5 | 4 | ENGL 1011 | Credits awarded as HUM. |
| University of Minnesota, Twin Cities Campus (MN) | 3–5 | 4 | COMP 1011 | Fulfills freshman writing requirement; 3 credits in English Lit 19994; fulfills literature requirement. |
| University of Missouri–Columbia (MO) | 4–5 | 6 | ENG 1000/ HUM elective | |
| University of Missouri–Kansas City (MO) | 4–5 | 4 | ENGL 204 & Humanities elective | |
| University of Missouri–Rolla (MO) | 3–5 | 3 | ENGL 20 | |
| University of Nebraska–Lincoln (NE) | 4–5 | 3 | ENGL 101 | |
| The University of North Carolina at Asheville (NC) | 5 | 4 | LANG 120 | |
| The University of North Carolina at Chapel Hill (NC) | 5 | 3 | ENGL 190 | |
| The University of North Carolina Wilmington (NC) | 3 | 6 | ENG 101 & ENG 110 | |
| | 4–5 | 6 | ENG 103 & ENG 110 | |
| University of North Florida (FL) | 3 | 3 | ENC 1101 | |
| | 4–5 | 6 | ENC 1101 & ENC 1102 | |
| University of Notre Dame (IN) | 4–5 | 3 | First Year Composition 13100 | |
| University of Oklahoma (OK) | 3–4 | | ENGL 1113 | |
| | 5 | | ENGL 1113 & ENGL 1123 | |
| University of Pennsylvania (PA) | 5 | | English Freshman Free | The English Freshman Free does not fulfill the college writing requirement. |

| School Name | Required Score | Credits Granted | Course Waived | Stipulations |
|---|---|---|---|---|
| University of Pittsburgh (PA) | 3–4 | 3 | ENGLIT 0000 | |
| | 5 | 6 | ENGCMP 0200 & ENGLIT 0000 | with 500 on verbal SAT |
| University of Puget Sound (WA) | 4–5 | | Elective | Credit is not allowed for both exams. |
| University of Redlands (CA) | 3–5 | | | |
| University of Rhode Island (RI) | 3–5 | 3 | Gen Ed Writing Requirement | |
| University of Richmond (VA) | 4–5 | 3 | ENGL 103 | |
| University of Rochester (NY) | 4–5 | 4 | | Upon completion of an English literature course with grade of "C" or better, four hours of elective English credit will be awarded (not for major). |
| University of St. Thomas (MN) | 3–5 | | ENG 104 | Partially fulfills the Literature and Writing requirement. |
| University of St. Thomas (TX) | 4–5 | | ENGL 1341 or ENGL 1342 | |
| University of San Diego (CA) | 3–5 | | | |
| The University of Scranton (PA) | 3–5 | 3–6 | | |
| University of South Carolina (SC) | 3–4 | | ENGL 101 | |
| | 5 | | ENGL 101 & ENGL 102 | |
| University of Southern California (CA) | 3–5 | 4 | | |
| The University of Tennessee at Chattanooga (TN) | 3 | 3 | ENGL 205 or ENGL 206 | |
| | 4–5 | 6 | ENGL 205 & ENGL 206 | |
| The University of Texas at Austin (TX) | 3 | | E 316K, CR | |
| | 4 | | E 316K, B | |
| | 5 | | E 316K, A | |
| The University of Texas at Dallas (TX) | 3 | | 3 SCH free electives | |
| | 4–5 | | RHET 1302 | |
| University of the Pacific (CA) | 4–5 | 4 | Varies | |

| School Name | Required Score | Credits Granted | Course Waived | Stipulations |
|---|---|---|---|---|
| University of the Sciences in Philadelphia (PA) | 4–5 | | | |
| University of Tulsa (OK) | 4–5 | 3 | ENGL 1053 | |
| University of Utah (UT) | 3–5 | 8 | Writing 2010 | |
| University of Virginia (VA) | 4–5 | 3 | ENLT 249 | |
| University of Washington (WA) | 4–5 | 5 | ENGL 109 | |
| University of Wisconsin–La Crosse (WI) | 3 | 3 | ENGL 110 | |
| | 4–5 | 3 | ENGL 110 & 300 level writing course | |
| University of Wisconsin–Madison (WI) | 3 | 3 | Literature Electives | |
| | 4–5 | 3 | Literature Electives | Exempt from GER Communication Part A. |
| University of Wisconsin–River Falls (WI) | 3 | 3 | English Elective | |
| | 4–5 | 3 | ENGL 241 | |
| Ursinus College (PA) | 4–5 | | | |
| Valparaiso University (IN) | 4–5 | 3 | ENGL 200 | |
| Vanderbilt University (TN) | 4–5 | 6 | ENGL 104W & ENGL 105W | |
| Vassar College (NY) | 4–5 | | | |
| Villanova University (PA) | 4–5 | | | |
| Virginia Military Institute (VA) | 3–5 | 6 | EN 101 & EN 102 | |
| Wabash College (IN) | 4–5 | | | |
| Wagner College (NY) | 4–5 | | | |
| Wake Forest University (NC) | 4–5 | 4 | ENG 111 | Only 4 total hours of ENG 111 credit will be awarded. |
| Wartburg College (IA) | 3 | | EN 150 | |
| | 4–5 | | EN 151 | |
| Washington & Jefferson College (PA) | 4–5 | | | |
| Washington and Lee University (VA) | 5 | 3 | ENG 11N | |
| Washington College (MD) | 4–5 | 8 | ENG 201 & ENG 202 | |

| School Name | Required Score | Credits Granted | Course Waived | Stipulations |
|---|---|---|---|---|
| Washington University in St. Louis (MO) | 5 | 3 | | 3 credits of elective credit (L13–0001) contingent upon completing L13–100 with a grade of B or better. Please note, no credit is given for writing or literature courses. |
| Wellesley College (MA) | 4–5 | | No exact equivalent | |
| Wells College (NY) | 4–5 | | | |
| Wesleyan College (GA) | 4–5 | | | |
| Wesleyan University (CT) | 4–5 | | | No more than one credit will be awarded even if students take both exams. |
| Western Washington University (WA) | 3 | 4 | Humanities GUR | Student may receive credits for either English exam, but not both. |
| | 4–5 | 8 | ENGL 101 & Humanities GUR | |
| Westminster College (UT) | 4–5 | 8 | ENGL 110 & ENGL 220 | |
| Westmont College (CA) | 4–5 | | | |
| Wheaton College (IL) | 3 | 2 | | |
| | 4–5 | 4 | | |
| Wheaton College (MA) | 4–5 | | | |
| Whitman College (WA) | 5 | 4 | None | |
| Whitworth College (WA) | 3–4 | 3 | ENGL 110 | |
| | 5 | 6 | ENGL 110 | |
| Willamette University (OR) | 4–5 | | ENGL 100 | Nonmajor credit in these departments. Contact Art, Environmental Science, French, Music, or Spanish departments regarding possible assignment of specific course equivalencies in these areas. |
| William Jewell College (MO) | 4–5 | 4 | GEN 102 & Elective | |
| Williams College (MA) | 5 | | ENGL 200 or 300 level | |
| Winona State University (MN) | 3–5 | | | |
| Wittenberg University (OH) | 4–5 | | | |
| Wofford College (SC) | 4–5 | 3 | ENG 102 | |
| Xavier University (OH) | 4–5 | 3 | ENGL 127 | |
| Yale University (CT) | 5 | | | |